THE LIFE OF SHERMAN COOLIDGE, ARAPAHO ACTIVIST

The Life of Sherman Coolidge, Arapaho Activist

Tadeusz Lewandowski

UNIVERSITY OF NEBRASKA PRESS

LINCOLN

The University of Nebraska Press is part of a land-
grant institution with campuses and programs
on the past, present, and future homelands of
the Pawnee, Ponca, Otoe-Missouria, Omaha,
Dakota, Lakota, Kaw, Cheyenne, and Arapaho
Peoples, as well as those of the relocated Ho-
Chunk, Sac and Fox, and Iowa Peoples.

Library of Congress Cataloging-in-Publication Data
Names: Lewandowski, Tadeusz, 1973– author.
Title: The life of Sherman Coolidge, Arapaho
activist / Tadeusz Lewandowski.
Description: Lincoln : University of Nebraska Press,
[2022] | Includes bibliographical references and index.
Identifiers: LCCN 2022003525
ISBN 9781496233479 (hardback)
ISBN 9781496233974 (epub)
ISBN 9781496233981 (pdf)
Subjects: LCSH: Coolidge, Sherman. | Episcopal
Church—United States—Clergy—Biography. |
Society of American Indians—History. |
Arapaho Indians—Biography. | Indians of North
America—Missions—History. | Indians of North
America—Religion. | Indigenous peoples—Cultural
assimilation—United States. |
Indians of North America—Government relations—
1869–1934. | Indians, Treatment of—United
States—History—19th century. | United States—
Race relations—History—19th century. |
BISAC: SOCIAL SCIENCE / Ethnic Studies /
American / Native American Studies
Classification: LCC E99.A7 L49 2022 |
DDC 978.004/97354092
[B]—dc23/eng/20220727
LC record available at https://lccn.loc.gov/2022003525

Set and designed in Adobe Caslon
Pro by Mikala R. Kolander.

For my dear wife, Marzena

The Indian must be made free. It sounds funny to me to say that because this land on which he lived from time immemorial has been the land of the brave and of the free, and my people enjoyed that freedom and they were monarchs, not slaves. They have been placed by this nation on reservations, and reservations are very much like prisons to these people who are so used to freedom. And the result has been that this independent, free, noble race has deteriorated until they are a caricature of what they were before they were placed on the reservation.

—Sherman Coolidge, 1913

CONTENTS

ILLUSTRATIONS

ACKNOWLEDGMENTS

There are many people I would like to thank for their help with completing this biography. Thank you to Matt Bokovoy, senior acquisitions editor at the University of Nebraska Press, and Heather Stauffer, associate acquisitions editor; Haley Mendlik, associate project editor; and Vicki Chamlee, copyeditor, for their work during the publishing process. I also thank Linda Hargrave, the archivist at St. John's Cathedral in Denver, and Marianna McJimsey, the parish historian and archivist at Grace and St. Stephen's Episcopal Church, Colorado Springs, for leading me to the Coolidge-Heinicke Collection at the Pioneers Museum, Colorado Springs. The museum's archivist, Hillary C. Mannion, was extremely generous with her time and did whatever she could to aid my research. Ms. Mannion was also kind enough to put me in touch with one of Sherman Coolidge's grandsons, Philip Heinicke, whom I thank heartily for sharing several magnificent family anecdotes. A big thank you, also, to Erinn Barnes, photo archivist at Pikes Peak Library District in Colorado Springs, for sharing her research with me. Thank you to Mark Thiel at the Marquette University Archives for somehow managing to get me exactly what I needed within days—despite his being quarantined at home. And the same big thank you to Rose Buchanan of the National Archives and Records Administration in Washington DC. Ms. Buchanan did me a great service when she somehow was able to locate a series of files vital to this biography when most government buildings were closed. I also thank Tom Rea, editor of WyoHistory.org; John Waggoner and Renah Loren Miller at the American Heritage Center, University of Wyoming; Rev. James Zotalis and Missy Donkers of the Faribault Cathedral, Minnesota;

and Rev. Ben Scott for the information and aid they gave me. Thank you to Tricia McEldowney, archivist and special collections librarian at the Warren Hunting Smith Library at Hobart College. As always, I thank my wife, Marzena Lewandowski, for her support; my mother, Linda Lewandowski, for reading and commenting on early drafts; and Jane Vavala of Hinkle Memorial Library in Alfred, New York, for her kind willingness to help me locate and gather sources. Finally, I am also grateful to the Wyoming State Historical Society for awarding me a 2020 Lola Homsher Research Grant, which funded the research for this biography.

* * *

I would like to express my deepest thanks to Dr. Jacek Furtak for rendering neurosurgical intervention with utter brilliance and great humanity. Without his extraordinary help, I would not be able to hold this book in my hands today.

THE LIFE OF
SHERMAN COOLIDGE,
ARAPAHO ACTIVIST

Prologue

On a cloudy spring morning in 1870, an Arapaho boy cowered next to his widowed mother, wondering whether he would live or die. Towering above him stood two Shoshone warriors, coolly assessing his physique. If they let him free, would he be able to exact revenge? How well could he shoot an arrow? Might he pose a threat? As they deliberated, the boy shivered intensely. In a desperate attempt to escape, he and a small band of women, children, and an elderly man had stumbled down the middle of a river, hoping to leave no tracks. Outrunning their assailants had proven impossible, as had hiding in the brush adjacent to the stream's banks. Now soaked, cold, and captured, the group offered no resistance. As the warriors decided who would live and who would not, a U.S. Army scout suddenly interceded. He insisted, forcefully, that the women and children be surrendered at nearby Camp Brown, one of several military bases that dotted Wyoming Territory. The elderly man received no such mercy. Before his shrieking wife and children, he was shot and scalped. At that, one of the warriors roughly lifted the Arapaho boy onto his horse and began to ride. Tears rolled down the boy's cheeks as he sat trapped in the large man's arms. The boy had already suffered many upheavals, having seen much of his family killed in warfare and raids. He had somehow survived, but the days among his tribe had ended. His mother, no longer able to protect him, would soon give him up to officers at Camp Brown, then depart seemingly forever. His life among whites would begin.[1]

When he was born in the early 1860s, the Arapaho boy's parents had named him Des-che-wa-wah, translated as "Runs On Top" or "Runs Mysteriously Over Ice," after his great-grandfather, a chief who once safely led his band over a frozen lake to elude an enemy war party.[2] By the time he died in 1932, Runs On Top was known throughout the United States as Sherman Coolidge, an adoptive son of a white military officer and his wife, an Episcopal canon, and a Native rights activist. What had unfolded in the interim was, in many respects, as remarkable as his survival that tragic morning in 1870. During the sixty-some intervening years, Coolidge had inhabited western plains and eastern cities, ridden in military campaigns with his foster father, escaped all manners of death, labored as a missionary to his tribe, fomented dangerous conspiracies, wed a fabulously wealthy New York heiress, met with presidents and congressmen, and become one of the nation's most prominent Indigenous persons as a leader of the Native-run reform group the Society of American Indians.

Upon Coolidge's death, the *Wyoming State Tribune* attempted in vain to encapsulate the breadth of his experience in one short column of newsprint. Perhaps realizing the folly of the endeavor, the paper's staff writer gave an account that briefly described his early life of "savage warfare" and his shocking marriage to a white woman. These dramatic and striking aspects of Coolidge's story, however, hardly provided the full picture; nor did the *Tribune*'s sole reference to his activism. "The solution of the Indian problem was one of the greatest desires of Dr. Coolidge's life," the paper explained, adding that "Coolidge himself could be taken as an example of his contentions of the complete adaptability of the Aboriginal Indian to the customs, civilization and culture of the white man."[3] This characterization, regrettably, elided every single complexity of Sherman Coolidge's thoughts on the Indian's place in America, but what could one expect? If the *Tribune*'s writer had failed to convey the intricacy of a multidimensional existence, the paper could be forgiven. Coolidge's panoramic life as a victim of the Indian Wars, a witness to the maladministration of the reservation system, a mediator between Native and white worlds, and an ultimate defender of Native rights and heritage had made him the literal embodiment of his epoch of American Indian history. That is a hard thing to communicate adequately in a mere paragraph.

Sherman Coolidge's life spanned what is known as the era of assimilation. Around the time he entered this world, Indian nations on the Great

Plains were struggling to subsist in a rapidly changing environment and were fighting fiercely to sustain their traditional lifeways in the face of Euro-American encroachment and forced treaties that left them marooned on reservations. As a cycle of brutal retaliation engulfed the West, violence often escalated to full-scale massacre. Though few in the East lamented the slaughter of "savage" Indians, Christian reformers, horrified by the seeming indifference of their government, sought a different solution. In 1869 President Ulysses S. Grant yielded to their pressure. Attempting to improve Native-white relations, he announced a "peace policy" that operated under a two-pronged strategy. First, a nonpartisan Board of Indian Commissioners would oversee the historically corrupt Department of the Interior's Office of Indian Affairs. Second, agents nominated by the board would ensure humane treatment for peaceable Indians, slated for assimilation through the guidance of missionaries on reservations.[4] A new chapter of colonial relations had begun.[5]

The Office of Indian Affairs, more often referred to as the Bureau of Indian Affairs or the Indian Bureau, played the main administrative role in this new scheme, holding Indigenous peoples confined under a wardship that denied basic freedoms and discouraged long-held cultural and religious traditions.[6] These policies found support among the largely Quaker Indian Rights Association (IRA), or Friends of the Indian, founded in Philadelphia in 1882. Smaller groups, such as the Women's National Indian Association and the Boston Indian Citizenship Association, advocated the same assimilationist goals.[7] Some of this work meant educating an American public that largely went by the dictum "The only good Indian is a dead Indian." In 1881 Helen Hunt Jackson, a member of the Boston Indian Citizenship Association, published *A Century of Dishonor*. The groundbreaking book cataloged the long list of U.S. treaty violations against Indigenous nations, simultaneously pleading for "a liberal and far-sighted policy looking to the education and civilization and possible citizenship of the Indian tribes." Hunt's admirable and rare humanity nevertheless contained ethnocentric assumptions of cultural superiority shared by her fellow reformers and Americans writ large. "Civilization," she wrote, was a "gift" to the "savage," and only "Christian influences" could lead Native peoples from "filth" into the "cleanliness" of modern life.[8]

U.S. Army officer Richard Henry Pratt seconded Jackson's sentiments. Born in 1840 in rural New York and brought up in Indiana, Pratt fought in the Civil War for the Union in his twenties, then traveled west to command a regiment of Buffalo soldiers in Oklahoma Territory. In 1874–75 he participated in the Red River War, an effort to force the Kiowas, Comanches, Southern Cheyennes, and Arapahos onto reservations. Some of the Indian captives were sent to Fort Marion, Florida, under his guard. Once there, Pratt made a startling realization: Native peoples, despite their "uncivilized" ways, were human. With the help of two New England schoolteachers, he formulated a course of education for his prisoners that was meant to impart Euro-American ways. His ostensible success persuaded the U.S. secretary of the interior Carl Schurz to support the creation of the first off-reservation, assimilationist boarding school for Indian children in Carlisle, Pennsylvania, on the site of an abandoned army barracks. In 1879 Pratt opened the doors of the Carlisle Indian Industrial School, an institution that promised to "kill the Indian and save the man" by educating Native children far away from their elders' "heathen" influence. Students sent east experienced a jarring and immediate transition. Their clothing was burned and their hair cut, with before-and-after photographs documenting the metamorphosis. The school's predominately vocational curriculum included marching and drills, and the compulsory adoption of Christianity. Native languages were banned.[9] This type of immersion in white culture, Pratt strenuously argued, was the only effective means to embed the "gift" of "civilization," to conquer the "savage," and to enable Indians to take their rightful place in Euro-American society.[10]

Pratt, the Indian Rights Association, and other Christian reformers envisioned a future in which Natives would become equal citizens. But this end was not thought possible if the prevailing reservation system held them back from "progress." The IRA, for instance, strongly advocated breaking up the communally held lands under the 1887 Dawes Act. The act promised to divide reservations in severalty, forcing Native families to move from a dependence on rations to a productive, self-sufficient existence based on farming. Individual lands were held in trust by the U.S. government for a period of twenty-five years, allowing Indians time to assimilate. "Surplus" lands were sold off to whites.[11] When the Department of the Interior deemed Natives "competent" for citizenship, a ceremony marked their transition. Secretary of the Interior Franklin Lane held the first one on the Yankton Reservation in South Dakota in 1916. A total of 150 honorees symbolically shot arrows into the sky, after which Lane declared to each: "You have shot your last arrow, that means you are no longer to live the life of an Indian. You are from this day forward to live the life of a white man."[12]

The motives behind such official policies were often altruistic, but the policies themselves had dire consequences for their intended beneficiaries. Boarding school life became a painful rite of passage for many Native children, and thousands did not survive. At the United States Indian Industrial Training School in Lawrence, Kansas—later renamed the Haskell Institute—inadequate nutrition, diseases such as measles, and cramped and unhygienic conditions resulted in over six hundred deaths.[13] The Haskell cemetery hence became the final resting place of small boys and girls, some of whom had arrived only months earlier. In 1888 students representing ten tribes went so far as to submit a petition inquiring about the appallingly high mortality rate. Nothing came of the effort.[14] Such was the case with many other government institutions where Indian children, separated from everything familiar, suffered under a regime meant to inculcate the values of a higher "civilization" that rarely fulfilled its promise.[15] Going back to the reservation after boarding school, unfortunately, only presented new problems. White education created a painful gulf between older and younger generations, and returned students found little official support back home. The Dawes Act, meanwhile, devastated the Native land base, resulting in an eventual loss of 86 million acres in total. This disastrous period of forced assimilation concluded in 1934, two years after Sherman Coolidge's death, with the Indian Reorganization Act. Taking a somewhat softer approach, the act restored some lands, dismantled Dawes Act allotments, and lifted bans on traditional Indigenous practices.[16]

Despite the many faults of the Indian Bureau's early policies, Coolidge endorsed the ultimate merits of assimilation for much of his life, whether as a missionary on the Shoshone and Arapaho Wind River Reservation in Wyoming, where he spent almost a quarter of a century attempting to convert his former tribe, or as the president of the Society of American Indians, the most visible Native-run reform group of the early 1900s.

Indeed, Coolidge once wrote that his duty as a missionary lay in educating "the weaker race of the inferior language, life, and religion into the better language, life and religion of the stronger race."[17] Thus, if one did not look deeper, the *Wyoming State Tribune*'s description of his "contentions of the complete adaptability of the Aboriginal Indian to the customs, civilization and culture of the white man" might be believed.[18] Yet in the end, these were not his contentions and should not be his epitaph. Instead, Coolidge's life was one of intellectual evolution, and his conclusions were a long time in the making. He may have begun his career arrogantly trying to fit his people into the mold of white society, but he ended it as a fierce critic of federal Indian policy and a defender of Native rights, having decided that Indians, in fact, were not the problem.

Astonishingly, Sherman Coolidge's story has never before been told.[19] And there is much to tell. Any one of his experiences with the late nineteenth-century Indian Wars, excruciating loss, treacherous conspiracy, corrupt power, or clashing cultures contained more drama than most lives as a whole. Coolidge also entered into a mixed-race marriage in an era of strict taboos against miscegenation, causing a national sensation. His wife, Grace Darling Wetherbee Coolidge, was in many ways a very brave and unconventional woman who rejected wealth and privilege in favor of an existence of greater meaning. An activist in her own right and a talented writer, Grace is indispensable to this biography. Some chapters are even told from her perspective, revealed in a rich epistolary record that provides an intimate view of her and her husband's lives, and of the tensions sometimes produced by their union. These letters and other scraps of paper—some collected by the Coolidges' grandchildren, others found in archives here and there—are all that remain of two lives lived fully on a vast continent of enormous contrasts. This biography seeks to do these two lives justice.

I

The Arapahos and Runs On Top

When Sherman Coolidge was a young man, he wrote the following words: "On a moon-lit night an Indian camp might be calm and quiet, the ponies tethered close by their owner's tepee, all resting peacefully—till the war-whoop and the sharp report of a rifle are heard, and the frightened people rush out for their lives, some to escape, some to be shot down and scalped, and others to fall under the cruel blow of the flashing tomahawk."[1] Coolidge was referring to his own experiences in the 1860s as a Northern Arapaho boy named Runs On Top, though the violence in America's newly declared Western Territories touched many Native peoples during that period. Why the Great Plains had devolved so precipitously into deadly warfare is a story of Euro-American invasion, dwindling natural resources, and long-standing animosities among tribal warrior cultures. Runs On Top's Arapahos were but one of the Indian nations enmeshed in a tragic cycle of retribution that only ceased with the U.S. government's final imposition of the reservation system in the 1890s. This forced confinement and loss of sovereignty proved a wrenching transition for a people who, for centuries, had migrated over vast distances.

The Arapaho people (the People with Many Tattoos) originally made their home in the Red River Valley, west of the Great Lakes in present-day Minnesota of the United States and Manitoba, Canada. For nearly three thousand years, they dwelled on the plains and in the woodlands, subsisting off abundant game and cultivating crops such as maize.[2] In the Arapahos' creation myth, the First Pipe Keeper, with the Flat Pipe in hand, existed alone upon an endless body of water and prayed to the Great Mystery above. The creator inspired the First Pipe Keeper to conceive of the duck and turtle, which searched under the water and brought up bits of dirt. Placing this dirt in the Flat Pipe, the First Pipe Keeper blew it north, south, east, and west, creating the earth, sun, moon, seasons, man and woman, and all creatures and plant life. When finished, the First Pipe Keeper taught religious rites to the people. The duck, turtle, and Flat Pipe were placed into a bundle, leaving the Arapahos—the descendants of the first man and woman—to care for them in sacred trust.[3] Each tribal band possessed a sacred Flat Pipe, wrapped in a bundle, for use on important ceremonial occasions. A lead rider held the Flat Pipe when the band traveled.[4]

In the late 1600s, the Arapahos, along with the Cheyennes and Dakotas, were pushed out of the Red River Valley by the large and powerful Ojibwe Nation, which had acquired firearms from French colonizers. The Arapahos moved on to the Great Plains, first inhabiting the northern region of Saskatchewan and areas to the south in today's Montana, Wyoming, and eastern South Dakota. There they lived a migratory, hunter-gatherer existence, facilitated by using dogs to transport possessions via travois. When the Arapahos acquired horses in the early 1700s, they became more mobile and more successful at hunting large game such as bison. They boiled or dried bison meat and sometimes combined it with fat and berries to make pemmican. Individual chiefs generally led Arapaho bands, though there was no centralized authority within the larger nation. Like other Plains Indians, the Arapahos adopted the Sun Dance as their principal religious ritual. Young men danced and offered sacrifices to the Great Mystery over three to four days of ceremonial fasting and prayer, displaying their devotion.[5] Much of Arapaho culture also revolved around the warrior, who kept the peace among bands and thwarted enemy incursions. Counting coup, or acts of bravery such as touching an enemy warrior with one's hand or bow and then escaping unscathed, were vital to gaining status. Young women, meanwhile, tanned skins, providing material for tepees, clothing, and other items. Men sometimes had more than one wife, though marriage was mostly matrilocal. A third recognized gender consisted of men who desired to be women. It was thought impossible for a woman to desire to be a man.[6] Arapaho bands of twenty to eighty families congregated in the summer, then dispersed in the winter to their favored campsites.[7] All Arapahos passed through the "four hills of life," a series of stages from babyhood to childhood and adulthood to old age, that reflected the four seasons. During these periods, the obligations, roles, and privileges assumed by individuals changed.[8]

After the Arapahos arrived on the Great Plains, they displaced many of the region's original inhabitants, such as the Shoshones, through violent conquest. They then migrated south as far as present-day Colorado, Oklahoma, and Kansas, and broke into two allied bands, the Northern and Southern Arapahos, that jointly operated on a terrain that stretched up through Wyoming to southern Montana.[9] Having carved out this territory in the early 1800s, the Arapahos allied with the Cheyennes and the Lakotas and Dakotas (or Sioux). Together, they repelled the Kiowas and Comanches from the south—only to make peace in 1840.[10] At this time, Euro-American encroachment in the West had not yet reached painfully disruptive levels, though the situation was rapidly changing. In the 1830s, white frontiersmen had established a series of trading posts on Arapaho and Cheyenne territory, including Fort Laramie in now southeastern Wyoming and Bent's Fort in now southeastern Colorado.[11] The Northern Arapahos traded goods at Laramie; the Southern Arapahos frequented Bent's. The arrangement solidified the growing division within the larger nation. While the Arapahos gained some initial benefit from their trade with whites, growing numbers of immigrants passing through the Great Plains to the continent's coastal regions eventually exerted a negative impact on the once-thriving biota. The California gold rush began mid-century, increasing traffic, dispersing bison herds, and reducing the availability of natural resources. Inevitably, the stress of deteriorating environmental conditions led the Arapahos, Cheyennes, and Lakotas to wage increased attacks on the pioneers and prospectors.[12] The U.S. government, too weak to exercise hegemonic military power throughout the West, had no option but to seek peace.

In the early fall of 1851, Washington called for treaty negotiations at Fort Laramie, which the military had recently purchased to protect passing wagon trains.[13] Eight Indian nations signed, including the Northern Arapahos, Cheyennes, Lakotas, Assiniboines, and Crows. The agreement established peaceful relations among all parties, officially designated specific lands to each signatory, and stipulated that the U.S. government could build forts and maintain trails in the region. The Indian nations retained the right to hunt, fish, and pass over the territories defined and did not surrender any land claims. As long as peace was maintained, Washington promised to pay annuities totaling $50,000 in the form of goods for ten years to each nation. The Arapahos and Cheyennes were to inhabit lands between the Platte and Arkansas Rivers and the Rocky Mountains, encompassing present-day eastern Colorado and southeastern Wyoming.[14] This fragile arrangement may have lasted longer had gold not been discovered in 1858 near what is now Denver, Colorado. Thousands of prospectors subsequently invaded these lands, degrading the environment and inviting violent conflict.[15] Undeterred, Washington declared Colorado a territory in 1861, opening the path to statehood.[16] That year, a portion of the Southern Arapaho chiefs ceded lands promised in 1851 for a small area between the Arkansas River and one of its tributaries, an intermittent stream named Sand Creek. Only a minority of the Southern Arapahos and Cheyennes signed the treaty. The Northern Arapahos did not sign at all.[17]

The 1861 agreement did little to defuse tensions between the Arapahos and the multiplying Euro-American immigrants now inhabiting the Arapahos' former lands. More ominously, the foreign presence became increasingly militarized as the Civil War raged in the continent's east. The Colorado Territory's volunteer forces fell under the command of Col. John Chivington, an avowed Indian hater. Acting on false claims that Indians had stolen cattle, he and the territorial governor, John Evans, launched attacks on the Cheyennes throughout 1864. Faced with the hostility of the new Colorado government, a large group of Southern Arapahos and Cheyennes under Chiefs Black Kettle and White Antelope sought a truce. Evans invited them to Fort Lyon, offering protection. Black Kettle arrived in late November and received assurances that his band, primarily composed of women, children, and elders camped near Sand Creek, would not be molested. After returning to his village, he flew a white flag and awaited a peace delegation. The next morning, Chivington's Colorado Volunteers charged without warning, slaughtering and mutilating whomever they encountered. Overwhelmed by five hundred soldiers armed with canons and lacking artillery themselves, Black Kettle's men offered little resistance. As many as 140 Arapahos and Cheyennes, most of them women and children, perished in an orgy of psychopathic violence. In celebration of their victory, American troops collected fingers and other body parts, including genitalia, and whole fetuses.[18] White Antelope's body was likewise desecrated.[19] Accompanied by six hundred stolen horses and mules, the Colorado Volunteers rode back to Denver adorned with newly won scalps. The items were later placed on display in the city's Apollo Theater.[20] Enraged, the Southern Arapahos and Cheyennes resolved to meet the Euro-American invasion with force. They began raiding stage-coach traffic, wagon trains, and supply lines along western trails with a new determination.[21] The 1864 Sand Creek Massacre, as it is known, had sparked a cycle of retaliation on the Plains that would ultimately engulf thousands of lives.

Several years prior to Sand Creek, most likely in 1860 or 1861, a Northern Arapaho boy was born along one of the branches of the Goose Creek, a tributary of the Tongue River that flows into the Wind River Basin in present-day Wyoming.[22] There lay the territory of a band that included his parents—Banasda (Big Heart), a warrior and council chief; and Ba-ahnoce (Turtle Woman). Banasda and Ba-ahnoce named their first-born child Des-che-wa-wah (Runs On Top or Runs Mysteriously Over Ice) after his great ancestor.[23] Runs On Top's younger brother was born four or five years later. Named Nee-netch-a (Little One Who Dies And Lives Again), he had the odd habit of crying and holding his breath until almost losing consciousness.[24] Nee-netch-a was later called Left Hand because he turned out to be left-handed. The boys' father also had a second wife, Ba-ahnoce's sister, who bore a son, Singing Beaver, prior to Runs On Top's birth, and a daughter, Sings First, somewhere between 1862 and '64.[25] White encroachment had not yet erased the Arapahos' migratory lifeways of hunting and gathering, and if only for a time, Banasda's children were afforded the stability and support common in traditional tribal societies.

Sherman Coolidge later wrote that his Indian childhood as "the favorite of indulgent parents and relatives" was often "happy."[26] His earliest recollection appears to have been waiting for his father to return from an eagle hunt. To procure feathers, Banasda had left camp, constructed a hide, baited a trap, and sat patiently with his bow and arrow over several days. Runs On Top, meanwhile, waited anxiously, peeking out of the tepee. When Banasda finally came walking back to camp with his quarry, Runs On Top, not knowing the word for eagle, shouted out in excitement, "Here comes father with crows on his back!"[27]

Runs On Top's mother taught him one supreme lesson, the "Rule of Civility," or, "Excuse yourself before going before anyone," which meant being reserved and polite, and never forcefully intruding.[28] Ba-ahnoce and her extended family nonetheless had a love of humor and a penchant for practical joking that resulted in some of Sherman Coolidge's fondest memories. When Runs On Top was about three or four, he received his first horse, a colt of just a few months. That spring, his mother, aunt, and grandmother began their annual collection of "buffalo berries," which produced a juice akin to pink lemonade. Excess berries were dried for the winter. As Ba-ahnoce finished packing the harvest into rawhide sacks and tying them to the horses, one last sack sat on the ground. Eager to tease her son, she lifted it up and placed it on his wobbly steed, which promptly fell over under the weight. Runs On Top exclaimed, "You killed my horse!" Ba-ahnoce quickly rescued the colt as everyone present burst out in laughter.[29]

Ba-ahnoce was not the only one fond of teasing Runs On Top. The boy suffered another such incident just after his brother Nee-netch-a's birth. At a council meeting, a young chief, wanting to have a bit of fun, challenged Runs On Top, then age five, to an arrow-shooting contest. The two competed to see who could shoot nearest a mark in the ground, with predictable results. Runs On Top lost his prized possessions—his bow and arrows—in the game. At first the boy managed to take the defeat gracefully, but that evening he broke down in tears. Ba-ahnoce tried to console him to no effect. She finally promised that if he went to sleep, his little brother would go and win the items back in the night. Unschooled in the powers of little brothers, Runs On Top believed his mother. The next morning, he awoke to find the bow and arrows placed beside him.[30] Such innocent stories of youth were, unfortunately, a prelude to a series of astonishing tragedies played out against the backdrop of the Indian Wars of the 1860s.[31] These inescapable conflicts would separate

Ba-ahnoce and Banasda's children from everything familiar within the first decade of their lives.

In the wake of the Sand Creek Massacre, the Southern Arapahos and Cheyennes departed Colorado Territory. Gathering disparate bands of Arapahos and Lakotas, they moved north, murdering settlers; attacking trains, ranches, army forts, and trading posts; and downing telegraph lines. By the summer of 1865, the bands had reached their destination, the Powder River and Tongue Basins in present-day Wyoming and Montana—lands that still offered plentiful bison for the hunt. Sustenance secured, they made contact with the Oglala and Brulé Lakotas, Northern Arapahos, and Cheyennes, and began plotting revenge for Sand Creek.[32] Three main bands of Northern Arapahos had by then emerged, led by Chiefs Friday (a fluent English speaker raised partially by whites), Black Bear (with whom Runs On Top's family lived), and Medicine Man, whose people held a long-standing, mutual antipathy toward the Eastern Shoshones.[33] In a collective decision, the Arapahos, Cheyennes, and Lakotas planned an attack on Platte Bridge Station, an army post that guarded a river crossing along the Oregon Trail. They struck in July 1865, killing over two dozen soldiers.[34] In response, the U.S. military mobilized the Powder River Expedition under Gen. Patrick E. Connor. His orders were simple: "You will not receive overtures of peace or submission from Indians, but will attack and kill every male Indian over twelve years of age."[35] This mandate was in fact exceeded.

In late August 1865, scouts led Connor's soldiers to a large Arapaho village under Black Bear and Medicine Man camping peacefully along the Tongue River. As Connor's surprise charge commenced covered by two howitzer cannons, Ba-ahnoce, seized by terror, grabbed Runs On Top and fled. Nee-netch-a, momentarily left behind, was thankfully scooped up and rescued by a cousin. Overwhelmed by the chaos, not everyone was able to reach safety. In the onslaught, Runs On Top's grandmother and aunt were shot while trying to escape. Many of the band's older men, women, and children perished in the same tragic manner. U.S. troops then captured a number of Arapahos, among them Runs On Top's female cousin, who was eventually released. Thirty-five warriors, including the boy's uncle, lay dead on the earth as the soldiers excitedly rounded up five hundred horses and mules as spoils of war. Sherman Coolidge later wrote of how his father, Banasda, had considered revenge and how the troops had departed, "rejoicing over their victory, the lives they had blighted, and the families they had broken up." Cholera and smallpox epidemics had already taken a drastic toll on the Northern Arapahos, who now numbered around a thousand people. Depleted, they were left dependent on the Lakotas and vulnerable to attacks by the Eastern Shoshones and their Bannock allies, both of whom nursed recriminations toward the People with Many Tattoos.[36]

Conflicts between the Arapahos and Shoshones had a long history. In the mid-1700s, pressure from the Arapahos, Cheyennes, and Lakotas had pushed the Shoshone Nation into the westernmost parts of present-day Wyoming and northern Idaho. The Eastern Shoshone, in particular, found it difficult to cope with Euro-American expansion in the late nineteenth century. The band's leader, Chief Washakie, understanding the powerful nature of the new arrivals, sought peace and protections.[37] Under his chiefdom, the Eastern Shoshones signed two treaties with Washington in the 1860s. The first, in 1863, established a 40 million–acre Eastern Shoshone Reservation, which included the Wind River Basin. The U.S. government secured several routes of travel through the area in return for annuities of $10 million over twenty years. The second treaty, cosigned with the Bannocks in 1868, severely reduced these lands to 3 million acres. The reservation's administrative center became Camp Brown, constructed in 1869 near present-day Lander, Wyoming, and the Eastern Shoshone Reservation was later renamed Wind River. One major problem nonetheless persisted. Approximately five thousand whites had settled on Shoshone lands during an 1862 gold rush. As a result, the bands continued to hunt and forage outside reservation boundaries, competing for diminishing resources with the Northern Arapahos.[38] Horses, needed to hunt bison, became a constant target of theft.[39]

Sometime in the early spring of 1867, Black Bear's band of Northern Arapahos struck camp in the Big Horn Basin and began to follow a large group of Crows, who had left days before for new grounds. Minor tensions arose when the Arapaho council differed over which route to take. Most of the men wanted to travel along the Big Horn River. A few others, Banasda included, argued that they should trace the Crows' route along a smaller stream through the hills. Several hundred Arapahos chose the river route. Banasda dissented and instead took his two wives and children along the Crows' path, accompanied by two other families. One warrior in the group had a pregnant wife and young son. None knew the danger that awaited.

At sunset on the first day, the small band pitched their three tepees on a site recently vacated by the Crows, by then ten miles ahead. The picturesque, circular clearing, enclosed by quaking aspens, boasted a convenient trail leading out to the smaller, half-frozen stream. On the bluffs behind the stream, the group looked across the valley and spotted around twenty-five Indians slaughtering a freshly killed bison. No one could determine their tribe. Thinking there were no hostiles in the area, the families assumed the men were friendly Crows. With no trepidation whatsoever, they ate dinner, enclosed their horses, and retreated to their tepees to bed down. As night descended and a bright moon rose in the clear sky, Runs On Top and his older half-brother, Singing Beaver, listened while Banasda told a series of vivid ghost stories. When the mysterious yarns had ended, Singing Beaver crawled under his buffalo robes and went to sleep. All was quiet and peaceful, but Runs On Top, excited by his father's supernatural tales, could not close his eyes. Instead, he sat there, watching the fire slowly expire in the center of the tepee. Just as he was about to lie down next to his older brother, Bannock war cries pierced the silence.

Those in Runs On Top's tepee immediately bolted up. Ba-ahnoce, with no time to think, snatched up her youngest son and, along with the others, slipped under the tepee's bottom into the aspens, escaping down the trail to the stream. Runs On Top, however, was left behind. Meanwhile, in one of the adjacent tepees, a warrior faced a choice. Stay and fight, or aid his pregnant wife and son to escape. He chose his family. The man in the third tepee did not deliberate and merely fled with his wife and children. Runs On Top, shocked by the suddenness of the attack, tried to gather himself. His first instinct was to follow his mother, but lifting the tepee's heavy hide with his small arms proved impossible. Panicked, he whirled around. Through the dying embers of the fire, he distinguished his father, methodically loading a rifle with a powder horn, intending to fight off the enemy so the others could flee. Banasda crouched near the tepee's entrance and ordered his son to run for the stream the moment he lifted the opening. As his father drew back the flap, Runs On Top dashed out into an eerie, empty stillness. Confusingly, no one appeared to be there. At the stream's bank, he came upon the pregnant woman, having broken through the ice into the water. Her husband was desperately trying to rescue her. Runs On Top could offer no help. He slid over the thin frozen crust onto the far bank of the stream, much as his ancestral namesake had done years ago, and began to run at full speed, calling out for his mother. A cloud drifted over the moon, engulfing the boy in darkness. Running blind, he abruptly hit what felt like another human being. It was Ba-ahnoce, who had not answered his cries for fear of giving away her location to the enemy. Reunited, Runs On Top and his mother, with Nee-netch-a in her arms, rushed over the frigid earth and headed, as best they knew, in the direction of the Crows' camp.

Hours later, mother and son had slowed their pace, each having worn through their moccasins. As the sun began to rise, an Indian boy unexpectedly emerged from a small cluster of pines, calling Ba-ahnoce's name. When he approached, she and Runs On Top recognized him as the son of their companions. His father and pregnant mother, it turned out, had managed to ford the icy stream and hide nearby. The boy explained that his mother had given birth during the night and could not be moved. With no other choice, Ba-ahnoce and her sons turned back to the trail, trudging without sustenance for almost a full day. Late in the afternoon, a large group of Indians appeared in the distance. As they quickly advanced, Ba-ahnoce realized, to her relief, that it was an Arapaho and Crow war party. Singing Beaver had run to the main camp so swiftly that he had already alerted the larger band about the raid. The warriors were searching for the attackers, determined to exact revenge. After questioning Ba-ahnoce, they instructed her to follow the trail to safety. She, Runs On Top, and Nee-netch-a continued walking for another full night. At one point, they stumbled upon a Crow man hunting horses. Unfortunately, he had no provisions to share. Another Crow helped them cross a partially frozen river and escorted them the rest of the way. When the exhausted trio reached the Crow camp at dawn, the women provided them with food and new moccasins, then directed them to the larger band of Arapahos.

Once among kinsmen, an uncle of Runs On Top's, Bald Head, took in Ba-ahnoce, allowing her and her boys to rest after the draining two-day ordeal. The two other families and relatives eventually reached the Arapaho camp, but when the war party returned, their news was crushing. The men had found Banasda dead, shot through the chest and covered in arrow and spear wounds. His murderers had neatly placed his body within a buffalo robe, neither scalped nor mutilated, out of respect for his bravery. All the tepees and horses had been stolen. The war party had buried Banasda and given up, unable to find the assailants. Years later, Sherman Coolidge learned that the Bannocks who had murdered his father had no intention of killing anyone that night. They had merely wanted to scare the families and steal their horses. Had Banasda retreated, he would have survived.[40] Instead, the family was shattered, and Runs On Top was left "the poorest of the very poor among his people and with a broken home." His only consolation remained "the memory of a loving parent, the bravest, the wisest, and the best of chiefs."[41] Ba-ahnoce, plunged into mourning, was left to care for her young boys and somehow recover. Regrettably, the mounting crisis on the plains was inconducive to healing.

The time following Banasda's death was one of increasing warfare. The Bozeman Trail, a newly carved offshoot of the Oregon Trail leading through the Powder River Basin to the gold fields in Montana Territory, became a flashpoint. In the summer of 1865, the U.S. military had deployed the punitive Powder River Expedition in response to raids by Lakotas, Cheyennes, and Arapahos. Having failed to secure the Indians' defeat, Washington sent out invitations for truce talks in the spring of 1866. When the tribes arrived at Fort Laramie, Brulé Lakota chief Spotted Tail showed a willingness to make peace. Oglala Lakota chief Red Cloud also appeared amenable. The main issue of contention became the Bozeman Trail. On the thirteenth day of negotiations, discussions broke down with the arrival of Col. Henry B. Carrington along with two battalions of over a thousand troops. Convinced that Carrington had come to take the Bozeman by force, Red Cloud refused further dialogue and departed. Washington would pay for this diplomatic blunder. In July Red Cloud, supported by the Northern Cheyennes and Arapahos, began attacking wagon trains along the Bozeman, stealing cattle, killing two men, and stopping most traffic.[42] Then in December 1866, a small group of Lakotas led by Crazy Horse lured a boastful and inexperienced captain, William Fetterman, into an ambush. Having given chase with his unit, Fetterman found himself surrounded by a massive Lakota, Cheyenne, and Arapaho war party. He and all eighty-one of his men died in a hail of arrows in the short space of twenty minutes. In revenge for Sand Creek, the Indians also mutilated the soldiers' bodies.[43]

Unable to conquer Red Cloud and his allies, Washington resorted to peace commissioners again in early 1868. The result of these overtures, the second Treaty of Fort Laramie, created the Great Sioux Reservation in the western half of present-day South Dakota, including the Black Hills. Washington also promised extensive material assistance and access to the hunting grounds of the Powder River Basin "so long as the buffalo may range thereon in such numbers as to justify the chase." The treaty did not, however, create a reservation for the Northern Arapahos. They instead agreed to settle among the Lakotas near the Yellowstone River in Montana Territory or in present-day Oklahoma alongside their Southern Arapaho and Cheyenne kinsfolk within a year.[44]

Despite the stipulations laid out at Laramie, the Arapaho chiefs preferred a reserve of their own. The Wind River Basin in Wyoming Territory, where the Eastern Shoshones spent their summers, was an attractive prospect. Hoping to come to some arrangement with their traditional enemies, the Northern Arapahos requested that Washington intercede. In early 1870, the United States brokered a treaty between the antagonists that included increased annuities for the Eastern Shoshones. Chief Washakie cautiously allowed the Arapahos a temporary home at Wind River, but when the bands began relocating in the spring, relations immediately deteriorated. Some settlers blamed the Arapahos, unjustifiably, for stealing horses and killing three miners in the town of Miner's Delight. The rumor incited hatred among the local white population, which raised an extra-military retaliatory force. Unaware of the sentiment against them, two small groups of Arapahos, mostly older men, women, and children led by Black Bear, broke off from the larger encampment in early April and made their way to Camp Brown to do some trading. Ba-ahnoce and her sons were among them, as were her sister's daughter, Sings First, and a small nephew named Cow-a-hay. On the morning of the eighth, they came under attack by Shoshones, Bannocks, and a 250-strong white mob led in part by an early settler in the region, Herman G. Nickerson. Black Bear was murdered along with over a dozen more Indians. Others escaped by quickly withdrawing to the Arapaho camp. Ba-ahnoce and her children, then resting in her tepee along the banks of the Popo Agie River, were left vulnerable.

Upon hearing the cries of the Bannock and Shoshone warriors, Ba-ahnoce, those under her care, and another family raced down the middle of the Popo Agie, hoping to avoid leaving tracks. An older boy drove the horses in the opposite direction as a decoy. Having run some distance, the breathless families, consisting of women, children, and an elderly man, took cover in an outgrowth of brush on the south side of the stream, believing falsely that they were out of sight. They hid there, silently shivering, trying to control their fear. Yet the tactic had failed. The Bannocks and Shoshones on horseback quickly spotted the group from a nearby ridge and rushed to surround them. Runs On Top huddled next to his mother as the warriors assessed his ability to take revenge. One remarked, "Look at his scalp, he is old enough to shoot us with an arrow." As they calmly debated whether to kill him, Ezac, a Shoshone scout employed by the U.S. military, interceded. Ezac insisted on taking captive the remaining three women and nine children, ages five to ten, for surrender at Camp Brown. Though the emaciated old man begged for his life to be spared as well, a warrior turned to him, shot him down, and removed his scalp in full view of his terrorized wife and children. A Shoshone named Kagavah then lifted Runs On Top and placed him on his horse. The boy sobbed violently all the way to Camp Brown.

Later that day, Ezac handed over his prisoners. Several officers went out to retrieve their worldly belongings, still sitting by the northern bank of the Popo Agie. When they returned, Ba-ahnoce pitched her tepee outside the garrison, gathered the children under her care, and waited for an army escort to return them all to the main Arapaho camp. Her niece, Sings First, had been taken by Ezac, though no one knew where.[45]

Despondent and traumatized, Ba-ahnoce sat outside the fort, perhaps considering the agonizing losses that had brought her to this awful point and the dim prospects offered by the future. Just then a concerned officer, Lt. Charles Frederick Larrabee, approached.

Cognizant of Ba-ahnoce's dire situation, Larrabee felt compelled to intervene. He asked to take her younger son, promising to provide Nee-netch-a a life more secure than she could guarantee. After much convincing, Ba-ahnoce reluctantly agreed, explaining that her husband had been killed and that she had little idea of what would become of her. She had one demand, however: Larrabee could have her younger child, but he would also have to take Runs On Top because he and his brother did not want to be separated. The youngest child in Ba-ahnoce's care, the five-year-old Cow-a-hay, needed a home as well. Larrabee, determined to help, persuaded a major at the camp named Russel and the resident surgeon, Dr. Shapleigh, to assume care of Cow-a-hay and Runs On Top, respectively.[46] Following several days at Camp Brown, soldiers returned Ba-ahnoce to her people under cover of night.[47] She left, no doubt, in a state of profound regret. The children she had given up lay in the hands of strangers. Would she ever see them again? Her oldest, Runs On Top, understood better than the others that the parting from Ba-ahnoce was, essentially, final. As a man, Sherman Coolidge never recorded any recollections of his mother's departure but did once admit that for days afterward he had wept and wept.[48]

2

New Life

Though Runs On Top was now safe at Camp Brown, Dr. Shapleigh, his new guardian, was a poor replacement for the mother and tribe he had lost. Both Lt. Larrabee and Maj. Russel took a genuine interest in the boys they adopted. Shapleigh was the exception. Nevertheless, the surgeon renamed Runs On Top William Tecumseh Sherman after the Union army general and the Shawnee chief who resisted Euro-American expansion in the early 1800s. Larrabee meanwhile renamed Runs On Top's brother, Nee-netch-a, Philip Sheridan Larrabee after the general who advocated the elimination of the American bison to subdue the Plains Indians. Russel named Runs On Top's cousin, Cow-a-hay, Louis D. Russel, with the last name taken from the officer who adopted him and the first from Russel's friend in New York. Nee-netch-a and Cow-a-hay were in responsible hands, but Shapleigh was a reluctant foster father from the start. He treated Runs On Top poorly and dressed him in nothing but a "bread cloth." Then, within less than a week's time, Shapleigh grew tired of tending to the boy altogether. This regrettable situation convinced Larrabee that new parents had to be found.[1]

Fortuitously, in May 1870 the Seventh Infantry began a march from Utah Territory to relieve troops stationed in Montana Territory and were joined by troops from Camp Brown. Among the Seventh was a young, mustached man, Lt. Charles Austin Coolidge, who would play a formative role in Runs On Top's life.[2] Born in 1844, Charles boasted Pilgrim lineage as a direct descendant of John Coolidge of Watertown, Massachusetts. Charles entered the U.S. Army as a private during the Civil War and, after helping suppress draft riots in Gettysburg, Pennsylvania, rose to the rank of second lieutenant. His unit served out the remainder of the war in New York; then it moved on to Florida, where the men spent the next five years. During this period, Charles met, courted, and married Sophie Wagner Lowry of Philadelphia, who was four years his junior. Sophie joined her husband when he was transferred to the West in 1870 and accompanied Charles as he marched to Montana Territory that spring.[3] After meeting Runs On Top and learning his story, Sophie prevailed upon her husband to adopt him.[4] Though she likely felt some sympathy for the Indian boy she so unexpectedly encountered, her initial instinct was not maternal. Sophie instead hoped that Runs On Top would become her "servant," good help being hard to find on the frontier.[5] When she asked Shapleigh whether she could take the child, he responded, "You can have him if you promise never to bring him back."[6]

Considering the near-constant death he had witnessed as a child, the separation from his mother and brother, and all the pain his circumstances entailed, one would expect little from Runs On Top but disconsolation and night terrors. "When I was first taken away," Coolidge later disclosed to an interviewer, "I cried every night for my own mother and my own people."[7] But slowly, Runs On Top, whom the Coolidges renamed Sherman, started to rebound. With his new guardians, he traveled north to Fort Ellis, where he began making friends.[8] He played with the other children at the fort, communicating with them (and his foster parents) in Plains Indian sign language, then commonly used by over 100,000 members of tribes such as the Arapahos, Lakotas, Kiowas, and Cheyennes. After being invited to several birthday parties, Sherman asked Sophie if he could host one himself. She agreed, and they chose to celebrate on February 22, George Washington's birth date.[9] This was apparently the first and final birthday Sherman enjoyed as a child.[10] The Coolidges seem to have treated their adopted servant with considerable formality and did not even bother giving him gifts for Christmas. This fact caused Sherman lingering pain later in life.[11]

Unbeknownst to Sherman, by the winter of 1870–71, his mother, Ba-ahnoce, had resolved to travel to Fort Shaw and see her sons. However, upon learning she would have to "pass through a country occupied by hostile Indians" to reach them, she abandoned her quest. Larrabee later got word from visiting Indians that Ba-ahnoce had instead "sent words of love" to her sons.[12] That same winter, the Coolidges were stationed at the Crow agency near present-day Livingstone, Montana, when a large group of tribesmen appeared to collect their annuities. Charles invited several of the men into his home, and Sophie sent them to the kitchen to get warm. Sherman stood at the kitchen door, peering at them quietly. One of the older men then noticed him and told the others, emphasizing his words in sign language, that Sherman reminded him of a boy he had once seen escaping with his mother from the Bannocks years before. It was the Crow who had been hunting horses and had directed Ba-ahnoce to the Crows' camp. Sherman understood his sign language and remembered him, but he was simply too shy to make himself known.[13] An opportunity for a reunion was thus missed.

The Coolidge family remained in Montana Territory until Charles received orders to return east for recruiting work in Cleveland, Ohio.[14] The family first made a short stay in Columbus, a place Sherman would later remember as his first encounter with urban civilization.[15] Sophie and Sherman then went on to New York City. When Charles followed is unclear. After settling in Manhattan on 144 West Forty-Sixth Street, Sophie enrolled Sherman in what one source calls "a school for colored children." He attended the segregated school for the three years his adoptive family spent in New York.[16] One day in class, Lt. Larrabee, then passing through the city, suddenly entered the doorway. Sherman recognized him at once and went over to greet him.[17] At home, Sherman was adored by Sophie's mother and her sister, Lena.[18] As any child would, he learned English rapidly, though he had trouble distinguishing between the *f* and *th* sounds. When asked what he was doing he would often reply, "Just washing my thace and hands."[19] He eventually developed native fluency but spoke with a few slightly accented consonants.[20] Sophie Coolidge also saw to Sherman's religious education. Bishop Horatio Southgate baptized him at Zion Church in midtown Manhattan, and from then on we can assume that he willingly attended regular Sunday services.[21]

When grown, Sherman Coolidge claimed that he first decided to become a priest and mediator between Natives and whites during his period in New York. One day on the street, he heard news of the defeat of U.S. forces in one of the battles of the Modoc War. The American press had exploded in fury, calling for the annihilation of all Indians in the West. The genocidal vitriol made Sherman realize the deep misunderstandings between the two adversaries, and he resolved to devote his life to ensuring peaceful relations. He later wrote:

> I knew then that the Indians did not understand the whites, and the whites did not understand the Indians, and that I did not think it was right to exterminate the Indians. I had lived several years among them as a child, and I knew them to be a peaceable and peace-loving people. I knew there were Indians who were friendly to the whites and whites who were friendly to Indians, and I also knew that there were a great many good white people, especially in the East. Many of those in the West were not of the best class of the white race. I made up my mind then that I would devote my life not only to preaching the Bible to my people but also in trying to make those two races understand each other.[22]

Sherman must have expressed as much to Sophie and those he knew at church. While in New York, Rev. George Geer of St. Timothy's Protestant Episcopal Church offered to send him west to study theology at Shattuck Military Academy in Faribault, Minnesota, all expenses paid. Sophie resisted, feeling that Sherman was too young to handle boarding school.[23]

In 1873 Charles Coolidge was transferred back to Fort Shaw, Montana Territory.[24] His family accompanied him. The move erased any nascent sense of predictability that Sherman, now in adolescence, may have enjoyed after three years in New York. In the Coolidges' relatively short absence, much had transpired in the West. At the start of 1871, the Northern Arapahos had forsaken Wind River for the Powder River Basin. Finding few bison to hunt, all the bands joined together. The collective leadership of Friday, Medicine Man, and a new chief, Black Coal (a blood relative of Sherman's), decided to draw their rations at the Red Cloud Agency near Laramie. Upon arrival, tensions quickly emerged between the Arapahos and Oglala Lakotas. Feeling unwelcome, the Arapahos returned to Powder River, from which they intermittently raided the Eastern Shoshones and the whites at Wind River. The Shoshones retaliated in kind. In the summer of 1874, Shoshone warriors and U.S. cavalry troops launched a sneak attack on an Arapaho village of approximately seven hundred people in the mountains between the Big Horn and Wind River areas, killing twenty-four Arapahos and stealing two hundred horses before retreating to Camp Brown.[25] Nevertheless, the Shoshones' cooperation with the military did little to secure Washington's promises to the tribe. Under a treaty ratified in June 1874, the Eastern Shoshones relinquished another 700,000 acres of their reserve, which was transferred to white squatters already dwelling there. In return, they received cattle and monies in annuities over five years. From that point, rations were delivered irregularly.[26]

What role Charles Coolidge played in the baleful Arapaho-Shoshone drama is difficult to determine, but he was a presence. Over the next decade and a half, he served at a series of forts throughout Minnesota, Montana, Wyoming, the Dakotas, and Colorado, attaining the rank of captain.[27] The Coolidge family spent the first three years at Fort Shaw, where Sherman attended the post school and performed daily chores for Sophie.[28] This pattern was disrupted by a sudden escalation of violence, caused by external pressure and growing hunger, between U.S. forces and the Lakotas in the summer of 1876. In 1874 Lt. Col. George Armstrong Custer had led an incursion into the Black Hills on the Great Sioux Reservation. He and his well-armed, thousand-man expedition verified the existence of gold deposits, inviting a small wave of prospectors.[29] Meanwhile, the Great Plains' bison population had been severely depleted due to an army policy of indiscriminate culling. As old lifeways became unsustainable, many Plains Indians turned to rations for survival.

Without a reservation of their own, the Northern Arapahos congregated every ten days at the new Red Cloud Agency in northwestern Nebraska to receive what was owed. The provisions were so meager and of such abysmal quality that eventually even Congress felt compelled to investigate. With no other choice, the Arapahos took to eating their horses and begging. Several children starved to death. By then, fewer than a thousand Northern Arapahos remained.[30]

Having demoralized the once-dominant Arapaho-Cheyenne-Lakota alliance, the U.S. government began wielding its growing power. Commissioners approached the Lakotas and asked to purchase the Black Hills. Red Cloud and several other leaders agreed, but Hunkpapa Lakota chiefs Sitting Bull and Crazy Horse remained in Powder River country, abhorring such notions. In June 1876 Custer attempted forcibly to relocate those Lakotas outside the reservation boundaries. He and most of his Seventh Cavalry perished in a reckless charge on a sizable Lakota and Cheyenne encampment on June 25, a bloody event known as the Battle of Little Big Horn.[31] Couriers alerted troops from Charles Coolidge's Fort Shaw unit, camped eighty miles away, to the situation, and the men immediately started marching. They arrived at the scene two days later and began burying the dead.[32] Sherman Coolidge, then about sixteen years old, declined to go with his foster father. He did, however, accompany Charles on expeditions against the Lakotas throughout the first half of 1877, likely acting as his servant.[33] Any recorded impressions have unfortunately been lost.

This period became an extremely difficult one for Sherman. Charles was convinced that his adoptive son had the makings of a soldier, but the death, horror, and separation Sherman had experienced as a child left him unreceptive to the idea. He still knew nothing about what happened to his brother Nee-netch-a; half-sister, Sings First; and cousin Cow-a-hay; likewise, he had no idea whether his mother was alive or dead. In one respect, it may have been better that Sherman did not know his half-sister's fate. Sources state that the Shoshone scout Ezac took Sings First to the town of Miner's Delight, where she narrowly avoided being tortured and burned at the stake thanks to the intervention of a white woman. Sings First was then sold for $100 to a man named John Felter, whose family apparently used her as a servant and provided her no education. She and Sherman, however, would in time meet again.[34]

Then suddenly in February 1876, Sherman had the chance to reconnect with his little brother, Nee-netch-a. Now about twelve years old and renamed Philip Sheridan Larrabee-Allen, Nee-netch-a was living happily in Matfield, Massachusetts. His foster parents, the Allens, were a long-established New England family with Pilgrim roots.[35] How Philip ended up in Massachusetts was a complicated story. After his initial adoption, Lt. Larrabee had sent Philip to Howard University, which was founded in Washington DC to educate freedmen after the Civil War. There, as Sherman later learned in a letter from Larrabee,

Philip had "made solid progress and was a general favorite with the teachers, and the scholars as well." One instructor, "a very highly cultivated lady teacher" named Isabel Barrows, had become "especially fond" of Philip and took him home to Massachusetts on vacations. Her husband Samuel June Barrows, a reporter and future congressman, loved the child and sang him to sleep every night. Philip also spent part of his summers with Larrabee's parents in Portland, Maine. In late 1875 or early 1876, James Madison Allen, a professor, and his wife, Sarah, asked Commissioner of Indian Affairs John Q. Smith if they could formally adopt Philip. How they came to know the boy is unclear. What is clear is that they felt Philip needed to be removed from Howard because he was "constantly worn out." The other students simply wanted to play with him all the time.[36]

Once in Massachusetts with the Allens, Philip wrote Sherman a letter that he kept until his death. In it, Philip asked his brother whether he knew of the famous Indians Samoset and Massasoit. "I am living where they used to live," he proudly announced. Philip went on to describe his new home and Mr. and Mrs. Allen, who "sometimes" played games with him. The Allens had a son, Ernest, and a daughter, Maribel, who had died. Philip had recently found "an arrowhead made by some Indian over two-hundred years ago." Mr. Allen had also gifted him a prism, which had become an object of fascination. "I like to study geography especially the maps." Philip continued, "I would like to study about the human body and mind." The Allen family had a strawberry patch, and Philip was looking forward to warmer weather, when they would plant some tomatoes and flowers. He had forgotten Sherman's Indian name and what he looked like, and asked that he send a photograph. Philip had also forgotten his father's name and wondered whether Sherman remembered him. He closed, "Much love for you from your brother, Philip S. Larrabee Allen."[37]

Sherman wrote back, but at some point, Philip stopped answering his letters. In February 1877, he finally learned why from Mrs. Allen. She and her husband had not responded because they "dreaded to break the news." Philip, it turned out, had suffered "a fit of sickness." For some time, it seemed he had recovered, but the Allens feared the worst. Mrs. Allen explained:

We saw however that he was tender, yet as we liked him so well, and he us, and we felt such a sympathy and kind feeling for all his race, we would not have him go away from us on account of his poor health, but all the more wanted him to stay—and he wanted to stay. So he was adopted as our own and *treated in every respect as if he had been our own flesh and blood!* Dear boy! We never knew a better boy—he was so high-minded, gentle, sensitive, generous and conscientious. But disease had fastened upon him, before he came to us; city life, close air, application to books in city schools etc. etc. seems to have laid the foundation for *consumption*; and all we could do to ward off the disease proved to no avail. After a month or two he lost his hearing mostly (from gathering in the ears) and gradually became feeble, and passed away to another life—where we trust there is no war, no sickness, no separation, and where he has found and joined his *dear father* and Em-min-ne-es-ka [the Arapaho word for God], and where he can watch over you and help you and guard and guide—till you join them in that happy world above. . . . He loved you much and wished you could be with him. His thoughts were with his father, and was pleased at the thought of meeting him. We did everything we could to make it pleasant, and we are glad we were permitted to come for him . . . Dear boy—an angel now—may he be with us all.[38]

The Allens had made a final effort to salvage Philip's health by going west, hoping that the fresh air of Indian Territory could heal his malady. The family began a journey to where Larrabee was stationed, intending to leave Philip with him to convalesce. Philip died en route in Gates County, Missouri, and was buried on a plot of land owned by the local postmaster. Larrabee later told Sherman, "If the little fellow had been my own child or brother I could not have grieved more."[39]

Philip's death devastated Sherman. He had lost his brother, whom he loved more than anyone.[40] Back at Fort Shaw with Charles, he reflected on both the overwhelming loss and the awful violence of the Lakota campaign. The series of skirmishes he had witnessed, known as the Great Sioux War of 1876–77, had ended in the Lakotas' crushing defeat. Faced with irresistible military force and starvation, the Lakotas, Northern Arapahos, and Cheyennes signed away their claims to the Black Hills. Sitting Bull escaped to Canada with a band of his followers; Crazy Horse surrendered, only to be fatally wounded by a prison guard. Under a postwar settlement, the Northern Arapahos were, again, left with no reserve of their own.[41]

Charles Coolidge had hoped that the experience of the war would start Sherman on a career in the military. Instead, it only fueled his desire for a life in the ministry. Though both Coolidges initially opposed the idea, Sophie came to respect Sherman's wishes, ultimately realizing that he was fit for a better life than that of a servant and that he should be able to make his own decisions. In early February 1877, she wrote to the Episcopal bishop of Minnesota and head of Shattuck Military Academy, Henry Benjamin Whipple, hoping to revive the church's offer to educate Sherman. Three months prior, she had heard Whipple speak inspiringly on the Indian question during a trip to Philadelphia.[42]

Sophie's choice of Whipple as a possible mentor was an obvious one. The bishop was a religious figure of national reputation and a noted advocate of humane Indian assimilation. In 1862 he had deeply alienated his own congregation by advocating for prisoners of war captured in the Dakota Uprising, a rebellion against the settler population of Minnesota incited by broken treaty stipulations. Whipple protested so vigorously against the forced removal and execution of those captured that his fellow bishops deemed him a fanatic.[43] His efforts, unsurprisingly, came to nothing. Under orders from President Abraham Lincoln, the U.S. Army executed thirty-eight Dakota warriors in a mass hanging—the largest in American history. The rest of the tribe was expelled. Lincoln simultaneously confiscated all Dakota territory in Minnesota, forcing the remainder of the Dakotas to escape west or to Canada.[44]

Despite Whipple's blatant humanitarianism, he survived as bishop and later joined the commission that brokered the peace following the Great Sioux War.[45] Sophie Coolidge's 1877 letter to him, excerpted, read:

My husband is an army officer belonging to the 7th Infantry now stationed in Montana. In the spring of 1870, I took into my family then in Utah Ty. an Indian boy of nine or ten years of age. He had been given to an officer in our regiment who tired of his bargain inside of a week, and gave him to me gladly. The boy is a son of an Arapahoe chief, a full blooded Indian though his life with civilized people has bleached him so he does not look it. My idea in taking him was to bring him up as a servant—which articles are scarce on the Frontier as you know. For that end he has been carefully trained and has also been sent to our Post schools, and can read, write, and cypher very well . . .

As the boy has developed, he seems to be above the position of a servant in every way. His taste for books and study is uncommon, and Mr. Coolidge and I have both thought it would be wrong to keep him in a menial position if we could give him the advantages of an education. We both think Sherman would in time ably fill the position of missionary, and my object in writing to you is to discover the plan of the mission college of which you have charge . . .

He is a good boy in every sense, reverent and devout, truthful to the letter, and I think it would be a great joy to him to know he was going to learn to teach his own people of a Saviour's love for them.[46]

Whipple responded within three weeks, suggesting that Sherman come to Shattuck Military Academy in Faribault, Minnesota. Sophie replied immediately, thanking him for "coming forward so generously in aid of my Indian boy." She then wrote Sherman, asking him "for a *deliberate* conscientious answer" to the offer.[47]

The exciting news that he could attend Shattuck pleased Sophie's "Indian boy" greatly, and he assured her of his seriousness. The return letter from Fort Shaw also revealed to what degree Sherman had imbibed Euro-American Christian norms and prejudices. "My dear Mrs. Coolidge," it began,

I received your letter safely, from which I learn of the opportunity I have to learn to be what I have been wishing for, for the last four or five years. It is a good a thing as I can do. If I go to Bishop Whipple's college I shall certainly do my best to enter into my studies with all my heart and soul. Still I may not be as good educated scholar as those that have already started to be educated for the same purpose, although I will do my very best, for I would gladly do something

30

toward having some of my race taught to believe in God. I know
how ignorant they are of the Bible and of Good. I expect I will have
to study hard in order to get along, but as I am fond of studying, I
think I will succeed in my studies. I will go down on my knees and
pray to God to help me, which I trust he will do in his great mercy
and goodness. I will do my best, for my pity at their ignorance of
God and of the Bible is so great that I will happily do all I can
possibly, to learn to learn to teach and preach the Gospel to them,
and if I succeed in doing this I would not ask for any better work
in this world.[48]

Sherman's willingness to attend Shattuck also partially satisfied Charles's
wish that he become an officer. Fortunately, Whipple acted generously in
offering a scholarship, though the Coolidges paid the costs of boarding and
school supplies.[49] As plans commenced for Sherman's trip to Faribault,
Sophie informed Whipple that they might not be able to care for her
foster son any longer due to the travel demands of life in the military.[50]
There was some irony in the situation. As Sherman was departing east
under the guidance of America's foremost voice for peace and reconciliation between Natives and whites, Charles Coolidge was embarking on
a starkly contrasting endeavor.

In May 1877, the Wal-lam-wat-kain Band of the Nez Perce, under
Chief Joseph, drew the ire of Washington. The larger Nez Perce Nation
had signed a treaty in 1855 establishing a reservation of 8 million acres in
the Idaho, Oregon, and Washington Territories. Following the discovery
of gold in 1863, commissioners forced another treaty upon the Nez Perce
that decreased the size of their reservation by 90 percent. Chief Joseph and
others refused to recognize the agreement and remained outside the new
boundaries. Joseph eventually agreed to move onto reservation lands in the
spring of 1877, but a desire for vengeance among several young warriors
resulted in the murder of whites in the area.[51] Knowing that the military
would seek retribution, Joseph attempted to surrender. Met by army gun-
fire, he and his band fought back, soundly defeating their attackers.[52] In
July Charles Coolidge's unit set out for the Rocky Mountains to kill or
subdue Joseph.[53] In fighting near the Lolo Pass, Idaho, Charles's thighs

and hand were badly wounded. Bleeding profusely, he carried on shooting until a fellow soldier told him to fall back, or he "would shoot the top of his [f—ing] head off." After wading through a river in retreat, Charles lay down under whatever shelter he could find, completely depleted.[54] He would have been killed if Patrick Rogan, another soldier, had not carried him away to safety.[55] Chief Joseph surrendered in October. Nonetheless, his dogged attempts to evade the U.S. military ultimately made him a national legend.[56] Even Sherman Coolidge counted himself among Joseph's admirers, once calling him the "red-skinned general who had made one of the greatest military campaigns in the history of the world's wars."[57]

Prior to Charles Coolidge's wounding, Bishop Whipple had secured Sherman's passage by rail and steamboat to Faribault.[58] Sherman left Montana Territory in the summer of 1877 and headed for the Ojibwe White Earth Agency in Minnesota, where he would lodge until the beginning of Shattuck's academic year. Sherman and a trunk of his belongings left Fort Shaw in the summer along with two guardians, Coolidge family friends Major Freeman and his wife. They rode to Fort Benton, Montana, and boarded a boat that ferried them to Bismarck, North Dakota, along the Missouri River. The group disembarked and settled into a train car that took them over a thousand miles to Detroit, Michigan, where the Freemans left Sherman to make his way by stagecoach to White Earth and his Ojibwe hosts. Sherman spent two months on the reservation at an Episcopal mission school. All went well, but he lost his precious rail ticket to Faribault. The money he had, it turned out, could not cover the rest of the journey, save the conveyance of his trunk by rail. Fortunately, he struck up a friendship with an amateur boatbuilder planning to float down the Mississippi to Iowa. The boatbuilder agreed to take Sherman as far as Minneapolis on condition that he would help row. After a grueling journey on sometimes rough waters, Sherman arrived in the city, walked to the train station, bought a ticket with his last pennies, and boarded the train to Faribault. When he finally located Shattuck Military Academy, he presented himself filthy and in tatters to the rector. Not long afterward, Sherman was happily reunited with his trunk.[59]

Shattuck, founded in 1858 as an Episcopal all-boys mission school and seminary, was then an "A class" military academy. As a cadet, Sherman likely slept in Shattuck Hall, built in 1866 to house the student body.[60] Thanks to the school's armaments training, he became a crack shot with an automatic rifle.[61] Charles and Sophie Coolidge took an active interest in Sherman's studies and corresponded with him often. Though Sophie sent "Love from Mamma," she expected Sherman to exercise strict discipline and achieve excellent results. When Sherman was ranked third in his class, Sophie asked, "Why weren't you first?" Another near catastrophe occurred when Sherman received a zero in recitation because he could not acquire the assigned book. Sophie advised: "Go to your teacher quietly and explain the matter to him—and ask him to give you an opportunity to make up that lesson by learning an extra one—and ask him to erase the zero if you do—as you are trying so hard to get perfect marks—I am so anxious that you should improve, Sherman, and send home reports that are *perfect* in everything. Certainly there is no reason your *conduct* should not always be marked perfect, because you know so well how to behave yourself."

Charles had similar expectations, insisting that Sherman "study arithmetic thoroughly and also grammar." He likewise hoped to hear of Sherman's "making an unprecedented success" as the "brightest, quick-witted, and energetic boy of the school." For Christmas, the Coolidge family reunited at the Hotel Windsor in St. Paul in 1878. Charles and Sophie then left to tour Europe in the spring of 1879, as Charles had been granted leave after his wounding. Sherman's parents urged him in a final letter before their departure "always to behave like a gentleman—and to be especially neat in your appearance."[62] Sherman stayed with friends that summer. When the Coolidges returned, they were ordered to Fort Snelling, Minnesota, where they could look after Sherman during school breaks. (They later moved on to Fort Laramie, Wyoming.)[63]

As graduation from Shattuck neared in 1880, Charles encouraged Sherman to transfer to the U.S. Military Academy at West Point, New York.[64] Sherman showed no interest and instead approached Whipple about studying for the ministry at Faribault's Seabury Divinity School.[65] "My people have never heard of the Savior," he purportedly stated. "If possible, I would like to become a minister and go back to tell my kinsmen of the love of Jesus Christ."[66] The bishop assented. At Seabury, Sherman's "devotion and piety won the esteem of the professors."[67] Whipple deemed his senior thesis one of the best.[68] Sherman graduated on June 1, 1884, at age twenty-four, with a bachelor's degree in divinity. Whipple personally ordained him as a deacon.[69]

For the next several months, Sherman assisted in church services in the immediate vicinity of Faribault, becoming a favorite among parishioners. Whipple could have kept his young apprentice in Minnesota, but he felt strongly that God had called him for a greater purpose as an Indian missionary.[70] "I believe it is God that calls you," one of his letters to Sherman stated.[71] The young deacon accepted Whipple's divination and began to prepare for the long journey back west after what he later called seven "happy school years."[72]

Runs On Top, a once-savage brother, would be returning, carrying with him the message of Christ and the mantle of Euro-American civilization. Expectations were high, but high expectations are easily dashed.

3

Return

During Sherman Coolidge's seven years in Minnesota, the people of his Northern Arapaho Nation had failed to secure a reservation of their own. In the wake of the Great Sioux War of 1876–77, a delegation of Northern Arapahos, Northern Cheyennes, and Lakotas traveled to Washington for a meeting with President Rutherford B. Hayes and Secretary of the Interior Carl Schurz. Among them were Red Cloud and the Northern Arapaho chief Black Coal, who had emerged as a primary leader. Before Hayes, Black Coal argued against sending his people to live with their Southern Arapaho kinsmen in Oklahoma. He stressed that his tribe was small and could be accommodated nearer their traditional territory. Hayes and his military advisers responded by arranging for the Arapahos to spend the winter on the Sweetwater River in Wyoming Territory in preparation for their permanent relocation. The bands would then move to the Eastern Shoshone Wind River Reservation and settle alongside their hereditary enemies. Whether this was possible remained an open question. At Hayes's behest, former Wind River agent James Irwin approached Washakie and other Shoshone chiefs in October 1877, requesting they permit the Northern Arapahos' presence. The leadership allegedly agreed but stressed that the stay be temporary. The Eastern Shoshones still argue today that the leadership withheld its full consent.

In the late autumn, Black Coal and his Northern Arapaho band set off for the Sweetwater, having been supplied with 155 cattle to sustain them. A month later, they had consumed all the cattle, and the U.S. military issued the tribe rifles for hunting. The Arapahos arrived at Wind River in March 1878 under army escort and made their way to Camp Brown, the agency's center, to collect rations. As more Arapahos continued to arrive, a series of meetings commenced between Washakie and Black Coal. Both sides hoped that another solution could be found and that the Arapahos could be again relocated.[1] This never occurred, and two formerly warring nations were left to make peace under the Indian Bureau's control.

In 1878 the challenges facing the Northern Arapahos were more daunting than ever. Black Coal's band established a tepee village at the confluence of the Wind and Popo Agie Rivers. Another band led by the warrior Sharp Nose (Sherman Coolidge's uncle) took up residence ten miles west on Little Wind River. The last band, led by Friday, camped west of Sharp Nose's band along the Little Wind. While solidarity still prevailed among the bands in the nation, their environs no longer offered a bounty. Game such as bison, elk, and deer had dwindled, and Indian Bureau's rations proved of scandalous quality. The political situation was perhaps worse. Those Northern Arapahos remaining, fewer than a thousand in number, had no treaty to secure the land on which they resided. Instead, they existed in an atmosphere of mutual recriminations adjacent the impatient Eastern Shoshones. Indian Bureau policy threatened both groups equally. Reservation populations held the legal status of dependent government wards, subject to an onslaught of dictates constructed to eradicate traditional practices and beliefs. Noncompliance meant punishment by reduced rations. The bureau's assimilationist program encouraged farming, though little of Wind River boasted suitable soil, and few desired to take up the plow. Efforts to force new lifeways on the Arapahos were coupled with attempts to "civilize" their children through Christian education. With the Indian Bureau's support, two schools operated on Wind River in the 1870s and '80s, with one run by Sherman Coolidge's Episcopalians and the other by Jesuits.[2] The Bureau of Catholic Indian Missions, established in 1874 to enlarge the church's influence on Indian reservations, oversaw the Jesuit mission.[3]

The Christian schools at Wind River constituted an affront to Arapaho and Shoshone beliefs and cultures. Instructors cut the students' hair and urged them to reject everything associated with their elders. The education received in return was inadequate and vocational in nature. Girls practiced the domestic arts; boys learned how to tend livestock and farm. Schooling began at age nine and lasted from three to six years. Even when male students graduated with some expertise, their success in farming remained elusive. Producing enough crops was simply impossible without the requisite heavy equipment. This grim fact left the Northern Arapahos reliant on substandard government rations of diminishing quantity. In 1883 the Wind River agent supplied one person with four pounds of beef for the week. By 1889 the amount had been reduced to one pound. Fortunately, some farming succeeded. In the 1880s, Sharp Nose and Black Coal established cooperative gardens along several rivers used for irrigation. Workers grew hay and vegetables, taking what they needed, then distributing the excess to the elderly and needy. These community projects, however, could only help so much. To receive more aid, the Northern Arapaho leadership had no choice but to comply with the Indian Bureau's rule. One tactic the tribe used was engaging in acts of goodwill that might influence the bureau agents and ensure the general welfare. In 1881 each chief sent a child to Richard Henry Pratt's Carlisle Indian Industrial School in Pennsylvania as a show of faith. The decision was tragic in one case. Sharp Nose's son died at the school in 1883. He received the news while guiding President Chester A. Arthur on a trip through Yellowstone. The composure and discipline he and the Northern Arapahos showed in the face of such events were nothing less than remarkable. Sharp Nose was never able to visit his son's grave in the East.[4]

These were the circumstances when Sherman Coolidge returned to Wind River in the fall of 1884.[5] He came directly from Colorado, where Whipple had initially sent him to work among the Southern Cheyennes.[6] The state's bishop, John Spalding, approved the move to Wyoming so Coolidge could be among his own people, whom he felt drawn to by ties that had not been erased during his many years among whites.[7] On his way, he stopped at Fort Laramie to visit his adoptive parents and to perform religious services for the soldiers and their families.[8] Charles Coolidge had fully recovered from his wounding by the Nez Perce and, unbeknownst to him, was about to embark on a new military operation. In September 1885, anti-Chinese riots broke out in Rock Springs, Wyoming, resulting in a massacre. White immigrant miners, resentful of the Union Pacific Coal Company for hiring lower-paid Chinese workers, marched on the city's Chinatown. Over the course of one day, rioters burned down eighty Chinese homes and lynched almost thirty persons while injuring fifteen. Hundreds of others fled. Charles's unit was summoned to restore order. Most federal troops departed weeks after the initial violence, but Charles and Sophie stayed in the city for another decade.[9] The Coolidges attended the Holy Communion Episcopal Church and were considered "a delightful couple" by the community. Sophie was known for her large hats and eccentric habit of traveling with a bottle of olives, one of her favorite foods. When meeting new people, she would employ her fashionably long hatpin to impale an olive from her bottle and offer it freely.[10]

Sherman Coolidge reached Fort Washakie (the renamed Camp Brown) on October 2, 1884, sincerely convinced that the adoption of Christianity and Euro-American culture was the only way to "uplift" his Arapaho kinsmen.[11] To his surprise, anxious relatives awaited him as he stepped out of the stagecoach that fall evening. Word had spread that the "Arapaho Whiteman," as he was called by his tribespeople, was on his way. The nickname reflected how some of the Arapahos might have viewed him suspiciously, but the welcome he received was enormously warm. Coolidge's arrival was a momentous event for one elderly woman, Runs On Top's mother, Ba-ahnoce, who had survived years of raids, war, and near starvation. Ba-ahnoce was standing there, waiting for her child at the stage post, and though impeded by age and partial blindness, she had walked there every day since hearing of his impending return.[12] Upon seeing Runs On Top, she exclaimed, "You are my son!"[13] Coolidge recognized her immediately, and they embraced in what must have been, by any standard, an emotional moment.[14] Ba-ahnoce was not alone in welcoming Runs On Top home. A succession of relatives lined up to hug him, each resting their heads on his shoulder and weeping.[15] Whipple later commented that Coolidge had been "welcomed as one from the dead."[16] Among the greeters was Coolidge's uncle Sharp Nose, one of the leading chiefs on the reservation.[17] It proved difficult, however, for Runs On Top to reconnect with his mother. They had been divided by time and cultural norms, and he perhaps felt a lingering resentment at having been given up as a child.[18] This wound eventually healed, and Runs On Top cared for Ba-ahnoce until her death, later expressing happiness at the pride she took in him.[19] She became one of the first people he baptized on the reservation.[20] Unfortunately, precious little information exists on this intriguing but no doubt difficult relationship.

Though Sherman Coolidge's return to Wind River brought him into contact with a people he had not lived among for fifteen years, an established Episcopalian infrastructure ensured his support. The Episcopalians had begun missionary work at Wind River in 1871, when Bishop George Randall of Colorado Territory helped found a day school for the Shoshones. This work continued until 1873, when a Shoshone Episcopal mission was officially established under Grant's peace policy near then Camp Brown, which had been vacated and moved fifteen miles northwest. Bishop Randall traveled to Wind River in 1873 but encountered considerable hardship. After delivering his sermon (his last), Randall and a small congregation of agency employees came under attack by a group of Arapaho warriors, who only retreated after wrongly assuming the group was armed. While returning by stagecoach to the train depot at Rawlings, Randall passed by the bodies of two women slain by the raiders. Randall died shortly after back in Colorado. The stress of the mission trip and the harsh weather had brought on a fatal bout of pneumonia.[21]

The prospects of the Episcopal mission at Wind River changed ten years later with the arrival of Rev. John Roberts in 1883. Roberts was, by that time, a long way from home. Born in 1853 in North Wales, he enjoyed a privileged upbringing, even earning a degree from St. David's College, Oxford. Called to do missionary work, Roberts traveled to the Bahamas in 1878 and was ordained as a priest in Nassau. After four years in the Caribbean, Roberts moved to the United States, leaving behind his fiancée, a church organist named Laura Brown. After meeting Bishop John Spalding, Roberts accepted an assignment among the Shoshones at Wind River. The last leg of his journey from Colorado took eight days by stage, during which he endured temperatures of sixty degrees below zero. Miraculously, he somehow avoided frostbite. Laura Brown, undeterred by Roberts's descriptions of Wyoming's weather and his warnings that she might not survive there at all, joined him on December 24, 1884. They married on Christmas Day and later raised five children despite leading very busy lives. Roberts established St. Michael's Mission seven miles west of Fort Washakie. His long list of duties included teaching at the Episcopal mission school and ministering to everyone within a 150-mile radius of the agency center. Eventually, a settlement grew around St. Michael's, now known as Ethete.[22]

In regular dispatches to the Episcopal periodical *Spirit of Missions*, Roberts reported on his activities. In early 1884, the mission school had eleven Indian children and five "half-breeds" boarding, along with eight day students. Some of these pupils could speak and read English, even the scripture, because they had gone to Carlisle in the East. Teaching took place five days a week, five hours a day. Church attendance was expected but not "compulsory." "Many of them are grown up," Roberts explained, "and compulsion, I find, has an undesirable effect on the Indian nature." Roberts's foremost problems at Wind River were the language barrier and the weather. He spoke no Indian tongues and needed an interpreter in his contacts with Shoshone and Arapaho elders. Every Sunday, he mounted his horse and rode to Lander for evening service. "This may not be practicable through the winter," he confided in one letter to the *Spirit of Missions*. "At this high altitude the cold after sundown is severe." Even worse, the trip took a full seven hours. Returning before midnight always proved impossible.[23] Roberts did have some help. He purchased a sturdy horse named Buckskin from an Arapaho in 1884. The hardy steed traveled thousands of miles in the "missionary cause" over the subsequent nine years. When Buckskin was ridden to exhaustion, Roberts's second horse, Chubby, bore her burden.[24]

By the end of 1884, the U.S. government had completed construction of the Wind River Industrial School at Fort Washakie, and it was large enough to accommodate two hundred students.[25] The institution made the Episcopal mission school in Ethete redundant, so Roberts ran a course of religious instruction outside of normal school hours.[26] He also served briefly as Wind River Industrial School's superintendent.[27] His wife, Laura, sometimes worked as an assistant teacher.[28] Considering his heavy schedule, Roberts was probably pleased to learn of Coolidge's imminent arrival. He complained in the *Spirit of Missions* that supervising the children "takes up my time from early morning to late night." Roberts was also tired of performing three services on Sundays and of making the thirty-mile round-trip ride to Lander.[29]

Ethelbert Talbot, the future Episcopal bishop of Wyoming and Idaho, expressed particular approval of the addition of another missionary at Wind River, writing to Coolidge, "May God bless, direct, and help you."[30] Talbot's daughter, Anne, would later become a lifelong friend of Sherman's. Though Coolidge had meager experience with missionary work, Bishops Talbot and Whipple did not want him "to be under Mr. Roberts in any slavish, or unfair" manner. True, Roberts was ultimately in charge, but he and Coolidge were bidden to "work as brothers."[31] Coolidge's appointment was a stroke of fortune because the Wind River Industrial School had recently grown to seventy-five pupils. One of the teachers, Mr. Jones, had just quit, "disheartened at the apparent small result of his self-sacrificing efforts to do good." Roberts admitted in the *Spirit of Missions* that he understood Jones's attitude. "The work is very discouraging," he wrote, "but I am confident that in due time an increase will be given by the LORD of the harvest." His hope may have been inspired by the twenty-two boys receiving religious instruction, some of whom could read "a little."[32] As one would expect, Roberts held a largely dismissive attitude of Arapaho and Shoshone religious practices. When allowed to view the sacred pipe ceremony of the Arapahos, he deemed the pipe "insignificant" but noted that it was "our duty not to ridicule their belief, but to show them the better way."[33] Sherman Coolidge would now be a major part of this effort.

Upon his arrival, Coolidge took up residence at the Fort Washakie Hotel and relieved Roberts of his extracurricular teaching duties. Unfortunately, he could not be counted on as a reliable interpreter. Over the years, he had completely forgotten Arapaho. Only after six months did Coolidge begin to reacquire some of his mother tongue, even regaining his native pronunciation.[34] That he made the effort to relearn his first language points to a desire to reconnect with his tribal identity, and though he had been away since age nine, correspondence suggests that Coolidge was able to draw rations along with the other Arapahos at the agency center.[35] In 1885 Bishop Spalding ordained Coolidge into the priesthood at St. Mark's Church in Cheyenne. Spalding later wrote of him: "He is received by them as one risen from the dead and is acquiring great influence over them. He trusts he will be able, through GOD's help, to lead many of them to the SAIVOUR who died for them, and to induce them to adopt Christian and civilized habits of life. Let us do all we can to support him and aid him in his efforts on behalf of these poor degraded heathens."[36] Following Spalding's visit, Reverend Coolidge took charge as the rector of the Church of the Redeemer at Fort Washakie, founded by Roberts in 1885 and constructed at a cost of $2,500—the grand sum having been donated entirely by one Philadelphia woman, Elizabeth Shields.[37] Coolidge's salary totaled $500 per annum.[38] Any spare time he had was spent flirting with female visitors from the East and preaching throughout the reservation in log cabins, tepees, and even the post office.[39]

Later in his life, Coolidge remarked that serving as a reservation missionary meant being a "judge, farmer, butcher, preacher, teacher, policeman, doctor, and everything else."[40] His efforts in these realms did gain at least some converts, resulting in a very small, mixed congregation of Arapahos and Shoshones. His services, according to Roberts, were "fairly attended." Coolidge's presence also seemed to draw more students to the reservation school, which was "prospering." The bulk of these new pupils were, in fact, Coolidge's relatives.

Though Roberts felt things at Wind River were proceeding well, he complained of certain challenges. "Missionary work among the Arapahoes is difficult," he wrote in the *Spirit of Missions*. "There is perhaps no tribe of Indians so tenacious of their traditions and clannish as they are." Such resistance was predictable in any Indian nation pressured to surrender long-held beliefs. There were, however, signs of what Roberts and Coolidge saw as "progress." Roberts proudly stated that twelve Arapahos and Shoshones had been taught to read St. Matthew's Gospel and were doing well in their "secular" and "industrial" training.[41] Three of their students had purportedly converted to Christianity, while Black Coal's son, Sumner Black Coal, had returned from Carlisle to assist with the government school's operations.[42]

That Coolidge's presence at Wind River increased student enrollment indicates, at least initially, he was respected as an effective mediator. Sometimes elders would address him by his father's name, Banasda, as a sign of respect for the son of a great warrior.[43] This dynamic would change over time as the Arapahos gradually tired of Coolidge's generally assimilationist mission and pro-government stances. Nonetheless, his first report to the *Spirit of Missions* revealed a burgeoning optimism, even if it was filled with typical references to the "poor uncivilized heathens" under his tutelage. "I find the Arapahoe and Shoshone children are docile and intelligent," he shared with readers, "[and] they learn very willingly and very readily." As such, the Wind River school was "doing as much good as any other institution of its class in the United States."

Coolidge also expanded on his activities outside of Indian education. By visiting tepees across the reservation and cultivating friendships, he "succeeded to obtain the promise of three Arapahoes to commence farming and continue until they have secured a home for themselves and their families." This success convinced Coolidge that greater proximity could allow him to lead by example. His plan—contingent on contributions—was to build a home near his uncle Sharp Nose's camp.[44] With his consistent presence assured, the Episcopal Church could be influenced to establish a mission there around which the Arapahos would permanently settle. Coolidge wrote Bishop Spalding on this matter in April 1885, laying out his strategy and requesting support. He insisted that the Arapahos at Wind River were amenable and that there was no other place where "savage men" and "heathen people" were "so favorably for the reception of the Gospel story of the love of God."[45]

Spalding responded enthusiastically to Coolidge's suggestions, instantly seeing the tactical advantage the outpost could offer in winning converts.[46] Coolidge's proposed homesite lay in the middle of the three main Arapaho camps, a location that would discourage other missionaries from poaching. The Episcopalians' main concern was a potential return of the Catholics. Father John Jutz, a German Jesuit, had established St. Stephens Indian Mission in the very same place earlier in 1884. He and Ursis Nunlist, another missionary, built a large, one-room building, only to leave the following year.[47] The Jesuits' departure elated Roberts. He wrote Bishop Spalding on August 4, 1885, announcing gleefully that the Catholics, through "their bigotry and rashness," had abandoned St. Stephens and that it was time to increase the Episcopalians' influence in the area. Spalding began soliciting money.[48] With Coolidge installed in their place, perhaps through "example and precept" he could work with the Natives and "lead them to a higher life."[49]

At Wind River, Coolidge also continued to receive support from his mentor, Henry Benjamin Whipple. At the 1885 annual convention of the Diocese of Minnesota, the bishop declared Coolidge "marked evidence of the Providence of God" and expressed the hope that "under God he will be the instrument to lead his people to the light of Christian civilization."[50] Whipple subsequently wrote the leading Episcopal journal, the *Churchman*, pleading for funds to ensure Coolidge a home among the Arapahos, a "poor people, who have suffered great things at our hands."[51] Such appeals prompted immediate donations. By the early fall of 1886, a stone dwelling had been built at the cost of $800. (Coolidge would later develop this land claim into his own ranch.) The money had been gathered in "small sums" from various "friends of Indians" in the eastern dioceses, including a $200 gift from Bishop Spalding himself.[52] In the *Spirit of Missions*, Coolidge thanked contributors for their "generous and prompt aid." He also assured readers that the "Arapahoes are in favor of civilization and Christianity," which were evident in their desire to farm, live in log houses, and send their children to school. "I have made some progress in question of my language," he added, "but until I have mastered it my chief work will be to advance the civilization of the tribe."[53]

Spalding had a slightly different conception. The bishop made clear that Fort Washakie was still Coolidge's parish and counseled him to avoid "intercourse only with the Indians" and instead to integrate himself within the white community.[54] His other advice, regarding the Wind River agent Col. Thomas M. Jones, read: "I hear you have got a good agent. Teach the Indians to trust him and the government to do right. Too complaining a spirit will bring them bad treatment."[55] This injunction would ultimately go unheeded, with disastrous consequences. Nonetheless, Coolidge's new missionary headquarters was completed just in time. The year 1886 saw the dreaded return of the Jesuits to St. Stephens, commencing a battle for souls that would, within a year, almost destroy Coolidge's career and, worse, almost get him killed.[56]

In a letter, Sherman Coolidge described his new home as "situated on the beautiful banks of Little Wind River, near the mouth of Trout Creek and half a mile from the celebrated Fort Washakie Hot Spring." The dwelling rested on 330 acres of "almost perfectly level" land, whose soil was so fertile it produced "a luxuriant growth of natural hay." Coolidge also shared his plans: "I am going to begin fencing it right away and I am also going to make an irrigation ditch into it as soon as I can. In doing this, I show the Indians by example as well as by precept, the beneficial outcome of industry and the dignity of labor under Christian Civilization."[57] Some neighbors were not as impressed as Coolidge had hoped. Years later, he admitted that he was "nearly assassinated," presumably by some Arapahos, for trying to divert water from the river for irrigation.[58] That a white man named Crawford had assisted him probably inflamed tensions.[59] Despite this setback, Coolidge claimed that the neighboring Arapahos had "taken advantage of the past mild winter by procuring and hauling logs and poles for fence and house purposes." They were therefore "working hard to advance themselves in every way in their power," even though life was "difficult under the existing circumstances."

These "circumstances" were indeed grave. Coolidge wrote of how the Arapahos "receive food every week from the government, but the rations they receive for the week can only last, at most, three days, so that what provisions are given them are sufficient to keep them alive for only half a week." He continued, "How many of them manage to exist is a mystery to me and to the white people of every class and occupation in this vicinity." Coolidge had witnessed that the Arapahos often had to sell their horses to survive and at times sold "their own daughters to wicked men" in exchange for "a mouthful of something to eat." Such conditions were all the more tragic because the Arapahos were "a noble people endowed with every capacity and capability" but were now "starving to death inch by inch, in sight of the American flag," as "helpless and despised wards."

Curiously, Coolidge believed that the only way out of this quagmire was to accelerate the government's broken assimilationist policy. Young Indians, he felt, had to be separated from reservation life for longer periods to counter the influence of their elders. One of the main dynamics he noted at Wind River was that returned students appeared "only half-educated and half civilized." When again among their people, they tended to "relapse into the old ways of wild and barbarous Indian life," victim to reservations that offered nothing but "a home in the shape of an Indian tepee and the simple and warm reception of their heathen uncivilized friends and relatives." Five or six years of schooling simply was not enough. Only "eight or twelve years of real social and religious training" could effectively counter "native influence."[60] Likely Coolidge was using his own life as a measure.

Coolidge elaborated on these issues in an 1887 piece for the *Churchman* that began with the abrupt admission that "a large majority" of Arapaho and Shoshone children sent to Carlisle in recent years had died. This was, of course, a devastating fact to many Indian parents. Coolidge's own brother had also been lost in the East, but that did not stop him from criticizing Indian parents, with their "limited range of thought," for refusing to send their sons and daughters to government boarding schools. One solution was on-reservation government schooling, though it entailed serious drawbacks. The Indian Bureau, described as "inextricably mixed up with politics, partisan changes, and a pernicious system of patronage," did not adequately support its "ill-paid and responsible employees." These Indian Service workers faced the daunting task of "overseeing starving human beings" in "a land bursting with plenty." By creating such conditions, the bureau actively stifled its wards' "progress." The best solution therefore resided in replacing government schools with on-reservation religious education. Whites skeptical of this policy or the Indians' "capacity to receive the Christian religion" were simply misguided. Thousands of "native heathens" had accepted Episcopal teachings, providing clear evidence that such doubts were unfounded. Many Native peoples had also rapidly risen from a "barbarian" to a "progressive" state. Seeing through this transformation required patience. The "cultivation of the industrial habits" and "enlargement of the mental powers" among a benighted people would take time but was inevitable.[61]

Coolidge's condemnation of the Indian Bureau amounted to a bold public act for a Native missionary residing on a reservation, even if his views echoed those of the Episcopal hierarchy. Ethelbert Talbot, elected as the first bishop of Wyoming and Idaho in 1886, regularly and roundly condemned the bureau's failures, blaming the "reservation system" for "the fact that the Indian has practically stood still." Talbot naturally abhorred the "savage customs" of Indigenous peoples and considered whites "stronger and more intelligent," but the "national shame" of America's broken treaties constituted an equal affront to his sensibilities. It was a "wonder," he wrote in his 1906 memoir *My People of the Plains*, "that after so many decades of such treatment" the Indians had not been "hopelessly ruined." Hope did, however, exist in the "tall, erect, broad shouldered, and full-chested" Sherman Coolidge, "an excellent illustration of what education and the refining influence of a Christian home may accomplish for the red-man."[62]

Though the Episcopal Church held him up as a model Indian returned to his people to impart the ways of Christ, Coolidge himself displayed an intense interest in the Arapaho culture he was chosen by God to eradicate. Part of this fascination can be accounted for by a desire to understand his origins, as anyone in his position would feel. Yet, the more Coolidge studied the more he came to question whether every aspect of Euro-American civilization was necessarily superior and whether every aspect of Arapaho life was necessarily degraded. For instance, Coolidge greatly admired Arapaho clothing, writing of the garb's "blankets of various, gay colors, bright bracelets, beautiful necklaces, moccasins covered with stained quills of the porcupine and beads which scintillate in the face of the sun."[63] Importantly, he began to perceive certain religious similarities. His journals noted how the Arapahos' religion was monotheistic, how they understood right and wrong, and how they forbade lying, idol worship, theft, and murder, just as the Ten Commandments do. Like Christians, the Arapahos also fasted, gave thanks, and prayed in solitude or with others on a hill or in a sacred tepee. Another revelation was that their language contained no profanity. It was simply impossible for an Arapaho to take the Lord's name in vain.[64] What perhaps struck Coolidge most, however, was the egalitarian nature of Arapaho society and its eschewing of worldly possessions or, put another way, its rejection of Euro-American materialism. These observations would appear in many of his later public statements and sermons.[65] Eventually, he even developed a theory that Adam and Eve had been Arapahos, though he shared it with few others.[66] Finally, Coolidge desired to preserve and promote Arapaho language and culture. In letters to William Jones, a friend from Seabury Divinity School, Sherman told of his plans to produce a manual of Arapaho and English conversation and a book on "the manners and customs" of the nation.[67] Unfortunately, neither idea came to fruition. Other work may have taken precedence.

At the end of the 1880s, Coolidge and Roberts inaugurated an Episcopal boarding school for girls with the blessing of Chief Washakie. Roberts cultivated a respectful relationship with the Shoshone chief, who donated 160 acres of land for the enterprise. Bishop Talbot raised funds for its construction and visited Wind River regularly. On one occasion, Washakie performed a war dance in his honor and prepared "two fat beeves" for a grand feast. Talbot eventually provided a full $2,000 for the school and lobbied in Washington for greater support. His actions sprang from his belief that it was "a sacred duty" of the Episcopal Church to aid Native peoples. The girls' school was thus named in his honor.[68] And the building only continued. Roberts also supervised the erection of a small log church near the girls' school grounds that served as a classroom and of a two-room log cabin maintained for visitors. Not long after, Fort Washakie supplanted Ethete as the Episcopal mission headquarters of Wind River.[69]

On the surface, then, everything appeared to be going well. In 1885 Talbot had urged Coolidge and Roberts to "work as brothers," and one might get the impression that they had.[70] In later years, Roberts and his wife, Laura, lauded Coolidge, remarking how he "was always a perfect gentleman, and said no evil thing about a living soul."[71] In truth, John and Laura Roberts (who treated most people with disdain) strongly disliked Coolidge, and he them.[72] Perhaps this was the result of a clash of personalities or methods, or perhaps it was racism, or perhaps Roberts—rather ironically—saw Coolidge as an interloper on the reservation, which for ten years had been his domain. This was, however, the least dangerous conflict that had arisen during Coolidge's first years back at Wind River. The others would soon result in his hasty departure.

4

Conspiracy, Exile, and the East

After Bishop John Spalding traveled to Wyoming Territory in 1885 for Sherman Coolidge's ordination, he had complimented Col. Thomas M. Jones, the "good agent" at Wind River, and advised Coolidge: "Teach the Indians to trust him and the government to do right. Too complaining a spirit will bring them bad treatment."[1] At first, Coolidge's relationship with Jones seemed friendly. In 1886 Jones, an Episcopalian, aided him in locating his half-sister, Sings First, following more than fifteen years of separation. Coolidge had heard she was living in Evanston, Wyoming, and Jones traveled there with a letter of introduction in both 1886 and 1887, with the latter trip reconnecting the siblings.[2] Jones also approved Coolidge's request to host "a white man," Mr. Crawford, on the reservation to help improve his land claim in the summer of 1886.[3] By early spring 1887, however, things had changed. Coolidge had become secretly angered with Jones and his wife, Mary, the head matron at the Wind River Industrial School, for what he viewed as her poor work ethic. The Jones family was not the only source of his frustration on the reservation. Coolidge had also grown irritated by the "conduct" of Reverend Roberts and was especially upset by the growing influence of the Jesuits at St. Stephens, led by Father Francis X. Kuppens, on what he felt was his rightful territory. Around this time, Coolidge began to deride Jones, Roberts, and the Jesuits in missives to his old friends in Faribault, Minnesota. One, F. L. Beane, tried to cheer him, writing, "I am very sorry that the Jesuits are trying to encroach on your field of labor, but once you speak the Arapahoe language fluently you will be sure to hold your own." Beane as well noted that tales of the Indian Bureau's maladministration were nothing new.[4] Coolidge appreciated his confidant's sympathy but decided to take matters into his own hands.

Everything started in November 1886, when Superintendent A. M. Johnson, a Southern Baptist minister, of Wind River Industrial School asked Commissioner of Indian Affairs John Atkins for permission to employ Coolidge as an assistant teacher. (It is possible that Agent Jones, persuaded by John Roberts, argued against the appointment.)[5] In his request, Johnson explained to Atkins that Coolidge "understands the Arapahoe, and the Indian sign language tolerably well, and for that reason he possesses superior qualifications for the work." His "moral character," importantly, showed "no blemish."[6] Atkins likely cared little if Coolidge spoke Arapaho, for the commissioner had already banned teaching in Indigenous languages in favor of an all-English school policy.[7] Nonetheless, the appointment proceeded, and Coolidge gave up his missionary stipend in favor of the $500 per annum government salary.[8] In gratitude to Johnson, he wrote Commissioner Atkins to ask that his new boss receive a raise to $1,200 per annum in recognition of his "rare qualifications" and the "marvelous improvement" his tenure had produced.[9] Johnson, just a week later, wrote Atkins of the remarkable work Coolidge had accomplished. "I have found him to be an indispensable factor in the enforcement of good discipline in the school," the letter explained. "Such was the looseness of the discipline on my arrival that boys went into the girls' dormitory almost every night and slept with the girls. I put a stop to it at once by putting the boys in the guardhouse and feeding them bread and water for a few days." Indian parents would come to complain, but Coolidge's "explanation was always satisfactory" because "being an Indian himself, his people believed what he said." As a result, discipline had even been improved to the levels of "the average white school," and the government institution had ceased functioning as (in his idiosyncratic spelling) a "hoar house."[10] Coolidge and Johnson, then, had become close, and their love of discipline was not all that bonded them. They both blamed the head matron, Mary Jones, for the lax atmosphere, and they both despised the Catholics at St. Stephens for encroaching on their chosen field.[11] In each case, Coolidge and Johnson were willing to take extreme measures to right perceived wrongs.

Sometime in the spring of 1887, Father Kuppens at St. Stephens began fencing in the mission's farm. He was "stopped immediately" by Arapaho chief Black Coal, "who told him he must not build any fence." According to a later affidavit taken by Agent Jones in his investigation, Kuppens and Black Coal "talked the matter over," and Kuppens, unwilling to "do anything that would create any ill feeling with the Indians," agreed to discuss the matter with Chief Washakie. Kuppens communicated to Washakie that Jones had given him 160 acres, "the same as any white man taking up land," and that he was building a school. The fenced land was "for raising grain and vegetables for food for the children." Washakie seemed "perfectly satisfied" and wondered why Black Coal "should find fault." Following a private meeting with Black Coal and Superintendent Johnson, Washakie abruptly changed his mind. Allegedly, Black Coal had convinced the Shoshone chief that Kuppens was in fact "fencing in the whole country."[12] This outrageous claim, it seems, had originated from Johnson and Coolidge, who had been turning Black Coal against the Jesuits for months. Later testimony by Henry Reed, an interpreter for the Arapahos, revealed that the two men had instructed Black Coal "not to give up the land to the Mission School" set aside by Jones, because the agent had "no right to go down to the Mission School and tell another man to fence up his [Black Coal's] land."

The effect of all these meetings was that Black Coal, Washakie, and Sharp Nose had become "very excited against" Jones.[13] Washakie himself stated that Johnson had accused Jones of treating the three chiefs "like dogs," which, regrettably, "made him feel bad."[14] One of Johnson's teachers even later swore that Coolidge, in reference to Jones's treatment of the Arapahos, had said, "There is no wonder that the Indians are driven to desperation and taking to the war path."[15] Jones left the reservation on April 14 for purposes that remain unclear. When he returned in early May, as he later wrote Bishop Whipple, he found that Coolidge and Johnson had been having "secret meetings with my Indians, and incited them to resist my authority, to have hard feelings to me and to the Gov't in order as I suppose to make the Catholics abandon their claim on the reservation." The situation had become so tense that Jones and the other agency employees spent several sleepless nights fearing "an uprising."[16]

Hoping that a show of force would discourage violence, the agent arrested one Arapaho chief for "insubordination and mutinous conduct." Jones then launched an investigation, interviewing people across the reservation and taking affidavits. His findings would soon put Coolidge and Johnson in a perilous position.[17]

Yet as dangerous as the conspiracy to undermine the St. Stephens Indian Mission was, Coolidge and Johnson were not done. The duo had also decided to strike at Agent Jones through his wife, Mary. Coolidge began gathering evidence in the form of incriminating incidents witnessed at the reservation school. In notes written to another agent, H. W. Wadsworth, he listed the sins, some of which, in truth, put the suspected offenders in a flattering light. Coolidge charged the Joneses with giving out clothing to students, including "new socks, mittens, scarfs, shoes, shirts, etc., when they were not needed." Worse, the couple had freed male and female students from the guardhouse when punished by other teachers at the school. These baleful inclinations toward leniency had resulted in chaos. The assistant matron, Miss Laura Smiley, had caught the Shoshone girls "swimming naked in the creek," and Mrs. Jones had, shockingly, not objected. Mrs. Jones had also taken a blasé attitude toward boys visiting the girls' dormitory, daring to remark, "Boys will be Boys," and "White boys would do the same." Several Shoshone girls had even been allowed to visit their families after being "denied the privilege." Perhaps most incendiary was Coolidge's claim that Mary Jones had suggested Miss Smiley could "help herself to unbleached muslin" from the warehouse. Mrs. Jones had allegedly requisitioned an amount of stove blacking polish from said warehouse, in effect stealing government property.[18]

In April 1887, Coolidge sent all this information to Commissioner Atkins, calling for Mary Jones's dismissal. He admitted that what he had to say was "disagreeable," but it was "the truth, pure and simple." During his time at the Wind River school, there had been "ample opportunity to observe the absolute necessity of a change in the matron."

Coolidge punctiliously detailed the reasons:

1st. Mrs. Mary E. Jones is totally unfit for the position as a matron because she is very impractical, she has no judgment, has no idea of discipline, has extravagant notions and ways, has an unhappy faculty of making remarks about others which is a source of mischief and confusion to the school, besides, she has a large family on her hands to draw her attentions away from the work of her position.

2nd. She looks upon her position as a *sinecure* and therefore does *practically nothing* for her annual salary of seven hundred and twenty ($720) dollars. . . . She claims that she has been excused from some of her duties as a matron by the Department.

3rd. As a result of her neglect or inability to do the work required by her position, through sickness or otherwise, the matron has been a great imposition upon the School, the Superintendent, the teachers, and especially, unjustly and grossly so upon the *assistant matron*, who has faithfully and devotedly attended to her own duties, besides, being compelled to do the work which the matron has left undone for twelve months.

This was hardly everything. Coolidge also complained that under the prevailing conditions, the school, "for all intents and purposes," had "no matron at all." Mrs. Jones refused to reside on the premises, against government policy, a fact that did not mask the larger issue of her being *"an unsuitable person for a matron in any case."* There had been a rumor that Agent Jones was "once ordered to have the matron resign" by the Department of the Interior, but no such thing had happened. The logical reason she survived, of course, was "on account of the matron being the *Agent's wife.*"

Coolidge sent his statement, "fervently hoping" that Commissioner Atkins would "take steps to remove this load of injustice and evil." He asked this not only for the sake of the school's employees but also for "the children of the tribe." His letter concluded with the promise that the majority of the school staff would corroborate his criticisms.[19] Another letter followed a week later in support of Miss Smiley, whom Agent Jones had immediately threatened to fire.[20] In his counterattack, Jones also gathered numerous affidavits concerning Coolidge's and Johnson's machinations against the Catholics. In Jones's report to the commissioner, he took care to include an affidavit from his own wife, claiming that

Superintendent Johnson had kept her on at the school despite having received the order to terminate her—an unlikely story, one might argue.[21]

Sherman Coolidge had a reason for writing to Atkins and praising Miss Smiley—a decidedly personal one at that. Later correspondence reveals that he and Miss Smiley had fallen in love and were planning marriage. This tender relationship, though, presented a vulnerable point at which to strike. Mary Jones, incensed at Coolidge's incendiary accusations, charged him and his fiancée with the salacious crime of "gross immorality," suggesting they had engaged in premarital intercourse. Coolidge now knew that he was in serious trouble. On May 8, he wrote to his mentor, Bishop Whipple, for the first time since his arrival at Wind River, preemptively defending his actions and character. Explaining that he had done nothing but his "duty," Coolidge condemned Mary Jones for her "utter disregard to truth, justice and decency." Agent Jones, meanwhile, had turned the local community and the Indian Bureau against him to such a degree that two agency employees had threatened his life. These efforts to "ruin" him were all the more outrageous considering that the Joneses professed to be Episcopalians.[22]

Two days later, the hammer fell. Agent Jones, having sent evidence from his investigations to Washington, saw no reason to delay in informing Coolidge and Johnson that their conspiracy had been foiled. They now stood charged with a violation of three sections of the U.S. Code in "inciting" Indians to "mutiny and insubordination" against the Bureau of Indian Affairs. Washington had granted Jones authority to "suspend and remove" both men from the reservation. Fortunately, he gave them a way to save face. Jones claimed he did not want his adversaries to be "humiliated by public arrest or trial by a U.S. Court," and if they would "quietly resign and leave the reservation," he would take no further actions against them. He even offered severance.[23] One naturally wonders if this eagerness to drop the matter stemmed from Mary Jones's alleged pilfering of government stock, but whatever its implications and defects, the letter had the intended effect. Both Coolidge and Johnson immediately tendered their resignations.[24]

A day later, Jones did something surprising. Having reconsidered the situation, he informed Coolidge that as long as he complied with "certain requirements," he could remain because, ultimately, Wind River was his "home."[25] Coolidge nonetheless rejected the proposition, understanding too well the "unfavorable condition of affairs." As quickly as he could, he hired a couple to take care of his property and made plans to head east for four or five years to pursue further studies. Coolidge also offered to purchase his home from the Episcopal Church. Where the money would come from he did not specify. Perhaps he had been able to save his salaries thanks to his free housing and government rations. Perhaps it was the coming severance. He resolved, though, to eventually return to Wind River when the "transitory" figures such as Jones and his wife had left the reservation and to erect a chapel for the Arapahos near his home.[26] Sherman Coolidge left Wind River three days later, vowing to Whipple that he would clear his name "if possible."[27] John Roberts wrote to Whipple the very next day, May 14, stressing that Coolidge's "unpleasant mess" was "the result of his own actions."[28]

Whatever the case, a hasty retreat was the correct choice. As Agent Jones explained to Commissioner Atkins, Coolidge's departure was "quite wise" in light of "the feelings of people outside the reservation." Settlers viewed the conflict with St. Stephens as one in which Coolidge had provoked violence against whites, thus putting their lives at risk. Jones stated honestly that he was unsure if it was safe for either Coolidge or Johnson to remain "after the evil influence they have had over my Indians." The public—probably due to Jones's efforts—had become "very much incensed against them."[29] Likewise, Jones's offer to allow Coolidge to remain should not be taken as a sign of affection. Instead, the agent viciously condemned Coolidge to Bishop Whipple in a lengthy missive. "I hate to have to say it but my regard for the truth compels me to do so," Jones announced. "This man is a failure and I fear that neither church, education or association can reform him." In treacherously allying himself with Johnson—a "confederate Baptist preacher," no less—Coolidge had become nothing more than "a disgrace to the church."[30]

With letters like Jones's coming in, Whipple and Spalding were left doing a sort of autopsy, sifting through any information that could fully explain what had transpired. John Roberts, for instance, did his best to excuse himself from any culpability in the scandal, claiming that any "suspicions" held by Coolidge against him were "erroneous" and that he had always been a "best friend" to the young man. Spalding then admitted to Whipple that for months Coolidge had been "doing nothing" on the reservation and that Roberts had in fact advocated for his transfer to the Wind River School "in order to get other work out of him." Spalding was still convinced, however, that Coolidge was "upright and good." More than likely, his wrongdoings had been committed under the corrupting influence of Superintendent Johnson and Miss Smiley.[31]

By the end of May, others had come forward in Coolidge's defense. H. B. Freeman, an old family friend with whom he had stayed just after leaving Wind River, wrote to Whipple and dismissed any notions that "gross immorality" had transpired with Miss Smiley. As evidence, Freeman noted that he had witnessed Coolidge "pass unscathed through temptations fully as great as any he may lately have endured." That the young missionary would jettison "so many years of work and discipline" after assuming a role in which "the capacity of his people for civilization was on trial" was unthinkable. It was more probable that his misfortunes resulted from honest work on behalf of Indian welfare—something that always elicited "hostility" from the bureau's power structure. Most interesting, though, were Freeman's comments on claims that Coolidge had been "lazy." "None of those who make this charge," he protested, "would stop to consider that until he was 12 or 14 years of age, Sherman had been taught that any kind of work was disgraceful, and that this idea had been inbred in him for many generations." Were one to consider this aspect of his character, they would immediately see that compared to his Arapaho brethren, Coolidge was "a marvel of industry and energy."[32]

Charles Coolidge, Sherman's adoptive father, concurred fully with Freeman. In a letter to Whipple, he regretted that Sherman had been "ill-adapted" to the "sharp scheming palpitations and the chicanery of an Indian Agency" and described how Sherman's "Indian nature" made him "slower and more deliberate" than a white man. Unfortunately, no one had considered this factor when he took up work at Wind River. Sherman required a "watchful eye," a "strong hand," and a "superior mind" to guide him, because he had not yet reached the same level "as men of our civilization." The best solution, therefore, was that Sherman be made an assistant to "some clergyman who would take an interest in him" and "spur him up to the requirements which a white congregation would require of him." Such tutelage would "brighten up his mind by the contact of civilization" and allow him to return to Wind River with the requisite skills once the time came.[33]

The racism displayed by Sherman Coolidge's sympathizers indicates a sad fact about his life. Even those who supported him and believed in him still saw him as innately inferior. How many such slights had he endured since his first contact with "civilization"? Had he ever felt at home in a society that deemed him as alien, as inherently "savage"? And one might also ask, how much of a role did racism play in his exile from Wind River? He had acted injudiciously, to say the least, in his conspiracy against St. Stephens. But even if he had not, would his complaints against Thomas and Mary Jones ever have been taken seriously? In the end, undoubtedly any Indian challenging a white bureau employee hazarded censure in what was a decidedly racist environment. Such an outcome was almost inevitable. And to make matters worse, John Roberts, Coolidge's "best friend" and Episcopalian brother, had openly sided with Agent Jones. As a final insult, Roberts then took over the vacant position of assistant teacher at Wind River's government school.[34] Coolidge, deeply embittered, meanwhile headed east, stopping in Minnesota to meet with Whipple and explain himself once more.[35] While in Faribault, Coolidge, wanting to get far away, matriculated at Hobart College in Geneva, New York, for graduate studies in theology. Immersing himself in study may have been the best salve for his battered soul. The St. Stephens debacle had been a major setback, professionally *and* personally. Whipple was likely understanding, but Coolidge's plans to marry his fiancée, Miss Smiley, had sadly been destroyed.

At some point in the early autumn of 1887, Sherman Coolidge arrived at Hobart College, ready to recommence life as a student. In his first week, he participated in a brutal orientation ritual called the cane rush in, of all places, the campus chapel.[36] Cane rushes, once widely practiced throughout the United States at prestigious academic institutions, began with a freshman student defiantly displaying a hard, wooden cane before the entire class of sophomores and teasing them to incite a fury. As the tension peaked, a sophomore would suddenly ejaculate, "Freshie's got a cane!"—signaling his classmates to rush the offending freshman. The freshmen's job was to block the sophomores by forming a V pattern around the student who held the cane. The two classes would then wrestle and throw punches, often drawing blood, until the cane-wielding freshman was pushed outside the chapel, where the sophomores could finally rip the cane away. If the freshman class managed to hold onto the cane, it won. Such cane rushes sometimes turned so violent that police were forced to intervene.[37] Coolidge—likely because of his imposing build and perhaps because he was Indian—was elected to hold the cane in his first days at Hobart. On the afternoon of the event, he became an immediate college legend when he put up a ferocious fight against the sophomores and at one point sat on a fellow student's head to immobilize him.[38] Coolidge only relinquished the cane when tackled by five students in unison. Whatever the popularity of the cane rush ritual, the vision of a Native man being attacked by a large group of whites is today more than irksome.

Nonetheless, his sensational performance in the cane rush won Coolidge the title of "most powerful man in the institution" and secured his status. Over the next two years, he became an active presence at Hobart and in the Geneva community.[39] Fortunately, school records and contemporaneous newspaper reports provide a brief picture of his activities. According to Hobart's yearbooks, as a freshman Coolidge joined the Pole Whist Club (for connoisseurs of fine dining) and served as an honorary member of the Hobart College Literary Society.[40] In his sophomore year, he was elected class historian.[41] More interesting were Coolidge's efforts to enlighten white audiences on the abilities of Native peoples. In July 1889, sponsored by one of the college's history professors, he offered public talks titled "Our Indian Problem" in one of the parlors of the Hygienic Institute on the Hobart campus. A local newspaper reported that his lecture was well attended and even featured live music.[42] Production values were important. Tickets cost a steep twenty-five cents.[43] No texts of Coolidge's summer lectures have survived, but their content is suggested by his appearance at the annual meeting of the Quaker-led Indian Rights Association, or Friends of the Indian, at Lake Mohonk, New York, in October 1889.

Sherman Coolidge's presence at Mohonk was most welcome. The organizing committee selected him to lead the opening prayer, thus exhibiting a shining example of what Euro-American education could accomplish in assimilating the Indian. Not long into the conference, future Massachusetts congressman Samuel June Barrows, who had cared for Coolidge's brother a decade earlier, casually approached him. As the two conversed, it slowly began to dawn on Barrows that Coolidge was the brother of the boy he had loved and mourned so many years ago. Barrows had carried a small portrait of Philip in a locket since the boy's death. That locket was around his neck at Lake Mohonk when he made the connection, much to both men's deep surprise. Coolidge and Barrows revealed the remarkable coincidence in a subsequent session, astonishing the crowd.[44]

For the Mohonk conference, Coolidge prepared a brief talk on Indian education. He thanked those who had gathered for their interest in saving a "helpless and perishing people," then related his own struggles to read and even to learn the alphabet as an eleven-year-old boy. Just as tears once rolled down his cheeks at his foster mother's insistence that he persevere, Indian children were now "crying for education." As the best solution to the "Indian problem," education allowed the Indian to "show his ability, his humanity, [and] his capability of mental culture." Deeming the Mohonk conference the "best pow-wow" he had ever attended, Coolidge explained his thankfulness by referencing Chief Washakie back at Wind River, stating, "I might express it in the way that an Indian expressed it once. A kindness had been shown to a chief of the reservation where I had been staying; and he said to the person that conveyed that kindness: 'Tell that person who sent me this gift that, when a Frenchman receives a kindness, he is thankful in his head. The head has a tongue: it can talk. But, when an Indian receives a kindness, he is thankful in his heart. His heart has no tongue: it cannot talk.'" Coolidge continued, "So it is with me to-night, but I have learned by education that there is a communication between the heart and the brain, and what the heart feels the brain can express through the tongue."[45]

Henry Kendall, a Pueblo Carlisle graduate, followed Coolidge at Mohonk. Kendall also spoke of his experiences as a young boy, trying to persuade his parents to allow him to study in a mission school in Albuquerque for the purpose of "self-improvement." When they finally relented, he was able to go to Pennsylvania and study under Richard Henry Pratt.

Kendall claimed that when he returned home after four years away, his parents "shed tears of joy" at the progress he had made and insisted that he continue his education in the East. His story was intended to dispel the myth that Indian children returned home with a sense of superiority. On the contrary, "since I have been separated from my parents," Kendall noted, "I respect them more and I love them more." His only worry was how the East would continue to affect his health. He prayed that he would be "spared by the Almighty."[46]

When the speech finished, Coolidge commented on how Kendall's feelings for his parents and people had grown, rather than diminished, after receiving his education. "I have experienced also the other side," he claimed, "that my people have received me after fourteen years of absence in civilization, and have looked up to me and been proud of me." This respect meant that when Coolidge made suggestions for improvements or courses of action, the Arapahos willingly listened, proving that older Indians "do not have prejudice always." Problems instead arose when "Indians are only allowed to stay a few years in the East," returning half-transformed with "only a smattering of education" (as Coolidge had discussed in his prior article for the *Churchman*). Such Indians often incurred the disapproval of their tribes for their incomplete mastery of "civilization." "But," Coolidge insisted, "when one is educated enough to stand his own ground and is recognized and encouraged by the white people there or in the East, then these people will have much pride and respect for him, and will heed his advice and his words." In an open display of patriotism, Coolidge concluded by calling on Dennison Wheelock, an Oneida cornet virtuoso associated with the Carlisle Indian Industrial School, to play "Taps" in honor of the military officers present.[47]

One might question Coolidge's claims regarding his influence over the Arapahos at Wind River, yet an incident from his time at Hobart indicates how they had certainly influenced him. One Sunday in New York, he was asked to give a sermon to "a very aristocratic church" that operated on a "pew-rent system." Wealthier worshipers paid for the privilege of proximity to the altar, while poorer members of the congregation were relegated to two pews placed in a rear corner. The idea offended Coolidge so greatly that he felt it impossible to worship there. He announced to the shocked congregants that he preferred the religion of his forefathers, the Arapahos, to a religion of "commerce" that was "auctioned off" to the highest bidder.[48] This striking example showed how Coolidge's first period back among his tribespeople had shaped his perspective. Yet despite this incident, Geneva's Episcopal community appreciated his work. The local press even deemed Coolidge "a favorite at college and among church people."[49]

Why, then, did Coolidge leave Hobart in the winter of 1889–90 in the midst of his junior year?[50] No surviving letters indicate the precise reason, but Coolidge's old nemesis, Agent Thomas M. Jones, had left his post at Wind River in 1889.[51] Perhaps the regime change prompted the Episcopal hierarchy to encourage Coolidge to return. Perhaps he had finally run through his savings. One wonders, though, if he really wanted to go back. In a letter from August 1889 to John Roberts, Coolidge stated that he would not return to Wind River until Bishop Talbot agreed to unspecified "conditions."[52] Likely, he wanted to ensure Roberts would have no power over him. Another later letter reveals that in Geneva, Coolidge had become engaged to a young woman named Grace.[53] One piece of church correspondence also indicates that as early as 1890, he had requested a new assignment in Indian Territory in Oklahoma but was ignored.[54]

Despite the mystery surrounding his embarking on a second tenure at Wind River, Coolidge was returning at a time when the Plains Indians were in a deep state of crisis, threatened by the loss of their land base and the tightening restrictions on religious and cultural practices. Even basic survival had become a challenge for those living under an Indian Bureau bureaucracy that provided poor rations and paltry material support. Faced with the vicissitudes of federal policy, the Northern Arapahos in particular needed an influential advocate who was capable of mediating among the U.S. government, the Eastern Shoshones, and themselves. At Mohonk, Coolidge had boasted of the respect he had won for his mastery of "civilization." But rather than becoming this advocate, he would work to implement the Indian Bureau's assimilationist program against the wishes and traditions of his kinsmen. Over Coolidge's second stay at Wind River, the affection he had once enjoyed would, for some, turn to deep and dangerous resentment, and in time would lead to his permanent departure.

5

Losing Ground

By the late 1880s, the injurious changes forced upon the Plains Indians by Euro-American expansionism had resulted in widespread desperation. The Ghost Dance movement, led by a Paiute messiah named Wovoka, promised to heal this suffering. Wovoka's vision foretold that if the Ghost Dance were performed, all Native peoples living and dead would be reunited, the past would be resurrected, the bison would return, and the whites would disappear.[1] This prospect was attractive to many, including the Northern Arapahos. There was danger, however, in openly practicing the new religion. Arapaho chiefs, especially, realized its provocative message could severely endanger relations with federal officials, who saw the movement as the beginning of a revolt. As guests on a reservation to which they held no title, caution was advisable. Regardless, by 1889 the Ghost Dance had become an established ritual at Wind River. Chiefs such as Sherman Coolidge's uncle Sharp Nose circumvented bureau hostility by making regular trips to Fort Washakie to assure the agents that no militant uprising would occur. Other tribes, such as the Oglalas and Brulés at Pine Ridge and Rosebud Indian Reservations, respectively, were less obliging. Among these Lakotas, the Ghost Dance spread rapidly. When they visited Wind River to confer with the Northern Arapahos about Wovoka's prophesy, leaders convinced officials that the discussions dealt with farming methods. In the summer of 1890, military and agency authorities learned that some on Wind River were taking part in the Ghost Dance. Fortunately, they believed it posed little threat.[2]

By winter, the evolving situation had become more unstable. The Ghost Dance movement had grown among the Lakotas, and at Pine Ridge, inexperienced Indian Bureau agent Daniel F. Royer became convinced that a rebellion was imminent.[3] Higher officials agreed, and in October 1890, troops appeared at Pine Ridge and Rosebud, prompting over two thousand Brulés and Oglalas to head north to O-ona-gazhee, a plateau in the Badlands.[4] Sitting Bull, who had returned from Canada in 1881, was subsequently killed in a botched arrest by Indian police at the Standing Rock Reservation on December 15. The Indian Bureau had willfully perceived him as a supporter of the Ghost Dance.[5] Sitting Bull's tragic demise inspired more Lakotas and some Cheyennes to leave reservation territory. During the confusion, the Seventh Cavalry stopped one band of 340 Miniconjou Lakotas en route to Pine Ridge and forced them to make camp along Wounded Knee Creek. The next day, December 29, American troops killed nearly half, including women and children, in the Wounded Knee Massacre. The horror of the act and an infusion of more troops ended the impasse. On January 15, 1891, the Lakotas surrendered and began an orderly return to Pine Ridge.[6] Military officials quickly ensured that the Arapahos would not engage in similar resistance. Tribal leaders, wary of conflict, convinced the War Department that they would refuse to take up arms or give shelter to refugees. Sharp Nose played an instrumental role in these talks. In secret, however, the Northern Arapahos continued to perform the Ghost Dance until 1893.[7]

The Wounded Knee Massacre represented, most horrifically, the dire situation of Native peoples countrywide. By the end of the nineteenth century, the combined population of Indian nations numbered fewer than a quarter of a million people. The census figure—the lowest ever— enforced the prevailing notion among Euro-Americans that Indigenous peoples were simply fated for extinction. Outside of the small Native rights and anthropological communities, most whites remained indifferent to the prospect.[8] The Northern Arapahos were not immune to the steep population decline. Within the first six years following their relocation to Wind River, their numbers had decreased more than 10 percent to just 823. Until the turn of the century, their deaths continued to outnumber births, and a high infant mortality rate resulted from the consumption of poor government rations and contact with European diseases. Economically, the Arapahos fared little better.[9] Men tried to earn money and support their families within the local settler community, often by cutting firewood. Others labored for reservation authorities. Many more went into debt while taking agency loans for basic necessities.[10] Despite these hardships, Indian Bureau agents and whites in the surrounding area continued to demand the opening of more reservation lands for purchase, leasing, and logging.[11]

Worsening matters, the Arapahos at Wind River came under a new threat toward the end of the 1880s—allotment. In 1887 the Dawes Severalty Act passed. Its aim was to divide communally owned reservation lands and foster a rapid transition to single-family farming. Plots allotted to individuals would be held in trust by the U.S. government for twenty-five years, ensuring that Natives would settle and not sell. Heads of families received 160 acres; single persons, 80. Those younger than eighteen years of age received a mere 40. "Surplus" lands, left over after allotment, were distributed for white settlement. This policy proved disastrous for Native communities. By 1932 the Dawes Act enabled the appropriation of 86 million acres of collectively owned reservation lands, or over 60 percent of the Indigenous land base.[12]

Individual land ownership, of course, was a foreign concept to the Northern Arapahos. The leaders at Wind River nonetheless exploited the Dawes Act partially to their advantage. In 1888 they agreed to accept the new scheme (eventually) on the condition of receiving increased rations, a herd of cattle, and monetary compensation. They also had another motive. Black Coal, Sharp Nose, and two other chiefs, White Horse and Eagle Head, well knew that Shoshone chief Washakie was lobbying the bureau for the Arapahos' removal from Wind River. Consenting to allotment strengthened their claim to remain amid increasing pressures.

In 1891 the U.S. government actively began pressing for a cession of more reservation land. Washakie, angered at the continuing encroachments, stated bitterly: "Twenty-two years ago, I first came here. I thought this land was mine. I always thought I owned it, or had an interest in it until today. Now the people who came here to stay with me quarrel with me, and with the men the Great Father has sent out here to treat with us." Nonetheless, he reluctantly agreed to relinquish the southern portion of the reserve. Black Coal initially declined, arguing vigorously that Wind

River be divided between the two tribes as a reward for the Arapahos' cooperation with the government. Black Coal's efforts resulted in the opening of a subagency on the eastern portion of Wind River, twenty-two miles from Fort Washakie.[13]

The atmosphere was therefore strained when Sherman Coolidge returned to the West months before Wounded Knee and again took up residence at the Fort Washakie Hotel.[14] None of his comments on the massacre, however, seem to have survived, and rather shockingly, his correspondence from the winter of 1890–91 betrays no trace of the incident.[15] Coolidge's Seabury friend, William Jones, wrote him on January 5, 1891, asking, "Are you still alive after all the turkey and rejoicing?"[16] Coolidge replied that his "Christmas went off nicely" and spoke of a "lovely party" thrown at the school.[17] At Wind River, his work had resumed as rector of the Church of the Redeemer. Coolidge also had two other chapels under his purview and a position with the Indian Service as an intermittent clerk.[18] He sometimes returned to his strategically placed missionary headquarters, though the home had grown "dilapidated."[19] The same could not be said of the agency center. In 1892 a new Wind River government school was completed near Fort Washakie that was later dubbed "Gravy High" in honor of its monotonous menu. The school boasted the typical government curriculum, replete with military drills and corporal punishment for infractions such as speaking Native languages.[20] Few Shoshone or Arapaho parents sent their children willingly.[21] Roberts's Episcopal mission and girls' school, named for Ethelbert Talbot and situated on the western half of the reservation, also continued its operations. The Catholic competition at St. Stephens held a monopoly on the eastern half, four miles below the new Arapaho subagency. Since St. Stephens's reopening in 1886, Black Coal and the Northern Arapahos had become skillful at manipulating the two Christian factions at Wind River. The chief requested that the Catholics pay for the use of reservation farming lands; then he repeatedly requested they relocate so he could recover the already tilled fields. The Catholics tolerated the subterfuge, hoping to dissuade Black Coal from seeking closer ties with the Episcopalians.[22]

Near the time of his return, Coolidge contributed to the 1890 Wyoming Indian census, then in preparation. In a section on Arapaho culture and traditions, he stressed what he saw as a resemblance between their religious beliefs and Christianity. Coolidge's discussion covered the Arapaho creation myth and the monotheistic nature of the Arapaho conception of God, demonstrating that the tribe could not be classified as "pagan." Instead, he wrote that the Arapahos conceived of an "omnipotent spirit" that had an "evil" counterpart similar to the devil. Much like Christians, Coolidge claimed, they believed "the good and bad on earth will be rewarded and punished beyond the grave," even though their "standard of right and wrong" was "far inferior to that of civilized people." With this basis in place, he argued that the Arapahos had "made a commendable start" and could "become intelligent and self-supporting Christian citizens." But the loss of old ways first had to be overcome. In the past, abundant game and "no fear or knowledge" of diseases such as tuberculosis meant the Arapahos could "lie in the bosom of mother earth almost with impunity, with only a blanket or skin between them and the ground." This life had now vanished, replaced with "defective" reservation conditions imposed by the Indian Bureau. In their struggle for survival, the Arapahos had been forced to consume any dead cows and horses they happened to find, not knowing if they had died of disease. When illness inevitably befell them, no "properly-constructed hospital" existed to offer lifesaving services.[23]

The grim reality presented in the Wyoming Indian census was something that Ethelbert Talbot thought Coolidge could somehow mitigate. In early 1890, the bishop sent him $100 "for the purchase of a good-sized horse" that was "large enough to carry a heavy man like [him] on his back."[24] Enhanced mobility meant greater reach. Roberts generally sent off good reports of Coolidge's work, but at least once Talbot became frustrated with the lack of information flowing from Wind River.[25] In July 1890, he scolded Coolidge for not telling him how often he was holding services or how much "progress" he was making with the Arapahos. "This is your main work," Talbot sternly reminded him, "and the only possible justification for your appointment there." Coolidge was ordered to try harder in contacting the tribe and to apply "all the ardor, enthusiasm and devotion" in his "nature" to missionary activities.[26] Whatever Coolidge offered in response must have satisfied the bishop. Months later, Talbot resumed sending congratulations on the "noble" efforts being made at Wind River, along with words of encouragement.[27] One letter urged Coolidge to "keep on my dear fellow until you can talk Arapahoe like a Dutch uncle and then we will convert the whole tribe."[28]

As a missionary of Native descent, deeply interested in his birth culture, Coolidge might have been expected to side with the Northern Arapahos against policies they clearly opposed. This was not the case. Instead, as a bureau employee, Coolidge aligned himself fully with the U.S. government in its developing crises with the reservation's population. The agent from 1893 to 1895, a former army officer named P. H. Ray, was especially adamant about assimilation to individualistic Euro-American ways. Ray imprisoned anyone practicing polygamy, banned freedom of assembly, and undercut the Arapaho chiefs' authority by prohibiting giveaways and distributing rations directly to heads of households.[29] Coolidge fully agreed with this program. Evidence is found in an 1893 issue of the *Colorado Magazine*, specifically in his article "The Indian of To-day," which he wrote at the editor's request.[30]

Coolidge's article discusses his thoughts on recruiting Indian soldiers for the U.S. military, a policy already in place at Fort Washakie under Agent Ray.[31] Along with explaining how military discipline could effectively "conquer the barbarian," Coolidge lays out his progressive philosophy of Native development in stark terms, striking for their unabashed patriotism and rigid belief in rapid assimilation. Coolidge begins by recognizing that the U.S. government had made "mistakes in its dealings with the nation's wards"—perhaps an allusion to Wounded Knee. One should never doubt, however, that it was "substantially a princely Government" striving "to do the fair thing by the Indians of this continent." The "fair thing" resided in granting U.S. citizenship and looking forward to a time of "advancement" when Indians and whites could "worship the true God together at the Christian altar." This goal could be achieved only by educating "the weaker race of the inferior language, life, and religion into the better language, life and religion of the stronger race." With this process complete, newly Christian Indians would never take up arms against one another, or Americans, again. The military, especially, could be counted on to transform "dusky warriors" through "civilized" influences under a larger Pax Americana. Unsurprisingly, Coolidge equates Arapaho life before the reservation era with constant violence and upheaval. His "dearest and nearest relatives," he recalls, had been "slain in all the horrors of savage hostilities." Three things had ensured his further existence: Charles Coolidge, the embodiment of the U.S. military; Sophie Coolidge, the woman who enabled him to study for the Episcopal ministry; and the United States, a "new order of a civilization" in "union with God through the Prince of Peace."[32] Given his precarious condition around the time he was adopted, one can comprehend Sherman Coolidge's gratitude.

Coolidge's perspective on Christian civilization versus heathen savagery offered little room for compromise. Unfortunately, compromise was greatly needed at Wind River. But instead of searching for a middle road with a people experiencing a difficult transitional period, Coolidge maintained his strict notions. In the process, he became less of an advocate for the Northern Arapahos than an abettor of Indian Bureau policy.

In October 1891, the first land cession council took place at Wind River. Washakie and his subchiefs complained bitterly of the government's agreement to an Arapaho subagency and objected to the Arapahos' presence at the negotiations. Nonetheless, commissioners convinced the tribes to cede half of Wind River for $600,000 under the threat that annuities and rations would cease entirely in 1900. Even the Indian Bureau objected to the enormity of the loss, though commissioners argued that reducing the reservation from 2 million acres to 700,000 would leave plenty of land, timber, and minerals in Indian hands. Simultaneous promises that every tribe member would become rich from incoming monies enabled the collection of enough signatures. Remarkably, senators in Washington then rejected the 1891 agreement, claiming an insufficient amount of land had been ceded.

A second set of commissioners went to work in 1893, demanding more territory. Black Coal resisted, pointing out that the new terms left his people without adequate pastures and woods to survive and grow in subsequent generations. He died that same year, depriving the Northern Arapahos of a strong and able negotiator. Lone Bear, a new leader, succeeded him. Rebuffed, the U.S. government bided its time, reapplying pressure in 1896 when James McLaughlin, a long-serving Indian agent who had ordered the arrest of Sitting Bull, convinced the Arapahos and Shoshones to cede the hot springs in the northeast of Wind River as well as ten square miles surrounding the area.[33] The springs, called the "Smoking Waters," were believed to have medicinal qualities. Local whites coveted them and had established a settlement nearby.[34] In April 1896, both tribes signed an agreement in return for $60,000 in annuities, with a portion designated for cattle purchases, over the next five years. These promised payments failed to materialize, resulting in deep anger. The Arapahos, at least, finally obtained the legal right to remain at Wind River under the agreement. Nevertheless, Washington sought further cessions.[35]

Throughout these pained negotiations, Sherman Coolidge took the position of the government.[36] Here, a schism developed in which he became a better advocate for the Northern Arapahos when off the reservation than on site. The *Churchman* records that throughout the later 1890s, Coolidge traveled extensively in the Midwest and East. In cities including New York, Chicago, Boston, Philadelphia, and Newark, he lectured on his work among the Arapahos to women's groups, Episcopal congregations, and oftentimes children's clubs.[37] At these gatherings, he effectively pleaded for greater material and educational aid for the Arapahos and the Shoshones alike, raising "large sums of money."[38] Coolidge's personality was the major factor in his success. Among listeners, he quickly became known for injecting doses of humor into his speeches, at one meeting referring to himself and a fellow priest as the "wild Indian and the wild Irishman." The *Church Standard* noted, "All who heard his address felt that if there were a few more just such 'wild Indians' in the Church, and speaking for their race, the Indian work would not languish."[39]

Indeed, Coolidge never failed to make a lasting impression on white audiences and to present a perspective anchored in his Native roots. At a meeting of the New York chapter of the National Women's Indian Association, he condemned, "in the best of English," prevailing stereotypes of Indian peoples, taking issue "with the often-expressed opinion that the Indian is naturally and incorrigibly 'dirty, lazy and good for nothing.'" Appearances to the contrary were "due to force of circumstances" rather than any "expression of inherent qualities." For instance, whites who went camping were often reduced to filth in a bit over a week despite their having soap. As for notions of Indian idleness, Coolidge stated that when the Arapahos and Shoshones received the incentive of government contracts for agricultural products and timber, they "went to work with a will." The most compelling aspect of Coolidge's lectures, however, was his own personal story. Attendees in New York were aware that under the aegis of a Christian mission he was appealing for scholarships for Shoshone girls whose fathers may have killed his family members. Coolidge reinforced his message of peace, reconciliation, and education with claims that the elder Arapahos at Wind River supported his work and looked forward to the advantages that Euro-American knowledge would bring. He claimed that a man named Bad Face, "an Indian some sixty years old," had one day gazed at the Wind River school building with "rapt attention." He then turned to Coolidge and said, "I was just thinking that if it were possible for me to be a boy again, how I would love to go to that school, but it is impossible; my daughter shall go and enjoy the advantages an education gives."[40]

Coolidge's lectures made a lasting impression on white audiences. Many of the ladies who attended became intensely curious about Coolidge himself and pursued him romantically within the confines of contemporary decorum. The same was true of many young women who visited Wind River in person to witness Coolidge's fieldwork. With so much attention, he sometimes juggled correspondences with more than one love interest at a time. The letters that survive provide a window into his life at Wind River and his outrageously flirtatious manner. In 1891 Coolidge began writing two women—Nettie Smith of Beloit, Wisconsin, and Rebecca Buttroff of Baltimore, Maryland.

The correspondence with Buttroff began around the spring of 1891, following her visit to Wind River. Her letters could be somewhat suggestive. "Oh; how I long to have a good long gallop with some nice gentle lad," she wrote in one, referencing her rides with Coolidge around the reservation.[41] Coolidge thanked her for the "*spicy*" letter and wished he could see her again.[42] Buttroff also missed him badly and expressed as much. "I am in receipt of your precious letter," she responded, "and my thoughts are carried back to the dear old days I spent in Wyoming, with all its charms, how much I want to be with you if only for the short second of a single moment. I might take a glance at you at least if no more but now I will imagine I am with you, and adore you with my sweetest sentiments." John Roberts had asked her to return to Wind River, but her family "bitterly" opposed it, perhaps because of her growing attachment to Coolidge. She conjectured openly if his last missive had been a "real *love letter*" but then admitted, "I am afraid I have said too much on this subject."[43]

Unfortunately, Buttroff soon afterward heard the frightful rumor that Coolidge had acquired another "admirer," a young woman named Miss Truby.[44] Coolidge brushed off the Truby gossip, stating that it was his business alone. Still, Buttroff's romantic feelings were ones he shared. "It goes without saying I wish not only your thought could be brought back here," he reassured her, "but also yourself to the present charms of Wyoming as well as to those of 'the dear old days.' . . . Yes, the wish is mutual if only it could be realized for one moment." The distance between them nonetheless posed a problem. Coolidge could wait for Buttroff to return to Wind River, but there was little he could do to bring her back. That was Roberts's domain.[45] As a result, the romance limped on for another two years, with intermittent expressions of devotion and a few fights over who appreciated whose letters more.[46] In Coolidge's last extant letter to Buttroff, addressed to "Dear Beckie," he acknowledged how it was "a delicate matter for a lady to correspond with a gentleman and not be sure it is agreeable." He guaranteed her it was and wondered if he was "*the right person*" to receive her confessional letters. Buttroff mentioned that she had a special question she wanted to ask him "sometime." Coolidge promised to answer, but then rather insensitively he went on to speak of two "pretty girls" from Philadelphia then at Fort Washakie. One, "blonde ecstasy," was the daughter of an officer; her friend was a "lovely brunette."[47] That ended things with Buttroff for good.[48]

Unbeknownst to Buttroff, her competition had also included another young woman, Nettie Smith. Coolidge and Smith began exchanging photographic portraits of each other as early as June 1891. He shared news with her of his sick horse, his interest in *Anna Karenina*, and the "so very pleasant" Buffalo soldiers at Fort Washakie. His letter as well disclosed a wish to see her again.[49] In one missive, Coolidge lamented his unrequited love for a woman he called "the blonde," a teacher who had come from the

East. Luckily, "Dr. Time" had "performed a miraculous cure," and he was no longer smitten. The recovery opened the door for a new relationship.[50] Smith soothed Coolidge's pain by suggesting they spend time together.[51] She continued to write until 1893, often insinuating romantic feelings harbored for years. Still, nothing came of the exchanges.[52] What factor race played in how and why these relationships ended is not reflected in any of the letters. The correspondence does, however, allow us to see that Coolidge's life at Wind River was not all drudgery, conspiracy, and missionary work. There was instead much leisure time to fill. One of Smith's letters asks Coolidge about his "animal hunting tour," filled with the "slaughter" of "defenseless little birds" rather than "human hearts."[53] Correspondence with yet another love interest, Cornelia Pond, shows that in summers Coolidge camped in the mountains, fished for trout, and hunted elk, deer, and bear with a friend who owned a large ranch. His services as a chaperone to young couples on picnics were also in high demand. He himself went riding by moonlight "innumerable times" with "young ladies." In the summer of 1896, Coolidge escorted Bishop Talbot on a week-long camping trip in a "beautiful spot" by a lake. Sometimes, Hobart alumni would visit, providing a chance to talk politics.[54]

Politics, both domestic and international, interested Coolidge greatly. At the outbreak of the Spanish-American War in 1898, he traveled to New York City. There, he argued publicly that Indians should be allowed to enlist in the military and take revenge on the Spanish, "who had brought the first white men to America."[55] Another personal connection to the war existed. Adoptive father Charles Coolidge had been called into active duty in Cuba.[56] Fortunately, he had enough time before his departure to travel to Columbus, Ohio, for the annual convention of the American Philatelic Society.[57] Once in Cuba, Charles, then a major, saw serious military action during the bombardments of El Caney and Santiago.[58] Promoted to lieutenant colonel, he then embarked for the Philippines to battle for yet another colonial possession. After expelling the Spanish, Charles took control of a jurisdiction with a population of fifty thousand people. His task, as he put it, was "teaching them to run a civil government." Unhappy with the conditions he encountered, Charles composed a letter to the *Spirit of Missions* encouraging the Episcopal

Church to intervene. "I want to have schools, especially English, but have no school-books," he wrote, adding that the Filipinos were "too poor to buy books." Charles had ordered soldiers into the local classrooms, but they fell short of being "first-class teachers." His hope was that female readers would travel to the Philippines and "enlighten the heathen in his blindness and ignorance," because only the "Great American Church" could seize the "golden opportunity" and finally "civilize this nation." The notes that accompanied Charles Coolidge's letter cited his "inherent capacity for doing good" and noted how he had adopted a young Indian boy in 1870.[59] In June 1900, Charles left the Philippines and embarked for China as part of an expeditionary force led by Col. Emerson Liscum that was meant to quell the Boxer Rebellion. Liscum's subsequent death left Charles temporarily in charge of allied forces in the region. As a result, he became the first American ever to enter the Forbidden City in Beijing—a remarkable distinction. Charles attained the of rank of colonel for his efforts in 1901.[60]

Back in the United States, Sherman Coolidge was meanwhile putting his effort into furthering Native rights nationally. During an 1898 trip to Washington DC, he encountered another prominent Native person with similar concerns, the Santee Dakota physician Charles Eastman.[61] Born in 1858 to Wak-anhdi Ota (Many Lightnings) and a half-white mother, Nancy Eastman, who died of strep throat at age twenty-eight, Charles had never expected to make a life in Euro-American society. Originally named Hakadah (Pitiful Last), he was renamed Ohiyesa (Winner) after his tribe's victory in a lacrosse match. In 1862 Lincoln sentenced Ohiyesa's father to death for participating in the Dakota Uprising in Minnesota. Assuming Many Lightnings had perished, Ohiyesa's uncle escaped north and raised the boy until age fifteen. Then one day, Many Lightnings suddenly appeared, having been pardoned by Lincoln. He practiced Christianity and called himself Jacob Eastman after his deceased wife. Jacob insisted that his son return with him to the Dakotas, where he had remade his life as a farmer. Ohiyesa thus became Charles Eastman and entered the Santee Normal School in Nebraska. Following a frustrating start, Charles proved an excellent student, eventually attending Dartmouth College and Boston University's medical school. Upon graduation, he took the post of an agency physician with the Indian Health Service at Pine Ridge Reservation, just prior to the Wounded Knee Massacre. He and his future wife, Elaine Goodale, the superintendent of Indian schools in the Dakotas, tended to the casualties, though Indian Bureau officials sealed off the area for three days and blocked the Eastmans' entry. Repulsed by the killings and the corrupt bureau, the Eastmans resigned. Charles opened an unsuccessful medical practice in Minneapolis but found better employment lecturing and organizing clubs for the Young Men's Christian Association (YMCA). In need of money, Charles and Elaine began to publish stories of his Dakota childhood, achieving some degree of fame.[62]

Coolidge and Eastman, then, had much in common, having spent their childhoods in Indian societies only to make painful transitions into the white world. During Coolidge's 1898 stay in Washington, they quickly—and impressively—managed to secure an audience with President William McKinley. The men, accompanied by Eastman's brother, John, a Presbyterian minister, seized the opportunity to lobby for better educational opportunities for Indians and for the standardization of the government's school system. McKinley showed minor interest and made vague promises. Following the meeting, Coolidge and the Eastman brothers discussed the need for a national Indian organization that could effectively influence government policy on a larger scale.[63] They concluded, though, that such a step was premature. In Eastman's words, the government was "not accustomed to allowing the Indian a voice in his affairs," while the movement, admittedly, had little chance with either Indians or the wider public. There also existed the "grave danger of arousing the antagonism of the Bureau," a risk none were willing to take. Coolidge and the Eastman brothers consequently decided to delay any action until circumstances appeared more congenial.[64] The wait would last over a decade.

In the 1890s, Coolidge maintained his relationship with Henry Whipple, who saw the publicity value of a Native priest. Whipple and the Episcopal Church continued to hold up Coolidge and his message of peace as "an example of the result of missionary work," hoping to gain greater support for their efforts on reservations.[65] Coolidge made appearances at annual Episcopal councils in Minnesota and occasionally preached alongside Whipple in the summer months.[66] These trips to the Midwest reinforced

Coolidge's optimistic news from Wind River, printed regularly in the *Spirit of Missions*. Reports from the 1896 volume described Bishop Talbot's recent stay. Talbot had confirmed five young men in the mission church and visited an Indian village to give a short speech. Coolidge explained to readers that while the Arapahos "had the reputation of being warlike and ferocious," they were in truth "a good-hearted and peace-loving people" who were making "progress" toward Christian living. Offering proof, he wrote of recently wedding an Arapaho couple and baptizing seven boys and girls.[67] John Roberts added his own news on the Shoshone girls' school, which had enrolled twenty-five students, twenty of whom were boarding. "We trust" he confided, "when the time comes for them to leave, that they will carry with them the light and blessings of true Christian Womanhood to their dark heathen homes."[68]

In 1898 Coolidge began constructing a pine log church for the Arapahos near his old home. By slowly soliciting funds, he was able to furnish the building with wood plank floors, new pews, and even an organ donated by an army surgeon in memory of his brother. The logs were squared with the Wind River Agency saw. Such features made the church, in Coolidge's words, a "rose in the desert of rude log cabins and mud roofs." Two bells, nestled atop the steeple, were engraved with the phrase "To the Prince of Peace." Coolidge wrote of how the bells would "ring out every Sunday to call the faithful together, to awaken the pagan, and to prick the conscience of the indifferent members, and the skeptics."[69] When not ministering there, he held services for Fort Washakie's Buffalo soldiers, whom he found "so very pleasant."[70]

Coolidge gained a valuable asset in 1899 with the arrival of Fremont Arthur, an Arapaho lay preacher who addressed potential converts in their native language. Arthur had raised money in the East for a new church near the camp of Yellow Calf, one of Coolidge's relatives. Named Our Father's House, the chapel later became part of St. Michael's Mission, which still stands today.[71] Thanks to Arthur's sermonizing, church attendance had risen, and according to Coolidge's reports, the "better class among the Indians" had come to "listen to the truths of the Gospel most willingly." Others, regrettably, continued to hold "tenaciously to their old traditions."[72] But there had been one hopeful sign. Plenty Bear, an Arapaho subchief, had attended one of Arthur's services. "Some don't believe in religion," Plenty Bear remarked afterward. "We Arapahoes have all believed in God from our youth, and when we hear the Word of God preached to us, we are glad. . . . We are especially glad to hear the good news of rising again from the dead. . . . I believe your teachings." This declaration assured Coolidge that "pure religion" would in time "greatly diminish ignorance and injurious superstition" on the reservation. When all the work was done, the Arapahos and Shoshones would be united in the "brotherhood of Christ" and "live side by side in peace and harmony." The only impediment remained the fact that "the Arapahoe thinks he is better than the Shoshone, and vice versa."[73] (Regrettably, Fremont Arthur died in 1901 of tuberculosis.)[74]

Sherman Coolidge's positive, even glowing dispatches from Wind River may have been effective in raising money but not in ameliorating—or even mitigating—the larger problems that came with forced assimilation: to name a few, poverty, disease, malnutrition, dispossession, and the basic curtailments on freedom under the Indian Bureau's wardship. In winters, the Arapahos still resorted to eating cattle and sheep herds dead of starvation and disease.[75] Infants frequently died of malnutrition.[76] When the Arapahos took ill from diseases such as tuberculosis, they refused to consult the reservation doctor. Though Coolidge secretly regarded the physician as a "very poor excuse of a man," he tried to "coax" and "induce" his tribespeople to seek treatment—always to no avail.[77] Because of such conditions, Coolidge had written harshly of the Indian Bureau in the 1887 *Churchman* and even in his contribution to the Wyoming Indian census of 1890. But by the mid-1890s, he had abandoned his public criticisms in favor of an exclusive focus on "progressive" government programs. Nowhere was this more evident than in the implementation of the Dawes Act.

In 1895 Coolidge's uncle Sharp Nose agreed with fifty leading Arapahos to begin the process of dividing reservation lands into individual plots. Moving slowly, the Northern Arapahos and the Indian Bureau struck a series of compromises. Sharp Nose requested that stone markers first be put in four corners of the reserve to delineate Arapaho territory, while the following year the leadership exploited the allotment issue by demanding a meeting in Washington to air the tribe's grievances. This back-and-forth continued until the Indian Bureau began maneuvering more aggressively.

In 1898 Wind River welcomed a new agent, Herman G. Nickerson, who had a shocking connection to Sherman Coolidge. Back in April 1870, he had led the vigilante army of whites against Black Bear's band of Arapahos in the very incident that resulted in Runs On Top's capture and surrender to the officers at Camp Brown. Having once tried to eliminate Indians through violence, Nickerson was now charged with seeing to their well-being. Upon assuming control of the reservation, the agent became increasingly anxious about the people's advancement toward "civilization." One of his projects was anglicizing the names on agency roll sheets. Arapaho chief Lone Bear, for instance, suddenly found himself listed as Lon Brown. Since most council chiefs opposed his ideas and—quite understandably—detested him, Nickerson disrupted the Arapahos' tribal structure as best he could to achieve desired results. Astonishingly, he found a loyal ally in Coolidge, whose life could have easily been ended by Nickerson's actions (or own hand) thirty years prior.[78]

Agent Nickerson's 1900 annual report to the Department of the Interior makes for interesting reading. His descriptions of Wind River revealed plainly how government mismanagement blocked the Indian Bureau's own agenda and how the Arapahos—while appearing compliant in hopes that conditions could be bettered—deeply resented Washington's interference in their lives. Nickerson stated that the "Indians on this reservation, realizing that their future prosperity depends largely upon agricultural pursuits, manifest a commendable interest in land and farming." Yet several obstacles thwarted this interest. Government employees chosen to teach new farming methods had no time to provide "the requisite attention," the result being that the "Indians break up and destroy much machinery." Another issue was soil fertility. Nickerson complained that no allotments had been made, yet at the same time he admitted that most terrain was "totally unfit for farming." Allotment, therefore, would only tie each family to "a worthless piece of land." In the realm of education, matters were worse. The government boarding school near Fort Washakie, with accommodations for 200 students, had an average attendance of only 125 due to the Indian parents' "deep-rooted prejudice" and their habit of "seeking to coax or steal [students] away" whenever possible. The school was meanwhile experiencing a high staff turnover, losing a newly hired superintendent every six months. Maintaining the school's hundred-acre farm had also become impossible due to a lack of manpower.[79] The acting superintendent, Edwin L. Chalcraft, elaborated on these failings, noting that the "absence of trees and shrubbery and being enclosed with very old barbed-wire fencing gives the school site a barren, uninviting appearance." The buildings themselves had begun to fall apart, having been "poorly constructed of soft brick."[80]

The one bright spot Nickerson designated was the work done at St. Stephens Indian Mission school, overseen by two Catholic priests and seven nuns, and at Roberts's Episcopal school for Shoshone girls. Nickerson deemed the "educational, industrial, and moral training of the pupils" at St. Stephens as "noteworthy and commendable," and stated that the Shoshone girls were "receiving an educational, industrial, and moral training that must redound to their welfare and advancement if conscientious and painstaking labor can aid them." Though such commendations suggested the efficacy of larger missionary work, the report openly contradicted Roberts's and Coolidge's accounts of steady "progress" toward Christianization in the *Spirit of Missions*. Nickerson wrote that "Christianizing and moralizing influence" on the Arapahos and Shoshones had garnered "poor success, as the effect is scarcely perceptible." This failure generated a robust workload for the agency police force, whose officers Nickerson could barely retain due to low pay. Their main tasks included expelling trespassers, confiscating firearms, preventing gambling, and, most ominously, tracking down runaways from the government school. All of these findings were regrettable, but the most glaringly dismal facts related to the tribes' health. Sanitary conditions were so poor that for every birth, there occurred eighteen deaths. A similarly high mortality rate among adults resulted from diseases such as tuberculosis. Nickerson assigned blame for the deaths among the young to inadequate "maternal care" rather than to the incremental reduction of already poor-quality rations. The tribes' financial status, meanwhile, remained weak because their lands were leased to white cattlemen at just one cent an acre. As a result of these circumstances, the July 1900 Wind River census recorded yet another population dip, with 801 Arapahos and 841 Shoshones, totaling just 1,642 persons.[81]

Within this mire of demoralizing circumstances, Nickerson and Coolidge saw only one path "forward"—allotment. There were nevertheless certain political mechanisms to overcome. In 1893 the Northern Arapahos had formed a chiefs' council consisting almost exclusively of former warriors from the two main villages. The Indian Bureau considered the small body a business council; the Arapahos saw it as their leadership. Nickerson found the council antagonistic to his policies and quickly acted to undermine its authority with the help of Coolidge. Together, the men took a divide-and-conquer approach, viewing the Northern Arapahos as older and younger factions that could be set against each other.[82] This method was particularly offensive to a people who had, for centuries, respected the hierarchy designated in the "four hills of life."[83] Nickerson first tried to undercut the elder chiefs by recruiting younger, more "progressive" tribe members for positions of control and status. This meant placing loyal Arapahos on the agency police force, which Nickerson directed to answer only to him, and selecting younger men for the tribal delegations to Washington. Nickerson also cut rations to those elder council chiefs he found uncooperative, and he circulated petitions on how leasing monies should be spent rather than deferring to the traditional tribal power structure.[84] The distribution of these monies constituted an important issue. After 1900 only the elderly and disabled were guaranteed rations at Wind River, increasing the Arapahos' dependence on leasing and the pressure to accept allotment.[85]

Of the two largest bands of Northern Arapahos, those in the northeast of Wind River appeared more tolerant of allotment. In 1901 Coolidge attempted to sour relations between them and the group to the south, informing the Indian Bureau that the "progressive" Upper Arapahos had rejected any authority of the Lower Arapaho chiefs and that allotment could proceed. His uncle Sharp Nose may have dissuaded him from this hazardous course had he not died the same year.[86] Predictably, relations swiftly became very tense on the reservation. In May the Arapahos began raiding settlers' stock in reaction to Nickerson's prohibition of the Sun Dance and to the bureau's failure to provide enough seed. The incident was reported in the *New York Times*, which noted that troops might have to intervene.[87] Matters worsened thanks to Coolidge's ill-conceived plan. When government surveyors appeared to begin allotment, both the upper and lower camps protested. The Shoshones meanwhile opposed allotting lands to the Arapahos entirely, though their influence had waned.[88] Washakie had died on February 20, 1900, soon after his famed conversion to Christianity, an event much celebrated in church literature. Roberts officiated the funeral.[89] Coolidge had come to admire Washakie tremendously and considered him, as he later wrote, "a personal friend."[90]

With the issue of allotment lingering, Nickerson continued to challenge the Arapaho leadership. In 1902 he stacked an approved delegation to Washington with chosen supporters, including Coolidge, even though he had little backing among his tribespeople. The dismayed Arapahos sought aid from the Catholics at St. Stephens. The Jesuits forwarded a letter from the leadership to Commissioner of Indian Affairs William Arthur Jones, stating that Nickerson had chosen "some friends of his that went already to Washington with him and did nothing for us or rather did us harm for they could not speak our heart."[91] Then the Catholics sought to rid the Arapahos and Shoshones of their agent entirely.

Nickerson's contract was due to expire on April 1, 1902. Alarmed at the prospect of being dismissed, he sprang into action. As the Arapahos described to the director of the Bureau of Catholic Indian Missions William H. Ketcham: "Now he wants the Indians to petition for him to be next in office, for this he had a meeting with the half-breeds to get their signature, then told the Shoshones to have a meeting so that they would petition for him but they said that they would not have him for anything." The Upper and Lower Arapahos promptly convened and decided they wanted Nickerson gone. In an act of defiance, they sent his petition back completely blank. Only a few policemen and some younger tribe members now supported the agent. Nickerson had even paid two Arapahos, Tall Indian and Herbert Welsh (Coolidge's half-white cousin), ten and two dollars, respectively, to lobby for him in the Arapaho camps. They generated paltry enthusiasm.[92] In the end, Director Ketcham personally intervened in Washington. His letter condemned Nickerson's "ungovernable temper, his harsh and tyrannical treatment of the Indians, and his use of abusive and profane language both to men and women, causing turbulence and friction all through his term of office, with the results that his management of Agency affairs has been anything but a success and that a large number of Indians are dissatisfied with him and opposed to his continuance as agent." Ketcham also revealed that Nickerson had bribed Indians with farm machinery to get signatures for his ill-fated petition.[93]

The Indian Bureau responded by replacing Nickerson with H. W. Wadsworth, but in hopes of pushing through allotment it refused to reshuffle the delegation. The elder chiefs on the council had still won a significant battle, while those who cooperated with Nickerson hastily retreated from public life. He himself was awarded with a new government position as a U.S. allotting agent. Wadsworth, to whom Coolidge had reached out in his doomed effort to oust Agent Jones in 1887, often complained of the "unprogressive" nature of the Arapahos' business council. Wisely, he did not act on his grievances. Nevertheless, the 1902 Nickerson debacle was a serious blow to any reputation Coolidge had managed to build at Wind River, laying bare the antagonism to his ideas of radical change among most Arapahos.[94] Failure in this realm, interestingly enough, was balanced by success in another. Amid the acrimony surrounding allotment, Coolidge met a young, idealistic woman named Grace Darling Wetherbee, "a New York society belle" who would eventually become his wife.[95] How Miss Wetherbee, an East Coast socialite of fabulous wealth, ended up marrying an Arapaho missionary on a distant Indian reservation is a story deserving of considerable attention. We now turn to her unexpected journey.

6

Grace

"I'm nearly bursting with delight for I don't see any reason why I shouldn't start for Wyo. a week from next Monday or Tuesday!!!!!!!! This statement warrants even more exclamation points, I think. To say I am glad is so inadequate, it is absolutely foolish."[1] Grace Darling Wetherbee wrote these words to her dearest friend, Anne Talbot, on July 4, 1896, in anticipation of a long-awaited and long-desired trip to the West, where she would finally see real Indians. Looking at Grace on the surface, one would wonder why she, a wealthy New Yorker, would have an interest in an uncomfortable stay on a reservation. Peering deeper into her life, one finds a woman of passion, intelligence, and empathy, afraid of little but a life without meaning. So who was Grace?

Born on July 25, 1873, in Auburndale, Massachusetts, Grace was the daughter of Gardner Wetherbee, the owner of the Hotel Manhattan, a sixteen-story building situated on Madison Avenue and Forty-Second Street, known as the tallest hotel in the world. Her mother, Hannah Nye Wetherbee, descended from a founding colonial family that included Coolidge ancestry. Well-known fixtures in New York high society, the Wetherbees inhabited a magnificent townhouse on Seventy-Second Street. As with many young women of her milieu, Grace was well traveled and well educated, having even studied in Paris.[2] When not abroad, she spent her evenings looking very refined in a box at the Metropolitan Opera House. Grace's knowledge of French and German heightened her appreciation of Gounod and Wagner, the latter being a particular favorite.[3] Such sensitivity did not extend to every aspect of her personality. Grace harbored many of the distinctive prejudices of her era and social class, holding Jewish and African Americans in absolute contempt.[4]

However typically decadent Grace Wetherbee's life might appear, a number of atypical qualities marked her character. As a young girl, she believed that she had a connection to Native peoples, whom she called "cousins."[5] She was equally certain that one day she would marry one.[6] In contrast, her sister, Alice, married Rudolph Festetics de Tolna, a Hungarian count, in an extravagant, much-publicized, nobility-packed wedding in Paris.[7] The women also differed in that Grace, unlike her sister, was one to question. She looked upon New York City as a place of unjust economic polarization, which was offensive to her "socialistic ideas."[8] And though her parents were not particularly religious, she displayed a strong devotion to the Episcopal Church, even undergoing baptism and confirmation in her twenties. All her time prior, she once wrote, had been "wasted."[9] She then began searching, with anxious seriousness, for something to fill her life. Grace was attractive, even "magnetic," as one acquaintance stated, but she eschewed marriage to, one assumes, a host of eligible upper-class suitors. Hannah Wetherbee was driven to distraction by her daughter's unwillingness to lead a conventional lifestyle, but this kind of existence was not what Grace wanted or needed. There had to be something greater, more profound, and more worthy of devotion outside the realms of pleasure, comfort, and leisure that her upbringing afforded.

Grace attended the Ogontz School for Young Ladies in Pennsylvania in the mid-1890s.[10] The exclusive private school, named for a Sandusky Indian chief, was then among the most prestigious in the nation.[11] While there, Grace met two young women who would introduce her to the West—Nellie Hart, whose father, the Reverend Dean Hart, ministered at Saint John's Episcopal Cathedral in Denver; and Anne Talbot, the daughter of Sherman Coolidge's superior, Bishop Ethelbert Talbot, then in Laramie.[12] Grace and Anne were especially close and may have roomed together at Ogontz. Anne and Nellie shared an interest in Indian welfare, and through their Episcopal network, Grace became involved in Indian missionary work. She first visited Nellie in Colorado and found the experience so overwhelming that only western landscapes could cheer her when away from the Metropolitan Opera.[13] In 1896

Grace visited Anne in Wyoming, where she met, and eventually married, Sherman Coolidge.[14]

Reading later accounts of Grace and Sherman's courtship, one would learn the following: After meeting at Wind River, the two "fell in love almost at once."[15] The couple subsequently maintained a regular correspondence until Sherman made the long trip to New York City, met Grace's parents, and humbly asked for her hand. Mr. Wetherbee, ever gracious, gladly gave his "full consent."[16] Grace's mother and several friends disagreed, but the couple, engaged and undeterred, embarked on a tour of Yellowstone.[17] In the summer of 1902, Grace returned to Wind River, where she helped John Roberts run a Sunday school.[18] Then in early October, Sherman and Grace decided they could no longer wait to marry.[19] Roberts, who officiated the ceremony, purportedly asked Grace, "And your family?" She responded, "If you don't marry us, someone else will."[20] The wedding, one reads, was attended by Grace's parents and Sherman's relatives. Sherman later told an interviewer, "When we were first married both sides of the new house were humorously dignified, my people boasting of my chieftain ancestry and Mrs. Coolidge's remembering that they were Wetherbees."[21]

This simple rendering, however, is not remotely true. The Coolidges' courtship lasted just a couple months, Gardner Wetherbee did not give his "full consent," neither Grace's relatives nor Sherman's attended their nuptials, and Roberts's opposition to marrying the couple was not so easily overcome. More important, though, is that the real story of Grace's journey to the altar is one of deep and painful turmoil, turmoil caused by another relationship that, to all appearances, might have had a different outcome had it occurred in a different time.

We can know Grace, even very well, through her extensive correspondence with Anne Talbot, who was two years her junior.[22] Many of Grace's letters have survived, thanks to Anne, though Grace seems to have lost, destroyed, or hidden the missives she received in return. Anne was a striking young woman with green eyes and auburn hair. These physical features inspired Grace to assign her a series of nicknames, including Red, Reddy, Red Top, Redhead, Redthing, Redheadedthing, Green Eyes, Green Eyed, Annie Green Eyed, and, inexplicably, Duckie. Several other names—Precious, Treasure, and Treasurer—rounded out the list. Grace called herself Gedy, apparently a play on her first two initials.

In the summer of 1896, Grace and her mother crossed the country through Wyoming to California.[23] Talbot was then living in Laramie with her parents, and Grace and her mother paid a short visit. It was then that Grace became acquainted with Sherman Coolidge, whom she took to calling Pokey, Cousin Pokey, or just plain Poke.[24] Anne herself introduced them one evening in the now-defunct town of Rongis along the old Oregon Trail on the banks of the Sweetwater River.[25] Coolidge was a very flirtatious man, yet no evidence appears in Grace's letters that she felt anything for him save friendship. She did however note his obvious "weakness for petticoats."[26] Grace also socialized with John and Laura Roberts. Over the late 1890s, they developed a relationship that would bring Grace back to Wyoming for missionary work in 1902.[27] During the interim, Grace sent Roberts regular donations, which he always acknowledged with thankful, detailed letters.[28] She apparently even met Chief Washakie, whom she liked tremendously.[29]

The letters Grace sent Anne after visiting Wyoming tell us a great deal about her lifestyle and personality. For instance, we know that she and her mother continued on their way to Pasadena, California, for several weeks of "splendid" horseback riding.[30] Grace was then rereading Henrik Ibsen's *A Doll's House*. The main protagonist, Nora, a proto-feminist who rejects a stultifying marriage, was one of Grace's favorite literary characters. Anne, who held more conservative views on domesticity, recommended a recent psychological study titled *Six Modern Women*, which argued that a lady who seeks education and artistic expression "unconsciously deprives herself of her womanliness."[31] Despite this difference in outlook, the two ladies planned to cross paths again in California, a prospect that excited Grace terribly.[32]

For some reason, leaving Anne in Wyoming had been difficult. In Pasadena, Grace felt a sudden and surprising bout of loneliness. "I am like Faust, triste et solitaire!" she confessed, referencing the popular Gounod opera.[33] To her, she and Anne had a rare connection. Grace wrote her friend:

I simply can't tell you how I felt when I opened yr. letter! I really didn't know I was so fond of you. . . . I feel as tho' I simply *must* see you. I have so many things that I want so much to talk. Just for my own selfish sake. There are so many important things that arise when one first begins to feel one's age, I want to talk about them with you. There is no good talking about all the little things, the drives I thought we could take together and all the hundred little things I had planned. It's too disappointing![34]

Also disappointing was the fact that their travel schedules, in the end, did not align. Anne became unwell, and a meeting in San Francisco proved impossible. Grace naturally understood but missed her friend all the same.

You old silly to get ill, and poor Gracie way off here and just aching to pet somebody. (You'd do.) There are moments, even, when the aching gets so pronounced (usually at night) that this foolish child pretends with the maddest glee that Annie is just on the other side of the bed. And what is the good of poking out yr. hand to feel for her when you know she is not there? It's a lovely game. . . . Oh, Annie, how I longed for you—It almost hurt—way down in my tummy. You know that place. What an Annie you are to me. What an Annie you are to me.

These longings had little chance of being fulfilled for some time. Grace's mother was arranging a long voyage to Europe for the summer months, putting off any foreseeable reunion.[35]

The Wetherbee ladies returned home to New York at the end of April. Grace set Anne aside and became intensely preoccupied with two matters—publishing a "clergyman story," possibly inspired by her meeting with Sherman Coolidge, and raising money for Greeks affected by the ultimately brief Greco-Turkish War that had recently ignited in Crete. Grace's concern for the latter stemmed from her having been "entangled in the meshes of a Platonic friendship" with a young Greek soldier—when, where, and how we do not know. The matter nonetheless affected her profoundly. Every night, she dreamed of "Greek hillsides covered with

Greek dead and everything gory and nasty!" More frustrating, she could not contact her soldier or know if he had been killed. All she could do was hang a Greek flag in her room, have the hotel orchestra play the Greek national anthem, donate clothing and her allowance to the Red Cross, and solicit monies.[36] This last effort failed miserably. She hung up boxes to collect pennies around the hotel, but those gathered were "mostly bad or Canadian." Faced with war abroad and indifference at home, Grace increasingly felt disgust for the world. "The whole Gk. affair is so disgraceful that I have lost faith in everybody," she confided to Anne. "I don't see how Christian countries can be such brutes, do you?" Still, were she not "destined to petticoats," Grace claimed she would definitely volunteer as a soldier.[37] That route blocked, she could at least take solace in the letters to Anne. "Isn't it nice we are scribbling so often," she asked. "I only hope it will continue for the next 50 years or so."[38] Instead, it would last forty.

On June 3, 1897, Grace and her mother sailed for Hamburg, Germany, where Mrs. Wetherbee planned to take "a horrid cure."[39] After touring France and Switzerland, they arrived in the Bohemian spa town of Karlsbad near the end of the month. Shopping was on the agenda; yet in the midst of luxury, Grace remained unimpressed. The locals, whom she deemed "hideous" and "degenerate," made her wonder how long "it must have taken to build up a Goethe a Wagner or a Beethoven." One day, a hotel clerk handed Grace a letter from Anne that immediately made her "wildly homesick for Wyoming" and the smell of sagebrush.[40] That was a world far away and about to get farther. Following Karlsbad, the Wetherbees traveled throughout Russia and England until the autumn, only then heading back to the United States. The trip distracted Grace from thoughts of Anne, as did the continuing correspondence with her Greek soldier. She received a telegram from him in the spring and started trading "fortnightly letters." Then, suddenly, she never mentioned him again. During this period, Anne missed her letters from Grace and feared there was some ill feeling. "But I never thought you bad, you darling!" Grace assured her, "How dare you say such things to me!" She also shared the news that Sherman "Pokey" Coolidge was in New York on church business.[41] As it turned out, he had arrived at the Wetherbees' door just before Easter 1897, only to find Grace absent. No meeting occurred.[42]

Pokey tried again to reach Grace in November 1897. She was off in the New Jersey countryside, but this time he left a note with his address. Grace wrote back, "I was torn between glee at knowing you were still alive and . . . sorrow at having been away when you called." Wanting to meet, she proposed a dinner with some friends, one of them "a nice girl" who would indulge his "weakness for petticoats."[43] Pokey's response was typically frisky. Repentant that he had no "plumes" to wear, he nevertheless expressed confidence that the "happiest moment" of his life was imminent. The ardent letter continued,

> I am burning with impatience for the time to come when I hope to have another sweet converse with you. I never hope for such a thing even in the wildest flights of my fancy. . . . I had heard you were abroad in Russia, and as I was about to apply to Uncle Sam for a position in the Russian Legation, I was informed that perhaps you would be in New York for the winter. There you are, and there you are. I was indeed happy when I heard at the Manhattan's that Neptune had brought you back safely across the salt seas, but my hopes were raised only to be dashed to pieces upon hearing that you were not in; but as the poet says:

> > Hope springs eternal in
> > the human breast,
> > Man never is, but always
> > to be blest

> And be blest if I don't think now that the agonizing pain of disappointment I endured was but a precursor of a greater rejoicing.

That was not all. The letter featured a sketch of a couple locked in a deep kiss, captioned with the phrase "Yum, Yum à la New York."[44]

As interested as Pokey appeared in Grace, she did not feverishly reciprocate his ardor. Dinner with her Indian "cousin" and friends had only one outcome—stimulating her to work for a new cause, the Arapahos at Wind River. She first purchased church pews and sent them across the country, and she even somehow collected enough money to obtain and transport a church organ.[45] But not long after, she grew impatient, deciding that "begging for the Arapahoes" was "awful work" and that "next time the Arapahoes can go hang!"[46] The city also posed certain distractions. One afternoon while out in Manhattan, there appeared "an awfully fascinating man-creature" on the train, much in the vein of a "Canadian hunter." Later that evening, Grace took a ferry around New York. While walking up and down the decks, she unexpectedly ran into her "hunter-man doing the same." "I was so sorry that circumstances over which I have no control," she lamented to Anne, "prevented my hailing him." As she ruefully observed, "Petticoats do shut us from so much."[47]

Fortunately, though, Anne would soon be nearby, thanks to her father's recent election as the bishop of central Pennsylvania. In 1898 the Talbot family moved east to the town of Bethlehem, just eighty-one miles from New York City.[48] Grace and Anne met in the fall, prompting Grace to express vague regrets:

> I had thought for a long time that we had come to the end of things. Oh, Duckie, the things I want to write you, but I expect I'd better wait till we can push and talk. But there are two big things which I must blame myself for, first, that I didn't remember that it is only a red haired child after all; and secondly, that you thought I felt as you said you did. Annie, it's not so. Will you believe me? I have thought about it so much and I am sure it is not so. I'm not going to talk about this anymore for it is almost impossible to write it.[49]

What Grace meant can only be guessed at, but she was clearly pained. Then, in December 1898, her mother fell seriously ill "with neuralgia of the stomach," experiencing "attacks of pain" quelled only by morphine. The illness distracted Grace from writing to Anne, who became "cross." The women had seen each other several times and had planned to attend the opera, but abruptly, Anne canceled.[50] Grace was devastated. "As for what's in the envelope," she dejectedly noted, "if you knew the horribly uncomfortable hours its contents have given me, you would for once in yr. life give me some definite proof that you like me a little bit. . . . I cannot bear to think there is even a possibility of yr. not coming on Friday morning, you know it will be weeks before we can see each other again . . . if you don't come." Grace understood the situation as dire. Anne was being courted by two young men—Tommy, last name unknown, and Francis Donaldson, whom she would eventually marry. "Reddy, come!" Grace implored. "Think what a few years we have to see each other in before the long separation. It's a thought that haunts me all the time. Of course the thing I wanted to say in this letter is what I have left unsaid, but you know what I have been thinking every time I have thought of you. Oh dear! There are such things I want to say but I mustn't."[51]

Anne's response, which may have been cold, forced Grace to plead for attention. "Reddy," she began, "I've always had a deadly feeling that to find a man as fine as a woman was impossible, is and ever more shall be— . . . Oh! despair! I wish you were here. Why haven't you written me for so long? I generally wander aimlessly about thinking of you. Please tell me in every letter that you love me—if you do. But I don't see how you can." Anne's reluctance to see Grace lasted for weeks. She even exacerbated matters by then discussing her relationship with Tommy. "It seems almost like hitting a man when he is down to talk about Tommy now," Grace objected, "but I have never been able to bring myself to believe that he could give you all your best part, yr. spirit part would demand, if not now anyway in the years to come. . . . If you knew how I feel writing you this—oh—surface letter when I want to say such other things! All I can think of just now is how much I want you—no, that's not quite all."[52] The intensity of these emotions even began to cause Grace nightmares.[53]

Anne finally agreed to travel to New York at the beginning of February 1899. Grace, elated, wrote, "Please do love me hard. I don't know why but I have a sort of cut loose feeling lately. Oh! do come! How shall we manage about sleeping???"[54] Yet, unfortunately, this anticipation made the meeting all the more crushing. Grace was "inexpressibly troubled" to learn that Anne had been in poor health, and she only longed for Anne more when she left. The women resolved, however, to see each other as often as possible.[55] They met again in late March, just before Anne had to leave for Missouri, likely for church work. When Anne said goodbye and boarded the train back to Bethlehem, Grace had an impulse to run after her, countered only by the thought of the "strange people" in the compartment. But Grace's letters seem to indicate that, perhaps, Anne's absence would be a relief.

It is true that we are not, either one of us, right, or when we are
together we could not be, and feel as we do. And yet it is so horrible
to think of wasting six months of these few, precious years. . . . I feel,
for my part, as tho' I had come to the foot of the mountain where
the real climbing must begin, as tho' all that had gone before had
only been the easy approaches and I know that the one way I can
possibly go is up the mountain side. I think just now that I have
come to the end of myself. All that myself can give me it has given
and now I want to make a place for something else, to annihilate
this self. When a time comes when I really love you better than I
do myself I want to go to you, to fly to you, Annie—only tonight
what I most want to do is to kiss you and kiss you—Let us both
pray for regeneration. But oh! to think that we—that I—have gone
on all these years and yet have come to nothing.[56]

The impending separation, it seems, had stirred Grace to reevaluate her
life and consider deeply what she wanted to accomplish. Perhaps during
the last meeting in New York, Anne had spoken to Grace about how their
relationship had to change and in doing so became a model to emulate
in religious devotion and self-control. "I'm trying very hard to be good,
Reddy," Grace wrote following the parting, "but you must tell me you
love me in every letter."

Grace had also decided that her life in Manhattan destroyed the spiritual
aspects of life that were, after all, paramount. She had to do something
in the outer world to express these convictions.

I believe I feel today past any fear of retracting, that the real life
is the life of the spirit that renunciation is gained and that the
eternal, the worthwhile, is not to be found here. If I believe truly, I
think I must act someday, don't you? Oh! Reddy, love me in spite
of everything. If you knew how it breaks my heart to think how I
have fallen short. But you do know. Having you here and at least
the change of trying for the great things to come I feel very rich,
even in spite of everything.

Earning Anne's love meant that Grace had to prove that she, too, could master her emotions and focus on matters of greater significance. Had any relationship between the two been revealed, the social and familial consequences would have been more than ruinous. "I want to tell you all I have been stopping to think, here about how I love you Reddy," Grace promised, "not how much, but how; only I think after all you know, and then how can I talk about it when you're not here? . . . Your trying-hard Gracie."[57]

By May 1899, Grace had found a way to channel her inner turbulence and cast off the constant pressure from her mother to enter a conventional upper-class marriage. The answer was to take control and do what she wanted most. "I have a very strange feeling, stronger than I have ever had it before," she divulged to Anne, "that I want the consecration, the setting apart, the being obviously what you are inwardly; making the business of yr. life what you most want to because it is not only because it is most worthwhile, but the only thing worth; feeling and acting in fact, like a man, and choosing my own vocation. I can't see that that is so much to ask, can you?"[58] Grace's choice of vocation would be in the church. Without the knowledge of her mother, she arranged to begin studies in the fall at St. Faith's Deaconess Training School in New York.[59] First, however, a long-planned summer vacation in the beloved West beckoned.

During the previous winter, Grace and her friends Nellie Hart and Dolly Waterfield had decided to visit Yellowstone and Colorado.[60] (Anne could not go because she and her parents were sailing for England.)[61] Grace's "soul rebelled against being in this dear ol' Wyoming as a tourist," but she managed nonetheless.[62] Grace had also decided to invite Pokey, whom she had recently seen in New York starring as a thieving Indian prince in an amateur performance of *The Great Ruby*, set in the British Raj. In a crucial scene with a Russian countess, his leading lady had refused to kiss him on stage, a fact that rendered Grace "aghast."[63] Through happenstance, Pokey was to be in Yellowstone that summer as well. Grace had been writing him infrequently. Her letters were very friendly but hardly romantic. In her invitation, she warned him that if they met for some hiking or riding, "anybody who goes lame or whose horse goes lame is to be shot and left behind." Also, there would be "no engaged couples allowed," and "twosing"—nineteenth-century slang for petting—would be "discouraged." "Of course, therefore," Grace joked, "you will go!!!!!"[64]

As usual, Pokey penned a bombastically flirtatious response. "Dear Cousin Grace," it read,

> ever since I wrote my last epistle to you, I have lived in hopes and was about to expire in despair when lo and behold! your letter was handed to me by the Assistant Post Master-general of the Fort Washakie Post Office Department. Now all is well with me. But, oh, Cousin! for a while a great black cloud hung its gloomy strength between me and the Eastern sky. My heart was like ice; I wished in the evening that it was morning and in the morning that it was evening. I was nigh to being crazy. My life was as emptiness and ashes to all people and all things. It was a black time to me. At last, I thought that, before I took the long trail on the Milky-way, I would make medicine and find out from the powers above if indeed the fair, the ever fair cousin of the "Manhattan" teepee had deserted me forever or no. So, one dark night, according to the sage directions of Weasel Bear (or Squaw Bear) who keeps the Sacred Pipe of the Arapahoes, I stood on the summit of the red-streaked hills across the river near my teepee and as I looked up to the glowing stars of the Great Spirit's medicine lodge I sang the mystic song and strange birds and animals came to me and told me in the voices of my ancestors that my pale-face Manhattan cousin who lives far away in the land of the rising sun would send me words written on paper the color of the everlasting sagebrush before many sleeps had come and gone. After that I was happy and felt as if I must continue to be happy as long as the grass grows and the water flows.

Having attained eternal contentment, Pokey declared he would be more than "willing to run the risk of becoming lame and being shot" to enjoy the company of such a "grand party." The rules also suited him fine; he was not "much given to twosing." In the envelope, Pokey enclosed some pressed sagebrush and a rattle from a rattlesnake with the note, "May you never get rattled."[65]

Grace and her friends arrived in Yellowstone in mid-August 1899. After a few days, she and Dolly insisted on climbing Mount Washburn without a guide, thinking claims the trail was "ambiguous" were just the "natural care of the tenderfoot." The women completed the ascent easily and were thrilled by the views of snow-capped mountains from the peak. After returning, they learned they were the first ever to do the hike without a guide.[66] This surprising news instilled in Grace an overconfidence that would soon place her in a very dangerous situation. But for the moment, there was still one problem at Yellowstone—no Pokey. Grace looked everywhere, but her efforts yielded nothing save a "frantic telegram" from Pokey, explaining that he had missed her at the Fountain Hotel and was on his way to Jackson's Hole.[67] Grace was "furious" but could do nothing more than reply. "I was like the shade of the classic Orpheus (only the other way around)," she explained to Pokey. "I peered into every camp, questioned every hotel and eating station and sent forth word by every passing tourist that if anybody saw a wandering parson on a dejected bay horse they were to tell him that his cousin was looking for him."[68] With no cousin to be found, she could only continue her travels. Her group left Wyoming for Colorado near the end of August.

Then it happened. Fresh off her triumph on Mount Washburn, Grace unwisely decided to conquer one of the surrounding mountains at Grand Lake with no guide and, this time, no companion. Her crisply drawn description of the experience to Anne reveals much of her determined and adventurous character, and warrants presentation in full:

> Reddy, I must confess to you the most hopeless, tenderfoot trick I did last week. Thought I'd climb a mountain which stood up in the sky very temptingly in front of the house. Started about ten with the kodak and two slices of bread. There was no trail and the timber was close and lots of fallen timber, but Bobbie Harrington had been to the top so I saw no reason why I shouldn't go too. Climbed till four when I got well above the timber and found a snow drift. Hadn't had any water all day. Choked down my bread and started for home. Allowed myself three hours to get down in. Didn't get quite to the top as I didn't dare allow the extra time it

would have taken. (Wish I'd gone now!) Came down, down, down through fallen timber. Finally got out on a point where I could get a view of the lake. Saw I was on the wrong spur and would come down way above the head of the lake. But there was nothing to do for it but go on. Found deer tracks and followed them down an old water course. Deer aren't particular about where they go, apparently. Down over rocks and fallen timber at a descent of 60 [degrees] at least, swinging downwards by holding one sapling then grabbing the next. Shirt torn, hand cut, head bumped. Bottom at last. Heard water. Listened. Found I was near the Upper Falls 5 miles from the lake and through the worst country in this region! It was then 6:30. Got down to the river. Long grass and swamp. Plunged along. Fell into holes. Butted through willows. Waded through the river. Got onto rocky spur of the opposite mountain. Lost my matches in the thicket. It got darker and darker. Kept getting into difficulties and having to go back and around. Had been climbing for ten hours and legs began to get revolutionary but I remembered the heroes of antiquity and struggled on. At last it got so dark that I fell down every step or two so I decided to make a night of it. No coat, no fire, wet feet, no gun and visions of Nellie worried at the other end. Couldn't even find a decent bed it was so dark. So lay down between logs on a spurt of rock with a few small pines nearby to climb in case of bears. Said my prayers, thought of you, remembered that certain seraphic individuals had once been lost not 15 minutes from home the other side of the lake, and went to sleep. Slept and shivered till 5 o'clock, when it was light enough to see a little. Then went on for two hours over rocks and rotten logs till I got to the lake. Prowled about a house, saw no one moving, so stole a boat and rowed the 2 miles home in frantic haste and landed on our beach in deep embarrassment. Three men out looking for me till 3 o'clock!! Now known about the lake as "the girl who spent the night out on the mountain." Now did you ever know of such an idiotic trick? Nothing to eat till 24 hours and sleeping out (the mud was frozen in the morning) without a coat doesn't sound pleasant but it really shows you what you can do at a pinch and it was a fine feeling of independence and, if I had not thought of being such a fool and of worrying everybody I should have quite enjoyed myself. There were moments, however, when I fully expected to be wakened by the tickling of whiskers of a mountain lion. But I had a plan! First snap the front of the kodak open in the creature's face, then make for the nearest pine!![69]

The night on the mountain could have deprived the world of a future deaconess and Sherman Coolidge of a future wife. Instead, it produced, in just a few pages of writing, a very telling sketch of Grace Darling Wetherbee.

7

Proving Herself

"Dearest Reddy," Grace wrote Anne in early October 1899, "I'm one day toward the Deaconate. I went down this morning in fear and trembling." This nervousness quickly turned to tedium. That day, the warden of St. Faith's Deaconess Training School, Dr. William Huntington, had offered an "exhortation" not unlike a "ramble." His strict message—that it was "very unseemly for deaconesses to think of marrying"—was tempered only by his opposition to "vows of celibacy." "Apparently," Grace commented, "the deaconess is encouraged to hope in the face of certain failure, predestined failure."[1]

The founders of St. Faith's probably had a different message in mind when they opened in 1891, as did the anonymous woman who donated the institution's first building—a gift she called "an act of Faith to a work of Faith." The school quickly became a well-known testing ground for young women wanting to express their religious convictions as missionaries and Christian educators. Its two-year curriculum included courses in theology, church history, and the Old and New Testaments, supplemented with ecclesiastical embroidery, home economics, and tailoring. Summer internships took place in churches and hospitals.[2] Students were expected to board, meaning that at the start of the semester Grace had to confess her intentions to her mother. Mrs. Wetherbee was not pleased, and initially, neither was Grace.[3] In the first year, she sometimes did poorly on her exams, and her modern ideas clashed with her instructors' conservatism.[4] At times, she was even officially "scolded" for her refusal to accept church doctrine in its entirety.[5]

Thankfully, other sources of stimulation existed. In November, Grace attended a football game between Princeton University and the Carlisle Indian Industrial School's formidable team. Grace went in "feeling quite Princetonian," but the moment "those pretty cousins came trotting in, looking so bow-legged and sweet," her heart "went promptly back to its proper sphere." Despite her ardent support, Carlisle lost. Nonetheless, the Indians "played fiercely," more than once "casually" hitting their "white brothers" so hard they flew through the air "head over heels." Most spectators cheered Carlisle's loss. "The small boys peeking thro' the holes in the fence and myself," Grace reported, "were for the Indians, but the populace, I regret to state, seemed to share the national prejudice."[6] Grace was working to mitigate this bias as best she could. Throughout the fall and winter, she gathered and sent large boxes of school supplies to Wind River, care of Reverend Roberts.[7] Her remaining time outside of class was spent caring for patients in a New York hospital.[8] Taking on this work, in particular, caused tensions with her mother.[9]

But it was Anne who became Grace's greatest distraction. The Talbots had returned from England in the fall and were again living in Bethlehem, Pennsylvania. Grace traveled to meet Anne in November, stirring up old feelings.[10] These yearnings were, to some degree, alleviated by the sense of purpose and self-worth Grace derived from her deaconess training. "Oh! Reddy," one letter read, "I felt very lonely in my bed. But it's finer than I can tell you to be working at something and toward something. I feel as tho' I was trying to get enough together to propose to my girl!" Grace proposed that they tour the West during their next vacation.[11] She would eventually travel there but alone, and for an entirely different purpose.

St. Faith's maintained connections to Grace's primary passion, Indian missions. In December 1899, the school held a "missionary week" that included an "Indian day." The head deaconess let Grace out of Greek so she could attend the lectures. William Hobart Hare, a onetime missionary bishop of the South Dakota diocese, spoke, as did Herbert Welsh, Coolidge's cousin from Wind River. The afternoon's proceedings convinced Grace that she had found her calling. "I just nearly died and wanted to get up and go out to them [Indians] so," she wrote Anne. "I never have felt half so strongly, in spite of myself, about anything in all my life as about going to them someday." There was simply no more useful way to spend her time on Earth. "I know I shall just have to," she continued. "I can't feel justified in dying till I've been."[12] Despite the excitement of this prospect, Grace remained largely bored by her studies. She complained of "dying of idleness" and hoped to be placed in the "alcoholic ward" of the hospital, where things often got "fierce."[13] Overnight visits with Anne relieved some ennui, and in May 1900 rumors swirled that Cousin Pokey was in town.[14] A friend had sighted "a large, fat Indian in clericals and surrounded by 3 white squaws walking up the avenue," but for whatever reason he had neglected to inform Grace of his presence. "Could it be?" she asked Anne. "And why shouldn't he let us know?"[15]

Due to a long gap in correspondence, we also do not know what Grace did for the next seven months. A later letter from Laura Roberts suggests that she and Anne may have spent some of this period in the Bahamas.[16] Grace's own letters to Anne only pick up in January 1901. Life then appeared much the same. Grace was still studying at St. Faith's, caring for the infirm, and seeing Anne, though work and school sometimes interfered. In one instance, Grace assured her, "I love you so much, Sweetie. Think about that whenever you think about me, will you? I may be seeming to take temperatures or give the weekly scrubbing but what I'm really busy at is loving my little Red, in a common place way, of course."[17] Grace's major ambition, however, was to spend the coming summer volunteering at an Indian mission. In the spring of 1901, she began sending out inquiries, only later asking Ms. Susan Trevor Knapp, the head deaconess, whether she could substitute Indian work for another stint in the hospital. When Grace received permission, she ran "like a shot" to the mission house. There was one opening in the West. No one else had applied, so she put forth her name. On the advice of the deaconess, Grace then wrote the bishop of Utah Abiel Leonard for a placement alongside Lucy Carter, whose work among the Utes in Utah had been featured in the *Spirit of Missions*.[18] In May 1901, Grace received word that she was welcome to come.[19]

Carter's invitation filled Grace with "the most unmixed desire to start for Utah on the spot." Two complications, unfortunately, dampened her exhilaration. Her arrival date had been set for June, meaning that she now had to endure three weeks of "sitting around." And when Grace received a letter from Anne, she remembered that it was her "little Reddy" whom she truly wanted.[20] Anne also wanted to meet, but Grace could not bear the emotional toll of their cyclical reunion and separation. "Don't ask me to come out again," she gently protested.

> Coming out only means coming away at the end. I don't feel half as lonely for you as I did before I went over. I hope you feel hopeful about us. I do, and it is so foolish not to just make ourselves so. I do need you so much every way, Reddy, and want you all the time. But let's not talk about it. It doesn't do any good. It's very lonely in my bed without any little Redhead in it. . . . Anyway, we must both think about the little house and maybe someday we can go and live in it together. . . . I love all of you, every bone.[21]

Anne may have nonetheless been hurt. In a subsequent letter, Grace acknowledged the greater difficulty of their situation and the pain it caused:

> I feel discouraged, too, and I don't see that there is much to hope for unless some great big change happens. I suppose that is possible, but I don't see any at this moment. Besides, no matter how unified we are or how happy together, there will always be the fear of yr. getting married hanging over head, at least. There will never be any security—then you will never like what I do. Perhaps there will be some way out of it, tho'. At any rate, I love you now as much as I'm capable of loving anybody and I've never had much practice in that sort of thing, and except children I never want anything more than you. Only I want a little, more of you!! . . . One thing I know and that is that I am not going to see you anymore as long as I do you harm.

Grace's plan was to socialize with others as much as she could while studying for her upcoming mission trip. This involved learning Ute sign language, learning the tribe's history, and making out her last will and testament.

All of Grace's preparations were advisable, especially putting down her last wishes. Indian reservations were tense places at the turn of the century, where violent rebellion in response to colonial rule often simmered. Grace was well aware. In her letter to Anne, she also enclosed a newspaper clipping from the *New York Times* titled "Indian Outbreak in Wyoming," which described the Arapahos killing settlers' farm stock in defiance of Agent Nickerson and his ban on the Sun Dance. The *Times* reported that government troops were preparing for any eventuality.[22] The Uintah and Ouray Reservation was likewise insecure. Disease, poverty, and bitterness at bureau restrictions were rampant there, though its agents tolerated the Sun Dance. The Ninth Cavalry nonetheless made regular patrols to prevent raids and arson.[23] No one knew the potential harm Grace was exposing herself to better than Lucy Carter. When Grace wrote her and asked to arrive early, Carter, who was then away from the Uintah agency center of Whiterocks, insisted that Grace wait until she could be there to ensure that Grace would be all right. Carter also requested "four pair of stockings" at twenty-five cents each and some writing materials.[24]

Nothing about the idea of missionary work on a distant Indian reservation pleased Grace's parents. Their opposition was so great that she wished not to return home. "Mother is very much upset," Grace complained to Anne. "It is disappointing. How I wish I never had to come back. If ever anybody ever had a millstone I'm sure I have. I don't think it is all selfishness, my wanting to get away, at least I hope not, for I do feel so more and more strongly that I can't ever get over anything as long as I stay in this atmosphere. There was a time when I didn't mind the rows so much except as they affected me, but now I know too well where they lead." Though Grace's actions left her parents dismayed and angered, she herself faced the real agony of leaving Anne. "Poor Reddy!" she wrote. "But I just can't think about going without you. It seems so far and I want you so all the time." Yet Grace saw Uintah as a trial, necessary if only to feel she had once done something useful. She had come away from her last meeting with Anne "discouraged" and anxious that she was "failing all the time." Grace had to prove her value by going west as a missionary. "If I could only be just good and helpful out there so I could be worth something when I see you again, I think you would love me more," she hoped. This negative mindset genuinely pained her. Grace admitted to "screaming and crying" while writing the letter.

And so Grace left, boarding a train in New York on Monday, June 3, 1901, at 5:30 p.m., for a four-day cross-country trip to Evanston, Wyoming.

Once there, she would visit Roberts before her train ride to Salt Lake City. She would get to the Uintah reservation by stagecoach. Grace took with her a massive trunk, a saddle, a blanket, and her "best clothes"—so many things she was afraid people would think she had "come to stay."[25] On the second day of the journey west, Grace woke up early and looked out the window to see Erie, Pennsylvania. After passing the city, the "big country" began to "spread out," getting "bigger and sweeter till it turned into prairie dogs and paintbrush."[26] Arriving in Evanston, Grace was welcomed by Dr. George Coolidge Hunting and his wife, Mary Grace, her hosts for the next few days. At Fort Washakie, Grace found Roberts and a group of schoolchildren waiting for her in front of the church. Cousin Pokey was also there, but no romantic sparks flew. Grace instead mentioned to Anne that after a tour of the government school, she was forced to listen to his evening sermon with some "regret."[27]

Relief came Sunday afternoon as Grace sat alone on a hillside among the sagebrush, watching a sheepherder. A sage chicken walked by with her little offspring. Grace picked one up, and the chick sat happily in her hand. The mother hen soon became "agitated," so Grace released it. From her vantage point, she could see the snowy Uintah mountains in the distance, the only physical barrier between her and the reservation where she would prove herself, a mere hundred miles away. Getting there, however, meant six hours by train to Salt Lake City, an overnight stay, and a thirty-six-hour stagecoach ride to Whiterocks. This was no "hopeful prospect" to an impatient missionary in training. Grace kept saying aloud, "If there was only a road or even a trail!" A passing woman suddenly answered, "Why there is a road!" The route, used primarily to transport iron ore, was just what Grace needed. She ran to the Huntings' home and "gently but persistently" convinced them not only to drive her to Whiterocks in their buckboard wagon but also to turn the outing into a two-week vacation. There would be snow on the way, and they expected to "strike drifts." With her usual insouciance, Grace thought these obstacles "just sporty." Everything about the West seemed so. After the first few days, she was convinced that she wanted to stay "for good and all." Grace told Anne, "I just can't live in a shut up town anymore. I am going to locate here just as soon as I am done at St. Faith's. We'll have our little house yet, precious!"[28]

On the trip over the snowy mountains to Utah, Grace and the Hunt-ings once got hopelessly lost and spent more than a few frigid nights in their tent. At one point they passed an abandoned cabin in which they slept next to their horses. The bedraggled party reached the Whiterocks mission in the third week of June, just as the Utes began performing the annual Sun Dance. Grace's response was fascination with what she called the "weirdest sight." The men, who had been dancing for two days without food or water, looked "haggard beyond words." Yet still, the atmosphere felt very welcoming. On the last day, the tribe gave away their horses to elders and visitors. Grace would have attended were it not for "a finger amputation." A Ute man had gotten "mixed up with a rope and a wild horse," and required her nursing skills. She later commented that "any self respecting hospital would have had a fit at the operation" performed in the front room of Miss Carter's small cabin. As they removed the finger, "a cat wandered around freely," and "an admiring group of friends stood around and watched the performance," walking in and out of the open door as they pleased. A young girl named Elsie, whose leg had been amputated, looked on from the corner with interest. The Ute man eventually lost consciousness and slept until evening, forcing everyone to dine outside. Grace called him "a nice Indian." The other Utes, she quickly concluded, were "not very good Indians."[29]

From the beginning, Grace had unrealistically high hopes, and after just a few days at Uintah, she decided that the work was "miserably discouraging."[30] Grace taught several classes at the Whiterocks agency school, where morale was exceedingly low.[31] Measles had killed seven-teen of its sixty-five students in 1901; as a result, parents were fearful, and attendance was sparse. Eventually, the Uintah agent began paying parents to enroll their children.[32] Grace also regretted the absence of an ordained priest.[33] Instead, there was a "dreadful" layman at the neighboring Ouray mission who enjoyed the respect of no one. Two Indians had died because he refused, for whatever reason, to admit them to the infirmary. Grace noted that the man "hurts the work so much." She could not understand why the bishop did not "see through him."[34] Miss Carter recognized the disadvantage of the situation, making her all the more determined to have Grace stay. Grace felt that without a priest, it was pointless.[35]

In a typical week, Grace visited the surrounding camps and hosted any Indians who appeared at the mission. On Sundays, she and Miss Carter held "a little service" for the students and agency employees, and Grace took charge of a Bible study class for the children.[36] She was also learning to cook and clean for the first time in her life. The experience was "thrilling," as was tending house, which was "such fun."[37] It also came as a "great surprise" that St. Faith's courses had been "tremendously helpful" in preparing for mission work. By August, Grace was certain she wanted to be a deaconess and that she would return to work under Roberts at Wind River once she graduated.[38] Another stay in Uintah was out of the question, no matter how much praise she received from Miss Carter. Ultimately, it was the feeling of usefulness that attracted her to the work. "I'm so thankful to have some excuse for living," Grace expressed to Anne.[39]

In her last dispatch from Uintah, Grace reported that she had run out of money.[40] Even if her parents had wanted to help, there was no way to do so. Whiterocks had nowhere to receive wire transfers.[41] Somehow, though, she managed to reach Denver by the end of October and make her way back to New York City. Grace "hated to leave Miss Carter to struggle on alone" and was moved when she "begged" her to return the next summer.[42] Life back in "civilization" quickly revealed its shortcomings. By November, Grace was unhappy she had returned to Manhattan, where she felt "horribly oppressed" by "everybody's lack of any sense of earnestness." In the West, everything had been "big and simple." Confronted with New York's "inequalities," she could not understand how people remained not only indifferent but also devoted to "heaping them higher." She observed, "The poor—poor people! There isn't much outlook for them."[43]

As the winter of 1901–2 approached, Grace began to reflect on her time at Uintah and her feelings for Anne, whom she had not yet seen. In a letter she explained:

> Oh, Reddy, this summer has taught me two things; first, that I can get along without you and second, that I'm "heap hungry" doing it. I used to think at Whiterocks that I could do without after all and I used to remember how bored you would be if you were there doing our stupid things and how you would wonder why I wasn't

and then I would get so promptly. But when I came away I wanted you *so* and every day now I turn to you and want to feel so only *half* without you, so incomplete, everything is fine but always lacks point; just you, Reddy. And yet, you were the one who saw first and knew that we must break off, but I think I've seen at last, Reddy, and now I feel as tho' I never wanted to see you again if ever there was going to be one word more added to all that has gone. I mean it, sweety. It is myself that I blame as I should and I don't know whether I am sure of myself or not, I don't think I'm sure. The same things give me the same frightened feelings they used to. I forgot them in Whiterocks and at St. Faith's but coming back into this house is like hearing an echo of it all again. I am trying to be good and fit myself for all I hope to do but, you know it isn't natural to me and I've never been brought up to it; but this I mean to do if I can find the strength for it, and that is to put my work before you. You know I didn't do that, and you can't serve two masters. But oh! My Reddy, how hungry I am for you this minute. For the sweet feel of you. I only want to tell you frankly, I'm desperately afraid, and of the same two things that used to be all the trouble to me in you. . . . I think, Reddy, (you must understand) that the only way I feel stronger about us now is that the horror of all that has happened has at last taken hold of me. I think that is all. But I'm your Gedy and nobody else's.[44]

Reddy, however, asked for a meeting, which only rekindled suppressed emotions. Grace later wrote, "I woke up all thru' the night feeling so sad that my little Reddy had gone away."[45]

Nonetheless, the reunion itself was very happy, with Grace writing that Anne was "the fine, wonderful Reddy of the old days again." Grace continued, "I don't know where you have come from, but I do know you have come. It's like having two Reddys, but both to be loved as one. I hope this isn't too subtle for your little pretty mind; it's very plain to mine!" What Grace again felt was a need to prove herself worthy of Anne's approval:

I'm overpowered with a sense of responsibility at the thought of living up to you and with abounding gratitude for you. Filled with a wild desire to do what you want in everything is your Gedy because she knows that you know right. That's the way I used to feel long ago but only vaguely because I didn't know you well, then only guessed what you might be. If I can only have you, and have you more fully, I shall never dream of wanting anybody else, ever. I think I might even reach a place where I would love everybody.

"Living up" to Anne meant returning to the West as a missionary. Grace wrote John Roberts, who agreed to accommodate her at Wind River that coming summer.[46]

In the spring of 1902, Grace resolved to purge her bank accounts and live a life better suited to her "socialistic ideas" at Fort Washakie. She asked Anne if she could give her access to what was left of her money, so Anne could send it to her "little by little" at Wind River. At this point, Grace's parents did not know she was planning to leave. James Bowen Funsten, the new bishop of Wyoming and Idaho, made a special visit to Grace's aunt Sarah and uncle Nye, helping to convince them that she would be safe. Funsten "inspired confidence," though Grace was less sure of her own ability to do the work.[47] Roberts had offered "the whole charge of the school" and asked her to bring others to help with responsibilities requiring three or four persons.[48] This challenge seemed daunting but not as fearful as the prospect of Mrs. Wetherbee's learning of these plans. Toward the end of March, her mother began to realize something suspicious was afoot, bringing down on Grace a "regular persecution." Grace's anticipation of her June departure was the only thing keeping her spirits up.[49] At the end of April, she graduated from St. Faith's, becoming an ordained deaconess.[50] She saw Anne for a "sweet last day" of "comfort" before boarding a train west and leaving behind an exasperated set of parents.[51]

Grace arrived at Fort Washakie in mid-June, ready to settle into a small, two-room log cabin with another young woman, Mary Bennet.[52] In a letter to Anne, Grace wrote, "You must remember all the time that I am trying to love you the way you want me to and that every day I sit still and think about you hard and am so sorry."[53] A part of their relationship had seemingly concluded. Grace's life as a missionary had begun.

8

Twosing

When Grace Darling Wetherbee arrived at Wind River in June 1902, the last thing on her mind was marriage, much less to Sherman Coolidge. Her foremost concerns—shelter and transport—were much more basic. John Roberts had not yet prepared the Fort Washakie mission's guest house of "rough logs," so Grace and her new housemate, Mary, slept elsewhere until a red cedar partition was installed to create separate rooms. Grace also asked that a large horizontal window be cut out to frame the mountain views and create "a sweet place to sit and sew or read." Roberts maintained that another window would make the house too cold, but she was happy to sacrifice for "those sweet mountains." Sherman meanwhile set about finding Grace a horse. He located a black-and-white pinto whose owner, an Arapaho named Sage, asked $25.[1] Negotiations fell through when Sage "accidentally shot himself in the eye."[2] Grace eventually ended up with an old racehorse named Foxy, reputed to be "a little bit crazy."[3]

Roberts had promised Grace a great deal of work, and in the beginning there was much to do. The mission school for girls housed a group of "real nice children." One, Delia, was "a perfect fiend." Throughout the day, she would appear at Grace's window, "make a sudden sally, as it were, and carry off any little trophy she happened to fancy, and then have to be chased, shrieking, all over the place." Grace labeled Delia a "war chief," considering her "much the nicest of the bunch." Overall, Wind River struck Grace as "lovely." The Arapahos were "real" and "nice," though the Shoshones were "magpies"—slang for "stupid people."[4] While making rounds at the agency, Grace met Sherman's half-sister, Sings First. Now named Julia Hereford, she was living at Fort Washakie and married to a

"Shoshone quarter-breed," John Hereford. Julia, whom Grace described as very attractive, had just given birth to a "cherub" named Sherman, soon to be baptized.[5] Grace's delight with the child was blighted only by Hereford's shocking habit of nursing her baby "freely in the gaze of the public" and at church services, no less.

Grace's duties at Fort Washakie consisted of seeking out children for the mission's Sunday school and visiting the Arapaho camps "to keep hold of the confirmed girls." She also did whatever possible to aid those Arapahos and Shoshones who had fallen ill. The work was demanding but invigorating. As Grace described to Anne,

> Talk about irons in the fire. Two Sunday schools, both weak, two parsons, with peculiarities, two tribes, heap nice, school children in school, school children in the camps, white people, half breeds, sick people, babies to be christened, such dusty churches—why I just dream of brooms! And it's so lovely to have them tell you they've been looking for a useful lady for ages and to be able to fall to, hit or miss, and take yr. personality with you. I feel about 20, wear corsets, and sit up as straight as a gopher, just for pure joy, and curl my hair!! Now could my own Red ask more of me?[6]

Grace's "joy" was mixed with a touch of confusion. She observed that Arapaho and Shoshone women regularly died in the camps for little perceptible reason. One evening, a funeral passed outside her cabin, filling the night with mournful singing and drumbeats. The constant death was inscrutable. "They go into a decline, just the way wild birds or plants die," she remarked to Anne. "Isn't it too queer to think of nature, or the primeval, or something, having such a hold over them? I suppose it is a sort of general tuberculosis." There was nothing one could do but bring food for the hungry or infirm. One case was "a little sick school girl" whom Grace knew from class.

Throughout her first month at Wind River, Grace saw little of Cousin Pokey, who spent most of his days in an old agency storehouse doing "apparently nothing" aside from keeping his "eye peeled for those who pass his windows." What contact they had Grace enjoyed, and her letters reveal a fast-growing appreciation for his company. In one, she regretted that Sherman visited only occasionally.[7] In another, she pronounced him "docility itself." Sherman's sermons had also improved from the improvised talks of years past. "Poke gave an awfully good address," Grace admitted, "written, I'm thankful to say." Beforehand, she had been "simply paralyzed for fear" that he had not "given it a thought before he got up." Sherman's disposition had likewise changed. Once "conceited," he now seemed much more serious in demeanor.[8] Grace soon began seeking out his company whenever she could, even if some aspects of his "dead proud" personality still grated. While on a group ride, he "behaved badly" and insisted on monopolizing her time. Yet, at the outing's end, he won back her affections by lending his horse, Prince, when Grace's began to run "frightfully rough." On another occasion, Sherman displayed his unflappable discretion during "a dark and terrible adventure." Grace and Mary had visited his half-sister one afternoon to inquire about a recently born baby. They found Hereford seated among giant piles of uniforms, weeping at the prospect of ironing them all in time for the agency's soldiers. Despite thinking Hereford below their station, Grace and Mary felt too guilty to leave. They remained for three hours, working "as hard as ever." At the moment of peak chaos, Sherman suddenly walked in the door. Grace related the scene to Anne:

> Talk about being embarrassed! First at being caught there, and then the way he must have felt about her. She calls him "Coolidge" half the time and says "for G's sake" and talks about things you don't exactly talk about in polite society. Well, I thought I'd die on the spot. I declare Poke's a gentleman, Red. He just gave me one wild look and then said, "Hullo," as cheerful as tho' it was the most natural thing in the world to find me ironing soldiers' stable jackets with the cats and the babies swarming. I stuck to the ironing and blessed Pokey for being such a dear.[9]

The afternoon affected Grace in another way. By the time she left, she had become desperately "baby hungry" from being around little Sherman.[10] She had as well concluded that "Indian babies are so much the nicest."[11]

Whether this desire for a baby influenced the development of Grace's relationship with Sherman, she does not say. But by late July, the two were meeting regularly, and Grace's letters began to take on, as she put it, an "Arapahoe tinge."[12] In the evenings, Sherman would arrive at the mission's cabin with "gold tipped cigs," which they leisurely smoked "behind lowered shades."[13] Not every encounter was so relaxing. When out riding together, just as dusk fell, "an old rattlesnake went off like an alarm clock" under Grace's horse. She leaped off and began to "fire" rocks at it until it appeared dead, then demanded Sherman's knife so she could cut off the rattle and send it to Anne as a trophy. He "coldly refused," fearing the snake might somehow bite. Grace turned increasingly "scornful," even comparing Sherman to some "squaws" they had met earlier in the day. After almost coming "to blows," she wrested the knife away. Darkness, however, had already descended. For some time, she unwisely felt around on the ground for the snake, but it had disappeared. This conflict quickly passed.

The same letter told of how on another evening, "sandwiched in between wild jokes," Sherman had suddenly opened up to Grace, telling her about "his Injun self." All his life, he had been discriminated against in one way or another, always made to feel like an inferior outsider. Grace, sitting alone with him while stitching an altar cloth, felt almost paralyzed. She wanted "to go and comfort him," but could not bring herself to move, slowly realizing his "pretty hard road to travel." Afterward, the two decided they were "just like Robinson Crusoe." With "no one else to play with," they "might as well play with each other." Influenced by Sherman, Grace began to consider relocating near the Arapahos; in her eyes Roberts neglected them at his mission.[14] Then things between the new friends took a new turn.

In late August, Grace posted a desperate missive to Anne, begging her to visit as soon as possible. Late one night, she and Sherman had become physical, leaving her "awfully mixed up." "Talk about principles," she wrote. "Did I ever have any?" The letter continued,

> How far can you let them go when they don't mean anything serious and you don't? I never let anybody before hold my hand a whole evening, or even a few minutes. I'm so afraid it seems flip, then I explain that I never did this way before, and I am convinced that makes it worse. I do get so horribly tangled. Every night that goes on and it was after midnight last night when it stopped and the

yellow puppy (the children gave him to me and he's such a foolish dear) and I got to bed. And *you* don't mind they're kissing you, do you? But I haven't reached that point—I won't say *yet*. Why should I? I had a narrow escape, but I tried the power of the human eye that Helen Copill used to bank so on in oral exams and it worked pretty well. But then the poor thing sat down and called itself a fool so many times that I almost did it myself after all.

The problem was not only one of boundaries. Grace feared that her actions had been "undignified" and "unwomanly." She admonished Anne for not being there to offer her own "little white hand" and ease her sense of isolation. Yet, her feelings that night did seem "serious." Grace felt that she and Sherman were "playing not with each other as objects, but together, each being subjects." The thought of harming Sherman also pained her. Out of carelessness, she had said something about his being "Injun," provoking a harsh lecture on the wrongs of harboring prejudice. "It hurt like fire," Grace admitted. "I told him he would never have a chance to hurt again and I meant it by Jove." Even so, Sherman avoided Grace for three full days before she, "pretty nearly sick," approached him to make amends. Now she was being careful to avoid offending his "so absurdly sensitive" feelings.[15]

The three-day tiff only intensified Sherman and Grace's emotions. They began twosing every night on a packing box outside Grace's cabin, as the "sweetest moon" shone above and coyotes howled a serenade in the distant hills. The "power of the human eye" had failed entirely. At first, Grace was "scared," feeling much like "Adam and Eve after the fall." Yet, the twosing had been "so natural and comfortable." She asked, "Red, do you think I'm an awful fool or maybe worse than that?" She queried further,

What's happened to me, I wonder? My convictions are, I think, the same, but it does seem so comfortable and natural I might as well buck at kissing you. But is it wrong to Sherman?

I honestly can't make myself care about him like he says he does about me and I tell him so every few rounds. Maybe we both like just the twosing. I guess it is because he's Injun that I feel so at home. They always have seemed more natural than just white people, tho'

I don't tell him that. Oh! yes. I did too, partly. And he said, well, wasn't he one? I said, yes, but how about the quarter of a million others? And he said something silly about the seventy million other whites in the country. You have to get up early to get ahead of these Arapahoes. . . . I wish you'd tell me what I'm doing, Reddy, and say a little prayer for my perplexity.

Grace's feelings for Sherman were not the only source of incertitude. What she felt for Anne had been so clear. Male sexuality did not elicit as strong a response, a factor that made the present situation all the more incomprehensible. "I wish I could fool myself but I can't," Grace lamented. She continued,

Don't you believe you better come out and take care of me? It looks like you had to me. My! but I wanted you that first night, I'm awfully green for my years. But I always thought men were just about like women. Indians don't seem to be, anyhow. Well, if I hadn't you, I never would dare go as far as I have. If you tell me to stop, I will. But it's awfully nice to have somebody to say good night to.

For heaven's sake, say something, Reddy. I wish I liked him like I do you. I guess there's something wrong with me. I want to like and I just plumb can't, only you, you old red headed sweety. Your perplexed Gedy.

This "perplexed" state was relatively short lived. Though Grace struggled over her attachment to Anne and no longer "felt fit for church," she soon resolved that her future resided with Sherman.[16]

At the end of August, Sherman proposed. Grace "almost died right there and then," but she told him she needed time instead. To Anne, she revealed not having "the vaguest idea" about her true feelings except for being "just dead comfortable and happy" whenever Sherman was near. It had to be because he was "Injun." Her giddy letter included these jokes: "What's your favorite season of the year, Reddy? Mine is Indian Summer! Ha! Ha! Ha!" Followed by, "And when I'm married, Reddy, I'll be half Arapahoe, which half, Reddy? My better half!"[17] Questionable humor aside, Sherman was impatient. Less than two weeks after his proposal, he "got rambunctious" and insisted on knowing Grace's answer. She did not have one but confessed to Anne that twosing with him "was so much realer than any (man) body" she had ever known.

By that point, Grace had time on her hands. For whatever reason, Roberts had stopped giving her much work. There was so little to do that she even considered returning to Uintah and Ouray Reservation to aid Lucy Carter. Grace had also come to view the girls' school, consisting of only fourteen students, a "most awful failure" compared to the government school with "the same church influence." Only her relationship with Sherman was keeping her at Wind River, yet she could not bring herself to accept his proposal. "I just can't open my mouth and say the word," Grace explained to Anne. "I feel just like a kite that is waiting for the wind to pick it up. I couldn't tell if you burned me at the stake whether I was going to say yes or no."[18]

A fortnight passed, and in late September, Grace finally "said the word" as she and Pokey sat on the packing box outside her cabin. Sherman responded by squeezing her so tightly she could barely breathe. Others on the reservation took the news as no surprise. For weeks, Sherman and Grace's budding passion had been treated like an open secret. A "sweet old Priest" at St. Stephens one day casually hinted at the obvious, asking Sherman, "Mr. Coolidge, do you know how many witnesses are necessary for a wedding in this state?" An awkward silence followed in which Grace "inwardly thanked heaven" that Pokey was an Arapaho "and so could keep his face straight as they gravely discussed the question." Then one day Grace's roommate, Mary, asked her "out right" after a long period of seeming to ignore Sherman's constant presence. Mrs. Roberts had even caught Sherman and Grace "in the act" (perhaps twosing again) while on a clandestine picnic. Any shroud of secrecy had been ripped to tatters, but Grace's first instinct was continued discretion. She wanted, especially, to hide the engagement from her parents and only inform them after the wedding.[19] News that she was marrying an Indian would only cause more distress to a mother afraid of having a "burnt child"—"burnt" meaning "disgraced."[20] Sherman objected, insistent on doing the "square thing" by writing Grace's father for permission.

The week Grace accepted Sherman's proposal, the couple rode down to inspect his old ranch. Grace found the cabin "sweet and homey," and much nicer than Sherman's off-putting descriptions. Returning that night to Fort Washakie, Grace grew annoyed at the slow pace and forced Sherman to take a shortcut at a gallop. Just when she "finally had the satisfaction of loping at a high rate of speed," she slammed "straight into a barbed wire fence." Her horse panicked and pulled her along over three posts. The lacerations, with one on her shin that reached the bone, "hurt like Sam Hill." She had to be bandaged the next day by an army surgeon. Still, the afternoon at the ranch had convinced Sherman and Grace that they should live there in the summers and establish a mission exclusively for the Arapahos. Sherman's vacation was due in October, giving them time for a honeymoon of home renovations. To Grace, it was all "such a sweet Injuny thing" that seemed like destiny. As a child she had said she would marry an Indian. Now she was. Their plans were set until a major obstacle presented itself.

Sherman and Grace wanted to be married at the Fort Washakie mission surrounded by a few select witnesses and a group of "Injun kids."[21] With Mary's help, Grace put together a white dress that looked "very respectable." Everyone, it appeared, supported her union with Sherman. Then two days before the wedding date, Sherman approached Roberts alone to ask about the ceremony. After a short discussion, he returned to Grace with a forlorn look. "Is it all right?" she asked. "No," he replied, "Mr. Roberts says he won't marry us." Grace was shocked. Sherman, having known Roberts for years, had expected as much. Roberts's objections varied. First, he made a fumbling excuse about needing two weeks' preparation. Then he insisted that Grace's father had to approve the marriage.

Grace was certain that Sherman had thrown "an Injun fit" and given up too easily. She was wrong. When she approached Roberts and "talked straight from the shoulder," he behaved like a "pope" judging "a run-away couple coming in off the streets." His only response was, "I shall telegraph your father." This dismissal, Grace ruefully noted, was "such an insult to Sherman." Though she condemned Roberts's "narrow mind," she could not supply her father's permission. Upon receiving Sherman's letter, Gardner Wetherbee had urged caution and asked that he and Grace contemplate the future at length. Roberts and his wife at least sensed the disappointment they had caused, so much so that Laura—who, as Grace put it, "never bothers being civil to anybody and rather doesn't like Sherman"—behaved "so sweet and good" to them. This fleeting manifestation of sympathy did not negate the fact that their wedding had been delayed indefinitely.

The possibility of no marriage almost destroyed Sherman. One night, he "went all to pieces" and "cried like a baby" in Grace's arms. She had not given up. Her suggestion was to travel to Lander, telegraph her father, and explain that after careful consideration they still wanted to wed. She and Sherman got in a horse cart and drove the seventy miles to the telegraph office. After a long and futile wait while the townsfolk ogled them, they retreated home, feeling "helpless and insulted." On the way back, the weather turned "cold and miserable." Suddenly, "a fearful rainstorm" broke out, and Sherman's horse, Prince, became so exhausted that he stumbled, almost upsetting the cart. Fearing a more serious accident, Sherman had to lead the beleaguered equine along the muddy road for the last two miles to the agency. The trio arrived "soaked and almost frozen," too exhausted to make it home. They took shelter at the government school for the night, hosted by the matron on duty. Back at the mission, everyone assumed they had eloped.[22]

Gardner Wetherbee's telegram came the next morning. It read: "Under the circumstances I withdraw my decision and leave the responsibility with you."[23] This reply did not satisfy Roberts. For years, he had taken a great deal of Gardner Wetherbee's money, and he was not about to repay this debt of gratitude by marrying his daughter to an Indian, even if Grace insisted her decision was final. Roberts's second refusal made Sherman "perfectly furious." In a heated conversation, Sherman told him that he and Grace would be leaving at daybreak for Casper. There, Sherman had a friend in the clergy who would perform the ceremony. Still, both Sherman and Grace privately worried about how relations in the East might view their elopement and how it might reflect on their characters. As it turned out, this anxiety was premature. Just as they were about to board the stage the next morning, Sherman got a message from Roberts saying that if the couple could produce a marriage license, he would marry them at once. Grace could not decipher why Roberts had suddenly changed his mind, other than it had dawned on him that she and Sherman really did want to get married and that her father's telegram relieved him of responsibility. It is also possible that Roberts feared some in the Episcopal Church might view his recalcitrance negatively. Whatever the reason, Sherman and Grace "piled in the cart" and headed back to Lander. They returned about ten hours later, at five in the evening, with marriage license in hand and led by "poor, tired Prince."[24]

At the mission, Sherman was tethering Prince to the hitching post when Roberts unexpectedly appeared. Awkward silence followed an exchange of good evenings. Roberts asked, "Won't you come in the house and have some supper?" Sherman and Grace declined. "When would you like to be married?" he ventured. "Right away Mr. Roberts!" came the answer. Roberts promptly left to notify the schoolchildren, who raced out of the dormitory, screaming, and began "violently" hugging the couple. Though the bride was wearing an "old black skirt and a red flannel waist with a button off and a hole in it," Sherman told her to forget the wedding dress. Grace was too exhausted to care. She entered the church to wait with the children while Sherman washed his face and hands. Somewhat refreshed, he appeared at the church door a moment later and rested his hat on a pile of firewood. Grace walked toward him, and they kissed and entered. The hasty ceremony concluded minutes later with the Shoshone girls hugging the "stuffing" out of the newlyweds.[25]

The Coolidges were finally married. The date was October 8, 1902.[26] Grace was nearing thirty years old; Sherman had reached forty. As their cart left Fort Washakie for the dilapidated ranch, the weather turned "mild," and a "lovely" moon sat in the heavens. Passing the government school, Grace remarked, "Wouldn't it be lovely if the band would only play for us?" An instant later, the voices of a student choir rang out: "John Brown's body lies a-mouldering in the grave!" Sherman and Grace convulsed with laughter. What happened later that evening, Grace never described for Anne.[27] Instead, her first postnuptial letter announced, "Since we have been married, we have been housecleaning to the exclusion of every other idea."[28]

The mixed-race marriage at Wind River between a New York heiress and an Indian priest was not something the American press would ignore.

Newspapers across the country marveled at how Grace Darling Wetherbee, a daughter of high society, had wed a "full-blooded Arapahoe" on
a distant Indian reservation. One paper even claimed that Sherman had
traded in his tepee for a modern home at his bride's behest.[29] The *New
York Times* also ran an article on the pair, claiming that Mr. Wetherbee
had, shockingly, given his "full consent."[30] The much smaller Geneva
press announced to its readers: "Well, he's married."[31] The most extensive
reporting on the "somewhat unexpected" union appeared in the *Denver
Post*, which commented that the news would "cause a sensation in New
York society circles [and] keep the tongues of the gossipers of Gotham
wagging for an indefinite period." The article described Grace's "palatial
residence" in the city and, again, suggested that Sherman had been living
in a tepee before the wedding. An interest in "Poor Lo" had brought the
"charming brunette" to Wyoming, where she had fallen in love with her
"dusky admirer." This "red-skinned missionary," now thankfully civilized,
had been born among the "savage and warlike Arapahoe," only to be
saved by the dashing army captain Charles Coolidge. Charles, though
very much alive, was erroneously declared dead. Nonetheless, the *Post*
correctly stated that Sherman Coolidge's life story provided "an excellent
subject for a novel."[32]

Sherman and Grace found such dramatic statements extremely amusing.
Friends sent newspaper clippings from across the country that Sherman
read aloud "with great unction" at the dinner table. The couple "joyfully"
whispered their favorite quote—"If the details could be known, the story
of their courtship would read like a chapter from a Romance"—in the
midst of "unromantic duties" such as washing dishes.[33] After reading one
melodramatic account of their marriage in a Cheyenne newspaper, they
both "pretty nearly busted."[34] Reactions to the marriage varied within
family and Episcopal circles. Ethelbert Talbot took credit for bringing
the two together but admitted "surprise." Warnings from Anne that they
might marry had fortunately mitigated the "shock" and thus enabled him
to "survive" the news.[35]

Coolidge's adoptive parents experienced no such brush with death.
By then, Charles had returned from fighting in the Spanish-American
War in Cuba and the Philippines.[36] He and Sophie were now living at

the Presidio in San Francisco, where Sophie became the center of the social scene after throwing a legendary Halloween party.[37] She also hosted a twelve-course luncheon for Gen. Arthur MacArthur Jr. and his wife. The *United States Army and Navy Journal and Gazette* deemed the event a smashing success and recognized Sophie as "the main spirit in the society of the Presidio." The gathering also gave her an opportunity to display her collection of "Oriental work," including the "finest silks of great value" that she had acquired in China.[38] Sophie's only care was occasional rheumatism, which forced the Coolidges to summer in San Rafael in hopes the weather would alleviate her pains.[39] (Charles retired from the military on August 10, 1903, at six o'clock in the evening. In a "touching ceremony" attended by a large group of officers and their wives, he "formally surrendered the regimental colors" to his successor. At the following reception, he proudly received "a beautiful silver loving cup standing about sixteen inches high surmounting an ebony pedestal about a foot high.")[40] Both elder Coolidges appear to have been thrilled by Sherman's marriage. Sophie sent her congratulations in a "sweetest kind of a letter."[41] No such letter arrived from anyone in Grace's family.

Before going to Wind River in 1902, Grace had turned to her uncle Nye and aunt Sarah for support and comfort while arguing with her parents. Bishop Funsten had even paid the couple a special visit to assure them Grace would be safe in Wyoming. News of Grace's wedding an Indian, however, mortified Aunt Sarah, who refused to write her niece. Uncle Nye was left to inform Grace of the acute distress she had caused. His letter, excerpted, read:

> Regarding your marriage, I know not what to say. That it was a complete surprise to me and, I need not repeat, to Aunt Sarah. As it was *un fait accompli* as we French scholars say before we knew anything about it, what could we say?
>
> That you have married a man of another race than your own is no more than your sister has done and as you are now in your thirtieth year you are supposed to have arrived at the years of discretion and at any rate know your own mind.

Considering all these circumstances, I concur with the opinion of your father that as the fact is a thing which cannot be recalled we had better accept the situation and say no more about the matter.

I shall certainly *never love you any less* for the step you have taken.

Possibly, I should have selected another choice for you but it may not have been so well as I understand you are more than satisfied.

Your father informed me that Mr. Coolidge is a gentleman of education and refinement, and as I doubt not he is a soldier of the Cross, and I *know you* are so perhaps we can all say it is well that it is so.

. . . Your Aunt Sarah has gone out, but I know she loves you no less than before and sends all good wishes.[42]

Such disapproval was a blow to Grace, as was learning how friends and relatives had to console her aunt. Only her father had written "nicely" but then went silent for a month. Grace complained of this treatment to Anne, even while admitting she expected nothing else.

Also galling were the racist comments that filtered out to Grace through Anne's letters. Many in her old social circle had questioned whether Sherman was "civilized or not." Some wondered what he wore for clothing. Others made "disgusting" remarks about what race their babies would be. Grace was deeply offended that anyone thought she would marry a "blanket Indian" but laughed off questions about Sherman's attire. (Every morning he chopped firewood in "pink-trimmed pajamas.") As for babies, Grace wrote, "You bet they'll be Injun if there ever should be any. Just like their mother and father." Ultimately, though, her response to everyone was, "Darn 'em! They can't talk that way about my husband to me, . . . not after the kind of song and dance I've had all my life."[43]

Despite her defiance, the opinion of one person remained deeply important to Grace. That was, of course, Anne's. Two weeks into her marriage, Grace experienced a moment of weakness when, one evening, Sherman began to sing "Oh, Come Ye to Bethlehem" at the dinner table. She felt "homesick" for Anne and began to weep. She tried to hide her tears, but Sherman noticed and comforted her. The next morning, he gave her one kiss from him and another from Anne.[44] Part of the problem sprung from Anne's refusal to say she was "glad" that Grace and Sherman had married—a vote of approval that Grace wanted to hear. Seeking approbation, she tried to convince Anne that Sherman suited her. "He's such a dear," she wrote, "I don't know just what I love in him—you asked me—he's got awfully sweet eyes, but I think what I love most is all the love he gives me. It's the sweetest thing. . . . Reddy, you wouldn't know me from my hubby's description of me."[45] One gathers from reading Grace's letters that Anne became jealous at these glowing accounts of life with a new partner.[46] In one letter, she played up her ill health to receive more attention.[47] Grace, in response, seemed to downplay her love for Sherman and the intensity of the relationship. She also suggested that Anne marry her male love interest, Francis Donaldson, and she eventually did two years later.[48]

Anne's behavior and her criticisms of Francis forced Grace, at times, to criticize Sherman as well:

> I despise Sherman too, quite frequently, and I never feel hot about him as I do about you. I don't love him any better and I don't think as well, anyway. I always tell him I don't. But what does it matter? He's my own Injun and we all have such worthless faults—a few more or less don't matter. Besides that, when you've once stood up there in church and said all those things and got their ring and their name you don't really despise them a bit. I tell you honestly, Reddy, I would have given every dear thing I have on this earth to have gotten out of marrying Sherman that week before we were married, ending two months ago today, anything under heaven. I thought all those dreadful things that happened to us were signs for me to break off. And there I was just helpless and all alone in the world to decide my fate and his. All on earth I could think of was running away. I couldn't sleep, I was wild. I give you my vow and honor if he hadn't been through so much of that kind of thing, I would have broken it off and flown.[49]

In other letters, Grace assured Anne that she remained paramount in her heart:

Do you know, Reddy, I think a friendship like ours is the best safeguard for married life any human creature could have. I find myself again and again in a thousand things thinking, "Why don't I feel this way about Sherman?" or "Why doesn't he make me feel so and so?" and then I think back to our failures and tests too. I'm horribly fond of you. I never knew just how fond till I got another person to measure by, for I really have never cared for anybody else one quarter as much as I have you. I haven't the vaguest idea which of you I am fondest of but I know that both of you together are all I want—of this generation, anyhow![50]

These doubts and her affections toward Anne did not mean Grace was now regretful. "But the very minute we were married," she emphasized, "when we were still driving down here with the tea kettle and the sauce pan of eggs all my doubts and nerves vanished and I've just been a happy Arapahoe squaw ever since."[51]

There was truth in these words. Remarkably, throughout the entirety of Sherman and Grace's ensuing marriage, nothing ever approaching a harsh word appears in their voluminous correspondence. Though her love for Sherman initially seemed weak, it would grow enormously over the decades. Meanwhile, the only reason Grace mentioned "despising" him in her early letters was his insistence that she make griddle cakes and rice pudding just like his adoptive mother had. How to hang the dish towels properly also remained a major point of contention. But as Grace had learned, "being married is forming a sort of mutual toleration society—at best—and, oh! by Jove, it's better than *not* being married."[52] And even if Grace had not won everyone's approval, Sherman's relatives had given her a warm welcome to the family. One day his distant cousin showed up at the ranch bearing this message: "All the Indians are glad of this marriage of Sherman's. They like you first rate. That's what they need, a nice woman."[53]

9

Death and Life

Around two weeks after Sherman Coolidge married at Wind River, he almost died. He and Grace had gone to Fort Washakie to collect a new bronco, and while "gaily driving" home to the ranch, the horse unexpectedly bolted up a bank and flung Sherman a good distance. The landing "pretty near busted his neck." For the next few days, Sherman remained so "suppressed" that even changing his own clothes was too painful. Nevertheless, he immediately threw himself into work on the ranch, ignoring the persistent ache in his shoulder. The Coolidges' cabin, situated "on the very edge of the very wildernesses" near the Little Wind River and "under the reddest red bluffs," was just a half a mile from the "Smoking Waters" hot springs and close to one of the Arapaho camps.[1] Distracted by these beautiful surroundings, Grace had initially thought the home lovely. After closer inspection, she labeled it "the worst looking place you ever saw."[2] Undaunted, she cleaned and organized the house's two rooms until they were "fixed up awfully homey and sweet."[3] Evenings, she and Sherman rested their feet on the wood-burning stove and relaxed over a cigarette.[4]

After a month of harnessing horses and chopping and carrying firewood, Sherman discovered he had broken his collar bone. The doctor recommended several weeks in a sling, leaving him "pretty helpless."[5] Fortunately, he had acquired some fresh reading material. Anne Talbot had sent Charles Eastman's *Indian Boyhood* as a gift. Grace commented that Sherman remembered "all those same things" but had become "too much of a white man" since. In later years, she would encourage him to write his own autobiography, but he never finished the project, save a few unpublished sketches.[6] Grace also had big plans for the ranch, including the addition of a large living room, a bedroom for visitors, and a "little garden place" south of the house.[7] All of these renovations were contingent on the availability of funds. Gardner Wetherbee no longer supported his daughter, meaning that the Coolidges mostly lived on Sherman's salary of less than $600 per annum, or a little over $17,000 today.[8]

The Coolidges' ranch sat five miles from a village that included members of Sherman's extended family. Some there took interest in his "progressive" teachings and Christian proselytizing, and treated Grace with kind respect. Occasionally, older men would address Sherman by the name Banasda as a sign of veneration for his father's deeds.[9] One of many regular visitors was a former Shoshone warrior named Kagavah, the very man who had captured Sherman and taken him to Camp Brown on his horse in the spring of 1870. Kagavah and Grace even laughingly discussed how Sherman cried all the way to the fort, while Sherman showed his erstwhile kidnapper his single portrait of his brother.[10] The loss of his brother still caused Sherman tremendous pain. One evening, Grace asked him "in a goofy moment" whether he loved her "better than anybody he ever had." Sherman replied, "Yes, Gedy, except." He stopped, and after a long pause Grace said, "Well . . . ?" He looked at her "so sweet and loving," and admitted, "Except little Phil."[11] How Sherman was able to reconcile with Kagavah, who once had almost killed him in cold blood, is astonishing, as was his willingness to share his brother's picture with the man. Perhaps, as Grace once commented when she was getting to know him, Sherman was indeed "docility itself."[12]

What relatives Sherman had left at Wind River also flocked to him. Members of his extended family, such as cousin Herbert Welsh, sometimes pitched their tepees in the ranch's corral even when they had log homes elsewhere. Among them were Yellow Calf and a headman named Mule, who claimed that the Arapahos were "all glad" Sherman had "taken up their work."[13] Meanwhile, the Arapaho church erected in 1898 also began attracting a handful of congregants.[14] Mule and Yellow Calf welcomed Christian services, discussed opening a school, and advocated building churches "all over the reservation." One day the two men related to Grace that "they had never understood about religion" before Sherman explained the similarities between Christianity and Arapaho beliefs. To them, he now "stood between them and the white people" as an effective mediator.[15]

During the first months on the ranch, the Coolidges acquired a bulldog and a litter of puppies that, to Sherman's chagrin, regularly made "little pools on the floor." Grace's response was, "Now what difference can it possibly make?"[16] Sherman called the bulldog Gros Ventre, a play on the name of an Arapaho tribe that had split from the larger nation years ago and on the phrase's translation from French, "fat stomach."[17] As the Coolidges settled, Grace noted in letters how Wind River was changing. The government boarding school now had electric lights, and "the Bell telephone" had arrived to great acclaim.[18]

Though Grace occasionally described life at Wind River in rhapsodic terms, there existed dangers and hardships. Winter nights were so brutal that the dogs had to sleep in the Coolidges' bed to keep from freezing.[19] Although Grace's habit was to sleep without covers, Sherman, in contrast, piled them all over himself.[20] Money was also an issue. Costly renovations to the ranch meant being "hard up." "Hardly a cent and all kinds of bills not paid," Grace told Anne in the spring of 1903. "I hope we'll never have another ruination year like this."[21] Escape from penury came days later with an unexpected transfer of $1,000 from Grace's mother. Before, they had not even $5 to their names. The cash infusion allowed the Coolidges to pay off their bills and begin an irrigation ditch, yet relations with their eastern relatives remained strained.[22] Still disapproving, Hannah Wetherbee hardly communicated with her daughter except by shipping items west. When Grace's furniture arrived, the sight of Sherman in her childhood bed made her feel "indecent."[23] This problem paled compared to events outside the ranch's boundaries. Grace recorded in a letter: "There have been horrible things happening around here lately. An Arapahoe woman tried to hang herself over a cliff. She had a row with her family. They found her almost dead, but she is feeling well. And a nice old Cheyenne woman who lives in a teepee alone near the Agency had her throat cut across twice Sunday night." At least, Grace mentioned in the very next line, the weather was "grand." She took the opportunity to visit the Arapaho camp and "squirt things" into the ear of a sick boy with an abscess.[24]

After being at Wind River almost a year, Grace had come to dislike the whites living outside the reservation's borders. She wrote of how they either hated the Indians out of jealousy for their government provisions or showed complete indifference.[25] Nor did Grace like the Buffalo soldiers at Fort Washakie, because she apparently thought they brought bad luck.[26] She had noticed, too, that the Arapahos bore ill will toward John Roberts, though she could not determine the precise reason.[27] Within a few years, this festering hostility would explode into murderous rage. For the moment, though, Sherman and Grace were generally happy at Wind River. They began expanding their home to include a room for Anne Talbot, who came to Wyoming in the summer of 1903 for what photographs indicate must have been a very pleasant visit.[28] Unfortunately, none of Grace's letters describe the time they spent together.

During the early 1900s, Sherman continued his trips east to raise money and advocate for the Arapahos and Shoshones at Wind River.[29] He traveled to Washington DC in October 1903 to attend the annual Episcopal missionary council and remained, according to the *Churchman*, "to speak on behalf of the Church's work among the Indians." The *Churchman* also called on Episcopal clergymen across the country to invite him to address their congregations, adding that "Mr. Coolidge speaks English excellently" to preempt inevitable doubts.[30] At the missionary council (attended by President Theodore Roosevelt), Coolidge lightly criticized the U.S. government by highlighting the ostensible need on reservations for the "moral" instruction that only Christian schools could provide. "Uncle Sam" had his place but was hardly "a baptized or communicant member of the Church." Those present applauded the remark and registered delight at Coolidge's tales of the "reconciliation of ancestral tribal hatreds wrought by Christian teaching."[31] Importantly, Coolidge did not spare criticism for the behavior of settlers. He stated that one of the primary reasons Native people felt skepticism toward Christianity was "the treatment accorded Indians by white men, who were naturally understood to be typical representatives of the Christian people."[32] Public talks in New York followed in November, though attendance was sometimes poor.[33] In December, Coolidge appeared at a meeting of the Indian Rights Association as a featured speaker.[34] He had kept in contact with the IRA since the 1890s, sometimes asking it to investigate matters affecting the Arapahos and Shoshones at Wind River.[35]

Grace also took an active part in the Indian reform movement. In 1904 she began lecturing with her husband, on one occasion discussing her reservation work before the Women's Auxiliary of the Central Pennsylvania Diocese at St. Luke's Church in Lebanon.[36] Grace's focus, however, was proselytizing at Wind River. Her article for the *Spirit of Missions* titled "An Arapahoe Christmas Tree" recorded these efforts to bring Christianity to her Indian neighbors. In December 1902, Grace and Sherman spontaneously decided to hold a Sunday post-Christmas celebration for some Arapaho children in headman Mule's village. They gathered candy, peanuts, toys, and a tree left over from a benefit at the agency church; loaded the goods into their wagon; and set off in a "howling wind storm," fording multiple rivers along the way. When they arrived, Mule, Herbert Welsh, and a young returned student named Bruce Goes Back gave the Coolidges a tour of the irrigation ditches under construction. The ditches meant "possible plenty instead of hunger" for both the villagers and their horses. The next morning, Grace and Sherman set up the tree in Mule's large cabin, hanging the candy and presents in little bags made of mosquito nets. A group of girls with "giggling little faces" entered after much anticipation. Sherman "made them a little Christmas talk," and together he and Grace distributed the gifts. In return, Mule presented Sherman with "a beautiful pair of moccasins." Grace wrote, "Many of the Arapahoes are very poor, but they are a progressive people." In the past, their energies made them "a terror to the people of this region." Now, these energies had been "thrown in the direction of improvement of themselves and of their land." The older generation had "told their war stories or danced their scalp dances." The younger generation showed the same pride in their irrigation ditches.[37]

Events such as the 1902 Christmas party had, of course, a missionary purpose. In a similar article from 1905, "A Christmas Tree that Bore Souls," Grace revealed the fruits of these labors. She reported that soon after the 1902 party, Mule and a larger group of Arapahos organized another tree ceremony in their council house in February 1903. Sherman officiated and upon Mule's request baptized him with several members of his family. Mule even encouraged older Arapahos to join him. Grace admitted that this act was unprecedented. Previously, Sherman had only managed to baptize schoolchildren "under Christian influence from six years of age." A year later, the Coolidges held another Christmas event, aided by boxes of toys from the Women's Auxiliary of Ohio. By the time it concluded, Sherman had baptized fifty-nine children with their parents' consent. Grace thanked those in the East who had donated. Such generosity was key to demonstrating the good that came with worshiping Christ. At Sunday school, her students had been discussing a section of the catechism reading, "That we may worship Him, serve Him, obey Him as we ought to do." The students understood the meanings of "worship" and "obey," but they were "perplexed" about the term "serve." "And how about the fifty-two dolls that came with your Christmas things?" Grace asked. "Who dressed them for you? And the hoods for the little children? And the candy? And the money to build your churches? What were the people doing who sent you all these things?" "Serving God," the students answered in unison. "Now," Grace explained, "if only we can teach these Indians to serve God, too, in the same way!"[38] Though her intentions were undoubtedly pure, there was some irony in a wealthy Euro-American woman instructing a tribal people on generosity.

Due to such reports, the Coolidges' marriage continued to attract attention in the press. An article titled "Society Belle Turns Squaw" described how Grace, a "beautiful and gifted girl" with all the "advantages of education and society," had thrown it all away to dress "as a squaw," having fully rejected "the conventions which govern white society." Though her friends opposed her engagement, she had purportedly threatened to elope, and all involved relented to her mad wishes. "Since that day," the article continued, "Mrs. Coolidge has lost many of the graces of the white woman of culture and education." She was nonetheless regarded as "a saint by the Indians" and "an angel of mercy" to the sick and unfortunate. As a result, Grace had "a look of supreme happiness in her eyes," appearing "entirely contented with her earnest, grave faced husband."[39] Despite the article's tone, there was truth to its account, particularly regarding Grace's devotion to the reservation's children.

Grace once wrote that "death is no more at home on the river Styx" than at Wind River, where Indians died at a rate twice that of surrounding settlers, and every mother had lost at least one child. When Indian parents passed away, the U.S. government refused to support their orphans. Grace regularly traversed the reservation, visiting villages with an interpreter or communicating in sign language and offering to take any children in need of guardianship.[40] She found, unsurprisingly, that few Arapahos were willing to give up an orphaned child to a white woman. In almost every case, parentless children were taken in by tribal members.[41] This disappointed Grace. She and Sherman, she wrote, were "pining for babies."[42] Grace, however, felt trepidation about procreating with Sherman. "You know, how from my tenderest youth I always meant to marry an Indian," she confided to Anne. "That's why—partly—I'm worried about the babies. I've always been afraid, horribly—that I won't have any."[43] The reasoning behind her irrational fear is not something Grace specified, but possibly it was inspired by contemporary taboos against miscegenation. Whatever the case, the Coolidges' attempts to create a family were, in fact, thwarted by a series of excruciating deaths.

By April 1903, Grace had apparently gotten pregnant. So great was her alienation from her mother that she preferred to have the baby at Wind River rather than travel to New York. The pregnancy, it turned out later, had either been misdiagnosed or ended in a miscarriage. The agency physician could not conclude which.[44] Her first child, an "awfully sweet" boy named Louis, came in April 1904. Grace kept Louis in a traditional Arapaho baby carrier and described him as "a regular old Mamma's boy" who loved to get "spoony" with her.[45] Grace delivered again that same year. The child was a girl she named Grace Anne for Anne Talbot.[46] Though Grace Anne was born prematurely, she appeared more than healthy and exited Grace's womb "just like a trout jumping," hitting the doctor in the arm. Several Arapahos commented that she looked like Sherman's mother. All was well until Louis, by then a "great big strong boy" of twenty-pounds, suddenly fell ill. For two weeks, it seemed as though he was teething. The Coolidges suspected pneumonia after his suffering refused to abate. Eventually, Louis's temperature exceeded 108 degrees, and Grace and Sherman brought him to Fort Washakie for care. The doctor there called him "the sickest baby he had ever seen." Louis died in a hotel room, "just after sunset," in the autumn of 1904. The cause was typhoid. Grace and Sherman took him home, dressed him, and buried him in a small coffin near the Arapaho church.

Grace wrote of her immense loss,

> It is the worst thing I ever had. I can't get used to it. It seems as tho' next summer he must come back again, or sometime. Think of a little baby going through all that great experience, all that suffering—and then death. Do you think he is a baby now? Or what? I will send you one of his pictures. I think you will want one. He was laughing right to me. All I want is to get him back—and I can't. . . . It seems as tho' somehow he must come back. But if I get another baby as I did him it can't be him, and if I have another it can't be. You think of everything and there is no way. Except to go to him. That is the only way I can ever have them both again. The thing now is to make the best come out of it. I feel all the time that the responsibility rests with me now to see that his death and his life too for that matter of that, were not in vain.

Grace resolved to find meaning in Louis's death by helping. "I feel that I want to spend all my time now that would have been spent on Louis on the Indians," she decided. "It is all I can do for him."

Louis's sister, Grace Anne, "still very little," had not taken ill. She provided great comfort, though Grace sometimes found it hard to look at her without yearning for Louis. Grace Anne was "very pretty" and "as smart as anything." She laughed constantly. Sherman, though bereft of his son, was "silly over her," especially because Grace Anne resembled a photograph of his late brother Philip. No matter what time of night, he always jumped out of bed to care for her when she cried.[47] The Coolidges called their daughter "Toots," as Grace clarified, "pronounced like loots."[48] Yet by the New Year, Grace Anne had become sick with a cough.[49] In the spring of 1905, just as her condition seemed to be improving, she succumbed to pneumonia. "We don't know what to do without a baby," Grace told Anne. "I am glad to say that in another 6 mos. I ought to have another."[50] The pregnancy provided hope, as did Sherman's unwavering faith in an afterlife and belief in destiny. Grace remarked that she could not have gone on without a husband so "sure of himself."[51]

Grace gave birth to a son, Philip, named after Sherman's brother, on October 17, 1905. He died twelve days later, on October 29, due to a congenital heart defect. "What will you say when I tell you that my little son is dead too?" Grace asked Anne. Her letter read:

> He was the fattest, healthiest, goodest baby you ever saw and no one can believe he is dead. The doctor says that valve that should close in a new born baby's heart didn't close properly in his case. He wasn't very well Saturday night, that is, he wouldn't nurse much, but we didn't think it was much. Sherman went to church as usual and the baby died about an hour before he came home. I was all alone with him. I thought he died a half an hour before he did, but I put him in a hot bath and revived him. He died in my arms. Before he did I Christened him. I was so afraid he would be different from the others. Do you think that was just as good as if Sherman had? It is funny we can't raise children, isn't it? You ought to see those three little graves in a row, Grace in the middle and the boys on the outside.[52]

Philip's death occurred at a time when difficulties were mounting. In the fall of 1905, the Coolidges ran out of money and were forced to sell a few of their horses and cattle. Grace even had to borrow money from Anne.[53] Relations with her parents had again soured. Both Hannah and Gardner had been "so nasty" about the deaths of their own grandchildren that Grace had hidden her pregnancy with Philip. Once he died, she could scarcely bring herself to tell her father. When she did, neither Gardner nor Hannah acknowledged the letter. "I think the time has come for me to break with them entirely," Grace, furious, stated to Anne. What hurt her more was Anne's continuing friendship with her parents. Grace tried to make her understand the wrong she was committing: "I am sorry you have been so intimate with them since I have been married. Either you can't know what my mother is or you can't really have much friendship for me. I don't see how you can help knowing what mother is for you knew when I lived at home. You can see for yourself I just can't feel the same toward you or dare talk openly to you while I know you are their friend. Perhaps when you are married you will understand these things better."[54] Remarkably, this harsh disagreement did not break up their long friendship.

Grace ultimately kept the promise she made when her son Louis died by doing whatever she could for Wind River's orphans. An issue of the *Spirit of Missions* dubbed her "God's own blessing sent to the Indian babies of the reservation," explaining that the children "she does not adopt she cares for in one way or another, and the Indian mothers bring their babies to her whenever they are ill."[55] In the spring of 1906, the Coolidges finally adopted an eight-year-old girl named Effie.[56] Born on April 8, 1898, to a white man and a Shoshone woman described as "slightly less than full blooded," Effie had been orphaned entirely.[57] Soon after, Grace and Sherman adopted six-year-old Virginia, just when Grace learned she was pregnant for the fourth time.[58] Virginia was born January 17, 1900. Her Arapaho mother, name unknown, had died, and her father, an Arapaho named Paul Revere, was a relation of Sherman's who was unable to care for her.[59] Both Effie and Virginia would later attend the famed Carlisle Indian Industrial School in Pennsylvania. Caring for the girls was not without difficulty. After joining the family, Effie contracted a virulent case of trachoma, a bacterial eye infection that causes a roughening of the inner eyelids and leads to blindness. Grace sought medical attention, and the doctor, alarmed, insisted on operating "there and then." His special "eye water" cure consisted of scraping off "all the granulations" from inside her eyelids and cleansing them thoroughly. Although Effie was administered an anesthetic, she "screamed and struggled dreadfully" throughout "an awfully bloody and nasty performance." There was no other option. Without the operation, she would have quickly lost her sight. Fortunately, Effie remembered nothing of the afternoon. Though she could not see for a day, the next morning she was as "plucky" as ever.[60]

Another near tragedy was averted in April 1906, when a devastating earthquake hit San Francisco and a consequent fire ravaged the city. Sherman's adoptive parents resided on Van Ness Avenue, and for weeks he was "pop sure" they were under "the ruins somewhere." As it turned out, the Coolidges lived "out so far that they didn't get burned up or shaken down." Only a few items in the house had been broken in the tremors. Looters stole a good number of their possessions, but in the end, "they came out alright." Grace almost seemed disappointed. She lamented that Charles Coolidge neglected to "tell us any gory particulars."[61] The experience was nonetheless traumatic. Wanting to avoid another catastrophe, Charles and Sophie relocated to much safer Detroit.[62] On one occasion Sherman visited them. Charles went on and on, boasting of how his ancestors had come over on the Mayflower. Sherman, not to be outdone, retorted, "Oh, that's nothing . . . mine were on the reception committee."[63] The quip would later be put to good use whenever Sherman met anyone who shared his surname.

On January 4, 1907, Grace gave birth to Sarah Lucy Coolidge in Salt Lake City, Utah, in St. Mark's Hospital, where her old friend George Hunting had become the superintendent. Sarah Lucy, named after Grace's aunt Sarah, would be the first of the Coolidges' biological children to survive to adulthood. Sherman and Grace also gave her an Arapaho name, Ja-issay, a romanization of Ce'isee, which means "comes back."[64] And while Sherman sometimes called her Little Pocahontas, he and Grace mostly called her Sallie.[65] She was apparently quite a vocal baby. "I hear a war whoop from the corner," Grace wrote in one letter.[66] Sallie's birth did much to make amends with Grace's aunt, who had so vigorously protested her marriage to "a man of another race."[67] "I feel very much complimented in having a little namesake," Aunt Sarah admitted upon hearing the news. "I hope she will live to be a great comfort to you. . . . I think you had a good deal of courage to take more children when you knew you had one coming." Whatever her faults, Aunt Sarah was right about that.[68]

Malcontents

As the Coolidges became immersed in reservation life in the early 1900s, they met and befriended a highly intelligent young man named Fayette Avery McKenzie. Born in 1872 to an upper-middle-class home in Pennsylvania, McKenzie had already compiled an impressive résumé. A graduate of Lehigh University, he had taught French, English, German, history, and economics at Juniata College before moving to the University of Pennsylvania in 1900. There, McKenzie chose Indian assimilation as the topic of his doctoral dissertation in sociology and economics. Convinced that he needed to learn more about Native peoples firsthand, he applied to the Indian Service and in 1903 signed a nine-month contract to teach at Wind River's government school. The 2,000-mile journey to Wyoming from Pennsylvania was less than pleasant. After arriving in Laramie by train, McKenzie traveled for five frigid days over 150 miles to reach Wind River by stage while accompanied by a coach-sick passenger who would not stop vomiting. Once there, McKenzie took up his teaching duties, overseeing a student body that had grown to 170 pupils. Other duties included playing the organ and piano at church services and tending the school's chickens.[1]

The Coolidges formed a solid relationship with McKenzie, judging by its long-lasting character.[2] One imagines the trio spoke often and seriously about Indian policy and about the prospects for a Native-run organization, which they would eventually inaugurate in 1911.[3] McKenzie used his experience in Wyoming to inform his 1906 dissertation, which argued for the type of assimilation Coolidge generally supported. McKenzie posited that under a program of white education, allotment, and citizenship, Indians could be rapidly integrated into Euro-American society.[4] He even suggested subsidies for white parents willing to adopt Indian children.[5] Such ideas, as well intentioned as they were, did little to assist McKenzie's Arapaho and Shoshone students at Wind River or their elders. At the time of his departure in 1904, the tribes were again facing intense pressure to cede lands to the U.S. government.

In the spring of 1904, Washington again sent Agent James McLaughlin to Wind River for another round of negotiations. McLaughlin explained that laws in the capital had changed since his last visit for cession talks in 1896, thus it was no longer possible to resist the government's plan to requisition parts of Indian reservations for white settlement. Any offer tendered should be accepted posthaste, lest Washington decide to act unilaterally and deny payment for lands that would be lost anyway. McLaughlin related the government's terms: cede 1.5 million acres on the northern side of the Wind River and receive a $1,000,000 payment. The massive cession amounted to two-thirds of the reservation. Only 800,000 acres would remain. Lone Bear, the Northern Arapaho head council chief, bristled at the proposal, feeling that the loss of acreage was too great and the compensation inadequate. The council fully agreed. Coolidge, attending the meeting at the government's behest, reinforced McLaughlin's message and advised the young men of the tribe to agree.[6] John Roberts likewise supported the cession and, one assumes, Coolidge's exploiting of the generational divide.[7] The Shoshone delegation, surprisingly, consented. Negotiations might have yielded more for the Arapahos if Lone Bear's wife had not suddenly become ill, precipitating his premature departure. In his absence, McLaughlin collected enough Arapaho and Shoshone signatures to seal the agreement. Congress ratified it on March 3, 1905, after amending it to include more lands that stretched to the southern limits of Wind River. Few Arapahos were pleased with this outcome, but Coolidge was.[8] He later received the land he had claimed under his ranch, encompassing a little over 73 acres, and another plot encompassing 240 acres near the Smoking Waters hot springs.[9]

In 1904 McLaughlin had made several pledges to soften the blow of the cession, including an offer of compensation for those removed from ceded lands, a government buyout of some sections of land, a $50 payment for each tribe member following the opening of the lands for white settlement, and an ability to earn monies from leasing ceded lands that would fund irrigation projects and secure tribal water rights. However, the version of the agreement that Congress passed in 1905 rescinded several of these promises. Washington negated its responsibility to buy and lease lands for the tribes' financial benefit and instead forced them to pay for surveying and irrigation services. The money they did receive would first go to the secretary of the interior, who would fund irrigation works, schools, livestock purchases, and rations at his discretion.[10]

Lone Bear and the leadership vigorously protested these changes, but to no avail. The Wind River irrigation system had been largely completed by 1905, but the government's changed terms meant that—contrary to the original agreement—Arapaho and Shoshone individuals now had to apply and pay for water rights. When in 1906 the government started allowing the sale of Dawes Act allotments, Arapaho farmers in need of money began to sell off land to non-Indians.[11] The $50 payments then became a point of contention. By 1906 the government had still not made the payments, and when it did, the Indian Bureau withheld monies designated for the tribes' children. Such frustrations, incurred by a people struggling to attain basics like proper nutrition, were not to be borne. Wind River's acting agent H. W. Wadsworth pleaded with the Indian Bureau to release the payments, citing the Arapahos' anger and noting that even John Roberts "was afraid of the lives of himself and family." The bureau declined and instead completed the allotment and opened "surplus" lands for white settlement.[12]

John Roberts was right to fear for his life. He and Coolidge had long faced fierce opposition in some quarters merely for their presence. In the *Spirit of Missions*, each had regularly claimed "progress" in ministering to a population that—at least in some measure—wished to emulate the virtues of white "civilization." Informed by these reports, the Most Reverend James Funsten, the bishop of Wyoming and Idaho, remained supportive of Roberts and Coolidge's work under the willful illusion that such "progress" was occurring.[13] In late 1905 Funsten wrote a lengthy piece for the *Outlook* titled "The Indian as a Worker." He began by praising the Indian Bureau's wardship of the Arapahos and Shoshones, presenting the Wind River land cession and allotment in highly positive terms. The "wild Indian," he claimed, was "passing away" in the wake of disappeared game and the "example of surrounding white men," who had inspired "a realization of the absolute necessity of work." The Arapahos, "far in advance of the Shoshones in intelligence," had also proven their superiority by constructing "neat log houses" and establishing farms. Especially impressive was the 1904 decision to cede part of Wind River in exchange for improvements in irrigation. This "cutting down of uselessly large reservations" was the best way of "bringing the Indians into the lines of the world's workers." And although Funsten admitted some Arapahos had protested, the "worthy among them" had nothing to fear as long as they adopted "American civilization."

Unwittingly, Funsten then exposed the opposition that existed to the "perfectly sane and reasonable policy" of allotment and cession. A group of "non-progressive Indians," in their "dread of the light of civilization and the restraint of law," had rejected and condemned the treaty. Fortunately, these "members of the heathen element" had been quelled by the "strong influence" of Sherman Coolidge, who found support among the younger tribal members that had been educated in white schools. Coolidge's and their collective efforts had "carried the day for progress." This was not to say that every problem had been overcome. Deep fissures existed in Arapaho society, but the answer was more, not less, "progress." Funsten had been "moved with pity at the sight of some Indian girls who had been trained in an Eastern school" and brought back to the reservation, "where absolutely nothing awaited them but to return to the dirty old tepee, or log house, to be the objects of ridicule to the old squaws, representing the most non-progressive element among the Indians." The government therefore had to guarantee such young graduates "protection and employment" so "new ideas and new hopes" would not drown in "a dirty and immoral Indian camp." Luckily, things were headed along the correct path. The "wild, savage, and murderous wanderers over the plains" no longer presented "a menace to the traveler and rancher." Instead, these same people could be found "working on their little places, planting fruit trees, building fences, cutting hay, and performing the useful arts of life." This transformation was proof that rapid assimilation could civilize even those who had almost killed Bishop Randall on his first visit to Camp Brown in 1873.[14]

The borderline insouciance to the generational discord and larger discontent at Wind River that Funsten demonstrated became harder to maintain a year later. Grace had previously sensed that the Arapahos disliked John Roberts. She in fact grossly underestimated their feelings.[15] In February 1907, the *Churchman* reported an incident that laid bare the acrimony many Arapahos felt toward not only Indian Bureau policy but also the Episcopal missionary presence. "Indian Troubles in Boise" explained how Wind River had been reduced with the consent of "progressive Indians." The "non-progressive heathen Indians" had "bitterly opposed" the move and grew angrier as whites began to settle on former reservation lands. Also at issue were the delayed payments of $50 per child. This tinderbox burst into flames one evening when John Roberts, riding home from Lander, neared the border of the reservation. A group of "Arapaho malcontents," as the *Churchman* put it, began pursuit, giving "every evidence of an intention of attacking him." Roberts hurriedly retreated to Lander, where he telephoned the commanding officer at Fort Washakie. While he waited, a detachment of soldiers raced to collect his wife and children, who were also in danger of assassination. The family later reunited at the agency center. At the time, Sherman Coolidge was in Salt Lake City, where Grace was giving birth to Sallie. Upon hearing the news, he immediately returned to exercise his purported "quieting influence" on the Arapahos. The *Churchman* estimated that still at large were perhaps as many as two hundred "malcontents," each of whom had been enraged by a recent ban on the Sun Dance.

The Roberts incident inspired horror in the surrounding white community. A local paper observed that if more attacks occurred, vigilante violence against the Arapahos would result.[16] But whatever the severity of their methods, the "malcontents" at Wind River had made their point. Arapaho tribal leaders met with McLaughlin soon afterward, airing their grievances concerning the children's $50 payments. The Indian Bureau released the monies—two years later.[17] Nonetheless, the Roberts family was able to return to Washakie and resume life as usual. Glowing accounts of Roberts's and Coolidge's missionary work continued to flow east for the next three years. Bishop Funsten's annual report on his district for 1906–7 made no mention of the attempt on Roberts's life, instead declaring that "work among the Indians is progressing in a satisfactory manner." The Shoshone girls' school named for Ethelbert Talbot had become "most prosperous," though disease presented a persistent problem. Mortality on the reservation had been high the previous winter, but all the girls had survived. The Shoshones, a report from Roberts admitted, remained "most difficult to lead to the light of Christianity and civilization."[18] Irrespective of their lack of interest, he and Coolidge began constructing even more new churches at Wind River that were funded by outside donations.[19] Funsten visited in 1908 and later wrote rapturously of the "excellent work" and "evidences of the civilization of the Indians."[20] Periodicals simultaneously boasted of Coolidge's having "gained a great influence over his fellow-tribesmen."[21] The last article to give this standard account of his missionary work, "Red Men of Wyoming," appeared in the September 1910 *Spirit of Missions*.[22]

None of these reports, however, especially those regarding Coolidge's high status on the reservation, were true. What little reliable information we have on his reputation at Wind River comes from the noted historian of the Arapahos Loretta Fowler. In the latter part of the twentieth century, Fowler spoke with Wind River elders who had known Coolidge. In 1982 she wrote that over time, the missionary had "increasingly lost the goodwill of his tribesmen and eventually the confidence of his superiors." Fowler as well states that by 1910, Coolidge had reached a "disheartened" state, brought on by frustrations with the Arapahos' rejection of his ideal of progress. Surprisingly, her investigation even revealed that "Coolidge often rebuked Arapahoes for allowing him to be captured." This "resentment," Fowler writes, "in part explains his seeming hostility to the tribe."[23] Oral histories also indicate that Coolidge was seen as someone who "became a white man but still had skin like an Indian." Meanwhile, he himself was no happier with his presence at Wind River than the Arapahos were. Negative feelings between him and Roberts, especially, caused constant tensions.

In May 1909, Nathaniel Seymour Thomas became the new bishop of Wyoming, replacing Funsten. Less than two weeks later, Coolidge wrote Thomas a long letter that announced his desire to "leave the field," insisting that only "new blood" could improve the situation at Wind River. What rankled him most deeply, however, was what he perceived as constant neglect by the Episcopal hierarchy, which had kept him in "a subordinate ecclesiastical position" to Roberts despite his "repeated requests and protests." Meanwhile, his salary was so small that he sometimes lived on government rations, and his efforts to raise money for a reservation hospital had come to nothing. Still, Coolidge was reluctant to abandon his life's work. "My home, tribe, the fruit and association of my life-work, in fact, all my interests would seem to be rooted and centered here," he explained to Thomas, "and under other circumstances I would not think of leaving; but under the conditions in which I have labored here during the 25 years of my ministry I feel I have done all I can." Coolidge suggested that if a replacement missionary could be found, he should be given exclusive charge of the Arapahos and permission to work independently from Roberts.[24]

Bishop Thomas responded with a compromise. Coolidge was to focus on his Arapahos, while Roberts was to handle the Shoshones—each with no interference from the other.[25] Unfortunately, the new arrangement did little to improve the hostile atmosphere at the missions. In the summer of 1910, Thomas received a long, written complaint signed by twenty church women about the "jealousies and misunderstandings" that were making Indian work at Wind River intolerable. The main source of discord was Roberts's initial refusal, eight years earlier, to marry the Coolidges.[26] Thomas acted quickly to defuse the situation. He had a choice: remove Coolidge or remove Roberts. He was not about to do the latter. In June 1910, Thomas instead informed Coolidge that Francis Key Brooke, the bishop of Oklahoma, had made a request. Brooke wanted Coolidge to relocate to the Cheyenne and Arapaho Indian Reservation in his state, where he would run the small Episcopal mission at Whirlwind. In breaking the news, Thomas stated that there was "nothing personal" in his approval of the transfer. "My only thought is for your own happiness and the success of the work," he insisted to Coolidge. "The work, I am convinced, will never be successful until there is harmony on the reservation," a "vain" hope as long as he and Roberts worked in the same field.[27] Thomas's advice to Coolidge regarding the transfer read: "You better accept it." The letter made two other things clear: the Episcopal Church had highly unrealistic expectations about converting the Arapahos and Shoshones, and the hierarchy favored Roberts. As a consolation, Thomas promised to purchase a house for Coolidge in Oklahoma so he would "not be out of pocket."[28]

Though in some way Coolidge's removal was a defeat, he and his family welcomed the news. Grace's letters indicate that she had become disenchanted with Wyoming and alienated from the Arapahos, whom she felt had come to dislike her.[29] Still, prior to Bishop Thomas's letter, the Coolidges did not seem to be planning on leaving Wind River. In January 1910, they had begun constructing an addition to their ranch.[30] They had also acquired a motor car. Sherman tried driving but gave up after crashing into a bridge the first day out. To his surprise, the car refused to stop when he cried, "Whoa!"[31]

Of course, a small number of Arapahos—headman Mule and his family, for instance, and Sherman's relations Herbert Welsh and Yellow Calf, who showed an interest in Christianity and farming—respected Coolidge, sought to emulate some of his ways, and lamented his departure.[32] But certainly the majority had rejected him and his message. While the Northern Arapahos often feigned compliance with Indian Bureau policy, allowed their children to attend reservation schools, and took aid from missionaries, the story of their lives at Wind River at the turn of the century is one of covert resistance and slow adaptation.

From the start of their reservation period, Northern Arapaho elders had done everything possible to preserve their cultural traditions, discouraging their children from following the ways of schoolteachers, missionaries, and agents. Lands allotted in severalty were worked collectively rather than by individual landholders, and the old system of reciprocity ensured that those with surpluses aided those in need. Reservation agents condemned this practice as "unprogressive" because it held back individuals from potentially becoming wealthy. It persisted nonetheless. The Arapahos also continued to observe the "four hills of life," though the process was sped up and modified to allow younger men into religious lodges and enjoy greater status. These practices ensured that new generations remained under the influence of the elders. Younger men seeking influence now followed the lead of council members, while the elders on the council negotiated as best they could with the Indian Bureau for higher land-leasing rates and greater material assistance. Often, children and adults did accept baptism, as Coolidge was fond of advertising; yet, in reality, the Arapahos did not forsake their religious traditions. Ritual leaders instead continued their ceremonies, changing them if necessary to assuage the bureau.[33]

Though Sherman Coolidge left Wind River in 1910, John Roberts remained until his death on January 22, 1949, having spent sixty-six years on the reservation. As he approached old age, the University of Wyoming and the Wyoming State legislature heaped honors upon him for the dedication exhibited in his life's work.[34] If Coolidge had once envisioned the same kind of public recognition as he departed for Oklahoma, he must have been sorely disappointed.

A New Mission, a New Society

As the Coolidges readied themselves for the change of mission at the beginning of 1910, Grace received word from New York that her mother, Hannah Nye Wetherbee, had died. Gardner Wetherbee wrote his daughter in Wyoming: "It does not seem possible that I have lost mama. I never thought that she would not outlive me. I feel so helpless without her."[1] Correspondence does not suggest that Grace attended the funeral. Instead, she planned a long stay in New York from late summer through winter to coincide with the start of Sherman's work in Oklahoma. Grace also arranged to visit Charles and Sophie Coolidge in Detroit on the way east. Sophie was ecstatic at the first opportunity to meet her granddaughter, Sallie. She and Charles were also pleased with the city, though Sophie expressed a hunger to see the West once more. A recent trip to the theater had stirred her nostalgia. "Sometimes I fairly *yearn* for the West and a glimpse of the mountains again," she told Grace. "I saw a play here a few weeks ago that opens with a scene in the Ute Pass at Colorado Springs and it moved me to tears. They seemed to have caught the very heart of the mountains and when the light of sunset gilded the tips of the snow-clad mountains I fairly gasped and the tears streamed down my face." True, Detroit had "many beauties," but in Sophie's eyes, "the port and the smoke and the impure air" constituted "great drawbacks."[2]

Sherman Coolidge meanwhile feared the drawbacks of Oklahoma. In letters to his new bishop, Francis Key Brooke, he inquired about the "hot country" and whether he would have a long vacation from the end of May till mid-September. Brooke preferred that he spend that time trying to convert Indians.[3] The bishop's only advice appears to have been, "Do all you can to keep the bills down."[4] When Coolidge arrived in September 1910, he was surprised at the extent of the "strictly enforced" Jim Crow law, relating to Grace how "whites and Indians have the same waiting rooms at depots and the same train privileges, but separate and distinct from the negroes." While coming into the state, he had passed the Chilocco Indian School, which was situated in the middle of nowhere. Nearby, surrounded by white tepees, a camp of Ponca Indians danced. The scene reminded Coolidge of Wind River. Wanting to be alone, he moved to an empty car designated for African Americans. A brakeman promptly ordered him out. Coolidge disapproved of Oklahoman apartheid, though he was happy to learn of the "strict law against liquor for all."[5] To his equal delight, everywhere he went, Indians approached him and asked his tribe.[6]

At the time, Oklahoma had the largest Indian population of all the states, accounting for one-third of Indigenous peoples in the country. The Episcopal hierarchy viewed missionary activities there as a prime opportunity.[7] According to the *Spirit of Missions*, Coolidge's assignment was to convert two hundred "blanket Indians who live in teepees and still cling to many of the old-time customs."[8] The church had rented (not bought) him a rickety house in the small city of Enid.[9] The abode lacked a bathtub and a convenient water supply. Wanting to bathe with greater ease, Coolidge promptly ordered a tub and windmill to pump the well.[10] His new workplace, St. Luke's Episcopal mission in Whirlwind located nine miles from Enid, had been founded by David Pendleton Oakerhater, a former Cheyenne warrior (and eventual Episcopal saint) who had converted to Christianity after being taken prisoner during the Red River War. St. Luke's sole missionary, Harriet M. Bedell, had been there for several years teaching the forty-some students at the day school. Like at Wind River, boys learned farming; girls, the domestic arts. Sports, like basketball, were encouraged. Coolidge took over some teaching duties and made scheduled visits to the Chilocco school, sixty miles away, as a guest lecturer.[11]

Miss Bedell and a few others had greeted Coolidge when he arrived at the station in Fay, Oklahoma. He became so distracted that he forgot his new dog, Shonie, which had made the trip with him. After taking him out of the baggage car, Coolidge jumped in the mission's buggy and began to depart. Fortunately, Shonie ran alongside the buggy and was eventually able to get his owner's attention. When they reached St. Luke's in Whirlwind, Coolidge's first impressions were highly favorable. He even remarked to Grace that he had "never received a nicer welcome anywhere." A white woman had given him a chicken, and an Arapaho woman had presented him with a "very nice watermelon." The Cheyenne congregants, thankfully, seemed "just like our Arapahoes." The mission roof may have leaked, but at least initially, Oklahoma appeared "a splendid field to do things in." Much of this enthusiasm was inspired by Miss Bedell, who glowingly complimented Coolidge's first sermon and tended to some "poison bites" he had suffered from a wasp or scorpion, neither could tell which.[12] Their budding relationship became a running joke between Sherman and Grace after he asked for "a good, white comb" from New York. It seems the one Miss Bedell owned had "sharp corners on the teeth" and caught her hair.[13] Sherman's request arrived near the time of the Coolidges' eighth wedding anniversary. In her reply, Grace fondly recalled listening to "John Brown's Body" on the wagon trip to the ranch years before but added, "I think you and Miss Bedell are getting too intimate exchanging opinions on the kinds of *combs* you like!!"[14] In a subsequent letter, she joked, "So you love Miss Bedell? Gee Wizz! I had better be hurrying up home."[15]

While Sherman settled in rural Enid, Grace, Sallie, and Virginia were experiencing all that modern New York City had to offer. (Effie, who was older, had been placed in All Saints School in Sioux Falls, South Dakota.)[16] In October, Gardener, Grace, and the girls attended an aviation show on Long Island. Though the ticket costs were "awful," everyone marveled at the "biplanes and monoplanes dashing about through the air in all directions," one ascending to four thousand feet in a bid to win the "altitude prize." "They were just specks in the blue," Grace wrote. "It was most awfully impressive when you stopped to remember there was a human being all alone up there."[17] Though Gardner Wetherbee missed his late wife, Grace suspected that he was secretly "blooming glad" about being able "to do as he pleases for the first time in 40 years."[18] Knowing of the city's delights and the luxurious conditions afforded by the Wetherbee townhouse, Sherman wondered openly how his family would adjust to "awfully crude and inconvenient" Oklahoma. Perhaps for this reason, Grace and the children did not relocate to Enid until the spring of 1911.[19]

Life in the East among the Wetherbees also had its hazards. Grace unwisely accepted an invitation to Massachusetts from Aunt Sarah, who had so strongly opposed her marriage.[20] As should have been expected, though, Sarah treated Sallie and Virginia contemptuously. The affront provoked one of the few declarations of disgust Sherman Coolidge ever committed to paper:

> I am disappointed that Sallie or Virgie were in the least in the way of your Aunt Sarah at any time. I am sorry you had at *any time to insist upon* your own child to be with you. I do not want you or the children to be subject to anything of that kind whatsoever in your trip East. You had a thousand times better leave the children at home where they belong and out of the way of some people. I had doubts or misgivings about your taking Virgie or Effie for the sake of, or in hope of, stirring up some generous or benevolent instinct in the breast of someone who ought to help you anyhow as Christians. . . . I did not think that your Aunt Sarah would at any time show, even if she felt it, any disposition of that sort after she invited you several times to come.[21]

Aunt Sarah's behavior appeared all the more inappropriate when contrasted with how Coolidge perceived Indian-white relations in Oklahoma. In late October, he attended an "intensely interesting" fair in the town of Weatherford, where several thousand Indians and whites held horse races and organized markets. Coolidge was pleasantly surprised by the "cordial attitude" between the two groups. One evening, he spoke at a banquet for Indian chiefs and local government officials. Despite the evident harmony, he worried for the future. In seven years, federal restrictions on selling Indian property would be lifted. The education of Indian children had to be improved so they could defend themselves as adults in America's capitalist economy.[22]

Life in Oklahoma was not all fair going. St. Luke's mission was a busy place. A wealthy woman had donated $2,000 for a new chapel, meaning

Coolidge had construction work to supervise. On a typical day, he taught U.S. history, geography, reading, and spelling. Military drills and religious instruction followed, plus a daily prayer meeting attended by a handful of whites. Lectures at Chilocco and visits to infirm Indians, such as an old woman who had fallen off a wagon, were part of his regular duties.[23] Bishop Brooke also expected Coolidge to minister to whites in different parishes—at his own cost. By the end of November, Coolidge had "had enough of it" and refused to continue.[24] Dissatisfaction only grew, as did his longing for his family. At times he missed them so much he wept. Therefore, by February 1911, after weeks of getting to bed late, fighting off a vicious cold, quarreling with the Episcopal rector in Enid, dealing with the "freeze one day sizzle the next" climate, suffering sleeplessness thanks to a loud cricket hiding somewhere in the bedroom, and battling an invincible flea infestation in his home, Coolidge decided Oklahoma was not for him.[25] He penned a resignation to Brooke; then he informed Grace that the "misery" was "almost over."[26]

Coolidge's letter revealed a startling primary cause for quitting—a soured relationship with his erstwhile "love," Miss Bedell. The bishop, shocked at the suddenness of the transfer request, objected. Coolidge countered that he was not being "abrupt or rash" and iterated his complaints: "Personally, I do not feel that Christian work can be done in the spirit in which Miss Bedell seems to carry on the mission be the fault whose it may. My position in regard to Whirlwind is utterly false. I am nominally in charge of the work; and while Miss Bedell wishes so to regard me, she resents anything I do to the smallest detail, which does not absolutely coincide with her method of thought. And she does not hesitate to express her feelings before school children, Indians, neighbors, or whoever happens to be present at the moment." Whether Miss Bedell knew of this strong reaction to her criticisms appears doubtful. She may have liked him greatly, but she had a tendency to smother. Regardless, Coolidge consented to speak about the matter with Brooke on his next visit and ultimately respect his conclusions.[27] He should have pressed harder. A full year would pass before the bishop approved the transfer.[28] One reason Coolidge consented to remain in Oklahoma so long was that he felt "in need." His letters to Grace spoke of "the *Mescal* and *Peyote* fight" unfolding on the Cheyenne and Arapaho Indian Reservation, a result of the peyote religion's spread among Oklahoma's Indians.[29]

Peyote itself was nothing new. The Spanish had written of the cactus hundreds of years before, having witnessed its ingestion among the Chichimecas in what became present-day Mexico. In the seventeenth and eighteenth centuries, the Coahuitecans, Hopis, and Taos employed peyote for both medicinal and spiritual purposes. The peyote religion, however, had developed toward the end of the nineteenth century among Plains Indians such as the Comanches, Kiowas, and Wichitas. These peoples established organized rituals that combined Native beliefs with elements of Christianity that were meant to foster intertribal solidarity and create a panacea for Euro-American colonialism. Many of the new adherents were graduates of Indian boarding schools.[30] Coolidge reported that on the Cheyenne and Arapaho Reservation, Cheyenne chief Three Fingers had held a peyote feast six miles from the Whirlwind mission. Those in attendance declared themselves "against all Christian missions" in reaction to a recent church council that resolved "*to fight their Peyote religion.*" This "religious war" had sharply decreased the numbers at the local Baptist mission. There, an "educated Cheyenne" named Philip Cook had been fired as an interpreter for supporting peyote. Coolidge feared that the Cheyennes would now "boycott the different denominations, including the Episcopalian."[31]

Around mid-April 1911, Grace and the children finally arrived in Enid. Judging from Grace's correspondence with Anne Talbot, none were impressed.[32] Grace found the climate too hot and lamented the town's lack of a "modern library."[33] Her only feeling in the run-up to the family's first Christmas in the "dismal, footless, friendless" town was "dread."[34] Early on, she was awakened one evening by a Cheyenne woman crying out in pain. "A woman died here day before yesterday in the camp having her first baby," she wrote Anne. "Doesn't that just go through you, tho!! I heard the woman wailing when I went up to bed, that was the first I knew about it. She was sick 8 days and the baby had been dead a long time." Grace was naturally aware of Sherman's conflicts with Miss Bedell, and by spring both Coolidges wanted to leave Oklahoma badly.[35] Sherman put in another request for a transfer, having decided that Faribault, Minnesota, was the best place to educate his children.[36] When summer vacation commenced in June, he took advantage and traveled to Geneva, New York, to speak at the annual Hobart reunion; then he went to Detroit to visit his adoptive parents.[37] Sherman was forced to return to Whirlwind in July, braving the scorching Oklahoma sun to oversee work on the new chapel. Though the two men hired for the job were known as the "Sober brothers," they had "to be watched" due to their lack of experience.[38] This was not likely how Sherman idealistically envisioned his missionary work as a young man. Yet however unpleasant life had become, there was hope ahead born of a discussion from long ago.

On October 17, 1911, Grace Coolidge wrote to Anne Talbot, "The thing Sherman went to is very interesting, I think. It is the first annual meeting of the American Indian Assoc. All the educated Indians in the country. Awfully good speaking and all that, Sherman said."[39] Grace was referring to the 1911 founding of the Society of American Indians (SAI), a Native-run organization whose presidency her husband would hold for the following five years. The idea, originating from a meeting between Sherman and Charles Eastman over a decade earlier, had come into being with the support of Fayette Avery McKenzie, an old friend from Wind River. Since leaving Wyoming, McKenzie had accomplished much. After taking a position as an assistant professor at Ohio State University–Columbus in 1905, he had become one of the few sociologists in the country advocating for the assimilation of the Native American population. In 1908, the year he received his PhD from the University of Pennsylvania, McKenzie self-published his doctoral thesis under the title *The American Indian in Relation to the White Population in the United States*. He argued that Indigenous peoples were readily adaptable to white society, a fact proven by figures such as Sherman Coolidge, who needed nothing but immersion to bring about his transformation. Through a well-implemented program of "civilization" that eliminated Native cultures and encouraged Euro-American education and U.S. citizenship, the same could be achieved among the larger Indian population.[40]

Late in the first decade of the 1900s, McKenzie invited prominent Native persons to lecture before his students at Ohio State. Among the first in November 1908 were Sherman Coolidge, Charles Eastman, and physician Carlos Montezuma.[41] By then, Eastman had earned a national reputation for the books he had coauthored with his wife, Elaine. They included *Indian Boyhood* (1902) and *Old Indian Days* (1906), which discussed his early life among the Dakotas and recorded their stories and value systems.[42] Carlos Montezuma had achieved much the same renown but for different reasons. His life mirrored Eastman's and Coolidge's in drama, tragedy, and sudden transition.

Born a Yavapai (a tribe associated with the Apaches) in present-day Arizona in the mid-1860s, Montezuma's childhood as Wassaja, meaning "Beckoning," was similar to that of Runs On Top—filled with raids and violence. In 1871 Pima warriors kidnapped Wassaja during a massacre and sold him for thirty silver dollars to Carlo Gentile, an itinerant Italian photographer. Gentile raised the boy as his son, naming him Carlos Montezuma after himself and the last of the Aztec chiefs. In the interim, Wassaja's mother was shot trying to recover her son; his father died in an epidemic. Unaware his parents were gone, Montezuma traveled the country with Gentile, who eventually placed him in the home of a Baptist minister in Urbana, Illinois. Montezuma flourished, graduating from Chicago Medical College in 1889. After his first attempt at establishing a practice in Chicago failed, he reluctantly joined the Indian Health Service. In 1893 he secured a post at Carlisle and remained there for three years, becoming lifelong friends with Richard Henry Pratt. Montezuma later opened a stable medical practice in Chicago and established himself as a notable lecturer on Indian assimilation. Like Pratt, he rejected everything associated with the Native past.[43] Mainstream periodicals lavished praise on the doctor, citing him as incontrovertible evidence that Indians could become valuable members of white society.[44]

Montezuma and McKenzie became particularly close. In 1908–9 the duo, through a letter-writing campaign, made two failed efforts to bring a national Indian organization into being.[45] Fortunately, the time was ripening for such an endeavor. A group of prominent African Americans founded the National Association for the Advancement of Colored

People in 1909, an event that convinced McKenzie to continue organiz-ing.[46] A Temporary Executive Committee (Coolidge was not involved) met at Ohio State in early April 1911 and formed the American Indian Association, which was later renamed the Society of American Indians to reflect its composition as a Native-run organization. The group, which included Montezuma and Eastman, planned an inaugural conference for Columbus Day (October 12) in Columbus, Ohio—the date and place being symbolic.[47] Sherman Coolidge, forty-three other Indians, and 125 white reformers responded to the conference call. Columbus's welcome was warm. At a gala evening hosted in the city's thirty-six-hundred-seat Memorial Hall, Dr. W. O. Thompson, president of Ohio State University, greeted the attendees. The governor of Ohio and the mayor of Columbus also appeared to express their support.[48] Advance press in one of the city's papers singled out Coolidge's life as one of "thrilling incident and sentiment," rivaled only by "the stories of redmen told by James Fenimore Cooper."[49]

The conference in Columbus brought together some of the most prom-inent Native persons in the United States, the majority of whom were prosperous, Christian, middle-class professionals. Many had experienced life in both the Native and white worlds, and had gone to off-reservation boarding schools. The membership generally accepted assimilationist imperatives but went by Native and American names.[50] (Coolidge, in this last respect, was an exception.) But while assimilation was a crucial goal, it did not signal prostrate deference to white supremacy or fawning approval of Euro-American culture. SAI reformers instead harshly censured aspects of white society and its treatment of Natives, and stressed that the "Indian has certain contributions of value to offer our government and our people."[51] Many leaders openly celebrated Native identity and sought cultural protections.[52] Modern scholars have referred to these figures as "Red Progressives," referencing the larger Progressive Era in which their activism took place.[53]

The intellectual context of the Progressive Era, of course, is vital to understanding the Society of American Indians. The SAI drew on the fervor for societal advancement emblematic of white, Protestant, middle-class reform movements that were so common in the early 1900s. Reform was sorely needed. By the end of the nineteenth century, unregulated capitalist development had begotten vast disparities in wealth, unbridled corporate power, entrenched government corruption, and significant societal ills. Advocating improvements fell under the discourse of "uplift" for individuals as well as for the entire nation. In part, this meant the founding of settlement houses, temperance activism, charity work, government regulation, and improved public education. By aiding the careworn multitudes and vanquishing municipal malfeasance, America could, almost teleologically, "progress" toward the ultimate fruits of ordered and transparent democracy.[54] And in truth, the Progressive Era saw significant strides forward in some areas, such as the extension of the franchise to women, the direct election of U.S. senators, the regulation of corporations, and the establishment of a graduated income tax.[55] Race relations were another matter. Purportedly scientific discourses of eugenics and social Darwinism were widely accepted in mainstream white society. Meanwhile, Jim Crow dominated in the South, informal segregation existed in the North, and fears of "race suicide" among white Protestants compelled Woodrow Wilson's administration to restrict Asian and Southern European immigration in the 1910s. Daniel Folkmar's *Dictionary of Races or Peoples*, published by the U.S. Government Printing Office, spelled out a defined racial hierarchy that placed Caucasians on top and Africans on the bottom.[56] American Indians were barely mentioned.[57]

Within these dominant discourses of progress and racism, the Society of American Indians attempted to demonstrate that Indians, contrary to prevailing stereotypes, were equals with whites. By organizing for the purpose of uplift, SAI leaders sought to prove Native peoples' inherent value and ensure that other Indians could enjoy the opportunity to excel in white society, just as they had. Among this illustrious assemblage were Indian Bureau accountant and suffragist Marie Baldwin (Ojibwe); Carlisle graduate and Indian Bureau supervisor of employment Charles E. Dagenett (Peoria); activist and intellectual Laura Cornelius Kellogg (Wisconsin Oneida); Yale graduate, educator, and Presbyterian minister Henry Roe Cloud (Ho-Chunk/Winnebego); and renowned artist Angel De Cora Deitz (Winnebago), who was the head of the Native Indian Arts Department at the Carlisle Indian Industrial School.[58]

Also in attendance were two future SAI presidents—the Omaha lawyer Thomas Sloan and the Seneca museologist Arthur C. Parker. Sloan had graduated valedictorian from the Hampton Institute in Virginia that was founded to educate freedmen after the Civil War. He gave up acceptance to Yale University to read law with Hiram Chase, another Omaha lawyer and SAI founder. Sloan fought for his ideals. At age seventeen, he had been jailed for protesting Omaha agency corruption. As a young man, he had successfully argued a case before the U.S. Supreme Court, incensed that the Indian Bureau had denied him an allotment on the Omaha Reservation in Nebraska. He also supported the growing peyote religion, a fact that alienated other society members.[59] Parker differed markedly from Sloan. He was born in 1881 on the Cattaraugus Reservation in New York, and his great uncle Ely S. Parker had been the commissioner of Indian affairs under Grant. As a young man, Arthur had considered entering the seminary until anthropology became a dominant interest. At twenty-five years old, he won a post at the New York State Museum in Albany after scoring first in an open exam. Parker maintained close ties with the Quaker-run Indian Rights Association, frequently attending its annual conferences at Lake Mohonk.[60] As a friend and confidant to Sherman Coolidge, he would become a central player in the Society of American Indians for its first seven years.

On the opening evening of the conference, Sherman Coolidge listened as Commissioner of Indian Affairs Robert G. Valentine gave a congratulatory address. Valentine praised the initiative taken by the founding members, expressing the hope that the society would "continue to broaden its membership till it includes every critic of the Government." He concluded, "We need an All-Indian public opinion."[61] As it happened, the SAI would provide many more than one. Over four days, delegates offered diverse papers on economic, educational, and legal issues affecting Native peoples. Laura Cornelius Kellogg presented "Industrial Organization for the Indian," a striking proposal for organizing reservations as communal, self-sufficient "industrial villages."[62] Marie Baldwin followed with "Modern Home Making and the Indian Woman," in which she argued for gender equality and praised the historical contributions of Native women to their societies.[63] Parker spoke on "The Philosophy of Indian

Education," contradicting any notion that the Indian be viewed "as an inferior" with respect to the Caucasian intellect and calling for the "teaching of independent action."[64]

Parker's paper invited much commentary from Sherman Coolidge, whose response gave those present the first taste of his polished public speaking and well-timed humor. "I wish to say in regard to the education of the Indian," he began, "that during the last forty years the process has been going on, and I think we have reached a time when the white people are pretty well educated to the fact that the Indian can be civilized, can be Christianized, can be a good man." Still, further education was needed to counter "false statements about the Indians in general." Coolidge related a cogent anecdote: "I know a white man among the Arapahoes who said, 'You can't educate the Arapahoe any more than you can the Ethiopian,' and I have heard friends of mine say I was educated because I was an Arapahoe smart enough to take all the studies and carry them through creditably, including the Latin and Greek languages; that the Arapahoe was the quickest to catch on; he had a quicker intellect than the Sioux and the Chippewa who were educated in the same schools. I believe there are many Chippewas, many Sioux just as smart as I am!" The joke drew laughter from the crowd, and Coolidge explained how such potential had to be encouraged. Reformers had to convince Indians "that they must compete in life's race, and in the condition of our American civilization."[65] The remarks were typical of Coolidge's progressive philosophy, yet in a subsequent session he took a stand for protecting elements of the past.

In her presentation on preserving "Native Indian Art," Angel De Cora Deitz spoke on the aesthetic sensibilities of Native peoples, noting how even basic articles of clothing contained symbolic and artistic content. She argued that decorative art and sign language had been "the two mediums of communication which were almost universal with the whole Indian race" and that each should stand as "a permanent record" in which all could take pride.[66] These observations prompted a long discussion in which Charles Eastman and others took part, mostly reinforcing the value of Native art. Eastman was particularly concerned that Indian art remain distinctive with respect to tribe and not be consumed under one heading. Horton G. Elm, another Native man, dissented and argued dismissively that Indians should abandon their artistic traditions in favor of Euro-American civilization. "The past is dead," he announced. "We as a people must think seriously and work seriously . . . and then as a race we will be thought of seriously and, therefore, seriously respected."[67]

Coolidge, despite his progressive tendencies, had an interest in Plains Indian sign language and an appreciation for Arapaho clothing.[68] "I wish to remind the last speaker that the race has the reputation of being too serious," he interjected. Laughter filled the auditorium. Coolidge then made a series of decidedly unprogressive statements that even included praise for Arapaho religion. "I am struck with the idea," he declared, "that we ought to preserve all that is best in Indian art, and that there is too much of a tendency to condemn all Indian things; that there are beautiful things among the Indians, as well as useful things." He described how his wife, Grace, a member of the "white race," carried their babies on traditional Arapaho cradle boards and adored her "beautiful" Arapaho moccasins, which she found superior to tight, store-bought footwear. "She says they are easy, and they are warm, and she likes to wear them," he explained, "and there is enough room so they don't hurt her feet." The remark drew a ripple of laughter from the crowd, and Coolidge concluded by citing his negative experience at Hobart with "pew-rent" churches and by praising the democratic nature of the Arapaho "sacred teepee," which he had used "not in the cause of the old religion of our people, which was not so very bad after all."[69]

Though Coolidge had a private history of appreciating Arapaho culture, his comments in Columbus appear somewhat surprising. In the 1890s, his public writings had expressed a belief that Indian ways and beliefs were inferior, even if he had encouraged whites to recognize the intelligence and ability of Native peoples. Now, surrounded by a group of outstanding American Indian professionals who took pride in the precontact past, Coolidge, perhaps under their influence, had begun to speak more freely on his sympathies.[70] This pride was collectively displayed in the conference's evening program of Indigenous music, which SAI members performed at Memorial Hall. A group of Ojibwe, Potawatomi, Oneida, Choctaw, and Nez Perce singers, joined by a male quartet from Carlisle, presented arrangements of Ojibwe and Omaha melodies, including

"Manitou Listens to Me" and "Canoeist's Love Song." In a highlight of
the program, Nez Perce performer Nora McFarland interpreted several
songs by the quartet in sign language as they sang.[71]

The next morning, a major session on legal and political obstacles faced
by Native peoples got underway, largely dominated by Thomas Sloan's
paper on the reservation system. His wide-ranging talk covered vital issues
relevant to the welfare of Native peoples, such as the "autocratic and arbi-
trary power" of superintendents who could declare Indians "incompetent"
without warning. Even in cases where Indians had been granted citizenship,
Sloan protested, "they are treated as arbitrarily as the subjects of the Czar
of Russia."[72] In the discussion that followed, Coolidge put forth his own
criticisms of the Indian Bureau, condemning how "the treaties we have
made are easily broken"—a staggering remark for someone who had so
enthusiastically supported land cessions at Wind River.

As Coolidge detailed his own frustrations over the legal status of
Native peoples, he could not help injecting a bit of humor. "Now I go on
lecture tours to Iowa and to Missouri," he told the meeting, "and I was
once asked to speak before the Teachers' Institute in one of the Missouri
towns, and they said to the audience, 'The Rev. Sherman Coolidge is with
us to-day and he will tell us about his people. He is a Cherokee.'" Such
misidentification was secondary. Coolidge described how after acquiring
an allotment at Wind River, he tried to sell it after leaving Wyoming.
To prove he was "competent" under the Dawes Act and receive permission, he had to send an application. The bureau assured him that due to
his reputation and achievements the process would take no longer than
three months. "I waited with the patience of an Indian," Coolidge said,
"and I am waiting yet. . . . I may have to go to the other lands, and wait
there." Then, during his wait, all the regulations on competency changed.
Exasperated, Coolidge gave up, consoled in that he had at least avoided
being taxed. Still, this advantage did not compensate for the legal limbo
in which Indians were held. "I do not know whether I am a citizen of
the United States or not," he confessed. "I am forty-eight years old,—
nearly half a century. I have been an educated, civilized man since I was
twenty-one, and before. Put that in your pipe of peace and smoke it."[73]

Smoke it or not, Coolidge's predicament was one the society would make a focus—that is, defining the legal status of Indians.

On the conference's final day, throngs lined up to hear a panel on moral and religious questions. Over two thousand whites listened to Coolidge and Henry Roe Cloud speak in Memorial Hall on the importance of faith and church groups to the movement for Native rights. The same day, Indian guest speakers reached approximately ten thousand congregants in churches throughout the city. This cooperative effort raised considerable monies for the SAI.[74] Over the run of sessions, Coolidge had also spoken at area churches, generating increased interest.[75] National and local press coverage was highly favorable.[76] Arthur C. Parker later quipped, "Columbus was this time discovered by the Indians and the town was surprised."[77]

During the conference, the SAI membership had met in private to elect its leaders. In the selection of executive chairman, Coolidge and Eastman were nominated but withdrew. Sloan's name was put forward, and he was eager for the position. In the voting, Coolidge placed second despite his protests. Sloan was elected chairman.[78] Much of the important work, such as ratifying a constitution and composing an official mission statement, was left unfinished as the members began returning home. Coolidge said goodbye to his adopted daughter, Virginia, who had accompanied him and helped considerably with organizational matters. He headed to Enid; she went to Carlisle for a three-year course of study.[79]

Coolidge must have been satisfied while returning to Oklahoma. The event had been a success by any measure, diminished only by the absence of Carlos Montezuma, who, fearful that the Indian Bureau was trying to undermine the SAI's independence, had chosen not to attend.[80] He would be back, however, arguing vigorously—and controversially—for the bureau's liquidation. Once in Enid, Coolidge had other concerns. There had been an outbreak of an unspecified illness on the reservation, and he was constantly on the move between Whirlwind and Chilocco.[81] Rarely at home during November and December, he missed his family greatly.[82] When he returned, the reunions with Grace must have been passionate. She became pregnant around New Year's 1911.[83] Perhaps that is why, in February 1912, she and the girls returned to her father's townhouse in New York City. That she detested Oklahoma may have also been a deciding factor.[84]

In Enid, Coolidge attended to SAI business as best he could. He began corresponding frequently with Arthur C. Parker, who took up the habit of addressing him as "Arapahoe," as Coolidge occasionally signed his letters.[85] Parker was jubilant at Coolidge's participation in the SAI but shared several apprehensions about the nascent direction of the organization. First, the membership, though "fine and select," were too few in number. Some also had "too radical ideas." Parker hoped that a group of five thousand individuals could be assembled to lend greater weight to the endeavor. As well, he expressed fear of "Government Domination" and, even worse, government opposition. Charles Dagenett, an Indian Bureau employee, had been elected the secretary-treasurer—an arrangement some found suspicious. Sloan had also been a controversial choice as the executive chairman because of his background in law. The Omaha lawyer had promised to resign if involved in any suit against the government, but Parker felt Sloan and Dagenett should both resign to eradicate any possible friction, even if it meant "bowing to unjust criticism." Parker insisted that he desired no office for himself, only the "great success for all of the Indians and their successful uniting in one organization."[86] Coolidge—to Parker's mind—was vital to this goal in several respects. Living in Oklahoma, with its large Indian population, he could provide outreach for the society and attract new members. He could also enhance public awareness by publishing widely in Episcopal journals.[87]

If Parker hoped to spur Coolidge into action, there was no need. He was already hard at work, writing churchmen and local papers, giving lectures around Enid, and handing out SAI literature to prospective members. "I will take every opportunity to make the Society known and get active members, both Indian and white," Coolidge assured Parker. "And if I can inspire confidence and interest in the Society and thereby aid it to fulfill its mission to the race and country, I shall feel that I had an excuse for living."[88]

Thankfully, the society also gave Coolidge an excuse to leave Oklahoma briefly in the new year. The leadership had begun the process of opening a Washington DC headquarters near the Indian Bureau, and in January

1912, Coolidge traveled to the offices to help compose the SAI constitution. As the first order of business, Charles Dagenett resigned his post as the secretary-treasurer, quashing anxieties that had arisen from his holding a government post. Parker was elected in Dagenett's stead, taking what would prove the most demanding role in the young association. The new SAI executive council included a president; a first vice president; three other vice presidents to oversee legislation, education, and membership; and a secretary-treasurer. Like Dagenett, Sloan, who had every right to claim the presidency, also resigned in the spirit of unity. Coolidge, having received the second-highest number of votes in Columbus, accepted the duties of temporary president.[89]

With the leadership question settled, Coolidge remained in Washington to speak at local churches, though he admitted to Grace that the thin crowds prevented "a howling success."[90] The highlight of the trip became a twenty-fifth anniversary celebration of the Dawes Act. Coolidge and the others rented a small fleet of "clean and comfortable" boats to sail down the Potomac to the Hampton Institute in Virginia. This part of the plan was ill advised. Because of the winter weather, they had "to plow through cakes of ice" the whole way. In an address before an audience of a thousand, including Commissioner Valentine, Coolidge became, in his words, "the orator of the day."[91] The event convinced him that the society was "going to exercise considerable influence."[92] This enthusiasm was only dampened by his impending return to Enid. He told Grace that he wanted to let the "Popes of Whirlwind . . . go to grass" and added, "I hate the idea of having to go back at all." Grace had already begun buying clothes for the coming baby and wondered if it was bad luck. "I do not feel at all superstitious on the subject," Sherman assured her.[93] Days later, he informed Bishop Brooke that he would be absent an additional two weeks.[94] Having granted his own reprieve, he made his way to Carlisle to visit Virginia; then he presumably went on to New York for a short visit with his family.[95]

The Coolidges reunited in Oklahoma in mid-March 1912, just when Sherman received the long-awaited news that Brooke had finally accepted his resignation.[96] After Easter, his new parish would be in Faribault, Minnesota. The bishop there had sent word that Coolidge would likely minister in Kenyon and Concord, two missions joined by a railroad.[97]

Grace feared that Miss Bedell would prevail upon Sherman to remain in Enid to fight the "mescal trouble" (meaning peyote), but he was adamant about moving.[98] "It is about time," he announced to Grace, "I took the bit in my mouth with a baby coming, children who can be educated in Faribault, a book to write, and the Indian Society to help." The "book to write" was his planned autobiography, which he promised to finish.[99]

Just as the Coolidges started discussing plans to leave Oklahoma, they received a large envelope in the mail from Arthur C. Parker. Inside they found the *Report of the Executive Council on the Proceedings of the First Annual Conference of the Society of American Indians.* The report detailed the society's inaugural gathering in Columbus and called on "all progressive Indians and friends of Indian progress" to aid in "promoting the highest interests of the Indian as a race and as an individual."[100] A new periodical edited by Parker, the *Quarterly Journal of the Society of American Indians,* would help define this mission toward winning Indians their citizenship.[101] A yearly subscription to the *Quarterly* cost a dollar, and SAI membership cost two. Junior membership, meant for students who would someday run the society, cost fifty cents. Sherman Coolidge promptly signed up each of his daughters.[102] For him, the Society of American Indians was that kind of very personal experience. Surrounded by distinguished Native colleagues, he would continue to refine his views while leading the organization through its most robust period of agitation. The future seemed bright.

1. Charles Coolidge in an undated photograph from the *Colorado Magazine*, 1893.

2. Sophie Coolidge in a portrait dated 1877. Courtesy of the Colorado Springs Pioneers Museum.

3. Sherman Coolidge as a cadet at Shattuck Military Academy, ca. late 1870s. Courtesy of the Colorado Springs Pioneers Museum.

4. A young Sherman Coolidge, pictured in clerical garb in the 1880s, from the *Colorado Magazine*, 1893.

5. Chief Sharp Nose photographed in U.S. Army captain's bars, 1884. Courtesy of the National Archives, Image 530817.

6. Carlisle Indian Industrial School founder Richard Henry Pratt in an undated photograph. Courtesy of Beinecke Rare Book and Manuscript Library, Yale University, Image 1026112.

7. Sherman Coolidge (*standing, far left*) and John Roberts (*seated, far right*) at the Shoshone Episcopal mission school at Fort Washakie, 1880s. Courtesy of the American Heritage Center, University of Wyoming.

8. Sherman Coolidge, Arapaho chief Black Coal (*seated, right*), and Painting Horse, 1880s. Courtesy of the American Heritage Center, University of Wyoming.

9. Sherman Coolidge photographed in 1902. Courtesy of the National Anthropological Archives, Smithsonian Institution, BAE GN 0001OB 06077500.

10. Grace Darling Wetherbee and her older sister, Alice Wetherbee, photographed in girlhood. Courtesy of the Colorado Springs Pioneers Museum.

L. ALMAN,   172 5TH AVE., N.Y.
AND NEWPORT, R.J.

11. (*left*) Grace Wetherbee photographed in 1890. Courtesy of the Colorado Springs Pioneers Museum.

12. (*above*) Grace Wetherbee pictured with a rifle on her first trip to Wyoming in 1897. Courtesy of the American Heritage Center, University of Wyoming.

13. (*left*) Hannah Nye Wetherbee in an undated photograph. Courtesy of the Colorado Springs Pioneers Museum.

14. (*above*) Grace Wetherbee (*left, holding a child*) with her students at the Shoshone mission school for girls, 1902. Courtesy of the American Heritage Center, University of Wyoming.

15. Sherman Coolidge with his arm in a sling after sustaining a broken collar bone in a horse-riding accident, 1902. Courtesy of the American Heritage Center, University of Wyoming.

16. Grace and Sherman Coolidge at home on the ranch shortly after their wedding, 1902. Courtesy of the American Heritage Center, University of Wyoming.

17. The Coolidges' Christmas wagon packed with toys, foodstuffs, and tree, ready to embark on a missionary trip to an Arapaho village, December 1902. Courtesy of the American Heritage Center, University of Wyoming.

18. Anne Talbot on her trip to visit the Coolidges in 1903. Courtesy of the American Heritage Center, University of Wyoming.

19. Sherman and one of his infant children (unidentified), ca. mid-1900s. Courtesy of the Colorado Springs Pioneers Museum.

20. Shoshone and Arapaho men voting to cede tribal lands under the McLaughlin Agreement, 1904. Sherman Coolidge (*right, front row*) is looking at the camera. Courtesy of the American Heritage Center, University of Wyoming.

21. Grace (*back*), Virginia (*left*), Effie (*right*), and Sallie Coolidge photographed together, ca. 1911. Courtesy of the Colorado Springs Pioneers Museum.

22. Charles Eastman photographed in a headdress, 1913. Courtesy of the National Anthropological Archives, Smithsonian Institution, BAE GN 3463.

23. Arthur C. Parker. The image is taken from the pamphlet *American Indian Freemasonry*, published in 1919.

24. Sallie and Rosie Coolidge, ca. 1915. Courtesy of the Colorado Springs Pioneers Museum.

25. Sherman Coolidge pictured in his fifties. Courtesy of the Colorado Springs Pioneers Museum.

26. Father Philip Gordon (*left*) and Carlos Montezuma photographed in 1918 on a tour of Ojibwe reservations in Minnesota and Wisconsin. Department of Special Collections and University Archives, Raynor Memorial Libraries, Marquette University, Image BCIM01238.

27. Thomas Sloan in a photograph published in the *American Indian Magazine*, 1920.

28. Gertrude Bonnin at the Catholic Sioux Congress, Standing Rock Reservation, 1922. Department of Special Collections and University Archives, Raynor Memorial Libraries, Marquette University, Image BCIM00684.

29. Henry Roe Cloud (*left*), Ruth Muskrat Bronson, and Sherman Coolidge (*right*) with President Calvin Coolidge, 1923. Courtesy of the Library of Congress Prints and Photographs Division, Washington DC.

30. Sherman Coolidge in old age. Courtesy of the Colorado Springs Pioneers Museum.

The Society Ascendant

"But oh! heavens, how glad we are to get rid of the place," Grace wrote to her dear friend, Anne Talbot, following her family's long-planned escape from Oklahoma.[1] The Coolidges had arrived in Faribault, Minnesota, in April 1912 and had begun house hunting.[2] They found only one room for rent, so they decided, presumably with help from Grace's father, to purchase a "sweet" seven-room home that was for sale in the suburbs. The house boasted a second floor and attic, a concrete basement, and a back balcony with a "fine view of the mill pond and several other things." The panorama was a welcome change from "flat" Oklahoma. There was, unfortunately, one "great drawback": the house would not be ready until June. In the interim, the Coolidges stayed in part of "an old fashioned roomy house belonging to an ancient friend of Sherman's." The move to Faribault had cheered Sallie in particular. She despised Enid so much that whenever the subject came up, she suggested, "Let's try not to think about Oklahoma anymore." On the final train trip out of Enid, a friendly passenger had asked her where she lived. She "solemnly" answered, "In Faribault, Minnesota." Life there was much improved. Sallie quickly befriended the girl next door and spent all her hours playing outside. "Praise be!" Grace wrote. "I can't imagine anything which would induce insanity sooner than to be shut up with Sallie in a small hotel room and engage in conversation with her exclusively for 14 hours out of the 24."[3]

For Sherman, returning to Faribault was like returning home. Only Henry Benjamin Whipple was missing. The bishop had died in 1901 at age seventy-nine, having outlived his designated successor.[4] Following his death, his widow, Evangeline Marrs Whipple, rekindled her old love affair with Rose Cleveland, who once served as the First Lady for her brother Grover. In 1910 the women relocated to Italy to live out their lives as partners under the Tuscan sun.[5]

Coolidge described his work in Faribault as ministering to "a mixed congregation of whites and Sioux Indians," and visiting missions throughout Minnesota. When delivering his sermons, as he once told a group of students at the Haskell Institute, "the whites sit on one side and the Indians on the other."[6] Gleaned from Episcopal literature, Coolidge also addressed various congregations about his "Indian work" in the local area.[7] While not traveling or preaching, domestic duties kept him busy. Grace had been pregnant since the winter of 1911, and on September 5, 1912, she gave birth to a daughter, Sophie Hope Austin Coolidge, named after Sherman's foster mother and father. The family later called her Rose, Rosie, or Rosebud.[8] Grace wrote to Anne, announcing, "All off! It's a girl." The letter described her arrival:

> Born the 5th at 6 p.m. sharp. Not much trouble, only a couple of rather vigorous hours after a morning of uncertain qualms. . . . I had the sweetest of doctors and the nicest and kindest of nurses and the baby is a cherub for all she is only getting half rations. Sleeps 5–6 hours at a stretch and at night!!! She's a really pretty little thing with a little black fur cap on her heady. Well, all we can do is to echo Sallie's prayer put up the evening the little sister was born: "Please give us another, a boy; and, thank you for this one." She is the fattest best looking baby I have had. No wonder I never felt her move. She never wiggles a finger now if just rolling her eyes will do.[9]

Less than a month after his daughter's birth, Sherman was called away from Faribault on other business. At the end of September, he boarded the train to Columbus, Ohio, the site of the second annual conference of the Society of American Indians.[10]

The selection of Columbus as a venue had been preceded by some controversy. Charles Dagenett had originally promoted Colorado Springs, Colorado, a suggestion Coolidge deemed objectionable.[11] The city council had offered an invitation in late 1911, contingent on the construction of an Indian camp in the nearby foothills. "I don't like the idea of segregating our kind of Indians in a camp because I believe they have had enough of the reservation systems," Coolidge complained to Parker, "and feathers and paint and tomahawk may amuse the pale face and hence the freak 'Indian' or 'Injun' must be put on exhibition, but I don't quite relish the idea of being used as an advertisement for a summer resort, or for drawing a crowd for a fair." If it had to be Colorado Springs, he preferred facilities in the town center.[12] Parker, who had previously approved of the venue, agreed to look elsewhere.[13] Columbus, with its already "awakened interest and strong supporters," presented a superior option.[14] And though Parker had much work to do in preparation, he was lifted by Coolidge's financial contributions and moral support.[15] "You say in cheering me on, 'Go to it, old boy,' the Secretary will go to it and go to it strong if he has to go alone," Parker wrote. "However with a president like the Arapahoe in the chair,—I mean in the harness, I have no fear of a lone trip to the goal where we shall find success."[16]

Parker had cause for optimism. Thanks to a massive letter-writing campaign, the society now totaled a hundred full voting members of Indian ancestry and twice as many nonvoting white associates.[17] Attendance was correspondingly high for the 1912 conference held between October 2 and 7. Most of the important figures appeared: Arthur C. Parker, Henry Roe Cloud, Thomas Sloan, Charles Dagenett, Laura Cornelius Kellogg, and Carlos Montezuma, who had rededicated himself to his own cocreation. Fayette McKenzie and Richard Henry Pratt, a new associate member, appeared as well. Charles Eastman declined his invitation and would not return to the society's fold for several years. Regrettably, he had decided the SAI did not fulfill his vision of an intertribal body of elected representatives. Columbus, however, did not care. The city welcomed the society once more, with local dignitaries and church leaders offering tributes.[18]

On the conference's first morning, the attendees walked from the luxurious Hotel Columbus to the First Congregational Church. Following a sermon by Minister Washington Gladden, Coolidge delivered a spontaneous opening address meant to "outline the mind of the conference and its objects" from "a patriotic viewpoint." In doing so, he compared the Indians' situation to that of the world's Jewish population, innocently portending the conspiracies of Jewish domination that would fuel the rise of fascism in Germany two decades later. Coolidge claimed that though Jews numbered just 1 million in the United States and 11 million around the globe, "they manage to multiply themselves by many times in their power and influence." Indians, "as a small remnant of a race and few in numbers," should take their example, reject a "clannish spirit," and "re-establish the land of our forefathers in a higher sense as the land and the home of the free." He stressed, "Let us have harmony. Without that, we can do nothing."[19]

Coolidge's call for harmony was immediately undermined in the conference's first session. Asa Hill, a young Mohawk man, argued that Indian Bureau policy erred for allowing Indian nations "to maintain their tribal communism and remain intact." While "old Indians" preferred this arrangement, younger, "more progressive Indians" understood the need "to be liberated from such an environment." Hill suggested a program of secular education, strict laws against premarital and extramarital sex, and the prohibition of alcohol. These steps would slowly wean Native peoples from wardship, old ways, and "moral death," and ultimately "help the Indians to become *not white men*, but good Indian citizens."[20] Carlos Montezuma, determined to make up for his absence the previous year, dominated the following discussions. Comparing the reservation to "a prison," he insisted that the Indian Bureau be dismantled. In reaction, Thomas Sloan pointed out the dangers of the bureau's hypothetical disappearance. Indians, he countered, should not suddenly be "scattered over the country" without preparation, not least because the Indian Bureau had "grown to be a necessity" that employed so many of them. Sloan did, however, complain that the "Indian who gets along with the reservation system is the idle, lazy man who has become dependent upon the grace of the Indian agent."[21] Among this variety of opinion, the society generally agreed that the Indian Bureau's wardship had to end—eventually. The questions were how and when.[22]

The following day, Coolidge gave his main address at the Columbus Chamber of Commerce.[23] His speech echoed the shared concerns over bureau wardship and laid out his vision of "Christian citizenship" as a goal for all Indians. Achieving this status required the essential steps of terminating both the Indian Bureau and wardship more generally. The

Indian should not remain "a political nondescript forever" or be treated like a "civic freak"; instead, the Indian should fill "a niche" in the American racial tapestry. For some, Coolidge admitted, the idea of Indian participation in American life was anathema. Citing the time-worn saying "The dead Indian is the only good Indian," he quickly added, "But so is the live one!" Impassioned, he continued:

> Who is this Indian? What is he? Where does he live? Above all, why is he a problem? If these questions were asked of the average white man, the answers would be both inaccurate and confusing. In our early school-days, the Indian was defined as a savage who lived by hunting and fishing; who lived in a wigwam or teepee. He was a fierce, ferocious, cruel, crafty, treacherous, blood-thirsty red devil! Exterminate him! Exterminate him! Again, he has been described as a dirty, lazy, shiftless loafer, beggar and drunkard. No wonder "the only good Indian is the dead one!"

But why had this reputation prevailed? The answer was retaliation. The Indian had fought the European invader's "policy of war and extermination," killing "white men and women and children." Yet, Coolidge wondered aloud to the predominantly white audience, "What would you have done?" The Indian was merely defending "his lands, his people and his teepee home." Now with this fight lost, the Indian had become a ward, forced to battle with new tools against their conquerors' "self-interest, deceit, scandal, cruelty, ambition and lust." Only through unity and political organization could Native peoples regain their natural right and adapt to the new ways of "a more numerous and progressive race." In this endeavor, Indians deserved aid. If treated as "human," they would become productive members of society as doctors, soldiers, teachers, clerks, and clergymen. With full acceptance and the granting of citizenship, each could proudly someday state, "*Civis Americanus sum*"—meaning "I am an American citizen."[24]

It is difficult to imagine that anyone in attendance was not moved by Coolidge's words. He had condemned Euro-American expansionism in more potent terms than ever, showing a new forcefulness in defending the primacy and integrity of Native peoples and their violent response to the Euro-American invasion. Yet, like the Coolidge of old, his solution lay in intertribal unity and absorption into larger white society through adherence to "progressive" Christian ideals. One listener was particularly impressed. Richard Henry Pratt later called the speech "as near being a classic as anything yet written by an Indian on Indian matters."[25] Pratt, too, shared his thoughts in Columbus, denouncing the land loss Indians had experienced, the Wild West shows, the government's control of Indian funds, and the Indian Bureau, which he termed a "manhood-destroying prison system."[26] Pratt's bitterness was in part personal. In 1904 he had been removed from Carlisle for his blunt criticism of the bureau. In his forced retirement, he had continued to lecture on Indian issues whenever and wherever he could.[27]

The presence of Pratt and Montezuma made for a fractious conference. As allies who shared the same disdain for Native cultures and the same desire for rapid assimilation through the bureau's abolition, both men argued passionately for their goals. In one session, Montezuma took offense to the idea that educated Indians should "go back" to the reservation to uplift and protect their kinfolk. "Better send every Indian away," he declared. "Get hold and send them to Germany, France, China, Alaska, Cuba, if you please, and then when they come back 15 or 20 years from now you will find them strong, a credit to the country, a help and an ornament to this race." Montezuma pointed to Carlisle's history as evidence this approach would work, referring to Pratt as "our good father." The speech stirred Coolidge so greatly that he motioned to "adopt General Pratt as an Indian." Sloan seconded, but Arthur C. Parker quashed the discussion by noting that Pratt was "already" an Indian.[28]

In the voting that concluded the conference, Coolidge and Parker retained their offices unopposed. Sloan was elected first vice president, but a fierce disagreement occurred when Dagenett was nominated for second vice president due to his position in the bureau. He was elected regardless.[29] Despite the intermittent conflict on display in Columbus, the 1912 conference of the Society of American Indians clarified key issues pertaining to the organization's goals. Attendees created an Indian Code Commission to "define more exactly the privileges and disabilities of the several classes of Indians in the United States" and based it on a bill previously introduced in Congress by SAI member Rep. Charles D. Carter (Chickasaw, D-OK) that meant to classify the legal status of Native peoples. The society also urged more Native participation in the bureau to ensure greater opportunities for educated Indians. Last, the society demanded equal representation on the Board of Indian Commissioners and a commissioner who proclaimed the "uplift and promotion of the Indian" as "his only concern." If the bureau's structure could not be immediately eliminated, perhaps it could be taken over, then gradually dismantled as the situation allowed.[30]

Following the Columbus meeting, Coolidge was "encouraged and confident" about the society's future. He wrote to Grace of how the "conference shows what the past year's work has accomplished."[31] After his return home to Faribault, he picked up his correspondence with Parker, who promised to avoid sharing the finer details of society business too frequently. Coolidge was often on the move during the winter, visiting Indian schools in Oklahoma and Kansas, and "hustling and sowing the good seed" for the society.[32] Parker hoped that despite being so busy, Coolidge had started his autobiography.[33] The book, though never written, could have had a premature ending.

In February 1913, the Coolidges woke up on a Sunday and, uncharacteristically, decided to skip church for a family outing in their horse-drawn buggy. Grace looked down to see if Rosebud was asleep just as they were headed downhill toward a railroad crossing. Then everything went black. Her explanation to Anne of what happened next told a harrowing story:

> Just a few lines to tell you that you nearly lost us all three weeks ago tomorrow. R.R. [railroad] crossing, express train, hit the back wheels of the buggy. I would have had Sherman send you a newspaper account only that it was too lurid. Rosebud, who was picked up on the ground with the back seat (on which she and I had been sitting!) wedged on top of her. They could hardly get her out. But she was absolutely unscratched. None of us were really badly hurt, tho' Sallie and I were pretty well out of business for a few days, and I guess no words could do justice to our appearance. We seem to have landed

on our faces. . . . I never saw the train coming, nor knew the least thing about it. S. was driving, we in the back. Wasn't that funny!

"Funny" or not, Grace, nose broken and eyes swollen shut, spent nearly two weeks in the hospital and several more immobile in bed. Initially doctors feared Sallie might die, but she rebounded quickly after a few nights of "terror" and was sent home seven days later. Only bruised eyes indicated she had been injured. Rosie, not even a year old, stayed with a family friend before Sherman, who had been knocked unconscious in the accident, returned home to care for her with the help of a nurse.[34] Thankfully, by mid-April, Grace was feeling "grand." The doctors had been certain her right eye was lost, but it had recovered "as good as new." Grace boasted to Anne, "As a family, we might be described as indestructible."[35] Sherman perhaps slightly disagreed. He described his "suffering from excruciating pains of sprained ankle, injured hip, and stiffened neck" to Parker, who later informed the "clan" of the accident while visiting the SAI offices in Washington.[36]

The Society of American Indians was at that time flourishing, and the planning of each yearly conference, traditionally held in October, was a task that had to be seen to six months ahead. In April 1913, while still in pain from his unpleasant encounter with the express train, Coolidge wrote Montezuma and Pratt, asking them to attend.[37] The SAI had chosen Denver, Colorado, as the next conference site, and Coolidge had joined the Colorado Publicity League to better promote the gathering. He shared some press clippings with Montezuma, noting that they showed "how the Denver people will treat us, not as monkeys or clowns or other circus freaks but as men and women leaders of our race working hard and honestly for our uplift and welfare." Coolidge had also been involved in talks concerning an Indian pageant. Here, too, he was optimistic, stating, "I believe the grand council they propose having will tend to make the different tribes feel that they are part of a great race and a great nation, instead of feeling that they are just a few poor Injuns on the reservation and on that, in some dark corner of the republic. It will do no harm to the uncivilized and uneducated to meet the civilized and educated, and to talk together about things in general for the good of all."[38] If this was how fellow members of the publicity league presented the plans, there had been a serious misunderstanding.

Coolidge became incensed in late May when Pratt, acting on intelligence from an unknown source, wrote to warn him that the Colorado Publicity League counted Buffalo Bill Cody, father of the Wild West show, as one of its members. Coolidge had known of but tolerated Cody's presence, but Coolidge had not known that the league intended to use the SAI conference to excite interest for a planned visit to the city by Cody's troop. Upon learning the news, Coolidge promptly resigned.[39] He relayed the incident to Montezuma, complaining of how the SAI had been "trapped." "There is a spider called the 'fish-spider,'" Coolidge elaborated, "[and] it fishes for little fishes and when the fish is caught, it's all up with the fish. Denver, Parker wrote me, was fishing to land us in 1915. Why? Ye gods and little fishes! 'To glut the savage eyes of' Denver's 'proud populace.' And what is the reason? Why, forsooth? We are Indians." With the preparatory work already completed, Coolidge decided the conference had to take place as planned, but, as he told Parker, they "must not compromise the principles of the Society" with such publicity stunts. Instead, "it must be all for the *honor of the race* and the good of the country."[40]

By August 1913, Coolidge and Parker had formulated a conference program and sent out thousands of circulars to boost attendance. One of Parker's plans was to place billboards on reservations with the assistance of SAI members in those communities.[41] Throughout the run-up to Denver, he sent Coolidge detailed letters about the society's finances and expenditures.[42] Parker admitted that he was exhausted, but he remained proud of the work already accomplished. "Our great value and our achievement," he declared, "lie in the fact that we are standing for the revitalization of the race by infusing in various individuals the feeling that they themselves must do for themselves and stand for themselves as free and independent men, and that we are struggling against the continuation of a policy that breeds dependent children who look forever to the fostering care of the 'Great White Father.'"[43]

Amid his intense labors, Parker was not above sharing salacious gossip. In a letter labeled "Private and Confidential," he informed Coolidge of Charles Dagenett's imminent "downfall." Dagenett had "become enamored with many young women," some of whom had suffered "persecution, dismissal from service and transfers at a great distance." One woman, Miss Denomie, even decided to resign "on account of his continued advances in the office." Parker admitted that the "most efficient and plucky" Miss Denomie was "not a perfect girl," but she was hardly at fault. Dagenett's unwanted attentions had caused such stress that she "lost complete control and let herself slide into a sort of a federation (socially) with Frank Shively, a Crow delegate and a man known as a smart fellow but a drunkard." Denomie continued to resist Dagenett, who eventually "got sore because she was surly to him." "Certain parties" were now gathering evidence against Dagenett, preparing to oust him from his position. Parker did not condone his behavior but nonetheless pledged to stay loyal to his colleague in honor of the work he had done for the society.[44] At the same time, Parker kept secret some of the criticism leveled at Coolidge by other members. For one, the Tuscarora ethnologist John Hewitt humorously deemed Coolidge a "microbe of inertia" for not making greater efforts to accomplish the society's goals.[45]

In July 1913, Coolidge received a letter from Wind River agent J. H. Norris, informing him that he had inherited his mother's 120-acre allotment.[46] Exactly when Ba-ahnoce died is unclear. Not long before Coolidge received Norris's letter, he was in Washington DC, trying to convince the commissioner of Indian affairs and the secretary of the interior to allow the SAI to be represented in "investigations of importance" by its legal aid division.[47] When mother and son had parted in April 1870 at Camp Brown, neither could have half-imagined the path Runs On Top's life would take. It remains unfortunate that Coolidge does not seem to have committed to paper his thoughts on his mother's death.

The third annual Society of American Indians conference got underway on October 14, 1913, in Denver and ran over six days. The theme, "What the Indian Can Do for Himself, for His Race and for His Country," reflected the ideals of patriotic self-help that the leadership cherished. The SAI had by then grown to around two hundred active full members and four hundred associates (one of whom was Grace Coolidge). While far below Parker's expressed desire for a five-thousand-strong membership, these numbers were certainly respectable. The conference resembled those in Columbus, where local officials welcomed the delegates, and the general public attended a "mass meeting." Church groups invited Indian speakers to Sunday services, and the SAI arranged an evening of "Indian entertainment" for the city. Among the membership, Montezuma was again notably absent—a fact that ensured greater harmony. Dagenett did appear, confounding Parker's predictions of a "downfall."[48] Fayette McKenzie, mostly known for his silent presence, gave a notable talk titled "The Cooperation of the Two Races." "Each race has despised and hated the other," he admitted in his opening statement, but whites had to strongly support Native peoples as a moral imperative, just as Indians had to accept a general reconciliation. Nevertheless, Indians should never forget their origins and never accept "second best" in trying to make their way in American society.[49]

Coolidge presented his main contribution, "The American Indian of Today," before the student body of the University of Denver. The brief speech, apparently tailored for the young white men in attendance, highlighted the Natives' participation in America's creation. Coolidge stressed that though the United States had once "pursued the policy of war and extermination," Indians had survived and begun to adapt to "European" ways. In spite of consistent ill treatment, Indigenous peoples had also fought alongside whites from the Revolutionary War to the Spanish-American War. "Even policemen on the reservations," Coolidge added, "have not held back when they were in duty bound to arrest friends, relatives, and even to kill them for the welfare of the citizenship of the United States." Coolidge's comments then took a personal turn, describing his childhood and his time as a missionary in Wyoming, telling a well-worn joke. When meeting another man named Coolidge, a bystander asked how they had ended up with the same last name. The man answered that it was of little consequence but took pains to distinguish himself from his Arapaho counterpart. "I'm a real Coolidge," he said. "My ancestors came over in the Mayflower." "Yes," Sherman responded, "but mine were on the reception committee when they arrived." The anecdote underscored the fact that at present, Natives and whites were "banded together for the honor of the race and for the good of the country." And with more Indians taking part in public life, they were now becoming aware of the duty to "become productive, useful men and women."[50]

Coolidge's patriotic speech—and the larger conference—had a reve-
latory effect on some among the white Denver audience. One Colorado
monthly ran a long article on the "remarkable gathering," which was
nothing like the expected "powwow of savages in war paint." Though
the reporter had spotted a few "blanket Indians," the others had been
"clad in tailor-made garments or 'store clothes.'" Also remarkable were
the attendees' complexions, some being "fair"; some "with faces almost
white, mantled by a rich red tinge"; and some having "a bronze copperish
color or a light brown." Yet, in every case, they were "thoughtful people"
who were "proud to call themselves Indians." The "orderly" nature of the
proceedings offered ample proof that the "sons of the warriors and chiefs
of a half-century ago" had made "commendable progress in the direction
of Christian civilization" and were not remotely "bloodthirsty." Not only
that, the reporter also remarked, the "tribesmen, young and old," were "not
lacking in a sense of humor." There had been "an occasional bit of hilarity,"
and "the women sometimes accused the men of teasing." Many of these
"dusky young women were decidedly attractive," making it clear "to the
bachelor observer that Cupid was at work among the good-looking young
folks of both sexes." Meanwhile, Sherman Coolidge best represented the
new Indian, thanks to his "overflowing geniality." As the president of the
Society of American Indians, he employed his "superior culture" to rally
whites to his cause and to encourage his own people to work for "the
honor of the race and the good of the country."[51]

Whatever the manner in which the Denver reporter expressed himself, his article provided a glimpse into how Coolidge was able to open
the minds of those white Americans who had never given a thought
to Native peoples outside of negative stereotypes. From the pulpits in
churches around Denver, Coolidge made this eloquent plea: "We ask you
to cooperate with us in bringing Christianity to both the Indians and
the white men. We ask you to allow us to cooperate with you. Help us to
protect what little remains to the Indian in land allotments, be brothers
and put your shoulder to the wheel and appeal to your government to
give us a chance. This is the land of our ancestors and we should be permitted to help govern it."[52] Few could reproach such a message. On this

note of reconciliation and mutual responsibility, the Denver conference concluded in a spirit of unity.

Parker later lauded the resulting platform as the best statement of the society's goals thus far. Collectively, the membership advocated the passage of two congressional bills—the Carter Code Bill, proposed by Representative Carter to define the legal status of Native peoples, and a second bill named after Rep. John H. Stephens (D-TX) that sought to open a court of claims that would allow Indian tribes to seek compensation for broken treaties. A call for improvements in Indian education rounded out the society's agenda. In the election of officers, Coolidge and Parker held their posts. On all counts, the society appeared ascendant, and the executive leadership decided to celebrate soon and in style with a gala banquet in—quite appropriately—the City of Brotherly Love.[53]

13

Harmony in Jeopardy

Tradition held that the Society of American Indians' executive committee gather every winter in Washington DC to regroup and discuss policy. Thrilled by the success of the third annual conference, Arthur C. Parker presented another idea, "a meeting of Indians and their friends" in the city of Philadelphia, home of the Indian Rights Association. If the occasion could attract "eastern Indians of influence," Parker speculated hopefully that the "attention of the public" might be captured.[1]

As Sherman Coolidge prepared to embark for the capital around the first anniversary of his family's buggy accident, another unexpected calamity occurred. On a snowy Minnesota evening with the temperature at twenty degrees below zero, he and Grace were awakened at midnight by the sounds of baby Rosebud, "coughing and strangling." Quickly realizing the room was filled with smoke, they leaped out of bed and stuck their heads out of the window, gasping for air. Sherman then "plunged downstairs into a sea of smoke," searching for the source of the fire. Unable to locate the cause, he franticly collected the children and ran to a small house on the property inhabited by the maid. Sound asleep, she refused to answer even after repeated banging on the door. Spotting a light on in a neighboring house, Sherman hastened over through the snow and burst in on a young couple twosing on a sofa while the girl's parents slept upstairs. He "dumped" the children and raced back to Grace, who was busy welcoming the fire brigade while also trying desperately to salvage a few essential items, including a batch of her writings. The firemen went to work, chopping "two big holes" in the house, one upstairs and one down. The source of the smoke quickly turned out to be a defective flue. The firemen ultimately caused more damage than the smoke, which had merely ruined some wallpaper in three downstairs rooms. Grace wrote of the aftermath, "We were insured and really got three rooms papered for nothing, but oh! the mess. Nearly 3 weeks cleaning up after a two hour fire! And you don't know what it is to keep Rosebud off newly varnished floors."[2] Yet Rosebud had been the real hero. Her crying had saved everyone from certain death by smoke inhalation, buttressing Grace's claims to having an "indestructible" family.[3]

Sherman Coolidge had little time to reflect. Just two days after the near tragedy, he left Faribault, bound for the Quaker City.[4] On Valentine's Day 1914, he and other prominent reformers in the Native rights movement convened at Philadelphia's Academy of Natural Sciences for three hours of lectures. Coolidge opened the afternoon with a convocation, Marie Baldwin spoke on "The Hopes and Aims of the Society," and Richard Henry Pratt discussed "Indian Transformation." Representatives of the Indian Bureau and the Indian Rights Association presented brief papers. The big event, a sumptuous feast at the Hotel Walton, took place that evening.[5] There, Coolidge conversed with the new commissioner of Indian affairs, Cato Sells, who appeared "heart and soul in the work."[6] After the gala, Coolidge joined Pratt on a round of visits to congressmen, only to learn that the prospects for the Stephens bill, meant to open a court of Indian claims, looked dim.[7] The situation was typical. A handful of government officials and politicians in Washington were happy to attend SAI functions and receive a bit of press, but when the time came to implement systemic change, little, if nothing, occurred.

Undeterred, Parker described the Philadelphia dinner in the *Quarterly Journal* as a "brilliant" affair in which Americans "red" and white met on an "equal basis" of "friendship and good citizenship."[8] The only note of discord had emanated from Carlos Montezuma's talk on the evils of the reservation system. While the doctor conceded that "America stands pre-eminent for the unity of races and freedom of the individual," he launched a full attack on the Indian Bureau for its "despotic powers" and "unscrupulous actions." Its abolishment, accompanied by the direct inclusion of Natives into mainstream Euro-American society, was the only rational answer to the Indian problem.[9] This anti-bureau sentiment would eventually inaugurate a factionalism that proved ruinous to the SAI.

Coolidge, though a friend of Montezuma's and a critic of the bureau's, expressed a different public tone during this period. Following the 1913 Denver conference, he appeared at the Monster Twentieth-Century Jubilee Convention of the Anti-Saloon League of America in Columbus, Ohio. Presumably asked to speak on temperance issues, Coolidge took the opportunity to humanize Native peoples before a wider audience, using humor and personal anecdotes to gain support for reform. His speech began with a simple statement: "The Indian must be made free." He explained the irony within: "It sounds funny to me to say that because this land on which he lived from time immemorial has been the land of the brave and of the free, and my people enjoyed that freedom and they were monarchs, not slaves. They have been placed by this nation on reservations, and reservations are very much like prisons to these people who are so used to freedom. And the result has been that this independent, free, noble race has deteriorated until they are a caricature of what they were before they were placed on the reservation." Coolidge then told the story of his early life and how after his adoption he had visited the very city in which he now addressed the crowd. "At that time," he related, "I could not speak a word of English. I knew 'yes' and 'no,' and sometimes I put them in the wrong place." Yet, on his second visit in 1908, he had spoken to the students at Ohio State University, only to return in 1911 and help launch the Society of American Indians, an organization seeking to "serve, whenever they can, all humanity." Having shared this personal journey, Coolidge asked for solidarity, understanding, and a recognition of commonality. Indians were "human beings" who, together with whites, had to fight society's ills, such as alcohol. Many troubles on Indian reservations had come "directly or indirectly through liquor," which itself had come from the "white man." Only by joining together could both Indians and whites "redeem" historical conflicts and improve the collective lot of Native peoples.[10]

As Coolidge became more adept at cajoling white audiences into seeing Indians with a new sympathy, in other forums he expressed himself with a critical intensity largely absent from his surviving statements pre-1911. While at Wind River, he had rarely written or spoken of the importance of understanding the broader Native perspective or openly condemned the aggression perpetrated by white society. But now, he had clearly altered his beliefs on the supposed virtue of Euro-America. His 1914 article for the *Quarterly Journal* distilled his maturing views, reproving the U.S. government for its "war and extermination policy" and rejecting the idea of the Indian as a "degraded savage." Coolidge criticized the "white invaders," whose mistaken sense of superiority had assumed that the Indian should "be pressed into the white man's preconceived mold." Herein resided the "deep-seated disease germ of the whole Indian problem" that had spread through the construction of the reservation system. Under its dictatorial auspices, the Indian had "so deteriorated we can hardly realize him as the same proud monarch of fifty years ago." That Indians enjoyed no control over their own monies constituted another major offense. The U.S. government held almost $1 billion in tribal property, including cash reserves of $60 million and forests worth $100 million. Yet, whites determined how the funds were appropriated, allowing resources to end up in the hands of corporations. It fell to the Society of American Indians to ensure, or at least question, government policies and expenditures. The precontact past was "beyond recall," but as adaptation began, Euro-American society had to respect the Indian's values and "blame him not if he refuses to become an imitation white man; if he bows not the knee to commercialism, or fails to admit that the white man is the ultimate model of the best citizenship or of noblest manhood."[11]

Having once deemed Indians "the weaker race of the inferior language, life, and religion," Coolidge had clearly evolved.[12] He now believed that Native peoples, with their communal values, had lessons to teach white society. After years of proselytizing unsuccessfully at Wind River, he finally understood and accepted that the vast majority of Indians simply wanted to retain their ways and beliefs, and should do so proudly. Why the change? Likely it was due to the influence of Charles Eastman and Arthur C. Parker. Eastman consistently promulgated the notion of the Indian as "the highest type of pagan" in body, mind, and spirit, while Parker venerated his Native ancestry and openly displayed a withering contempt for the unethical nature of American capitalism.[13]

Coolidge's criticisms of white society also came partially from personal sources. Over the course of his adult life, he had become increasingly troubled by his own standing under U.S. law. In an article in the *Quarterly Journal*, Parker even employed Coolidge's story to demonstrate the labyrinthine complexity Indians faced in determining their legal status. The absurdity was dizzying. As an Arapaho, Coolidge came from a formerly independent tribe. Once that tribe entered into a treaty with Washington, it acknowledged U.S. sovereignty, making Coolidge a ward. Following his adoption, Coolidge lived life like any other American, even voting in Minnesota toward the end of his school days because the state considered him a natural-born citizen. Thinking he *was* a citizen, Coolidge returned to Wyoming, only to find himself classified as a ward under treaties signed before his birth. After taking an allotment at Wind River, he assumed that he was a land-owning citizen under the 1887 Dawes Act.

However, Coolidge soon learned that though he might be a U.S. citizen, he was not considered a citizen of Wyoming because he resided on an Indian reservation. He tried to vote, but his ballot was invalidated. In the meantime, the 1906 Burke Act passed, suspending the sale of allotments until their owners were found "competent" by the Indian Bureau. The new law meant that Coolidge could not be a U.S. citizen (if he ever had been) until he proved his "competency." His status changed yet again when he relocated to Oklahoma. Entering as a ward, Coolidge became a citizen under state law after two years of living independently. He voted legally. Yet when he decided to sell his allotment in Wyoming, he had to apply to the Wind River agent to be declared "competent." The agent promised a speedy process, which halted when the forms Coolidge submitted were annulled after a change in the procedure.

Parker injected some humor into his lengthy explication, noting that when Coolidge learned from his superintendent that the laws governing competency had changed, he "resisted any attempt at expletives" with "clerical fortitude" and calmly answered, "Well, my mind has changed too." Now living in Minnesota, Coolidge could vote and pay taxes, but his lands and his children's tribal monies were held in trust because in Wyoming he and his children remained wards. Coolidge's case, Parker pointed out, was not only an indignity but also a legal limbo that had to be remedied by the Carter Code Bill, which the Society of American Indians endorsed at the 1912 and 1913 conferences.[14]

Coolidge and Parker had already made some headway to this effect. In 1913 they befriended the sympathetic senator Robert Latham Owen (D-OK), whose mother was part Cherokee. Respectful of his roots, Owen had represented the Cherokees in successful claims against the U.S. government and became wealthy in the process. More important, he served on the Senate Committee on Indian Affairs. To Coolidge and Parker, Owen's support augured well for the future.[15] Both men, however, were fatigued. Parker admitted in a letter that he should no longer continue as SAI secretary for the good of his health.[16] Coolidge meanwhile expressed concerns that the leadership appeared too static. The organization's constitution stated that members could remain in their positions for two years, but Coolidge, despite fears over appearances, felt that the society should retain talented officers whenever possible. "We must use the best we have to give good impression and yet guard against having the same bunch trotted out," he divulged to Montezuma. "I am against a 'merry-go-round' policy, although I do think we ought to make use of the very best material we have for the main officers and keep a good one on for more."[17] Parker had differing worries regarding the leadership structure. Its "democratic nature" and "lack of centralized authority," he believed, were "spelling ruin" and preventing the SAI from moving forward.[18]

In the summer of 1914, Coolidge decided to take a long break. He, Grace, and the children headed to Wind River. Writing to Montezuma, Sherman was proud to report that "I am camping here among the Wyoming mountains with my family and on the reservation of my people, the Arapahoes."[19] Possibly, the Coolidge family had not spent quality private time together since the SAI's founding. Virginia had gone to Carlisle in 1911. Effie had followed in early fall 1913.[20] The Wind River vacation also alleviated some of the overwhelming tedium Grace felt in Faribault. She called the city the "land of the Lotus eaters," referencing the Greek myth of an island populated by lazy, apathetic addicts.[21] "It is awfully hard to write letters from Faribault," she once mentioned to Anne. "When you once get settled here you never can remember that there is anywhere else or any past beyond the day you got here and began to hibernate."[22] After only a year in the city, Grace had felt the "moss" beginning to grow on her.[23] The one bright spot was the friendly neighbors. It was nice to be liked "after ten years of the other thing" at Wind River.[24] But when Sherman left for his trips and conferences, Grace stayed at home, "a martyr to babes and food."[25]

Rarely one to let circumstances defeat her, Grace fought boredom with her pen. Drawing on her life at the ranch, she composed sketches of her time in Wyoming and sent them to publishers. In 1912 and 1913, some of her stories appeared in prestigious and well-circulated periodicals such as *Collier's* and the *Outlook*. Her pieces told of the near starvation, premature death, and profound grief many Arapahos suffered at the loss of their old ways and the plundering of their environment.[26] Grace continued to write throughout her time in Faribault. Her children's book, *Paddy-Paws: Four Adventures of the Prairie Dog with a Red Coat*, was published by Rand McNally in 1914. Her *Teepee Neighbors*, twenty-nine vignettes based on the daily life and people of Wind River, came out in 1917. In one story, an Indian father appears to go insane trying to provide food for his family. In another, Grace travels off the reservation with a little Arapaho boy, who is distressed to learn that whites do not cherish children. In yet another, a boy experiences abuse at the government boarding school.[27]

Finding a publisher for these sketches entailed considerable difficulty. Most editors insisted that no one would want to read such depressing material.[28] Grace acknowledged the grim nature of the stories and how it affected salability, but insisted she could not present the "crushing and appalling" truth otherwise. The preface condemned the failures of the reservation system, asking why Indian children and the elderly had to "die for want to medicine and surgery, and food and nursing" when they had millions in the U.S. Treasury. Grace also pointed to the dictatorial aspects of the Indian Bureau's power structure, which allowed agents to imprison Indians indefinitely with no recourse to bail or legal representation. These agents wielded ultimate control over a confined population menaced by occupying soldiers who preyed on Indian girls. *Teepee Neighbors* drew praise from H. L. Mencken, who noted its "great quality of pity" and "moving" simplicity.[29] Grace dedicated the book to the Society of American Indians, "the truest expression and the brightest present hope of the Indian People."[30]

Unfortunately, hope failed to appear at the 1914 SAI annual meeting. Coolidge may have feared as much beforehand. In the run-up, he corresponded frequently with Montezuma, sending him information on prospective members, talking up the conference, and insisting that he "help to make it a success."[31] The gathering ran from October 6 to October 10 in Madison, Wisconsin. Montezuma made the trip, as did other key members. Coolidge's daughter Sallie attended as a junior member.[32] All this would suggest that the society was healthy, were it not for the desolate portrait later offered in the *Quarterly Journal*. In previous years, Parker had devoted space to even the minutiae of proceedings. The Madison conference received a short comment noting the pervasive "gloom" among the attendees. One reason for their mood was the society's insolvency. Both full and associate members had pledged enough contributions in the conference's first hour to keep the organization afloat, but the larger SAI platform appeared doomed. The Carter Code Bill had not passed, nor had a court of tribal claims been established. Considering such inertia, the conference's primary questions were, "Can we solve our problems; and if we do, will it all be worthwhile?" Parker offered scant detail on the solutions proffered, instead declaring that "the right path was chosen." This seemingly meant that previous officers had been reelected, and each remained motivated. Still, Parker wondered whether the SAI would merely struggle on with a "small company of the faithful" or whether the leading figures would receive support from an engaged rank-and-file membership.[33]

To breathe new life into the society's legislative agenda, the leadership at Madison decided to make an appeal to the highest level of government.[34] The executive committee set about soliciting a meeting with President Wilson to present the SAI's two primary concerns—a commission to codify the legal status of Native peoples and the Indian court of claims.[35] Members had some trepidation about contacting the White House. Wilson had recently rebuffed the Negro Equal Rights League, having taken offense to their request for an audience. The backlash from reform groups, Parker hoped, would force Wilson to "demonstrate that he can receive delegations with courtesy and sympathy." The society could take advantage of this "psychological moment" as long as they were careful not to incur the ire of the Indian Bureau.[36] Wilson, it turned out, was relatively cordial to the SAI's overtures. He set the meeting's time and date for 12:15 p.m., December 10, 1914.

That morning, Coolidge, Parker, and the SAI leadership exited Washington's Hotel Powhatan and walked briskly to the White House. Wilson summoned the group into a reception room, where he and the society's main advocate in the Senate, Robert Owen, awaited them. Oneida cornet virtuoso Dennison Wheelock read a two-page petition detailing the legislative steps needed to define the legal status of Indigenous peoples and settle Indian claims. Wilson remained silent but appeared "impressed." Coolidge gave a short speech explaining the aims of the society, and Rep. Charles D. Carter followed up with some remarks. As the time allotted for the delegation rapidly came to a close, Wilson admitted never devoting any "special thought to the Indian" but swore to give their concerns "his most earnest consideration." At that, the delegates retreated to their hotel for an "informal conference." The banquet's party favors, "small Indian war clubs tied with white ribbons," delighted everyone.[37] That evening, Wilson dictated a letter to Parker iterating his earnest interest but promising nothing.[38] Nothing is what followed. Though the society's leadership had fleetingly occupied the halls of power, Wilson was unwilling to take up their cause.[39]

The inconsequential meeting with the president behind them, Coolidge and Parker turned their attention toward planning the next SAI conference, vetting sites such as San Francisco and Oklahoma City.[40] They very quickly decided on Lawrence, Kansas, convinced that the central location held the greatest potential for attracting delegates. Coolidge resolutely vowed, "I shall do all I can to make the Lawrence Conference as great a success as possible."[41] Parker, however, was in pain. Succumbing to the stresses of running the *Quarterly Journal* and performing his duties as secretary-treasurer, he suggested the office be split.[42] Coolidge agreed but insisted that any new officer be "in harmony with the spirit of the Society and the movement." He, too, had expended much energy and had donated funds for the SAI's benefit. The "ideal," he wrote, was for the leadership "to devote all their time to the work."[43] This wish was entirely unrealistic. The other officers had demanding careers, and the society was so poor that even employing part-time stenographers stretched the budget. Still, as Coolidge shared with Montezuma, the SAI could only flourish if everyone followed his example.

I am working every day, and most days all day, to drum up members for the organization, and seeing individual Indians, and correspond- ing with many of them, besides writing articles, making addresses to Whites and Indians in more or less large groups, in my clubs and social gatherings, on the street or on the train, at home and in church, first, last, and all the time, the Society of American Indians and my race are uppermost. If every Indian mother's son in the Society could say the same thing and say it truthfully, I believe the Society of American Indians would be irresistible and have ample in the treasury.[44]

The doctor could offer sympathy, though he was truthfully overwhelmed by deep frustrations of his own.

Since the early 1900s, Montezuma had been reconnecting with his past, making annual trips to Arizona and redeveloping bonds with surviving relatives. Over these years, he had become involved in securing water rights for the Yavapai on the Fort McDowell Reservation. The Indian Bureau and the Arizona agents, always wary of outside interference, viewed Montezuma as threatening. His letter-writing campaigns, public criticisms, and congressional testimony had convinced even the neighboring Pima Indians, who had kidnapped and sold Wassaja as a boy, to solicit his help in resisting the government's designs on their lands.[45]

In April 1915, Montezuma asked Coolidge's assistance in convincing the bureau to allow him to visit several reservations. In either a delaying tactic or a plain attempt to thwart him, Commissioner Cato Sells insisted that Montezuma first travel to Washington and explain himself, because "a visit of this sort by a representative of the Society might complicate matters." Coolidge let the matter drop, leaving his friend furious at Sells's comment.[46] "Right here," Montezuma told Coolidge, "I emphatically suggest that the Society act independently. Is the Society dictated by the Indian bureau what we must do? If it is, the Society is not an indepen- dent organization." Without representatives on the reservations, there was plainly no way to obtain reliable, firsthand information. Coolidge's unwillingness to fight harder offended Montezuma. "For myself, I do not ask it," he protested, "but when I am working for the Indians, it is the duty of the Society to back me up."[47] The mounting anger expressed in his letter would soon explode into an open campaign to chastise the SAI for its inaction on the issue of the bureau's abolition.

In the summer of 1915, Coolidge was intensely busy, visiting Lac du Flambeau, Wisconsin, to meet with Ojibwe returned students; Estes Park, Colorado, to speak at a YMCA conference; and San Francisco, California, to participate in the Congress on Indian Progress at the invitation of Charles Dagenett.[48] On the way to California, Coolidge passed through Wyoming. Peering out the train window, he hoped to catch a glimpse of Lander or Laramie. When he arrived in San Francisco, Dagenett greeted him, then quickly departed for the East, where his mother had taken seriously ill. Left alone, Coolidge needed a means to travel the city. He considered buying a fancy, horse-drawn Studebaker for $90 but balked at the price. A secondhand buggy for $10 would have to do. Though he missed his family terribly, Coolidge delivered a series of speeches at churches and before Indian students throughout mid-August while at times accompanied by Cato Sells.[49] Coolidge was disgusted to learn that in California, nearly 20 percent of the surviving Indian population, some two thousand people, remained "landless and homeless." At later public events, he publicized the fact that many were "so poor that they are eating grasshoppers to keep alive"—a terrible irony "in a State bursting with plenty." Likewise dismaying, Coolidge discovered that many returned students in California trying to make their way in white society felt mistreated by "people who called themselves Christians and who turned a cold shoulder to them," leveling quite a rebuke against the white community.[50]

When Coolidge returned to Faribault in late August, he prepared to leave once more and attend the Society of American Indians' fifth annual conference in Lawrence, Kansas. The city was home to the second-largest, off-reservation Indian boarding school, the Haskell Institute, where a portion of the sessions were planned. Haskell boasted a questionable legacy. In the 1880s mortality was so high that some entering students survived as little as a few months, falling victim to measles and pneumonia. Conditions had improved slightly by the 1910s but not much. In 1912 a group of students sent a petition to the commissioner of Indian affairs requesting that the school be discontinued. Haskell superintendent John

R. Wise, deeply embarrassed, began a series of interrogations, ultimately concluding that the petition had been sent by a student who had been forced to attend against that student's will.[51] These incidents did not bother the SAI delegates. In 1913 Arthur C. Parker had been contacted by a Kickapoo Indian, Scho-tha, who wrote to the society and hoped the leadership would intervene to free his son from Haskell for a brief stay at home. Scho-tha complained that his reservation agent had "deceived" him and that efforts to see his son had been blocked. As requested, Parker did raise the issue with Wise, suggesting that it was "better for the boy" to be kept at Haskell.[52] Wise may have liked Parker, but he feared holding the SAI meeting at the school, even suggesting to Coolidge that it might "stir up insubordinate spirit."[53]

The fifth annual conference began on September 28, 1915, and ran to October 3. Although the turnout totaled a mere eighty-five members, the number was greater than at Madison, and important figures such as Montezuma, Baldwin, Dagenett, Roe Cloud, and Sloan all attended.[54] Parker had invited President Wilson, who graciously declined but asked that his "very great interest in everything that affects the welfare and advancement of the American Indians" be noted.[55] Associate member Richard Henry Pratt made the trip to Kansas, ever loyal to the cause Wilson took care to ignore. Among the attendees at Lawrence were two new faces—Gertrude Bonnin, a Yankton Dakota woman, and Philip Gordon, an Ojibwe Catholic priest then serving as Haskell's chaplain.

Bonnin's route to Kansas reflected the magnitude of her intelligence and determination. Born in 1876 on the Yankton Reservation of South Dakota, she had gone to a Quaker boarding school in Indiana at age eight, suffering all the cultural dislocation and homesickness one would expect. She fought through it all to establish herself as a writer in Boston after an eighteen-month stint at Carlisle—a period she did not recall fondly. Under the pen name Zitkala-Ša (Red Bird in Lakota), Bonnin pilloried the school in three semi-autobiographical stories for the *Atlantic Monthly* in early 1900. Following a brief engagement to Carlos Montezuma, she rejected East Coast society, married an Indian Service clerk at Yankton, and in 1902 relocated to Uintah and Ouray Reservation in Utah. At Uintah, Bonnin taught at the same Whiterocks school that Grace Coolidge had two years earlier. Later, she inaugurated a community center movement to aid the Utes through organization and self-help.[56] Philip Gordon, by contrast, had led a privileged life as the favorite son of a well-established French-Ojibwe dynasty in Wisconsin. In 1913 after years of extensive travel and education in Europe, at only twenty-eight years old, he became the first Indigenous person ordained a Catholic priest in the United States. After working as an assistant missionary on the Ojibwe reservations in his home state, Gordon had been chosen by the Bureau of Catholic Indian Missions to oversee religious instruction at Haskell. He had arrived less than a month before the SAI conference.[57]

In their society debuts, Gordon spoke on moral responsibility; Bonnin, on her community center work at Uintah.[58] Judging by the published papers, Sherman Coolidge did not play a large role at Lawrence aside from a talk on the evils of liquor and an informal meeting with Haskell's student body.[59] The students heard stories of his recent sojourn to California, where he had met a group of Paiute children on a playground. The Paiutes, Coolidge noted, were often "looked down upon by humanity" as "Diggers." But when he asked the boys what they would do with a "white man's chance" in life, one of them replied, "Yes; give us half the white man's chance and we will take the other half." "That is the spirit of those Digger Indians," Coolidge mused, while exhorting the Indian students at Haskell to "take a stand" with the SAI to secure a bright future.[60] The future of the society itself, however, looked dark.

Some very contentious things were said at Lawrence. Referencing these disputes in the *Quarterly Journal*, Parker indicated the "danger" of "overriding all rules, principles and universal interests" in favor of "personal or private interest."[61] He was alluding to two issues that would destroy the society by the end of the decade, with the first being the ceremonial use of peyote. Several active Omaha peyotists had attended, as had Thomas Sloan, a supporter of the religion. It is likely that they collectively requested that the society intervene to shield them from the persecution of reservation agents or even Christian missionaries.[62] Wanting to avoid controversy, Parker neatly omitted these discussions from the pages of the *Quarterly*. The second issue, the Indian Bureau's abolition, was harder to ignore. The very loud and very passionate Carlos Montezuma had made quite an impression at Lawrence with his conference address, "Let My People Go," which appeared in the *American Indian Magazine* (the renamed *Quarterly*) five months later. The essay was Montezuma's clarion call to liberate Indians from a reservation system that held them as "prisoners" under the Indian Bureau, whose "slimy clutches of horrid greed" usurped lands and devoured property. Some of the blame for this abomination lay at the feet of the Society of American Indians' leaders, who, complacent in their relative freedom, had renounced their mission. Montezuma asked his fellow members to support a congressional bill to abolish the bureau, insisting that only this radical step could win Natives their liberty and allow their progress within white society. However politically suicidal the measure, Montezuma's conviction that freed Indigenous peoples would, without question, excel in Euro-American society revealed his degree of faith in his brethren. Indians had "a running chance with the public," he stated, "but no chance with the Indian Bureau."[63]

Montezuma's attacks at Lawrence left more than a few mouths agape. Parker called the response "a riot." No record of Coolidge's reaction appears in the *American Indian Magazine*, but his correspondence with Parker indicates that a tussle ensued between Coolidge and Montezuma, in which the latter found himself roundly humiliated. Eight months later, Parker was still going on about how the doctor had "not yet recovered from the stinging effect" of Coolidge's "squelching" at Haskell.[64] Neither Coolidge nor Parker were great fans of the bureau, but for their taste, Montezuma had simply gone too far. They saw the SAI as a watchdog that was meant to work with the bureau and influence policy for the better, not as a movement whose goal was to attack and overthrow it.[65] Philip Gordon, by contrast, was utterly convinced.[66] The young priest threw his support behind the bureau's abolition, nominating Thomas Sloan for SAI president.[67] Gordon and Sloan's attempt to dethrone Coolidge failed but not by much. In the voting, he barely retained his position for the fourth time. Sloan was relegated to vice president on legislation; Parker was reelected SAI secretary. Per his request, the duties of treasurer devolved to Indian Bureau accountant Marie Baldwin, whose expertise was needed to straighten out the organization's finances.[68] Regardless, the Montezuma-Sloan-Gordon triumvirate had not surrendered its quest to see the bureau liquidated. Over the coming years, the men would make their presence felt.

Coolidge's private feelings on the society's growing discord can be gleaned from Grace's correspondence. She had accompanied Sherman to Lawrence and looked on in horror as the gathering devolved into "quite a stormy meeting." Both she and Sherman were dismayed by what they perceived as "wire pulling and electioneering." Together they blamed the "very clever" Philip Gordon, who was "backed by the bad element of the society." They were pleased, though, in noting that the predominantly Roman Catholic SAI membership had chosen Sherman as president. Grace nevertheless wondered why some did not understand the "purely altruistic and philanthropic" nature of the society and hence chose to use their membership for "personal ends." Fortunately, she felt there was still cause to be "encouraged." The Coolidges remained convinced that the SAI was "shaping Indian ends in a really remarkable way." The Indian Bureau seemed to advocate every reform suggested at the conferences as if it was its own. As long as progress occurred, Sherman and Grace did not "give a whoop for the glory."[69]

One hardly notices these fast-growing conflicts in the official Lawrence platform, which was published later in 1915. The moderate demands mirrored those of previous conferences: the creation of a court of claims under the Stephens bill and "a careful and wise definition of Indian status" under the Carter Code Bill, which was now supplemented by a call for Indian citizenship. Other items included a reorganization of Indian education and improvements in hygiene inspections on reservations. Finally, the society recognized the groundswell of temperance organizing throughout the nation, requesting the "suppression of liquor in the Indian country."[70] Coolidge had likely suggested this initiative. Since his 1913 appearance at the Anti-Saloon League conference in Columbus, he had been counseling Indian students against alcohol, "the Indian's greatest enemy." At Carlisle, he had discussed how "poisonous liquor destroys human life" and asked that the standards of the past be respected. "The Indians used to just bar their tent doors with a stick and everything was safe," he reminded them. "But now, the doors have to be locked, and then, sometimes, someone breaks in and steals." This could not continue. The "honor" of Indian ancestors had to be upheld.[71]

But while those in the society certainly agreed with these sentiments, the issues of peyote and bureau abolition that came to the fore at Lawrence were another matter. Parker left Kansas deeply troubled, and in the wake of the conference he pleaded for "harmonious action along the lines of great principles" in an editorial for the *American Indian Magazine*. "Insistence on a certain political policy not general in its application," he warned, "will prove fatal."[72] He was quite correct. His appeal echoed Coolidge's in his first speech as SAI president in 1912. "Let us have harmony," he had entreated. "Without that, we can do nothing."[73] He, too, was quite correct.

14

State of Chaos, State of War

Arthur C. Parker wasted little time in expressing his fears to Sherman Coolidge concerning the "seeming attempts to overthrow the principles of the Society" made by Carlos Montezuma, Philip Gordon, and Thomas Sloan at the Lawrence conference.[1] This "strange combination" of allies, he claimed, each bore "a special grouch against the Bureau." Montezuma had been thwarted by the commissioner of Indian affairs in his effort to legally represent the Yavapai and Apaches, Gordon despised the bureau because his brother had died without receiving his trust fund, and Sloan had been trying, unsuccessfully, to be appointed commissioner himself for several years. "These facts as I have given them to you," Parker cautioned Coolidge, "are confidential." Fortunately, he had good news to share as well. Parker had recently traveled to New York's scenic Lake Mohonk for the annual conference of the Indian Rights Association. There, he had read the Lawrence platform and spoken "for several hours" with Commissioner Cato Sells, who had offered his support for the society's goals. Sells also expressed his irritation with Sloan, an admission that gave Parker a "considerable thrill of pleasure." Both men shared a dislike for the Omaha attorney. Parker felt Sloan kept company with "questionable characters" (meaning peyotists); Sells bristled at Sloan's unabashed criticisms of the bureau. Luckily, there were ways to defuse Sloan if he got too out of hand. The society could merely "repudiate" his actions or subtlety exclude him. As such, the next conference would be a small one, mainly for the "thinking people." Anyone seeking "disputes" would be discouraged from attending.[2] In truth, much was at stake. Parker suspected that Sloan was attempting a takeover of the society, and a well-connected friend had mentioned that "if the present management of the Society was destroyed it was: 'Good Bye to the power of the SAI.'"[3]

While Parker's notes to Coolidge sometimes appear duplicitous or even conspiratorial, there existed another side to their partnership. Over the years, the pair had been working diligently to remedy problems that both Indian nations and individuals had presented to the society. The annual gatherings, with their largely ineffectual speeches, debates, and platforms, had been one matter, but behind the scenes, Coolidge and Parker had intervened in a variety of cases—both legal and personal—that required action. In just one letter from December 1915, Parker listed for Coolidge the status of sixteen incidents that were either resolved or still under SAI scrutiny. Together, the duo had aided the Crow Nation with regulations affecting its reservation school and leasing of lands; petitioned the Indian Bureau to investigate various issues concerning the Potawatomi, Ojibwes, Brulés, Senecas, and Choctaws; and compelled the Bureau of Municipal Research of New York to conduct a study on the Indian Bureau's inefficiency. Coolidge had also made a point of advocating for the Arapahos and Shoshones at Wind River, notifying the bureau of their "destitution."[4] This was not his only concern. Having supported the controversial land cessions in the 1890s and early 1900s, Coolidge was now fighting for the peoples' compensation and the continuation of the tribes' water rights. Through Senator Owen and another ally, Sen. Paul O. Husting (D-WI), Coolidge was able to demand the attention of the Senate Committee on Indian Affairs and at least try to hold the bureau accountable for its egregious mismanagement of the reservation system.

In a 1916 letter read aloud at a Senate committee hearing, Coolidge painted a stark portrait of the situation at Wind River. For years, the residents had watched as whites settled on ceded lands for which recompence was still pending. Both the Arapahos and the Shoshones wanted the cession canceled and the lands returned. Meanwhile, the agent was failing to protect lands allotted to "the aged, widows, orphans, minors, and persons who by force of circumstances are absent from the reservation." In these cases, allotment owners were facing a December 1916 deadline to show they had made use of the land and then apply for water rights. Missing the deadline meant the lands would lose considerable value. Leasing to acquire water rights was one option, but many Indians were suspicious of agreements made with the help of the agent and were unwilling to go through the process of seeking written consent from Washington. Coolidge hoped that the Senate committee could compel the bureau to secure water rights for allottees at Wind River and to study the idea of reverting some of the unoccupied ceded lands. His letter also exposed "an old story." Many Arapahos and Shoshones, "driven by hunger," regularly "ate sheep and stock that had died from disease." In one case, thousands of sheep had drowned in flooding caused by an early winter thaw. The event had been "a godsend" to a people facing chronic undernourishment. Assistant Commissioner of Indian Affairs E. B. Merritt brushed off the criticisms, maintaining to the committee that Coolidge was "mistaken" and that the bureau had not been neglectful of leasing or water rights. Merritt also ignored the allegations of chronic hunger.[5]

Coolidge's own fortunes presented a tremendous contrast to the poverty many Native peoples endured in the 1910s. Following the death of Grace's mother, her father began keeping his daughter in some comfort, allowing the Coolidges a much better standard of living than that afforded by a missionary's salary. Then on March 24, 1916, Gardner Wetherbee died in Manhattan at age eighty-two.[6] Upon receiving the news, Grace traveled to New York with Sallie and Rosie. Following a large funeral in the city, mourners took a private train to Kensico Cemetery in Valhalla, Westchester County, for the interment. With the Wetherbee townhouse for sale, Grace and the children stayed with Anne Talbot in the village of Tuckahoe, "a sweet place out of the racket of NY."[7] At the reading of the will, Grace learned that she had inherited over $1 million, nearly $25 million in today's terms. More was to come later.[8] When she told Sherman the news, Grace doubted that there would be "anymore dealings with the family," suggesting the gulf between her values and those of her wealthy relatives. She lamented "the end of all the old life" but was happy to be in Tuckahoe with Anne; her husband, Donald; and the children.[9] Sallie was now nine. Rosie was four and capable of causing trouble. One night, Grace could not get her to bed down. When ordered to sleep "for the 1000th time," Rosie protested, indignantly, "I *am* asleep."[10] Grace spent a month in the East, taking a trip to Atlantic City with Virginia and Effie, still studying at Carlisle.[11]

Once at home again in Faribault, Grace and Sherman began planning to settle elsewhere and to found an orphanage for Indian children. Colorado Springs was first in their mind. "No fun being a millionaire here," Grace joked in a letter to Anne.[12] Though Sherman could have given up the church and led a life of leisure, he held church posts until his death. And there was also his work with the society.

On September 26, 1916, the SAI met in Cedar Rapids, Iowa, for its annual conference. Sponsors included the Quaker Oats Company.[13] Over four days at Coe College, delegates sought to mend the rifts that had appeared at Lawrence—by exclusion. Coolidge and Parker had chosen the remote location to discourage the attendance of the more bothersome members.[14] In one case, the tactic worked. Sloan, upset with the leadership and the choice of venue, did not appear.[15] Montezuma and Gordon bucked expectations and made the long trip west. Still, as Parker desired, turnout was poor. Unfortunately, so was the society. The treasury had reverted to its usual state following the flush of donations at Lawrence.[16] In another worrying sign, Coolidge had been wrestling with the idea of resigning his presidency since the summer. Parker, alarmed, had insisted that any decision be put off, but the stress of the position had become too enervating for Coolidge. For Parker, it was much the same. In an effort at commiseration, he admitted, "I can also say that while I do remain in this position my personal welfare is entirely neglected."[17]

Coolidge's own exhaustion and the difficulties facing the SAI prompted a reflective convocation on the conference's first morning. His speech referenced the experimental nature of the society and how that experiment was still in the "process of formation." In essence, the membership had undertaken the work of several established Indian rights associations, religious groups, and the U.S. government itself. The society had also striven to respect, preserve, and showcase the best of Native cultures while trying to solve the "problem into which the race has been thrust by the white race." Given the enormity of these tasks, it was no surprise that challenges had presented themselves. The question was whether these challenges would lead to the "destruction and shame of the Indians." Recourse to "destructive criticism, muckraking or abolishing," Coolidge noted, only detracted from the "strength and harmony" needed for success. Without a concerted effort to make the government act toward a path to citizen-ship, Indians would remain in "a state of chaos."[18] If Coolidge thought his plea for unity would preclude a repeat of the divisive grievances aired at Lawrence, he had erred.

From the start, the issues Coolidge and Parker hoped to avoid—the bureau's abolition and the peyote religion—quickly became the main focus of the conference. Concerning the latter point, those voicing opinions sided mostly with the leadership. White associate member and bureau employee Henry Larson denounced peyote as a "drug" that "demoralizes, destroys or degrades" the mind and body.[19] Richard Henry Pratt, compar-ing Indians to "weak children," called on the government to take hold of peyote "by the throat and drive it out" by any means necessary. As such, he advocated passage of the Gandy bill (named for Rep. H. L. Gandy [D-SD]), which sought national prohibition.[20] Gertrude Bonnin, who since 1913 had watched peyote spread on the Uintah Reservation, lent her support to Pratt's sentiments. She had already launched an anti-peyote crusade across the West with the help of the Indian Rights Association and local temperance groups, publishing pamphlets on the alleged sexual immorality, family strife, addiction, and even death by overdose caused by the cactus.[21] Carlisle graduate Delos Lone Wolf was the one person to defend the peyote religion at Cedar Rapids. He scoffed at the idea that peyote was "killing Indians," announcing that, as a Kiowa and a Christian, he had been ingesting the cactus for fifteen years without incident. Peyote was instead a way to reach "lost Indians." With its aid, he had converted "the hardest cases that the missionary or anyone else could not reach."[22] Lone Wolf persuaded few, and at the conference's end, the SAI called for a legislative ban.[23] Yet, even with the peyote issue contained, the conference quickly devolved into the chaos Coolidge had feared.

Carlos Montezuma had come to Cedar Rapids with more than a few things to say. Courting controversy, he unabashedly declared that "Indian employees in the service of the Indian Bureau could not be loyal to the Indian race and to their real interests." Coolidge immediately took issue, retorting, "I do not know how many times I must get up and say that I believe an Indian who is a Government employee can be loyal to his race and at the same time be loyal to his Government." Caught off guard by the equation of the government with the Indian Bureau, Montezuma rushed to clarify his thoughts. "The Indian Bureau," he rejoined, "not the Government." "The Government is represented by the Indian Bureau," countered Coolidge, invoking the blanket patriotism to which many SAI members deferred. Montezuma, in turn, objected to being put in the "very embarrassing position" of criticizing the government when he had merely meant to criticize "the system" of the bureau. After more heated back-and-forth, Coolidge lost patience. Defending his association with the Indian Bureau and the substance of his own life, he told the doctor, "I think the Indian Bureau has its work to do and we have our work to do and I would like as much as possible to cooperate with it as I would like to work with any other organization or institution that is trying to do anything for the Indians. . . . That is why I work when I can in favor of the race, at all times. . . . I worked as an Arapahoe Indian, a full-blood—just as full blood as Dr. Montezuma ever dared to be. . . . I have not suffered for nothing, for I have suffered for my race." The speech briefly silenced Montezuma, but Philip Gordon quickly revived the subject, denying that "a member in the employment of the Government is at the same time loyal to this Society." Falsely equating support for the bureau's abolition with membership in the SAI, he suggested that no government employee could speak freely without fear of repercussions.

Incensed at Gordon's claims, Indian Bureau accountant Marie Baldwin interjected. "I do not know," she insisted, "where at any time the Government clerk does not dare to say just what he thinks about the Indian Bureau." Baldwin herself had expressed support for the bureau's liquidation on many occasions, but she understood there were still "Indians who are not ready now to be put out in the world to take care of themselves." The ideal was to work for a day when there would be "no need" for a bureau. Gertrude Bonnin, whose husband worked for the Indian Service, agreed. She noted that it was silly to suspect that "just out of consideration of holding a job and getting a very small salary," a Native bureau employee would stay silent on an important issue. Most Indians she knew in the service were highly educated and only labored in the "wilderness"— meaning reservations—"from a sense of duty." Coolidge then moved to terminate the discussion, asking, "Is it right for us to act this way?" All present sought "the same end" of alleviating the "state of chaos" in Indian affairs, but wardship had to be maintained until all Indians could survive without government paternalism. In seeking to abolish the bureau, the society had to "take care and do not abolish the Indians." Coolidge added, "That has been tried many times, and it has failed."[24]

At one point in the debate, Montezuma jumped out of his chair. Waving his arms, he shouted at Coolidge, "I am an Apache . . . and you are an Arapahoe. I can lick you. My tribe has licked your tribe before." Coolidge, standing at least a head taller than Montezuma, coolly replied, "Well, I am from Missouri."[25] The quick retort, meaning something like "So let's see you try" in its allusion to the "Show-Me" state, caused an uproar of laughter, breaking the tension. Reporters, insensitive to the humor of the moment, seized on the incident as good copy. One headline read, "Tribal War Averted at Indian Meeting."[26] War had been averted but not disagreement. Despite Coolidge's pleas for decorum, Montezuma and Gordon refused to moderate their views. In prepared remarks, Gordon once more asserted that the SAI should "go on record as opposed to the system."[27] Montezuma, offering sharper criticism, accused the leadership of timidity in the face of problems that demanded "radical" solutions. If the society wanted to "get into the right road," there was no choice but to condemn the bureau.[28]

Outside of such dramatics, Coolidge secured meaningful press coverage at Cedar Rapids. According to news reports, he spoke before hundreds of "leading citizens" and students in the Coe College chapel, discussing the society and illustrating his points with "amusing" stories that "kept the audience laughing."[29] Later on, Coolidge sat before a gathering of locals at the Hotel Montrose for an in-depth interview with one of the city's papers. In recounting his life story and sharing his ambitions for reform, he elicited understanding from an audience that was generally prejudiced against Indigenous peoples. Coolidge claimed that while "the civilization of the Indians" was nearing conclusion, greater measures were needed to bridge cultural misunderstandings. "The European found the Indian with his own civilization," he explained, "but the European looked on the Indian's civilization as different from his, therefore inferior." Though they boasted a long and independent history, Natives had been forced to become "an imitation white man." Expecting an ancient people to remake their ways within several generations had simply been folly. Coolidge nevertheless hoped that through government cooperation with the SAI, this process could be humanely expedited. When complete, the society could "write a new history of the Indian with honor to himself and the nation."[30]

To this effect, Cedar Rapids delegates put forth a final conference platform that reaffirmed earlier principles but added several crucial items. Bowing to the "radicals," as Montezuma and Gordon were now dubbed, the leadership called for the dismantling of the Indian Bureau following a settlement of all claims. The time had come for Native peoples to be "invested with the full privileges of citizens." Also significant, the society pushed for the passage of the Gandy bill, citing the "baneful effects" of peyote ingestion on Indians' health and morals. In the election of officers, Coolidge declined to seek another term as president. He gave no official reason for his abdication, nor did the *American Indian Magazine*. Out of respect for his past service, the membership declared him honorary president "by acclamation." Baldwin stayed on as treasurer, Bonnin took the post of secretary, and Parker, despite his comparative youth, was elected president, saving the conference for the moderates.[31]

Sherman Coolidge left Iowa displeased with Montezuma and dejected by the poor turnout.[32] His destination was not home but Wind River, where he had business. At Fort Washakie, people appeared friendly and asked him whether he was returning for good. Yet, when he gave a sermon, only a handful of Arapahos and Shoshones came to listen. The slight made him feel "depressed and sad." Not even his relation Yellow Calf bothered to attend, choosing instead to stay home, "feasting and smoking." The peyote religion had spread at Wind River, with Roberts and his missionaries helpless to curb its popularity. And, as in the past, many Arapahos were still "complaining of being hard up and hungry."[33] In truth, little had improved economically. Lumber companies consistently violated contracts on the reservation. The one bright spot was that the situation with water rights now seemed satisfactory.[34] To his credit, Coolidge did what he could, sending out word that he would take in any orphaned child in need of a home.[35] Some Arapahos contacted him, and for a time he planned to assume legal guardianship of several children, including a boy the age of Runs On Top when he embarked on his new life.[36] For an unexplained reason, the adoptions were never completed, though Coolidge did vaguely reference problematic bureaucratic procedures in his letters.[37] The only bright prospect for Wind River was the discovery of oil, which could mean potential wealth for the tribes if the resources were managed fairly.[38] Coolidge left after several weeks, alone and saddened. However, he did leave a U.S. citizen, having been declared "competent" for the full title to his allotments. After years away, the ranch he had developed in the 1880s and lived on until 1910 was finally legally his. Alluding to a widely practiced ritual in which newly "competent" Indians would fire arrows into the air to signify having left behind the old life, Sherman jokingly wrote to Grace, "I have shot my last arrow and taken hold of the plow."[39]

Bad news awaited, courtesy of Carlos Montezuma, when Coolidge returned to Faribault. Nursing wounds from Cedar Rapids, the Yavapai firebrand had publicly repudiated the society and openly criticized Coolidge in his Indian rights journal, *Wassaja*. The personal attack read: "Ex-President Coolidge of the Society of American Indians says that he can be loyal to the Indian race and at the same time serve the Indian Bureau. *Wassaja* wonders if he serves God and the Devil in the same way."[40] This was no friendly barb. Montezuma only recommitted to the SAI thanks to the persuasion of his ex-fiancée, Gertrude Bonnin. By missive, while soothing his battered ego, she implored him to recognize that the society had "not sold out to the Bureau."[41] This effort at reconciliation succeeded, though scars lingered.[42] Coolidge's withdrawal from his role in the SAI leadership had opened the door to a factionalism that would subsume the organization and sadly spell its ultimate demise.

The battles within the Society of American Indians were of slight consequence in comparison to unfolding world events. In 1914 the Great War had commenced in Europe following the assassination of Archduke Franz Ferdinand, presumptive heir to the Austro-Hungarian throne, by a Serbian nationalist. The U.S. government and public had initially taken an isolationist stance. President Wilson even won reelection with the slogan "He Kept Us out of War." Yet, once reinstalled in the White

House, Wilson radically changed his rhetoric, contending in his inaugural speech that America's "fortunes as a nation" hinged on the outcome of the international struggle. Following the destruction of several U.S. ships by German submarines in February 1917 and the sensational decoding of the Zimmerman telegram, in which Germany encouraged Mexico to invade the United States, Congress declared war on April 6.[43] Many Americans, however, remained unconvinced. By mid-May, only seventy-three thousand men had volunteered for military service, far fewer than the million deemed necessary for victory.[44] Congress moved with uncharacteristic swiftness. The Selective Service Act, the first draft since the Civil War, passed on May 18.[45]

Cognizant of Americans' opposition to involvement in an overseas conflict, the Wilson administration created the Committee on Public Information (cpi) to influence public opinion. The cpi employed propaganda in the form of posters, pamphlets, rallies, and slogans such as "100% American," stoking hatred for Kaiser Wilhelm II and all things German. The response was enthusiastic.[46] In April 1918, for example, an Illinois mob publicly lynched German-born Robert Prager as police calmly observed. Prager was suspected of holding left-wing, and therefore anti-American, views. After a jury acquitted his murderers, one member declared, "Well, I guess nobody can say we aren't loyal now."[47] The *Washington Post* promptly lauded the trial's outcome as "a healthful and wholesome awakening in the interior of the country."[48] Federal legislation lent legitimacy to such vigilante actions. The 1917 Espionage Act introduced prison sentences for activities construed as anti-war, while the 1918 Sedition Act criminalized "disloyal, profane, scurrilous, or abusive language" regarding the government and national symbols.[49] Persecution also extended to pacifists, labor unions, and left-wing leaders, all common targets of the American Protective League, a 250,000-man-strong volunteer policing organization that monitored citizens through illegal searches and raids, and reported directly to the Bureau of Investigation, the precursor of the Federal Bureau of Investigation.[50] Socialist leader and presidential candidate Eugene Debs found himself sentenced to a decade in prison after allegedly advocating draft evasion in June 1918.[51] American progressivism had devolved into American jingoism, and the cause had come from within.

American progressives collectively supported intervention in the Great War, believing that militarization could have positive consequences for everyday life.[52] Progressive icon Walter Lippmann, who helped create the CPI, wrote in the *New Republic* of how the war represented an opportunity to organize the nation at a new level of efficiency and to create unity in combating social inequities. Bonded through common endeavor, Americans would better regulate business, enact beneficial labor legislation, and perhaps nationalize private trusts for the public good. Even conscription was seen as having the benefit of "smashing all the petty class distinctions that now divide, and prompting a brand of real democracy."[53] Like their progressive Euro-American counterparts, the Society of American Indians also looked on the bright side of war, certain that if Natives contributed they would be recognized as equals and rewarded with U.S. citizenship. Parker, in particular, spearheaded this initiative, promoting military service in the pages of the *American Indian Magazine*.[54] There was basis for his hope. Just months after America intervened, Rep. Carl Hayden (D-AZ) introduced an Indian citizenship bill in the House. Though it failed to pass, SAI member Rep. Charles D. Carter commenced work on a new bill. None of this is to say that the society held one perspective on the war. In fact, the issue of how Native soldiers would serve caused considerable division.

Just after the passage of the Selective Service Act, Commissioner of Indian Affairs Cato Sells began aggressively recruiting on reservations. Native Americans, especially young men who had been boarding school educated, volunteered in great numbers. Their motivations ranged from patriotism and warrior traditions to economic incentives. While the SAI did not question the rightness of the recruiting methods, one question lingered. Under recommendation of the Board of Indian Commissioners, Sells sought Indian men for service in segregated units.[55] Montezuma and Gordon supported the policy.[56] Parker was skeptical, despite a friend's having mentioned to him, "Think of it! Ten thousand painted Indians decked in their war regalia, yelling their peculiar and blood-curdling yells, swooping down in a cavalry charge upon the Prussians! Wow, there's an idea for you to give the Kaiser chills and fever!"[57] Gertrude Bonnin, perhaps more than any, objected to this vision. She dubbed segregated

Indian units a "walking reservation," fearful the U.S. government had embarked on a "scheme to utterly annihilate the Red Man, by a whole-sale slaughter!"[58] Once the War Department dropped the proposal, the Society of American Indians, Coolidge included, fervently endorsed Indian participation.[59] The *American Indian Magazine* suggested he and Gordon serve as army chaplains.[60] Coolidge recommended Parker join the war effort as an officer.[61] He need not have. Parker was already hard at work, cooperating with the government and informing on any Indians in New York who were not yet registered for the draft.[62] Indian blood, it appeared, was an appropriate trade for the hope, someday, of Indian citizenship.

Sherman Coolidge was a Christian who had seen firsthand the consequences of war and violence. The tragic events of his childhood had informed his life's work as a seeker of peace and reconciliation among Indians and whites, and among Indians themselves. But as the adopted son of a military officer and avowed patriot, he fully supported the U.S. intervention in Europe as well as segregated Indian units. One article from the period remarked on how Coolidge "thrills with pride at the way his people have rallied to the cause of humanity in the present conflict." The most effective way to demonstrate Indian virtues, he argued, was through a "Noble Red Man Regiment." Indians, "proud and high spirited," were "naturally warriors" with "education and athletic training equal to the Anglo Saxon." Coolidge asked, "Would not a Red regiment of Indian braves add glory to our history just as regiments of the Scottish Highlanders do to theirs?"[63]

There is a remote possibility, however, that Sherman Coolidge's initial views on the war contained greater nuance. Grace's views certainly did. By January 1916, she had become disgusted with Germany's conduct but remained neutral, convinced that all nations were capable of "actively carrying out the policy of frightfulness." She elaborated on these views to Anne Talbot: "The Germans are the ones just now and as such I regard them as hateful antis. It may be us, next time. And this also I believe: Our hatred, which is stirred up and awakened by the present mad behavior of mankind, should be directed against not any one people, but against war, militarism, itself. That's the whole crux of being neutral. I mean I think so!"[64] As the war dragged on, Grace became more and more interested in "honest pacifism" and more and more alarmed by the intolerance of the wider American public.[65] In mid-1917 the pacifist bishop of Utah, Paul Jones, had been forced to flee California after participating in a small peace gathering in Pasadena. Jones was later forced to resign after an investigation by a special committee of the House of Bishops.[66] Grace called the events "a rather disgraceful straw" and rejected the notion that being a pacifist was tantamount to being "pro-German." Her disappointment was compounded when Jones subsequently declined to stand up proudly for his beliefs in public.[67] Unfortunately, Sherman's reaction appears lost.

In the summer of 1917, plans for the annual Society of American Indians conference were underway, with the location of Oklahoma City and the theme, "The American Indian in Patriotism, Production, Progress."[68] Parker, however, began to have second thoughts. Out of fear that the issues of bureau abolition, peyote, and the war might lead to another tussle as experienced in Cedar Rapids, he "postponed" the conference, citing the national emergency. In a letter that reflected the zeitgeist, he wrote Coolidge that it was probably best to hold conferences every three years and to shift the society's focus to "propaganda" that would encourage "loyal cooperation with the better things in the country." This way, the "hounds of evil" (Montezuma, Gordon, and Sloan) could be neutralized as a force in decision-making. After all, there was no reason to give "certain malcontents and peyote-drug defending lawyers" with "ulterior motives" greater opportunity for attack. Ultimately, it mattered little if the "Gordon-Monteys may yell."[69] Though Parker kept Coolidge informed on all society matters and even deferred to his advice as if he were still president, Coolidge had retreated from such controversies.[70] In the fall of 1916 and early spring of 1917, the Coolidge family traveled throughout the West for pleasure, including a long stay in Santa Barbara, California.[71] Then in mid-1917, Sherman was named a canon at St. Matthew's Cathedral in Laramie, Wyoming.[72] He traveled there alone, as he had to Oklahoma, to assess whether the post and city would suit him, while Grace continued her vacation in California. One morning while she and the children were approaching the picturesque city of Trinidad, the train suddenly stopped. Grace said, "I don't think this is Trinidad yet." "No," agreed Rosie, "this is some other Dad."[73]

Meanwhile, in Wyoming, Coolidge became distracted from his new post by a shameful situation involving one of his adopted daughters. In early September 1917, Virginia had been admitted to the nursing program at Wyoming General Hospital in Rock Springs. The head of the hospital was glad to have her, but the interim head nurse, Miss McDonough, refused to work with an Indian and wrote an "ugly letter" to Grace about Virginia's "nationality." McDonough was replaced after the head nurse, Miss Reed, returned to work. This change only made things worse. Playing on the racism of her fellow nurses, McDonough engineered a walkout. When the nursing staff demanded McDonough's reinstatement, even the governor of the state, Frank L. Houx, became involved. Horrified by the strike, he briefly considered firing every single nurse. A lack of qualified replacements precluded this measure. Coolidge arrived in Rock Springs near the end of September and, in a private meeting with the hospital head, told McDonough that "there should be no discrimination against Indians" and "that if Virgie was excluded she and the nurses and the hospital would inflict a wound which no surgeon or medicine could heal." After a lengthy berating, McDonough relented and even admitted that Virginia had "shown herself superior to the rest of the nurses." Coolidge hoped that the "difficulty" had "blown over quietly" but threatened to go to "higher authorities" if matters did not improve. Remarkably, Virginia had remained entirely unaware that she was the cause of the strike and was "happy and doing her work."[74] Sherman left "quite sure" that she would receive "decent treatment."[75] Only a month later did Virginia learn from Grace the cause of the walkout.[76] She resolved to stay and by all accounts did excellent and dedicated work.[77] Nonetheless, Grace aptly labeled the entire incident "a disgusting mess."[78] Perhaps because of lingering racist behavior, Virginia moved on to a hospital in Casper in 1921.[79]

Just after the Rock Springs hospital incident had been concluded, Grace urged Sherman to finally record his childhood in an autobiography. "You ought to have a lot of time and leisure for sitting in Sheridan," she observed. "Why not go down to the public stenographer in Sheridan and let her take down your 'recollections' and get that job really done this winter." She continued, "Do, Sherman. You owe it to the children."[80] Unfortunately, he became distracted, and he had only a handful of stories that Grace typed up years later. The cause of the distraction was the news that his and his family's allotments at Wind River had been "pronounced oil land." Coolidge quickly set about arranging oil leases for Virginia and Effie.[81] The government had offered an eighth royalty to the Arapahos, possibly ensuring future wealth.[82] Then in February 1918, Dr. George Hunting, the Episcopal bishop of Nevada, suddenly contacted Sherman and requested that he come "help out with his Indian work." Grace, Sallie, and Rosie traveled to Reno, where the family commenced "a good six months trial" to assess whether the city was an appropriate place to settle.[83] Within a month, Grace decided that Reno was as "nondescript and uninteresting" as Oklahoma, and the demands of Sherman's missionary activities were too onerous.[84] She explained to Anne Talbot that while the thousands of Indians in Nevada were "much in need of something," the work no longer appealed. "But, oh! my dear," she wrote, "how my heart does sink at being back in the old church grooves again! where the little is so important and the fundamentals are overlooked." Mainly, she wanted Sherman "to have work" in a stable and stimulating environment for the children. The family had been "drifting," which was "bad business" for all concerned, and Sherman's work for the SAI did not fill his time.[85] Settling in Denver looked like the best option.[86]

Throughout this period of transition, the Coolidges continued to support the Society of American Indians.[87] Their donations especially kept the *American Indian Magazine* afloat.[88] Though Parker was grateful, he was also unhappy as president. Hoping Coolidge would return, Parker commented that it was "too bad" that he was no longer serving.[89] Given the state of the society, Coolidge did not share such nostalgia for the old days. The decision to cancel the 1917 conference had been met with outrage in some quarters. Though Gordon stayed silent, Montezuma, suspicious that the Indian Bureau had a hand in the cancellation, did not. His journal, *Wassaja*, questioned whether Indians, held in bondage by the U.S. government, should submit to the draft. After calling "Indian Bureauism" the "Kaiserism of America," Montezuma was investigated by the Bureau of Investigation and forced to disavow his views in a written statement.[90] In contrast, Coolidge was busy enjoying himself. In June 1918 he attended the annual Hobart reunion in Geneva, New York, and was thrilled when a former classmate approached and asked, "Do you remember when you sat on my head at the cane rush to keep me down?"[91] Soon after, Coolidge received an urgent letter from Gertrude Bonnin, beseeching him to "preside" at the annual SAI conference planned for the fall in Pierre, South Dakota. Bonnin was deeply troubled because Arthur C. Parker intended to withdraw, leaving the society vulnerable to the radicalism of Philip Gordon.[92] Coolidge agreed and, reinvigorated, secretly resolved to win back the presidency.

The 1918 SAI conference began September 25, just as the Spanish influenza pandemic was reaching the East Coast after months of ravaging Europe. Without Bonnin, no such meeting would have occurred. A year prior, she had moved to Washington DC to better aid the society and was dedicating every ounce of her energy to the work. The same could not be said of Parker. As expected, he stayed far away, claiming that his duties at the New York Museum prohibited his attendance. In truth, he had given up, fearful he would not be reelected. The vacuum caused by Parker's absence was filled by Charles Eastman, who, after six years, had finally recommitted to the society he had help found. Eastman's presence was almost an anomaly. Fewer than thirty full members bothered to make the trip to Pierre.[93] The tone, however, was surprisingly civil. Even Montezuma, realizing the polarizing nature of his behavior, had published a pre-conference appeal in *Wassaja* for the membership to leave "ill feeling at home."[94] Coolidge was stunned at Montezuma's and Gordon's "changed attitude" and at how they treated him so respectfully. Each also talked of having read *Teepee Neighbors*. Sherman noted to Grace that the book, "no doubt, showed them that we know a thing or two about Indians and Indian Affairs on the reservations."[95] Regardless, no compliments could paper over the fact that the SAI was unravelling, though none would have known it from the first night's festivities.

In Pierre's opera house, Coolidge hosted an evening rally that opened with a local military band playing "Over There." Montezuma, the first speaker, told the story of his childhood, assuring the audience that though he was an Apache, he was "perfectly tame." Bonnin, donned in buckskin, followed with a poetry recital. Coolidge brought the evening to a close with a speech praising Indian contributions to the war effort, proudly announcing that nine thousand Natives were serving in the military.[96] This number accounted for 25 percent of all Indian men, 10 percent higher than the proportion of whites serving.[97] Coolidge likewise boasted that Indians had bought thousands of dollars of war bonds while also increasing their crop production to meet war needs. There was nevertheless an important political point to make: Indians were fighting to make the world safe for democracy. "Are you going, after the war," Coolidge asked, "to make democracy safe for the Indian?"[98]

Coolidge's question was pertinent. At the time of the Great War, half of the Indian population lived under noncitizen wardship status, overseen by the Indian Bureau on reservations. Montezuma addressed this fact with a fervid speech titled "Abolish the Indian Bureau," which repeated the arguments he had been making for years. As usual, not everyone was pleased. One associate member, Mrs. Rhoads, thoroughly denounced him for "poisoning the good work of the Indian department."[99] Thanks to the radicals, however, the membership voted for a resolution to abolish the bureau at the conference's end. In the election of officers, Coolidge attempted his comeback but was soundly defeated in his bids for president, then for first vice president. Instead, Charles Eastman took the SAI presidency, while Bonnin took the post of secretary-treasurer, forcing out Marie Baldwin, who did not attend. As secretary-treasurer, Bonnin lost no time in declaring herself editor of the *American Indian Magazine*. Having orchestrated the conference almost single-handedly, she had now taken over most of the vital leadership functions. Still desiring some influence on policy, Coolidge ended up as the chairman of the advisory board, a minor role.[100]

The 1918 SAI platform, published in the fall, reflected the resolution made in Pierre for the immediate abolition of the bureau. Coolidge did not agree, but he and the radical membership were unified on one matter: the SAI unanimously demanded an improvement of the Indian's legal status following the war as a top priority, with citizenship being the goal.[101] The conference also made another thing clear: Sherman Coolidge's time had passed. This fact may have been perceived as a victory by some, but in marginalizing him, the SAI had marginalized itself. Calling so strenuously for the Indian Bureau's abolition had alienated those few in Washington who were willing to help. In 1918 the SAI had even failed in a collective effort to stop the Carlisle Indian Industrial School from being converted into a military hospital.[102] Coolidge, though, applauded the closure on the grounds that now Indian children might be sent to public schools.[103]

Weeks after returning home to Reno, Coolidge was walking down the street when he heard bells and whistles sound throughout the city. As he strolled about wondering why, a man informed him that Germany had requested negotiations for an armistice. The Great War was ending, but the Spanish influenza pandemic was beginning in earnest. In letters written to Grace following the Pierre conference, Sherman shared his thoughts on the society's direction and noted the multiplying signs of the virus's spread.[104] Whether Bonnin and Eastman would succeed as leaders was unclear. "Well, I shall be friendly to them and watch closely their sayings and doings," he told Grace, "for the sake of keeping the Society alive. . . . We all tremble for the outcome; still, we must wait and see."[105] In the meantime, he noted that Reno had taken on a surreal atmosphere as one after another institution fell under quarantine. Coolidge was scheduled to give speeches at schools that were now closed. Cinemas and even churches were shut as well. Children and teachers were "glad of the vacation," but the university had been forced to isolate four hundred students on campus. Thankfully, the Red Cross was diligently producing face masks. Some citizens had even taken to wearing them on the streets. Although Reno had only one flu death, responsible public officials were wisely exercising caution in the run-up to the November 1918 elections.[106] When on election day fourteen new cases appeared, the city's Board of Health immediately tightened measures to reduce risk.[107] The Spanish influenza affected the Society of American Indians in a very personal way. Angel De Cora Deitz and Charles Eastman's daughter, Irene, both died.[108] Gertrude Bonnin also caught the virus but survived.[109] Before the pandemic abated in the summer of 1919, Grace, Sallie, and Rosie had each fallen ill. Sallie and Rosie had to be hospitalized, with Rosie later suffering "a light touch of pneumonia." Grace recovered in bed.[110]

In July of that year, Effie, who had returned to Wyoming, married an Ojibwe man named George W. Tibbets. The whole family, including Virginia, who was still working in Rock Springs, gathered in the state for the wedding. After the "simple and casual" ceremony concluded, everyone enjoyed a tour through the Tetons.[111] Virginia married a year later, in 1920, though few details on the nuptials seem to exist. After the wedding, she spent three weeks in Colorado with the rest of her family. Grace was very proud of her, writing, "Really, I never felt more pleased about any one than I did her. She has developed wonderfully, loves her work and is so satisfied in it. She is living with a purpose now instead of just drifting. It is wonderfully satisfactory. They speak highly of her at the hospital and evidently she is just where she ought to be."[112]

When the Society of American Indians met in Minneapolis, Minnesota, in 1919 for the annual conference, Sherman Coolidge attended, hoping with a few others that they could counteract the influence of the radicals. Once again, Montezuma and Gordon triumphed, electing the pro-peyote, anti-bureau Thomas Sloan as president.[113] Eastman lost by a wide margin, as did Gertrude Bonnin's husband, Raymond, whom she had nominated in a desperate bid to challenge Sloan. Coolidge had always envisioned a moderate SAI that could promote a new view of Native peoples to the public and influence the Indian Bureau through persuasion and cooperation. Montezuma, Gordon, and Sloan all had valid concerns, but their work was not constructive. They had disaffected the SAI's main membership pool—the Indians employed with the bureau—through an application of rigid ideology.[114] Even Gordon admitted that abolishing the body would mean somehow finding work for three thousand of its Native employees, who for a decade had made up around half of the workforce.[115] None of this mattered in the voting. Coolidge was forced to watch as the Society of American Indians destroyed itself through a mixture of factionalism and ideological jockeying.

The election of Sloan resulted in one important casualty. Gertrude Bonnin, though reelected as the secretary-treasurer, refused any involvement in an organization headed by a man who condoned peyote. She announced her resignation on health grounds but vowed that "if there is any Indian council in the United States that asks me to go there, in justice for the Indian, I will be there and I will not ask them to see that I will not go to jail."[116] Whether anyone knew it or not, the moment these words exited her mouth the Society of American Indians was finished.

Minus Bonnin's full-time commitment to the day-to-day dirty work in Washington DC, no one was running the organization. Charles Eastman, unhappy at being unseated, left soon after, depriving the SAI of a famous figurehead.[117] Coolidge maintained his membership and took a ceremonial place on the advisory board, but he had entirely ceased to be a factor.[118] Throughout 1919, not even one mention of him appeared in the *American Indian Magazine*.

The slogan of the Minneapolis conference had been "American Citizenship for Indians." While discussing Native participation in the Great War in Pierre, South Dakota, the previous year, Coolidge had asked an opera house full of whites, "Are you going, after the war, to make democracy safe for the Indian?"[119] The SAI leadership, broadly, had believed that patriotic Indian participation would bring political change. Instead, it brought death. Native American soldiers in Europe suffered a 5 percent mortality rate, which was 400 percent greater than that of their white comrades. Some nations lost 10–14 percent of their young men. One reason for the high Indian death rate was disease; another was that white military commanders pushed Indians into dangerous roles as scouts and messengers.[120] The primary benefit from their war service came after the conflict, when the Indian Bureau relaxed bans on Indian dances and celebrations. This decision led to a resurgence of repressed traditions and rituals, some of which young people on the reservations had never experienced.[121]

There is strong evidence that Coolidge later regretted his support for the First World War. In one of his sermons from the 1920s, he stated that the "proudest militaristic nations in the world took a pacifist Jewish peasant for their guide and easily reconciled His teachings with bombs, poison gas, secret treaties, and all the lies of official propaganda."[122] Why he did not take this stance from the beginning can only be guessed, but hindsight is often clearer.

The war, then, had no immediate effect on the legal status of Indians. For years during Coolidge's presidency, he and his fellow activists had called on Congress to better define the legal status of Native peoples under the Carter Code Bill and to open a court of Indian claims under the Stephens bill. No such thing happened. In 1917 and 1918, both Indian citizenship bills had died. There was simply little interest in Washington, much less political will to support the effort. And if Coolidge still desired to fight for citizenship, no adequate vessel in which to do so existed. Even the Indian Rights Association, one of the SAI's original supporters, had by this point largely repudiated the organization.[123] All that was left was a handful of ideologically driven men, all abhorred by the Indian Bureau's power structure that they sought, in vain, to terminate. Returning home from Minnesota, the state where he had studied for the ministry and prepared for his life as an Indian missionary, Sherman Coolidge must have felt pangs of regret at how his grand ideas of Christianization and "progress" had come to so very little. The Society of American Indians, having once held the promise that a greater mission could be accomplished, had now failed as well.

Epilogue

By the end of 1918, the Coolidge family had once again relocated, escaping Reno for Denver, Colorado, though the move suffered delays due to the influenza pandemic.[1] The family's new address was Colorado Boulevard, adjacent a large park complex surrounding the Denver Museum of Nature and Science.[2] Grace described the house, decorated with her vast collection of Navajo blankets, as "homey and attractive," and the neighborhood as "lovely." She also appreciated the climate. Throughout the first winter, they only once had to use chains on their car tires and rarely had to use a blanket to keep warm while driving.[3] Sherman also liked the city. His new post as a canon at Denver's Saint John's Cathedral, formerly Saint John's Church in the Wilderness, allowed him to keep busy with frequent church activities and conventions.[4] But a year after settling, Grace decided that despite its excellent maids and dining, Denver had many of the "drawbacks" of New York City. She found making tea dates tiresome, preferring to socialize spontaneously, and the mountains surrounding the city were too far away to enjoy. Though the family was reluctant to move again, Colorado Springs seemed a better place to build a new home.[5] Grace claimed that if she had her choice, she would return to Wyoming and live on a ranch, but "the practical side of the things, the schools and the hard work, etc.," dissuaded her.[6]

Despite the outcome of the 1919 Society of American Indians conference in Minneapolis, Sherman had not given up on Native rights activism. In November 1920, he was one of just eight SAI members to appear in St. Louis, Missouri, along with Montezuma, Gordon, and Sloan, who was futilely seeking an appointment as the commissioner of Indian affairs under the Warren G. Harding administration. The 1921 conference in Detroit fared no better. There, the leadership attempted to boost its numbers by inviting several Indian fraternal organizations "for the purpose of solving the problem of the best interest of the Red Race."[7] Yet again, only Coolidge and six other society members came to hear Sloan make another call for the Indian Bureau's abolition. Sessions were badly attended. At one point, someone suggested they all just go home.[8] The new SAI secretary, Thomas Bishop, summed up the meeting as a "fiasco." For Coolidge, however, the Detroit conference yielded some benefit. The Teepee Order, one of the fraternal organizations that attended, invited him to join. Soon after, he was elected Great Incohonee, or "president." Though the Teepee Order was more of a social club than a political organ, the group adopted a platform similar to the SAI's, stressing the need for citizenship and a court of claims though making no mention of the bureau's abolition or peyote.

After Coolidge and other important full members left, the Society of American Indians struggled on for two more years. In the fall of 1922, the society held a conference in Kansas City, Missouri. Numbers were again very low. Montezuma criticized Sloan for holding on to the presidency. Sloan countered that no one else was left to nominate in his place. By that point, the Yavapai doctor was gravely ill with tuberculosis and only months from death. In December he left Chicago for Arizona, the land of his birth. Having fought for Yavapai land and water rights over the decades, he died among his people on January 31, 1923, in a small hut on the Fort McDowell Reservation. One of Montezuma's last wishes was that the 1923 SAI conference proceed in Chicago. When the event took place in September, the city's paper billed it as a banquet to "entertain twenty-five Indian chiefs."[9] Any political significance was lost on the public, even if Sloan again spoke of the bureau's abolition and the need for Indian citizenship. Philip Gordon was elected the last president. From that point on, the Society of American Indians existed in name only.[10] Charles H. Burke, the commissioner of Indian affairs for much of the 1920s, referred to the once-lauded intertribal endeavor as "a very much discredited organization."[11]

The society's demise came during a decade when Coolidge and the former leadership could have, through concentrated action, helped greatly in the fight for Native rights. In 1921 newly installed president Harding appointed Sen. Albert B. Fall (R-NM) as his secretary of the interior. Fall had little sympathy for Indigenous peoples and happily supported any legislation expropriating Indian property. When Sen. Holm O. Bursum (R-NM) introduced a bill allowing long-term residents of his state to claim communally owned Pueblo lands, Fall approved. He then declared reservations established by executive order "public lands," opening approximately 22 million unallotted acres for gas and oil drilling.[12] Similar machinations were occurring in Oklahoma. In 1910 Coolidge had worried what would happen when federal restrictions were lifted on the sale of Indian property.[13] By the 1920s, grafters in the state had colluded with a corrupt judiciary to engineer a guardianship system that deprived Indians of oil profits from their lands, resorting even to child murder to achieve control over monies.[14]

Reform groups quickly mobilized. The Indian Rights Association and General Federation of Women's Clubs, whose Indian Welfare Committee now included Gertrude Bonnin, worked together to found the American Indian Defense Association. John Collier, a passionate Native rights activist who would later become the commissioner of Indian affairs under President Franklin D. Roosevelt, headed the new organization.[15] Its campaign achieved some successes. The Bursum bill was defeated, and fortuitously in 1923 Fall was convicted of taking bribes for oil leases in the Teapot Dome scandal. Fall's successor, Hubert Work, was eager to allay outstanding concerns. After taking office, he created the Committee of One Hundred, which was tasked with investigating reservation conditions and making recommendations for improvements to federal Indian policy. The committee included both Indigenous and white reformers, such as Charles Eastman, Philip Gordon, Henry Roe Cloud, Arthur C. Parker, and, of course, Sherman Coolidge.[16]

In mid-December 1923, with Parker presiding as chairman, the Committee of One Hundred gathered in Washington to draft a series of resolutions. The members called for better schooling, financial support for Indian students pursuing higher education, the establishment of a court of tribal claims, the lifting of Indian Bureau bans on religious practices (peyotism excepted), and the termination of court proceedings designed to expropriate reservation lands demarcated by executive order.[17] Sherman Coolidge, accompanied by the Cherokee poet, educator, and activist Ruth Muskrat Bronson, presented a book to President Calvin Coolidge the same month in a public ceremony.[18] The two men had met several years before when Calvin Coolidge was the governor of Massachusetts. One news report recorded that the governor had exclaimed, "An Indian, named Coolidge! Why, all the Coolidges I have ever heard of were New Englanders whose ancestors came over on the Mayflower." The remark opened the door for Sherman's well-worn but ever-gentle statement of primacy, "My ancestors were on the reception committee which met them."[19]

One would be tempted to view Sherman Coolidge's meeting with the president in December 1923 as the culmination of his career in Native rights activism. Yet, unfortunately, the Committee of One Hundred's report had virtually no effect, save preparing the ground for future investigations.[20] The committee had even stopped short of recommending citizenship, fearing that it would endanger some of the protections wardship offered to Indian property.[21] Just a year later, however, Sen. Robert La Follette (P-WI) and Sen. Burton K. Wheeler (D-MT) sponsored a bill to extend U.S. citizenship to all Native peoples. In May 1924, the Indian Citizenship Act passed both houses and became law the following month.[22] None of Sherman Coolidge's immediate comments on the act appear to have survived. Coolidge's friend Richard Henry Pratt died weeks before the bill's passage, having never seen the conclusion of the work he began in the 1870s.[23] Four years later, John D. Rockefeller subsidized a large-scale study of reservation conditions, resulting in the 1928 Meriam Report (named after its director, Lewis Meriam). The scandalous facts the survey uncovered led President Herbert Hoover to appoint two members of the Indian Rights Association as the commissioner and the assistant commissioner of Indian affairs. The Meriam Report's true influence was later felt in the 1930s, when the Roosevelt administration pushed through substantial reforms in federal Indian policy, with John Collier as the commissioner of Indian affairs.[24]

Sherman Coolidge's private life during the 1920s was one of travel, semi-retirement, and, unfortunately, significant tragedy. There was a long family trip by ocean liner to Europe in the summer of 1924, with stays in

Norway, England, and France. Grace was "charmed" that they departed from Quebec, thereby "avoiding simultaneously 3 days of open ocean *and* the N.Y. Jews."[25] In the summer of 1920, the Coolidge family made a summer trip to Alaska, where everyone reveled in the "gloriously beautiful" landscapes and ate moose.[26] That fall after their return, Effie gave birth to a baby boy who lived but a few hours.[27] Grace wrote that she would have "given anything to have kept this trouble" from her adopted daughter. The infant's death was a prelude to successive misfortunes. Effie later suffered from mental illness and remained under the care of physicians until her death, the date of which is unknown.[28] In 1922 Sherman underwent an operation for unspecified reasons. While on the table, he began hemorrhaging badly. Doctors stopped the bleeding, only for it to reoccur hours later and then inexplicably disappear. Sherman then battled pneumonia throughout a long recovery, the first time Grace had ever seen him "gloomy and pepless."[29] Due to Sherman's compromised health, the Coolidges left Denver for an affluent neighborhood in Colorado Springs in 1923. The move was even reported in the *Colorado Springs Gazette*, which referred to Coolidge as a "full-blooded Navajo."[30] The family's multilevel, Spanish-style home still stands on Third Street and Mesa Avenue, and features a tiled roof and a sleeping porch. Sherman requisitioned a large corner room on the ground floor for his den.[31] Wanting to keep busy, he took the position of honorary canon at the city's Church of the Good Shepherd.[32] He rode to work on the city's now-defunct streetcar. His dog, named Old Chow, met him every day to escort him home.[33]

Coolidge's brief flirtation with death in 1922 was followed by a very serious matter concerning Virginia. That year, she had moved to New York City, where she was offered a nursing position.[34] Whatever occurred during the next two years is unclear, but in the spring of 1924, she was committed to Bellevue Hospital and pronounced insane after threatening to commit murder.[35] She died on November 18, 1925, in New York City. No cause of death was recorded.[36] While Virginia suffered mentally, Sallie began suffering physically. She had dealt with poor health for much of her childhood. Now doctors recommended an operation to remove part of her intestine. Grace refused, and luckily Sallie's health improved to the point where she could attend college. In the summer of 1925, the Coolidges took in a young Indian girl from Idaho who was sick with tuberculosis. The stay in Colorado Springs did her so well that Grace did not want to send her back to boarding school. The girl was "awfully nice and awfully smart," and provided "a good example to foolish Rosie, who toils not."[37]

As a canon of the Church of the Good Shepherd, Sherman Coolidge's life calmed considerably. Outside of his Sunday duties, he ran a small oil business on his lands in Wyoming.[38] Colorado church archives contain little information on Coolidge, save scattered reports of his public lectures in which he discussed his childhood "with great feeling" and presented "the Indian's side of the question in a most interesting and entertaining manner."[39] Several books from the period also record his witticisms.[40] One on Shoshone folklore from 1923 described this incident: "A woman in the East once asked Sherman Coolidge whether the Indians to whom he belonged were cultured or well read. 'My people!' replied he, 'Why, they are the best red men in the world!'"[41] On another occasion, a woman asked Coolidge what the title of canon meant. He replied, "Big gun."[42] Grace recorded one of Sherman's observations in a letter to Anne Talbot while preparing for Christmas in 1925: "I assure you buying, wrapping, filling, tagging, keeping straight, and finally delivering 60 stockings is— well, H—. And as Sherman says, isn't it funny that H. never stands for heaven!"[43] During these years, Coolidge also kept active memberships in a number of national and local academic societies, including the Anthropological Society of Washington, the American Economic Association, the National Education Association, the Kiwanis Club, and the State Historical and Natural History Society of Colorado.[44] At one point, he tried to join the Improved Order of Red Men, only to be rejected due to his Native ancestry. Unbeknownst to him, the organization did not accept Indians.[45] In the 1920s, Sherman and Grace learned that the maiden name of Grace's grandmother was Coolidge. Sherman was delighted, purportedly exclaiming, "My two daughters have a blood right to the name Coolidge!"[46]

Perhaps the most interesting bit of information on Coolidge that surfaces from the 1920s is his founding of the American Indian Film Company. In one of the last issues of the *American Indian Magazine*, he ran an announcement titled "Scenario Wanted for Great Indian Film." The company sought "to produce a photo play that shall to the fullest possible extent reveal both the primitive and modern life of the American Indian." Believing that "no one person can evolve such a comprehensive scenario," Coolidge invited readers to submit ideas for the venture, promising "fair remuneration." The concept behind the planned film was to depict the "picturesque and poetic elements in early tribal life," then go forward in time to reveal the "Indian's part in American civilization, culminating with his splendid achievements in the late world war." The film was to star the Creek-Cherokee soprano Tsianina Redfeather Blackstone, famous for her national tours with the composer Charles Wakefield Cadman. The rest of the cast and even the company's shareholders would be predominantly Indian.[47] While the film was never produced, its overarching goal reflected Coolidge's lifelong quest to counter ignorant public perceptions of Native peoples.[48]

This goal was also reflected in Coolidge's occasional public appearances during the 1920s. In a 1927 open forum at the Colorado Springs courthouse, "Christianity and the Indians," Coolidge explained to those gathered: "The Indian is a subject foreign to most of the American people for they are so engrossed, in material things that they don't give much thought to other things. . . . Even religion, the most important thing is put in the background. I was born a little savage, but I always resented that term being applied to my people because I know they are peace-loving, hospitable, generous and deeply religious. Yet they have been called 'Red Devils.'" Along these lines, Coolidge declared openly that "the Indian is more religious than the white man," pointing to the fact that the Arapahos never took "the name of God in vain." Profanity was nonexistent before white contact, though Indians admittedly now used it "very artistically." The Sun Dance, finally, was no pagan ritual but instead a "deeply religious observance." And still, 350,000 Indians remained "under direct control of the government," which hoarded Indian monies.[49]

Similar sentiments are found in Coolidge's sermons from the decade. One titled "Ye Cannot Serve God and Mammon" elaborated on the dictum that "there is no compromise between the love for God and love for riches" from a Native perspective. Though wealthy himself, Coolidge condemned how "Europeanized" civilization demanded a "cut throat

principle" that caused "cruel strife among men with its intendant greed."
Whites, encouraged by the economic system, willingly killed for material
gain. Indians may have killed for revenge but never for riches. In this way,
"the Indian *lived* his religion," believing it "*vital*" to every part of his life
rather than just as a Sunday outing.[50] Having spent the first part of his
career in the church trying to teach Indians to be like whites, Coolidge
had largely reversed his thinking and was now counseling whites to be
more like Indians.

Toward the end of his life, Coolidge indulged his appreciation for Native
spirituality by sometimes visiting Wind River to observe the Arapahos
performing the annual Sun Dance.[51] He had also struck on nonpolitical
solutions to the Indian problem. First, assimilation could best be achieved
through intermarriage.[52] Coolidge noted that he and Grace had encountered strong resistance to their union, but "those things pass when there is
a true mating." He claimed, "On the great Happy Hunting Ground, we are
all going to be surprised at the racial diversity of the chosen."[53] Another
solution was education. "The government has millions of dollars belonging
to the Indians," he stated publicly in the 1920s. "If it would let loose of
that, many an Indian man and woman would be glad to attend a college
and a university, and this money could be put to no better purpose."[54]

On June 1, 1926, Charles Austin Coolidge, the man who so radically
changed the course of Runs On Top's life, died in Detroit's Grace Hospital
at age eighty-two after suffering a stroke. Following a full military service
at the city's Episcopal Christ Church, Charles's remains were sent for burial
to Arlington National Cemetery in Virginia. Charles had been a regular
fixture in Michigan's veteran's association and had even devoted his time
to the Boy Scouts.[55] Following the funeral, Sophie Coolidge relocated to
Washington DC. As her health began to fail and death neared, Sherman
traveled east to say a final goodbye. The *Washington Times* covered the visit,
commenting on the "touching scene" of Sherman's leaving his adoptive
mother, perhaps for the last time.[56] Sophie then surprised everyone by
living another three years. She expired at age eighty-five on January 26,
1934, and was interred at Arlington with her husband.[57]

In 1928 Sherman and Grace placed Sallie, then twenty-one, and Rosie,
sixteen, in schools in California. Sallie, having graduated from Cheyenne

Mountain High School in 1925, took an apartment in Pasadena. Rosie entered the Girls' Collegiate School in Glendora, where she initially battled a severe bout of homesickness.[58] Before dropping the girls in California, the family traveled to Honolulu. While there, they went to "a rather second class theatre filled with Jap kids shrieking with delight when the brave soldiers saved the fair heroine from the cruel aborigines." Grace got "quite an ethnological kick out of that."[59]

With the children away, a new period began. Grace wrote Anne Talbot, "Sherman and I are really quite enjoying arranging our own lives and eating what we please after long years of slavery to the young."[60] The couple continued to travel in the early 1930s. Sherman attended Hobart commencements, where decades ago he had dazzled classmates with his athletic performance in the cane rush.[61] He and Grace sailed again to Alaska in 1931 and visited Wyoming to observe the Sun Dance.[62] At Wind River, they often felt a certain nostalgia that provoked "spells of talking about building up the ranch and going back for a while every year." But Grace knew it was merely talk. "You can't go back and recapture vanished phases of life," she mused in one letter. "The thing has to flow on, and if you hold it back you only make backwaters."[63] Expressing this arguable truth, she had little inkling that a major phase of her life would soon end. Sherman was just months from death. For several years, he had experienced bouts of dizziness that "tortured" him and periodic heart palpitations that made him "miserable."[64] Doctors suggested a warmer climate, so in late 1931 he joined Sallie in Los Angeles, where she had settled.[65] Grace saw him off at the train station.[66]

When Sherman arrived in California, Sallie sensed he knew death was imminent but was "quite sure he didn't mind." After Christmas, he entered a hospital for observation. During tests, he experienced heart failure but quickly rebounded. Sherman seemed stable, and Grace decided not to travel to Los Angeles herself. Then one evening, his condition suddenly deteriorated. Sallie was called to the hospital around midnight, only to learn her father had drifted out of consciousness.

Several hours later, on January 24, 1932, Sherman Runs On Top Coolidge passed away in his sleep. Grace received the news by telephone. Her first thought was to bury her husband at Wind River, perhaps in the little church cemetery alongside the infant children they had lost so long ago. She quickly decided against it, realizing the daunting challenges presented by the Wyoming winter and the frozen ground. Instead, mourners gathered in Colorado Springs on a bitterly cold day.[67] The Episcopal bishop of Colorado Irving P. Johnson delivered Canon Coolidge's eulogy. Regrettably, his remarks contained the kind of undercurrents of racism and ethnocentrism the deceased had fought against much of his life. "He seemed to embody peace and goodwill toward all men in spite of all the injuries which his race had received from the white man," Johnson noted. "There was no bitterness in his soul. He had a genial humor and a desire to serve which endeared him to us all. He was a witness to the power of the gospel which could produce in one who was born in a teepee the grace to become the peer of any of us as a Christian gentleman and a godly priest."[68] As the bishop spoke these words, a host of obituaries ran in papers from New York to Wyoming.[69] Printed tributes to Coolidge's career afterward appeared in Episcopal literature.[70]

Grace wrote her own tribute to Sherman in a letter to Anne following the service. "I am beginning to see daylight and now I don't know what to do with myself," she began. "This place suddenly doesn't seem to be a home anymore; just a house. Sherman was always here the steady one." Grace continued, "Sherman was always very calm and sure in his feelings; the thing that I fear and dread is not in any sense death, but horrors. I used always to be afraid when he came in late for dinner, for instance, that he had fallen in the street or been struck by a machine. You know how he always drifted along. People here used to tell me how they would honk at him—usually in vain." Grace was satisfied, though, that she had made Sherman's life "richer and happier." She remarked to Anne, "Isn't it funny to think that you were the one who first brought us together? At Rongis that night. Do you remember? I can't write one other word." Daughter Rosie, evoking her late father's sense of humor, gave her own tribute. "Papa was witty and funny and had a good clear mind and a personality that everybody remembers with pleasure," she told her mother one afternoon. "Maybe if he had lived on longer all that might have changed."[71]

Had Sherman Coolidge lived just a few years more, he would have witnessed the significant changes brought about by Roosevelt's appointment of John Collier as the commissioner of Indian affairs in 1933. The following year, Congress passed the Indian Reorganization Act, or Indian New Deal. This long-overdue reform of federal Indian policy dismantled Dawes Act allotments and allowed tribal lands to be merged, owned, and managed cooperatively while ensuring greater tribal autonomy through the election of governments empowered to negotiate with Washington. The act also offered low-interest loans, restored 2 million acres to reservation lands, supported on-reservation day schools, and liquidated many boarding schools. Likewise, Indian cultural and religious expression finally received protections, and Indians took a greater role in running the Indian Bureau. These reforms represented a significant break from the era of assimilation begun by President Ulysses Grant's peace policy in the late 1860s, very near the time of Runs On Top's adoption into white society.[72]

Though she left no commentary, Grace Darling Wetherbee Coolidge did live to see these changes. Following Sherman's death, she moved three blocks from her home into Colorado Springs' Broadmoor Hotel and traveled for some years, visiting Honolulu and California.[73] Her life was not as long as one would expect. In November 1937, Grace sustained a broken hip and remained bedridden until her death on December 28, 1937, at age sixty-four.[74] Three bishops traveled to Colorado to attend her funeral, reflecting the depth of her lifelong charity work.[75] Before her death, Grace saw both of her daughters begin their adult lives and was happy that each married "in a nice painless way" devoid of fanfare.[76] Sallie became an artist and in 1934 married a Hopi silversmith named Homer Vance, with whom she opened Coolidge Indian Crafts, a jewelry store in Hollywood. She later divorced and married Chief Jesse Rowlodge in Oklahoma, bravely overcoming her hatred for the state. Rosie meanwhile proved a talented writer in high school and studied English at Colorado College. In 1934 she eloped with her classmate Alfred Heinicke, with whom she had four children.[77] As a mother, she insisted that her offspring adhere strictly to her mother's sometimes idiosyncratic pronunciation. "Faarest" referred to any large collection of trees. "Baam" referred to any type of lotion.[78] Both Rosie and Sallie died far too young due to poor health. Sallie passed away on November 4, 1953, at age forty-six; Rosie on October 15, 1966, at age fifty-four.[79] Today, both lay buried nearby their parents.[80] Adoptive grandmother Sophie Coolidge had written of them years before, "Both girls are very intelligent and well-educated and proud of their Indian blood."[81]

Sophie's description, one might suggest, was Sherman Coolidge's ideal for American Indians in the twentieth century and beyond as a proud assimilated citizenry, ever cognizant of and identified by their lineage and heritage. But implicit in this philosophy of assimilation was the idea that as Indians adapted to new circumstances, the United States would adapt to Indians. Assimilation required a communal, pluralistic America that accepted Natives as equals and embraced them with respect, tolerance, and understanding. In shedding rank materialism, avarice, racism, and prejudice, this America would embody the democratic ideals preached within the national narrative and reject any discourse that deemed a good Indian a dead one. Here, education was crucial not only for Indians but also for whites.

The irony of Coolidge's career is that he began his life's work as a missionary, striving to instruct and transform Indians for inclusion in white "civilization." He largely failed, only to do his most laudable work in trying to enlighten whites to the Indian's humanity. With simple messages such as "Indians are human beings," Coolidge, within the restrictive terms and context of his era, became an able advocate for Native peoples in seeking to change negative perceptions and forcing whites to see matters from a different perspective. And though his brand of "progressive" Christian assimilation is no longer palatable, Coolidge's constructive work as a lecturer, representative, and advocate cannot be denied.

Sherman Coolidge's ultimate legacy, however, is his role as one of the originators of intertribal activism. The Society of American Indians, for all its internal disputes, represented a collective step forward in cementing solidarity and securing Native rights through organization, and it was one of many small but important forces that made the Indian Reorganization Act possible. The Indian New Deal was hardly perfect, but it did amount to some progress in the positive sense. Sherman Coolidge helped bring about this transformation in America's treatment of Indians, and perhaps, in time, his vision of a nation expunged of racism, prejudice, and intolerance will be fulfilled.

NOTES

PROLOGUE

1. Grace Coolidge to Anne Talbot, January 15, 1903; Sherman Coolidge, "The Death of Brave Heart (Great Heart)"; "Early Life of Rev. T. Sherman Coolidge"; and Sherman Coolidge, "A Sketch from Real Life"—all from the Coolidge-Heinicke Collection, Colorado Springs Pioneers Museum (hereafter CHC). See also Markley and Crofts, *Walk Softly*, 143–44.

2. Ellis, *Pioneers*, 13–14.

3. "Canon Coolidge Is Claimed by Death," *Wyoming State Tribune*, January 25, 1932, Sherman Coolidge Biographical File, American Heritage Center, University of Wyoming–Laramie (hereafter AHC). Sherman Coolidge in fact held no doctorate.

4. Adams, *Education for Extinction*, 8–10.

5. For greater elucidation on the nature of American expansionism, see the discussion of settler colonialism in Wolfe, "Settler Colonialism."

6. This status of Native wardship became official in 1871 with the advent of the Indian Appropriations Act. See Schultz et al., *Encyclopedia of Minorities*, 631. The Office of Indian Affairs was created in 1824 as a branch of the U.S. Department of the Interior. Though the office was officially renamed the Bureau of Indian Affairs in 1947, the terms "Office of Indian Affairs," "Indian Office," "Bureau of Indian Affairs," and "Indian Bureau" have often been used interchangeably. This monograph uses "Indian Bureau" or "bureau" because the titles appear in most of this biography's primary source material—despite its dating from before 1947. See C. L. Henson, "From War to Self-Determination: A History of the Bureau of Indian Affairs," *American Studies Today Online*, accessed April 27, 2020, http://www.americansc.org.uk /Online/indians.htm.

7. Adams, *Education for Extinction*, 8–10; and Hertzberg, *American Indian Identity*, 20.

8. Jackson, *Century of Dishonor*, 1–2.

9. Fear-Segal, "Nineteenth-Century Indian Education"; and Speroff, *Carlos Montezuma, MD*, 44–52.

10. Pratt, "Origin and History," 110.

11. Hoxie, *Final Promise*, 75–76.

12. Maroukis, *We Are Not a Vanishing People*, 151.

13. Child, *Boarding School Seasons*, 27, 30, 33; and Smith, *Indigenous People and Boarding Schools*, 7.

14. Milk, *Haskell Institute*, 76–77, 127–67.

15. For other accounts of the boarding school experience, see, for instance, Adams, *Education for Extinction*; Archuleta, Child, and Lomawaima, *Away from Home*; and Trafzer, Keller, and Sisquoc, *Boarding School Blues*.

16. Speroff, *Carlos Montezuma, MD*, 69, 372–73; and Taylor, *New Deal*, 12–13.

17. Coolidge, "Indian of To-Day," 93.

18. "Canon Coolidge Is Claimed by Death," AHC.

19. That Sherman Coolidge has been denied scholarly attention is evident from searches performed on Project Muse and JSTOR, which do not list a single academic paper written on him. Scattered information on Coolidge is primarily found in Hertzberg, *American Indian Identity*; and to a lesser degree in Maroukis, *We Are Not a Vanishing People*. The sole reprints of one of Coolidge's writings, "The Function of the Society of American Indians" (1914), appears in Peyer, *American Indian Nonfiction*, 345–49; and Peyer, *What the Elders Wrote*, 159–62. Otherwise, Coolidge has garnered virtually no scholarly attention for his long presidency of the Society of American Indians (SAI). Many other SAI leaders, such as Seneca anthropologist Arthur C. Parker, Yavapai medical doctor Carlos Montezuma, Santee Dakota writer and physician Charles Eastman, Ho-Chunk/Winnebago Presbyterian minister and educator Henry Roe Cloud, Winnebago artist Angel De Cora Deitz, Yankton Dakota writer and activist Gertrude Bonnin (Zitkala-Ša), and Ojibwe Catholic priest Philip Gordon, have been the subjects of detailed scholarly biographies. Even the educator Chauncey Yellow Robe (Sicangu Lakota), certainly a minor figure, has been treated in a full-length biography. Lack of recognition for Coolidge's importance to the intertribal activism of the Progressive Era is, therefore, glaringly unjust. For biographical treatments of Parker, Montezuma, Eastman, Roe Cloud, De Cora Deitz, Bonnin, Gordon, and Yellow Robe, see, respectively: Porter, *To Be Indian*; Iverson, *Carlos Montezuma*; Speroff, *Carlos Montezuma, MD*; Pfister, *Yale Indian*; Wilson, *Ohiyesa*; Messer, *Henry Roe Cloud*; Ramirez, *Standing Up to Colonial Power*; Waggoner, *Fire Light*; Lewandowski, *Red Bird, Red Power*; Lewandowski, *Ojibwe, Activist, Priest*; and Messer, *Chauncey Yellow Robe*. Why Coolidge has so long languished in the shadows of these figures

is hard to determine. One may conclude that among an illustrious group of Native intellectuals boasting large personalities and radically differing political agendas, Coolidge has been overlooked because he eschewed the kind of dramatics and polarization encouraged by some of the SAI's cliques in matters concerning the Bureau of Indian Affairs and the peyote religion. Amid these debates, Coolidge sought to be a moderating influence. See the discussion in Hertzberg, *American Indian Identity*, 45, for comments on Coolidge's "rather phlegmatic" temperament.

I. THE ARAPAHOS AND RUNS ON TOP

1. Coolidge "Indian of To-Day," 88.
2. Fowler, *The Arapaho*, 17; and Pritzker, *Native American Encyclopedia*, 279, 391.
3. Fowler, *The Arapaho*, 13.
4. Pritzker, *Native American Encyclopedia*, 289.
5. Fowler, *The Arapaho*, 14–18. In the Sun Dance, the central element is a pole that stands in the middle of the Mystery Hoop. Young men are tethered to the pole, and they sometimes offer parts of their flesh as sacrifices by pulling away until the skin breaks. Another element is a sweat lodge, used for purification. The ceremony includes an intercessor, who supervises the dancing and acts as an intermediary between Earth and the Great Mystery. Other holy men lead the dancers and care for the pipes and other items used in the ceremony. Women who have achieved status in the tribe sometimes provide moral support to the ceremony's dancers. See Jorgenson, *Sun Dance Religion*, 16–18.
6. Kroeber, *The Arapaho*, 19–20.
7. Fowler, *The Arapaho*, 18.
8. Anderson, *Four Hills of Life*, 94–96.
9. Fowler, *The Arapaho*, 16–18. At this time, a band of Arapahos called the Gros Ventre split from the Northern and Southern Arapahos from the main tribe and became a member of the Blackfeet Confederacy. See Pritzker, *Native American Encyclopedia*, 319.
10. Fowler, "Arapaho," in Demallie, *Plains*, 842.
11. Fowler, *The Arapaho*, 17; and Pritzker, *Native American Encyclopedia*, 306, 329.
12. Fowler, *Arapahoe Politics*, 22–25, 33–35, 37.
13. National Park Service, "Fort Laramie: Crossroads of a Nation Moving West," last updated March 31, 2015, https://www.nps.gov/fola/learn/historyculture/index.htm.
14. Klapper, "Treaty of Fort Laramie with the Sioux, etc., 1851," in *Indian Affairs*, 2:594–95.
15. Fowler, *Arapahoe Politics*, 35.

16. Stone, *History of Colorado*, 1:172.
17. Fowler, *Arapahoe Politics*, 42–44; and Klapper, "Treaty with the Arapaho and Cheyenne, 1861," in *Indian Affairs*, 2:807–11.
18. Hatch, *Black Kettle*, 108–84; and Thompson, *Civil War History*, 375–76.
19. Hoig, *Sand Creek Massacre*, 153.
20. Treuer, *Atlas of Indian Nations*, 134.
21. Fowler, *Arapahoe Politics*, 39; and Thompson, *Civil War History*, 376.
22. See Coolidge, "Sketch from Real Life," CHC. This handwritten document gives Coolidge's birthplace at Goose Creek and birth year as 1860. This birthdate or 1861 makes greatest sense when considering the events of 1860s and the preponderance of evidence for his age. For reasons unclear, Coolidge listed his birth year as 1863 in 1922. See "Hobart Centennial Fund Campaign," 1922, Sherman Coolidge Files, Warren Hunting Smith Library, Geneva NY (hereafter WHSL). The questionnaire also designates his birthplace as Goose Creek, Wyoming. Coolidge later mentioned being born along Goose Creek in 1913; see Coolidge, "American Indians," 251. Sherman Coolidge, in "Sherman Coolidge Autobiographical Notes," CHC, likewise lists his birthplace as Goose Creek. The place of his birth may have also been along the Tongue River, a tributary of the Yellowstone. Two sources mention the Tongue River: Myfanway Thomas Goodnough, "Sherman Coolidge," AHC; and "Escaped Massacre to Be Taken by White Folk and Educated for Ministry—Story of an Indian Boy," Society of American Indians Papers, Cornell University Library, Ithaca (hereafter PSAI). In other sources, Coolidge's birth year varies, with the earliest of date being 1860. See Markley and Crofts, *Walk Softly*, 144.
23. Ellis, *Pioneers*, 13–14.
24. See Sherman Coolidge, "A Little Gambler," CHC. Also see Goodnough, "Sherman Coolidge," AHC; "Canon Coolidge Is Claimed by Death," AHC; and "Full-Blood Indian Now a Missionary: Rev. Sherman Coolidge Arapahoe, Taken Prisoner as a Boy, Here for Conference Fell into Hands of Lieut., Now Gen. C. A. Coolidge, Well-Known in Columbus" (1911), PSAI. "Swiftest Runner" is also a translation that appears for Coolidge's name, for example, in Marion Gustin, "Arapaho Is Distinguished Churchman," WHSL. Also see Van Orsdale, "Rev. Sherman Coolidge, D.D."
25. Coolidge, "Death of Brave Heart," CHC; and Coolidge, "Early Life of Rev. T. Sherman Coolidge," CHC. A search on the website Find a Grave turned up an entry for Julia Felter Hereford, Sings First's name later in life, who was born July 15, 1864, at Fort Washakie and was later buried in the cemetery there. She lived to age eighty-two, dying on September 9, 1946. See "Julia Felter Hereford," accessed June 20, 2020, https://www.findagrave.com

/memorial/146659844/julia-hereford. The other preceding sources cited suggest she was born earlier.

26. Sherman Coolidge, "The Colt," CHC; and Coolidge, "Sketch from Real Life," CHC.

27. Sherman Coolidge, "Crow and Eagle," CHC.

28. Coolidge, "Sherman Coolidge Autobiographical Notes," CHC.

29. Coolidge, "The Colt," CHC.

30. Coolidge, "Little Gambler," CHC; and Ellis, *Pioneers*, 14.

31. A single source records that when Runs On Top was perhaps four years old, he had his first encounter with the Eastern Shoshones. One evening, a group of warriors raided his camp, killing indiscriminately until the Arapahos offered resistance. The incident is not corroborated elsewhere. See Goodnough, "Sherman Coolidge," AHC.

32. Wagner, *Powder River Odyssey*, 23–24, 28.

33. Cornell, introduction to *Teepee Neighbors*, by Coolidge, xxii; and Fowler, *Arapahoe Politics*, 43.

34. Wagner, *Powder River Odyssey*, 28.

35. Quoted in Cozzens, *Eyewitnesses to the Indian Wars*, 4:6.

36. The quote and details concerning Coolidge's family are taken from Coolidge, "Sketch from Early Life," CHC. See Fowler, *Arapahoe Politics*, 42–44, for the remaining information.

37. Office of Archeology and Historic Preservation, "Shoshone Episcopal Mission"; Stamm, *People of the Wind River*, 3–11, 25; and Urbanek, *Chief Washakie*, 28.

38. Brown, *Fetterman Massacre*, 13–14; Fowler, *Arapahoe Politics*, 48; Klapper, "Treaty with the Eastern Shoshoni, 1863" in *Indian Affairs*, 848–49; Klapper, "Treaty with the Eastern Band Shoshoni and Bannock, 1868," in *Indian Affairs*, 2:1020–22; and Stamm, *People of the Wind River*, 41–42, 51. Camp Brown was located near what is now the city of Lander, Wyoming. Camp Brown, originally named Camp Augur after Gen. Christopher C. Augur, was renamed in 1870. The name change was made in honor of Capt. Frederick H. Brown, whom the Lakotas killed in the Fetterman fight on December 21, 1866 (discussed later in this biography). See Kathy Weiser, "Camp Augur, Wyoming," Legends of America, updated December 2020, https://www.legendsofamerica.com/camp-augur-wyoming/; and Hebard, *Marking the Oregon Trail*, 10. Although Wind River Reservation did not become the official name of the Eastern Shoshone Reservation until the 1930s, the name is used henceforth in this biography to avoid confusion. See "The Arapaho Arrive: Two Nations on One Reservation," WyoHistory.org, June 23, 2018, https://www.wyohistory.org/encyclopedia/arapaho-arrive-two-nations-one-reservation#_ftnref1.

39. Stamm, *People of the Wind River*, 220.
40. Coolidge, "Sketch from Real Life," CHC; Coolidge, "Death of Brave Heart," CHC; and Ellis, *Pioneers*, 14. Coolidge writes in "Death of Brave Heart" that he learned the Bannocks had only wanted the horses from a white scout at Fort Washakie. He does not specify when he learned that, only saying "many years" after his return to the reservation. For reasons unknown, Sings First is not mentioned in the account of Banasda's death. Coolidge does mention that the children of the aunt slain by American soldiers were with them when attacked.
41. Coolidge, "Indian of To-Day," 88.
42. Olson, *Red Cloud*, 27–45.
43. Lazarus, *Black Hills/White Justice*, 38–39.
44. Pritzker, *Native American Encyclopedia*, 329; and Klapper, "Treaty with the Sioux—Brulé, Oglala, etc., and Arapahoe," in *Indian Affairs*, 2:998–1007.
45. The account of the events of April 8, 1870, is based on several sources from CHC: Coolidge, "Early Life of Rev. T. Sherman Coolidge"; Coolidge, "Sketch from Real Life"; and Charles Frederick Larrabee to Sherman Coolidge, May 31, 1887. Also see Duncombe, "Northern Arapahoe Experience," 184–86; Fowler, *Arapahoe Politics*, 47–48; Goodnough, "Sherman Coolidge," AHC; Markley and Crofts, *Walk Softly*, 143–44; and Stamm, *People of the Wind River*, 56–57, 220. Markley and Croft's account is derived from Rev. John Roberts's writings on Coolidge's early life, published in *A Round Robin to the Junior Auxiliary* on July 9, 1893. Coolidge spoke of his near-death incident at the annual meeting of the Women's National Indian Association in 1904. See "Annual Meeting," 10. The article states that Coolidge mentioned how he "was stood up to see if he was big enough to kill"; then it goes on to note how "he is working on the very spot his life was saved." The same story appears in "An Indian Boy, Slated for Death at Fort Brown, Where This City Now Stands, Now Minister of Gospel," AHC. Also see Olden, *Shoshone Folk Lore*, 57–58. The information on Kagavah is taken from G. Coolidge to A. Talbot, January 15, 1903, CHC.
46. Larrabee to Coolidge, May 31, 1887, CHC; and "Early Life of Rev. T. Sherman Coolidge," CHC.
47. Coolidge, "Sketch from Real Life," CHC; and "Early Life of Rev. T. Sherman Coolidge," CHC.
48. Reid, "Westerners," 47.

2. NEW LIFE

1. Cornell, "Coolidge, Sherman," in Birchfield, *Encyclopedia of North American Indians*, 133; Sophie Coolidge (hereafter S. Coolidge) to Grace Hebard, December 29, 1930, Coll. 400008, Grace Raymond Hebard Papers, American Heritage Center, University of Wyoming–Laramie (hereafter GHP);

Larrabee to Coolidge, May 31, 1887, CHC; and Maroukis, *Peyote and the Yankton Sioux*, 21–23.

2. "Early Life of Rev. T. Sherman Coolidge," CHC; and Van Orsdale, "Rev. Sherman Coolidge, D.D.," 85.

3. "General Coolidge Dies; Was in Three Wars," Arlington National Cemetery, November 11, 2007, http://www.arlingtoncemetery.net/cacoolidge.htm. Also see "Sophia Wagner Lowry Coolidge," Find a Grave, accessed June 18, 2020, https://www.findagrave.com/memorial/49170435/sophia-wager-coolidge.

4. Van Orsdale, "Rev. Sherman Coolidge, D.D.," 85.

5. S. Coolidge to H. Whipple, February 4, 1877, Henry Benjamin Whipple Papers, Gale Family Library, Minnesota Historical Society, St. Paul (hereafter HWP).

6. "Canon Coolidge Pays His Debt of Love: Colorado Minster Visits White Foster Mother in Washington," *Washington Post*, June 26, 1931, CHC.

7. Reid, "Westerners," 47.

8. See Coolidge to Hebard, December 29, 1930, GHP. Sophie Coolidge writes, "We were never stationed at Washakie. Our post was Fort Ellis Montana at the end of that march of a month and then the Crow Agency at the Yellowstone from whence we . . ." The surviving fragment of the letter cuts off there.

9. Coolidge, "American Indian of Today"; and Van Orsdale, "Rev. Sherman Coolidge, D.D.," 86. Van Orsdale states that the Coolidge family lived at Fort Ellis. Van Orsdale served with Charles Coolidge in the Seventh Infantry and was his good friend. See *United States Army and Navy Journal*, January 1903, 454. Also see Ellis, *Pioneers*, 15; and Tomkins, *Universal Indian Sign Language*, 7.

10. G. Coolidge to A. Talbot, February 26, 1903, CHC.

11. G. Coolidge to A. Talbot, December 27, 1902, CHC.

12. Larrabee to Coolidge, May 31, 1887, CHC.

13. Coolidge, "Death of Big Heart (Brave Heart)," CHC.

14. Ellis, *Pioneers*, 15; Van Orsdale, "Rev. Sherman Coolidge, D.D.," 86; and "Early Life of Rev. T. Sherman Coolidge," CHC.

15. "Indian Society Is Welcomed to City," 120.

16. Van Orsdale, "Rev. Sherman Coolidge, D.D.," 86. For the Coolidges' presumed address, see S. Coolidge to Whipple, February 4, 1877, HWP.

17. Larrabee to Coolidge, May 31, 1887, CHC. Coolidge and Larrabee (who later worked for the Bureau of Indian Affairs in Washington DC) kept in touch until at least 1895. See Larrabee to Sherman Coolidge, April 12, 1895, CHC. The letter discusses a planned meeting at the Indian Bureau in Washington.

18. G. Coolidge to A. Talbot, May 29, 1902, CHC.

19. G. Coolidge to A. Talbot, May 29, 1902, CHC.

20. Philip Heinicke, email to author, December 16, 2020.

21. S. Coolidge to H. Whipple, February 4, 1877, HWP; Ellis, *Pioneers*, 15; and Van Orsdale, "Rev. Sherman Coolidge, D.D.," 86.

22. Coolidge, "American Indians," 253.

23. S. Coolidge to Whipple, February 4, 1877, HWP.

24. Van Orsdale, "Rev. Sherman Coolidge, D.D.," 86.

25. Fowler, *Arapahoe Politics*, 49–51; and Reid, "Westerners," 47. In 1871 the Southern Arapahos settled with the Southern Cheyennes in Indian Territory, Oklahoma. They numbered approximately 1,650 people and took up residence at the Darlington Agency on the North Canadian River. See Fowler, *The Arapaho*, 91.

26. Stamm, *People of the Wind River*, 92–96.

27. "General Coolidge Dies; Was in Three Wars." The obituary states: "When appointed a Captain, [Charles Coolidge] served in Montana, Dakota, Fort Snelling, Fort Russell, Rock Springs, Wyoming, and Fort Logan near Denver."

28. Van Orsdale, "Rev. Sherman Coolidge, D.D.," 86.

29. Hedren, *Powder River*, 36; and Ostler, *Plains Sioux*, 60.

30. Fowler, *Arapahoe Politics*, 52–53.

31. Carlson, *Plains Indians*, 142, 150–62; and Ostler, *Plains Sioux*, 77, 144. Under a postwar settlement, the Lakotas also gave up the Powder River hunting grounds in present-day Wyoming and Montana.

32. Ellis, *Pioneers*, 15; and Philbrick, *Last Stand*, 255–66.

33. Coolidge, "Sherman Coolidge Autobiographical Notes," CHC. Coolidge writes of the Battle of Little Big Horn: "I was never on the ground. . . . I chose not to go up. Glad I didn't." Also see Gustin, "Arapaho Is Distinguished Churchman," WHSL. Gustin was an acquaintance of Coolidge's from his later years in Colorado.

34. "Sketch from Real Life," CHC, explains: "Sherman's half-sister was with Ezac, the scout, who went to Miner's Delight and joined the Bannocks and Shoshones. There she was in imminent danger of being put to torture— burned alive at the stake—but was saved by the intervention of a white boy and his aunt and finally adopted by Mr. and Mrs. John Felter, with whom she went to Evanston, where she was found by her brother fifteen years later. She married a white man and is the mother of two sons." Goodnough, however, tells a more disturbing story: "The life history of Mrs. Hereford was far different from that of her distinguished brother, for it was filled with sordidness and tragedy. She was sold for a hundred dollars, when but a mere child to a man named Felter and lived for years in Evanston, Wyoming,

where we were well acquainted with her. Now married to John Hereford, a mixed breed of the Shoshone tribe, she lives on the reservation with her two daughters, both of whom have been residents of Rock Springs. Nellie, married to a white man, a Mr. Scott, who was a contractor, and the other daughter went back to her tribe, reverting to the blanket state." See also Goodnough, "Sherman Coolidge," AHC.

35. Philip Sheridan Larrabee-Allen and Sarah Allen to Coolidge, February 16, 1876, CHC.

36. Larrabee to Coolidge, May 31, 1887, CHC. Also see Sarah Allen to Coolidge, February 11, 1877, CHC, which mentions that Philip came to live with the Allens in January 1876. Samuel June Barrows was born in 1845 in New York City and was a graduate of Harvard Divinity School. The *Tribune* asked Barrows to cover Custer's movements in the summer of 1876. His wife, Isabel, thought the assignment too dangerous and insisted he stay home. Her adamance extended Barrows's life considerably. Barrows later became deeply concerned with the treatment of Native peoples and the amelioration of reservations conditions, hence his membership in the Indian Rights Association. Isabel C. Barrows, in *Sunny Life*, tells a different story of Philip's life in the East, though it is less credible than the primary source correspondence cited earlier. She records that when Samuel Barrows had been a correspondent for the *New York Tribune* in the summers of 1873 and '74, he had accompanied Custer's expeditions into Yellowstone and the Black Hills. When he returned east, he arrived with a small Arapaho boy who had been offered to him by Gen. Oliver Otis Howard, then conducting the campaign against the Nez Perce in which Charles Coolidge was wounded. The Barrows family grew to love the child and saw to his education. Every night Samuel would sing him to sleep. At age ten, the boy contracted tuberculosis and died. From then on, Samuel carried a small portrait of the boy in a locket. See Barrows, *Sunny Life*, 1, 51, 69, 91, 149. The letters written by Sarah Allen and Charles Larrabee seem to offer a much more reliable account of Philip's sad fate.

37. Larrabee-Allen and Sarah Allen to Coolidge, February 16, 1876, CHC. The Allens were a long-established family, and their house had been built in the mid-1700s by an ancestor. An enclosure to the letter from Sarah Allen to Coolidge explained the history of Massasoit and Samoset excerpted from a book called *Indian Biographies*. She hoped Sherman would continue to write to his brother. Philip also mentioned that he was planning to write Larrabee, who was in Indian Territory fighting the Modocs.

38. Sarah Allen to Coolidge, February 11, 1877, CHC. Italics in original. For the translation of Em-min-ne-es-ka, see Coolidge, "Indians in Wyoming, 1890," in U.S. Census Bureau, *Report on Indians Taxed*, 10:628.

39. Larrabee to Coolidge, May 31, 1887, CHC. Larrabee did not know what happened to Louis, but he had a photo of Philip and offered to send a copy.

40. See G. Coolidge to A. Talbot, November 25, 1902, CHC. The letter is quoted later.

41. Carlson, *Plains Indians*, 142–57, 159–62; Fowler, *Arapahoe Politics*, 64–65; Ostler, *Plains Sioux*, 77, 144; and Powers, *Killing of Crazy Horse*, 410–13.

42. S. Coolidge to Whipple, February 4, 1877, HWP (the letter appears to have been sent from 144 West Forty-Sixth Street, Manhattan); Goodnough, "Sherman Coolidge," AHC; Gustin, "Arapaho Is Distinguished Churchman," WHSL; Whipple, *Lights and Shadows of a Long Episcopate*, 163; and Van Orsdale, "Rev. Sherman Coolidge, D.D.," 86.

43. "Henry Benjamin Whipple: Biographical Note," Minnesota Historical Society, St. Paul, accessed March 22, 2020, http://www2.mnhs.org/library /findaids/P0823.xml. Born in 1822 to a prosperous family of New York merchants, Whipple was educated at private schools but failed to graduate from college due to poor health. His father dabbled in Democratic politics, often lobbying for improvements in Indian policy. Whipple led a conventional life for some years, marrying and working in the family business. Convinced there was greater meaning to pursue, he began studying for the Episcopal ministry in 1848. He was ordained as a deacon the following year and as a priest in 1850. As the rector of the Zion Church in the wealthy parish of Rome, New York, Whipple directed his energies into charitable efforts in behalf of the indigent. In 1857 he moved his family to Chicago and founded the Church of the Holy Communion on the city's derelict south side. Whipple's congregation consisted of rough laborers and vagabonds. In his spare time, he ministered to the city's prison population. In the summer of 1859, Whipple was elected bishop of Minnesota, a position he would hold until his death. The Episcopal Church's presence in the state was then little more than a few missionary outposts, which Whipple developed into a thriving diocese based in Faribault. He traveled and preached extensively in the first years, cultivating an intense interest in Indian welfare. In 1862 he began construction on the Cathedral of Our Merciful Saviour, laying the first cornerstone himself.

44. See Pritzker, *Native American Encyclopedia*, 317. Whipple also wrote the preface to Jackson's *Century of Dishonor*. "The sad revelation of broken faith, of violated treaties, and of inhuman deeds of violence," he predicted, "will bring a flush of shame to the cheeks of those who love their country" (page ix).

45. "Henry Benjamin Whipple."

46. S. Coolidge to Whipple, February 4, 1877, HWP.

47. S. Coolidge to Whipple, February 25, 1877, HWP.

48. Coolidge to S. Coolidge, March 25, 1877, HWP.

49. Information on how and when Sherman Coolidge's education was decided upon is gleaned from these three incomplete and sometimes contradictory sources: Gustin, "Arapaho Is Distinguished Churchman," WHSL; Van Orsdale, "Rev. Sherman Coolidge, D.D.," 86; and Whipple, *Lights and Shadows*, 163. Sophie Coolidge references Sherman Coolidge's scholarship in a letter to Grace Hebard. See S. Coolidge to Hebard, December 29, 1930, GHP.

50. S. Coolidge to Whipple, February 25, 1877, HWP; and Gustin, "Arapaho Is Distinguished Churchman," WHSL.

51. Wilkinson, *Blood Struggle*, 40–41.

52. McDermott, *Forlorn Hope*, 81–83.

53. "General Coolidge Dies; Was in Three Wars."

54. "Publisher's Notes," in Coolidge, *Teepee Neighbors*, 3–4; and *United States Army and Navy Journal*, September 1894, 55.

55. "Brig. Gen. Charles Coolidge Dies in Detroit, Mich.," *Rock Springs Miner*, June 25, 1926, GHP.

56. Wells, "Nez Perce and Their Way."

57. Coolidge, "Sherman Coolidge Autobiographical Notes," CHC. Coolidge notes here that he later knew friends of Chief Joseph's, two men named Looking Glass and Amos.

58. Whipple, *Lights and Shadows*, 163.

59. Ellis, *Pioneers*, 16; and Gustin, "Arapaho Is Distinguished Churchman," WHSL.

60. "Our History," Shattuck–St. Mary's, accessed March 23, 2020, https://www.s-sm.org/about-us/our-history/.

61. Parker, "Editorial Comment," 18.

62. All letters quoted are found in Ellis, *Pioneers*, 13–16. In the only one dated December 20, 1878, Sophie explains to Sherman how to travel to St. Paul for Christmas and sends "Love from Mamma." Italics in original.

63. S. Coolidge to Hebard, December 29, 1930, GHP.

64. Reid, "Westerners," 47.

65. Whipple, *Lights and Shadows*, 162–63.

66. Whipple, "Bishop Whipple's Address," in *Journal of the Proceedings*, 32.

67. Whipple, *Lights and Shadows*, 162–63.

68. Allen, *And the Wilderness Shall Blossom*, 193.

69. Whipple, "Bishop Whipple's Address," in *Journal of the Proceedings*, 32.

70. Gustin, "Arapaho Is Distinguished Churchman," WHSL; Van Orsdale, "Rev. Sherman Coolidge, D.D.," 86; and Whipple, *Lights and Shadows*, 162–63.

71. Whipple to Coolidge, ca. Fall 1884, CHC.
72. Coolidge to Arthur C. Parker, March 7, 1913, PSAI.

3. RETURN

1. Fowler, *Arapahoe Politics*, 63–65; and Stamm, *People of the Wind River*, 128–29.
2. Fowler, *The Arapaho*, 59–61; and Reid, "Westerners," 47.
3. See Kevin Abing, introduction to "Directors of the Bureau of Catholic Indian Missions," 1994, https://www.marquette.edu/library/archives/Mss/BCIM/BCIM-SC1-directors.pdf, Bureau of the Catholic Indian Missions Records, Raynor Memorial Libraries, Marquette University Archives, Milwaukee (hereafter BCIM); and Mark Thiel, "The Bureau of Catholic Indian Missions: 140 Years of Action," PowerPoint prepared for the Tekawitha Conference, Fargo, North Dakota, July 24, 2014, https://www.marquette.edu/library/archives/Mss/bcim/documents/bcimsc1pictureHistory.pdf, BCIM.
4. Fowler, *The Arapaho*, 63–78; and Geoffrey O'Gara, "From Wind River to Carlisle: Indian Boarding Schools in Wyoming and the Nation," WyoHistory.org, May 28, 2019, https://www.wyohistory.org/encyclopedia/wind-river-carlisle-indian-boarding-schools-wyoming-and-nation. The information on how many government employees worked at Wind River is based on figures from Coolidge, "Indians in Wyoming, 1890," in U.S. Census Bureau, *Report on Indians Taxed*, 10:630.
5. Coolidge, "Report from Sherman Coolidge," August 1886, 57.
6. Whipple, "Bishop Whipple's Address," in *Journal of the Proceedings*, 44.
7. Stamm, *People of the Wind River*, 220.
8. See S. Coolidge to Hebard, December 29, 1930, GHP.
9. Larson, *History of Wyoming*, 141–43.
10. Goodnough, "Sherman Coolidge," AHC.
11. Coolidge, "Report from Sherman Coolidge," 57. Here Coolidge provides the date of his arrival at Wind River. Also see Weiser, "Camp Augur, Wyoming"; and Ellis, *Pioneers*, 17.
12. Goodnough, "Sherman Coolidge," AHC; and Whipple, "Worthy Object," 96. Goodnough records Coolidge's nickname a bit differently, as "Whiteman Arapahoe."
13. Ellis, *Pioneers*, 18; and Whipple, *Lights and Shadows*, 163.
14. Goodnough, "Sherman Coolidge," AHC; and Reid, "Westerners," 47.
15. Markley and Crofts, *Walk Softly*, 145–46. Uncle Bald Head, who took in Ba-ahnoce after her husband was killed, lived a long life and may have been among the relatives who greeted Coolidge upon his return. See Coolidge, "Death of Brave Heart," CHC.
16. Whipple, "Bishop Whipple's Address," in *Journal of the Proceedings*, 32.

17. Stam, *People of the Wind River*, 222.
18. See Cornell, "Coolidge, Sherman," in Birchfield, *Encyclopedia of North American Indians*, 133; and Fowler, *Arapahoe Politics*, 107, 324n59.
19. See Reid, "Westerners," 47. Coolidge is quoted as saying, "When I became a man I went back as teacher and missionary to the Arapahoes in the Wind River country of Wyoming, and there was my mother. She knew me and I knew her instantly. She called me her son and was proud of me, and I was able to help her till she died. Now I go back to see my foster parents and they call me their son and are proud of me. I am very glad for it all."
20. Ellis, *Pioneers*, 18.
21. Coolidge, "Indian of To-Day," 91; "Bishop Randall," *New York Times*, September 29, 1873; and James Bowen Funsten, "The Indian as a Worker," *Outlook*, December 1905, 877–78.
22. Coolidge, "Indian of To-Day," 91; Markley and Crofts, *Walk Softly*, 151–52; Warren Murphy, "The Reverend John Roberts, Missionary to the Eastern Shoshone and Northern Arapaho Tribes," WyoHistory.org, November 8, 2014, https://www.wyohistory.org/encyclopedia/reverend-john-roberts-missionary -eastern-shoshone-and-northern-arapaho-tribes; Office of Archeology and Historic Preservation, "Shoshone Episcopal Mission"; and Stamm, *People of the Wind River*, 220. A report by Roberts from early 1883 states that he had been running a Sunday and day school while also performing services for local Indians, soldiers at Fort Washakie, and settlers living outside the reservation. See Roberts, "Report from John Roberts," June 1884, 281.
23. Roberts, "Report from John Roberts," March 1884, 125–26.
24. Markley and Crofts, *Walk Softly*, 113–14; and Talbot, "Shoshone Indian School," 125.
25. Roberts, "Report from John Roberts," March 1884, 125–26.
26. See Roberts, "Report from John Roberts," March 1896, 118. Though the report is from 1896, his "Report from John Roberts," March 1884, notes that the government has built the school's new building. Also see Roberts, "Report from John Roberts," September 1885, 467.
27. Duncombe, "Church and the Native American Arapahoes," 357.
28. A. M. Johnson to John DeWitt Clinton Atkins, November 19, 1886, Microfilm P2187, Letters Received by the Commissioner of Indian Affairs, 1881–1907, Records of the Bureau of Indian Affairs, National Archives and Records Administration, Washington DC (hereafter RBIA).
29. Roberts, "Report from John Roberts," September 1885, 467.
30. Ethelbert Talbot to Coolidge, November 1, 1884, CHC.
31. Whipple to Coolidge, ca. Fall 1884, CHC.
32. Roberts, "Report from John Roberts," September 1885, 467.

33. Quoted in Duncombe, "Church and the Native American Arapahoes," 359.
34. Coolidge, "Report from Sherman Coolidge," August 1886, 424; and Spalding, "First Annual Report," 587. Also see Stamm, *People of the Wind River*, 220. Stamm records that Coolidge could no longer communicate in his Native language, though Fowler writes of how Coolidge acted as an interpreter for the government in the early 1900s. See Fowler, *Arapahoe Politics*, 95.
35. Spalding to Whipple, August 25, 1884, HWP.
36. Spalding, "Second Annual Report of the Jurisdiction," 617–18.
37. Spalding, "Second Annual Report," in *Annual Report*, 90. The Church of the Redeemer at Fort Washakie was completed in September 1885.
38. Spalding, "Second Annual Report," in *Annual Report*, 618.
39. Coolidge, "Indian of To-Day," 91–92; and Goodnough, "Sherman Coolidge," AHC. Also see Coolidge to William Jones, December 23, 1886, CHC. Jones was a close friend from Seabury Divinity School with whom Coolidge often discussed women. Jones asks in the letter, "Who are the other young ladies who are your companions at table and the favored butts of your jokes and teasing?"
40. *Report of the Executive Council*, 127.
41. Roberts, "Report from John Roberts," July 1885, 363–64.
42. Stamm, *People of the Wind River*, 220.
43. Coolidge, "Death of Brave Heart," CHC.
44. Coolidge, "Report from Sherman Coolidge," August 1885, 424–25.
45. The quotes are taken from Coolidge, "Report from Sherman Coolidge," August 1885, 425, though the letter to Bishop Spalding repeats the same sentiments. See Coolidge to Spalding, April 23, 1885, quoted in Markley and Crofts, *Walk Softly*, 99.
46. See Spalding, "Remarkable Opportunity," 208.
47. Stamm, *People of the Wind River*, 222.
48. Roberts's letter is quoted in Spalding, "Remarkable Opportunity," 208. Also see "St. Stephens Indian Mission: Our History," accessed April 16, 2020, https://saintstephensmission.com/our-history/.
49. It appears that the original plan was to purchase St. Stephens, though the transaction never occurred. Roberts discussed the practical motivations for living near Sharp Nose in the *Spirit of Missions*, noting how Coolidge "hopes soon to have a little dwelling at the Arapahoe camp, where he will be in the midst of his people, and endeavor, by example and precept, to lead them to a higher life." See Roberts, "Letter," 534.
50. Whipple, "Bishop Whipple's Address," 32.
51. Whipple, "Worthy Object," 96. The letter repeats Coolidge's nickname, "Arapahoe Whiteman."

52. Spalding, "Second Annual Report," in *Annual Report*, 90.

53. Coolidge, "Report from Sherman Coolidge," August 1886, 57.

54. John Spalding to Coolidge, October 2, 1885, CHC.

55. Spalding to Coolidge, December 1885, CHC.

56. Stamm, *People of the Wind River*, 222.

57. The quotes concerning Coolidge's home appear to be taken from a letter from Coolidge to Charles and Sophie Coolidge, ca. Fall 1885, quoted in Ellis, *Pioneers*, 17. Ellis, unfortunately, provides no concrete citation.

58. "Canon Coolidge Pays His Debt of Love," CHC. The 1931 *Washington Post* article, based on an interview with Coolidge, claimed: "During the first days, Canon Coolidge was nearly assassinated because of his work in taking over some of the Indian land for irrigation purposes." No other corroborating evidence for this incident appears to exist.

59. See Coolidge to Thomas M. Jones, July 16, 1886, RBIA.

60. Ellis, *Pioneers*, 17–18.

61. Sherman Coolidge, "Education of Indians," 594–95.

62. Talbot, *My People of the Plains*, 15, 247–49.

63. Coolidge to G. Coolidge, ca. January 1899, CHC.

64. Coolidge, "Sherman Coolidge Autobiographical Notes," CHC.

65. Sherman Coolidge, "Ye Cannot Serve God and Mammon," ca. 1920s, CHC; and *Report of the Executive Council*, 91–92.

66. See G. Coolidge to A. Talbot, August 25, 1902, CHC.

67. Coolidge to William Jones, May 24, 1886, CHC; and Coolidge to Jones, December 23, 1886, CHC. The quote is from the last letter. Coolidge and Jones were very close and often discussed their desires for female companionship and marriage. See Jones to Coolidge, October 22, 1890, CHC.

68. Talbot, "Second Annual Report," in *Annual Report*, 87. Also see Coolidge, "Indian of To-Day," 91–92; Goodnough, "Sherman Coolidge," AHC; Murphy, "Reverend John Roberts"; and Office of Archeology and Historic Preservation, "Shoshone Episcopal Mission." Construction of the girls' boarding school began in 1888. Later, an act of Congress and the consent of the Arapaho and Shoshone Tribal Councils in 1909 allowed the transfer of the title of the land to the Episcopal Church. This process was only completed in 1909. Talbot was the former bishop of the Episcopal Diocese of Central Pennsylvania before his move to Wyoming.

69. Coolidge, "Indian of To-Day," 92; Goodnough, "Sherman Coolidge," AHC; and Office of Archeology and Historic Preservation, "Shoshone Episcopal Mission."

70. Whipple to Coolidge, ca. Fall 1884, CHC.

71. See Goodnough, "Sherman Coolidge," AHC.

72. See Coolidge to William Jones, December 23, 1886, CHC; and G. Coolidge to A. Talbot, October 22, 1902, CHC.

4. CONSPIRACY, EXILE, AND THE EAST

1. Spalding to Coolidge, December 1885, CHC.
2. See Coolidge to Thomas Jones, April 7, 1887, CHC. Unfortunately, no information seems to exist on Sherman Coolidge's reunion with his half-sister.
3. Coolidge to Thomas M. Jones, July 16, 1886, RBIA.
4. F. L. Beane to Coolidge, April 21, 1887, CHC. Also see Coolidge to Jones, December 23, 1886, CHC; and Stamm, *People of the Wind River*, 286n44.
5. Coolidge to Whipple, May 8, 1887, HWP.
6. A. M. Johnson to John Atkins, November 19, 1886, RBIA; and Spalding to Coolidge, March 19, 1887, CHC.
7. See Linn et al., "Challenges of Enduring Language Programs," in *Indigenous Languages*, ed. Burnaby and Reyhner, http://jan.ucc.nau.edu/jar/ilac/ilac_13.pdf.
8. Coolidge to Whipple, May 8, 1887, HWP.
9. Coolidge to Atkins, December 10, 1886, RBIA. The letter also requested that Johnson stay in his present position rather than being transferred to another reservation in Washington state.
10. Johnson to Atkins, December 17, 1886, RBIA.
11. Coolidge to Atkins, April 5, 1887, RBIA; and Coolidge to Atkins, April 12, 1887, RBIA.
12. Affidavit of A. D. Lane, May 3, 1887, RBIA.
13. Affidavit of Henry Reed, May 3, 1887, RBIA.
14. Affidavit of Washakie, May 3, 1887, RBIA.
15. Affidavit of G. B. Jones, May 3, 1887, RBIA.
16. Jones to Whipple, May 15, 1887, HWP.
17. Thomas M. Jones, "Stating the Conditions of Affairs in Wind River School on His Return to the Agency," May 3, 1887, RBIA.
18. Sherman Coolidge, "Notes on an Indian Agent," 1887, CHC.
19. Coolidge to Atkins, April 5, 1887, RBIA. Italics in the original.
20. Coolidge to Atkins, April 12, 1887, RBIA.
21. Affidavit of Mary E. Jones, May 3, 1887, RBIA.
22. Coolidge to Whipple, May 8, 1887, HWP.
23. Copy of letter from Jones to Johnson (and Coolidge), May 10, 1887, RBIA.
24. Coolidge to Atkins, May 10, 1887, RBIA; and Johnson to Atkins, May 10, 1887, RBIA.
25. Copy of Jones to Coolidge, May 11, 1887, RBIA.
26. Coolidge to Spalding, May 10, 1887, HWP.

27. Coolidge to Whipple, May 18, 1887, HWP.

28. Roberts to Whipple, May 14, 1887, HWP.

29. Jones to Atkins, May 11, 1887, RBIA.

30. Jones to Whipple, May 15, 1887, HWP.

31. Spalding to Whipple, May 1887, HWP. Also see Spalding to Whipple, August 25, 1884, HWP.

32. H. B. Freeman to Whipple, May 24, 1887, HWP. Freeman may have been the same man that chaperoned Coolidge on part of his trip to Minnesota in 1877. He does not identify himself as holding a military rank in his letter, however.

33. C. Coolidge to Whipple, May 30, 1887, HWP.

34. Jones to Atkins, May 11, 1887, RBIA.

35. Coolidge to Spalding, May 10, 1887, HWP.

36. Ellis, *Pioneers*, 16; and "News Condensed," *Geneva Daily Times*, January 12, 1904, 1. "Sherman Coolidge Autobiographical Notes," CHC, seems to suggest that Coolidge visited his foster parents around the time of Hobart's commencement in June.

37. "The Story of Cane-Rush," accessed March 22, 2020, https://cs.nyu.edu/courses/spring09/v22.0380-001/maw410/nyu_Student_Traditions/canerushstory.html.

38. Coolidge to Grace Coolidge, June 15, 1918, CHC.

39. "News Condensed," 1.

40. "Ye Jolly Juniors," *The Echo*, 1889, 83, WHSL; and "An Adventure of St. Valentine's Eve," *The Echo*, 90, WHSL.

41. *The Echo*, 1890, 27, WHSL.

42. "Home and Vicinity," *Geneva Daily Gazette*, July 26, 1889, 3.

43. *Geneva Advertiser*, July 23, 1889, 3.

44. Barrows, *Proceedings*, 5. Also see Coolidge, "Indian Speeches," in Barrows, *Proceedings*, 98.

45. Coolidge, "Indian Speeches," in Barrows, *Proceedings*, 98.

46. Henry Kendall, "Indian Speeches," in Barrows, *Proceedings*, 99–100.

47. Coolidge, "Indian Speeches," 100. Some might wonder whether Coolidge was playing the "good" Indian here and using performance strategies that are discussed in Ramirez, *Standing Up to Colonial Power*, 4, such as acting white while he was not white. Others might simply take Coolidge's patriotism at face value.

48. *Report of the Executive Council*, 91–92.

49. "Rev. Sherman Coolidge Married," *Geneva Advertiser-Gazette*, October 28, 1902, 2.

50. Ellis, *Pioneers*, 16; and Coolidge to Arthur C. Parker, March 7, 1913, PSAI.

51. "Thomas M. Jones," accessed August 15, 2020, http://penelope.uchicago
    .edu/Thayer/E/Gazetteer/Places/America/United_States/Army/USMA
    /Cullums_Register/1625.html.
52. Duncombe, "Church and the Native American Arapahoes," 365.
53. G. Coolidge to A. Talbot, November 25, 1902, CHC.
54. Henry Niles Pierce to Coolidge, 1890, CHC. Cited in Barnes, "Between Two
    Worlds," 16.

5. LOSING GROUND

1. Greene, *American Carnage*, 69–70.
2. Fowler, *Arapahoe Politics*, 102.
3. Greene, *American Carnage*, 96–104.
4. Carlson, *Plains Indians*, 175–80.
5. Yenne, *Sitting Bull*, 241–46, 270–74.
6. Carlson, *Plains Indians*, 179–82.
7. Fowler, *Arapahoe Politics*, 102. One source indicates that Sherman Coolidge
   performed some interpreting work for Smithsonian ethnologist James
   Mooney in his study of the Ghost Dance. See Hertzberg, *American Indian
   Identity*, 45.
8. Meisenheimer, "Regionalist Bodies/Embodied Regions," in *Breaking Boundaries*, ed. Inness and Royer, 114–15; and Meyers, *Converging Stories*, 111.
9. Fowler, *Arapahoe Politics*, 91.
10. Fowler, *The Arapaho*, 63.
11. Fowler, *Arapahoe Politics*, 91.
12. Speroff, *Carlos Montezuma, MD*, 67–69.
13. Fowler, *Arapahoe Politics*, 91, 100. Also see Nickerson, "Report Concerning
    Indians," in U.S. Department of the Interior, *Annual Reports*, 414.
14. It is very difficult to determine when Coolidge returned to Wind River.
    Church correspondence seems to indicate that he returned in January 1890.
    See Talbot to Coolidge, January 29, 1890, CHC; and Talbot, "Fourth Annual
    Report," in *Annual* Report, 81. Also see Coolidge to Rebecca Buttroff,
    August 20, 1894, CHC, for information on his living quarters.
15. Only in his "Sherman Coolidge Autobiographical Notes," CHC, does
    Coolidge mention that some of those Lakotas who survived Wounded Knee
    later became "strong Christians." No other comment could be found.
16. Jones to Coolidge, January 5, 1891, CHC.
17. Coolidge to Jones, January 26, 1891, CHC. Coolidge had one connection to
    Wounded Knee. In the aftermath of the Seventh Cavalry's massacre, troops
    discovered a baby girl under the body of her dead mother, who had been
    shot twice in the chest by an American soldier. Named Zintka Lanuna, or

"Lost Bird," the baby was adopted as a "curio" by Brig. Gen. Leonard Wright Colby of the Nebraska National Guard and his wife, Clara. Lost Bird's subsequent childhood in Washington DC proved exceedingly difficult. She faced prejudice in public schools, a fact that contributed to her expulsion on several occasions. In 1904 Sherman Coolidge, who knew the Colbys, suggested sending Lost Bird to the government-funded All Saints' School in South Dakota, overseen by Willian Hobart Hare, the first Episcopal bishop of that state. Lost Bird's parents accepted Coolidge's advice, and the girl thrived until an illness forced her to return to her adoptive mother. Leonard Colby had by then mostly deserted his family after impregnating a seventeen-year-old-German girl hired as a governess. Clara Colby sent Lost Bird to be educated at Haskell in 1908. She arrived pregnant and was dismissed. Leonard was likely the father. Lost Bird eventually ran away to seek acceptance on the Lakota reservations. There she visited her mother's mass gravesite and wept. The Lakotas, however, saw her as a stranger and ignored her pleas for help. She returned to Oregon and married a man who left her with syphilis, and from that point Lost Bird's life became one of illness and poverty. She married an abusive rodeo performer and died in California of the Spanish flu in 1920. Coolidge's recommended enrollment at All Saints' may have been the happiest period of her life. See "Worth Knowing About," 8. In the early 1990s, Lost Bird's body was exhumed and reburied at Pine Ridge, with grand funeral rites, near the resting place of her mother. Also see Agonito, *Brave Hearts*, 241–51; and Smith, "Lost Bird."

18. Gustin, "Arapaho Is Distinguished Churchman," WHSL.
19. Coolidge to Rebecca Buttroff, August 20, 1894, CHC.
20. O'Gara, "From Wind River to Carlisle."
21. Nickerson, "Report Concerning Indians," in U.S. Department of the Interior, *Annual Reports*, 415.
22. Fowler, *The Arapaho*, 78.
23. Coolidge, "Indians in Wyoming, 1890," in U.S. Census Bureau, *Report on Indians Taxed*, 10:628–29. On one page, Coolidge is included in a photograph with Black Coal and an Arapaho man named Painting Horse. The image appears in this volume.
24. Talbot to Coolidge, February 24, 1890, CHC.
25. Talbot to Coolidge, January 29, 1890, CHC.
26. Talbot to Coolidge, July 21, 1890, CHC.
27. Talbot to Coolidge, October 31, 1890, CHC.
28. Talbot to Coolidge, April 20, 1892, CHC.
29. Fowler, *Arapahoe Politics*, 97.

30. Coolidge, "Indian of To-Day," 87. The same May 1893 issue of the *Colorado Magazine* featured a short biography of Coolidge that Capt. J. T. Van Orsdale wrote to introduce him to the local public. See Van Orsdale, "Rev. Sherman Coolidge, D.D.," 85–86. Van Orsdale served with Charles Coolidge in the Seventh Infantry. See *United States Army and Navy Journal*, January 1903, 454.

31. Fowler, *Arapahoe Politics*, 97.

32. Coolidge, "Indian of To-Day," 87–94.

33. Fowler, *Arapahoe Politics*, 92–94; and Utley, *Last Days*, 146–57.

34. "Shoshone Agency," 162.

35. Fowler, *The Arapaho*, 73.

36. Fowler, *Arapahoe Politics*, 105.

37. See "Diocese News," April 1885, 494–95, 586; "Diocese News," May 1885, 658; "Chicago," 727; "Pennsylvania," 444; "Connecticut Letter," 91; "Educational Notes," 15; and *United States Army and Navy Journal*, March 1895, 452.

38. See "Chicago Letter," 91; and "Church Periodical Club," 441. For the "large sums of money" quote, see Goodnough, "Sherman Coolidge," AHC.

39. "Newark," 169.

40. "News and Notes," 5.

41. Rebecca Buttroff to Coolidge, June 8, 1891, CHC. Buttroff opens the letter by apologizing for her "long silence." She feared that Coolidge might have taken offense to her letter, later asking, "Have I offended you in my last?" She also told him she was "anxiously awaiting a reply." See Buttroff to Coolidge, August 23, 1891, CHC.

42. Coolidge to Buttroff, October 17, 1891, CHC. Italics in original.

43. Buttroff to Coolidge, November 22, 1891, CHC. Italics in original.

44. Buttroff to Coolidge, ca. December 1891, CHC.

45. Coolidge to Buttroff, January 3, 1892, CHC.

46. Buttroff to Coolidge, June 20, 1894, CHC.

47. Coolidge to Buttroff, August 20, 1894, CHC. Italics in original.

48. See Buttroff to Coolidge, ca. March 1899, CHC. The letter indicates that Buttroff had taken a teaching position at Carlisle, but it contains no grand romantic gestures.

49. Coolidge to Nettie Smith, June 1, 1891, CHC; and Coolidge to Smith, July 3, 1891, CHC.

50. Coolidge to Smith, September 31, 1891, CHC.

51. Smith to Coolidge, ca. September 31, 1891, CHC.

52. Smith to Coolidge, December 2, 1891, CHC; and Smith to Coolidge, January 17, 1893, CHC.

53. Smith to Coolidge, August 13, 1892, CHC.

54. Coolidge to Cornelia Pond, October 27, 1896, CHC.

55. See G. Coolidge to A. Talbot, May 27, 1898, CHC.

56. Goodnough, "Sherman Coolidge," AHC. In the early 1890s, the Coolidges had been transferred to Fort Logan, Colorado. In the fall of 1894, Sophie sailed across the Atlantic to France on the *La Touraine* with her sister. They wintered in Paris. See *United States Army and Navy Journal*, October 1894, 85.

57. "Full-Blood Indian Now a Missionary," PSAI.

58. See "General Coolidge Dies; Was in Three Wars."

59. See "News and Notes of the Month," 304. Though in 1899 the U.S. Commission to the Philippines found the colony to be majority Catholic, American Episcopalians heeded calls such as Charles's, sending missionaries in force until the country's independence was declared in 1946. See U.S. Senate, *Report of the Philippine Commission*, 4:109–10. The report states that at the time, 6.5 million Filipino Catholics and 1.5 million "idolaters and Mohammedans . . . are still to be civilized" (page 111). Also see Douglas, "'Light to the Nations.'"

60. See "Col. Meade Invalided at Home," *New York Times*, July 27, 1900; and "General Coolidge Dies; Was in Three Wars."

61. Coolidge, "American Indians," 253.

62. Hertzberg, *American Indian Identity*, 38–41; Eick, *They Met at Wounded Knee*, 5–6; and Miller, "Charles Alexander Eastman," in Liberty, *American Indian Intellectuals*, 61–70. Charles Eastman was raised by his Dakota grandmother at his dying mother's request. Eastman's half-white mother, Mary Nancy Eastman, was named Wakantakawin, or "Winona." Winona means "first-born daughter" in Dakota.

63. Coolidge, "American Indians," 253. Coolidge dates the meeting with McKinley at the time of the Spanish-American War.

64. Eastman, *Indian of Today*, 131.

65. "Annual Diocesan Council," 1–2.

66. *Journal of the Forty-First Annual Council*, 54.

67. Coolidge, "Report from Sherman Coolidge," March 1896, 118.

68. Roberts, "Report from John Roberts," March 1896, 118.

69. Coolidge, "Report from Sherman Coolidge," December 1898, 598; and Coolidge, "Report from Sherman Coolidge," May 1899, 229.

70. Coolidge, "Report from Sherman Coolidge," July 1897, 550; Coolidge to Nettie Smith, June 1, 1891, CHC; and Coolidge to Smith, July 3, 1891, CHC.

71. Duncombe, "Church and the Native American Arapahoes," 365.

72. Coolidge, "Report from Sherman Coolidge," January 1899, 14; and Roberts, "Report from John Roberts," August 1899, 408.

73. Coolidge, "Report from Sherman Coolidge," January 1899, 598. Arthur apparently had his own camp where he sought converts. He and Coolidge

seem to have been close. A letter discusses visiting Arthur and "four Cut-throat men" he was hosting from Pine Ridge. See Coolidge to G. Coolidge, January 19, 1899, CHC.

74. Markley and Crofts, *Walk Softly*, 85.

75. U.S. Senate Committee on Indian Affairs, *Hearings*, 93–95. Here, Coolidge discusses how the Northern Arapahos had been forced to eat drowned sheep and diseased cattle. Also see "Terrible Plight of Indians: Forced to Eat Cattle Dead of Starvation," *National Humane Review*, August 1920, 149. The article cites Grace Coolidge: "Mrs. Sherman Coolidge, whose husband is an Arapahoe Indian of Wyoming, has written that the Indians of the Wind River reservation, Wyoming, have had to resort to eating such food. She has made no such report this winter, but in the past. Rev. Sherman Coolidge is a resident of Denver, Colo."

76. Coolidge, "Wanted: To Save the Babies," 19.

77. *Report of the Executive Council*, 127.

78. Fowler, *Arapahoe Politics*, 97.

79. Nickerson, "Report Concerning Indians," in U.S. Department of the Interior, *Annual Reports*, 414.

80. Chalcraft, "Report of Superintendent," in U.S. Department of the Interior, *Annual Reports*, 415–16.

81. Nickerson, "Report Concerning Indians," in U.S. Department of the Interior, *Annual Reports*, 414–15.

82. Fowler, *Arapahoe Politics*, 99, 106.

83. Fowler, *The Arapaho*, 23.

84. Fowler, *Arapahoe Politics*, 106.

85. Fowler, *The Arapaho*, 63.

86. Fowler, *Arapahoe Politics*, 106.

87. See the *New York Times* clipping, "Indian Outbreak in Wyoming: Arapa-hoe Braves Kill Stock and Defy Government Agent," included in Grace Coolidge's letter to Anne Talbot, ca. May 1901, CHC.

88. Fowler, *Arapahoe Politics*, 106.

89. Markley and Crofts, *Walk Softly*, 147; and "Shoshone Indians," 599. For a discussion of Washakie's birth year, perhaps 1809, see Stamm, *People of the Wind River*, 25.

90. Coolidge to Hebard, January 20, 1926, AHC.

91. Fowler, *Arapahoe Politics*, 106–7.

92. George Garfield (on behalf of the Arapaho council) to William H. Ketcham, January 12, 1902, BCIM. Herbert Welsh is mentioned as being Coolidge's half-white cousin in G. Coolidge to A. Talbot, November 25, 1902, CHC.

93. Ketcham to F. P. Sansone, February 11, 1902, BCIM; and Garfield to Ketcham, January 12, 1902, BCIM.

94. Fowler, *Arapahoe Politics*, 106–7; and *Progressive Men of the State of Wyoming*, 115.

95. "Society Girl's Heart and Hand Captured by an Indian," *Denver Post*, October 24, 1902, AHC; and *Report of the Executive*, 92.

6. GRACE

1. G. Coolidge to A. Talbot, July 4, 1896, CHC.

2. "The Coolidge Family," Finding Aid, CHC; Ellis, *Pioneers*, 18; "Publisher's Notes," in Coolidge, *Teepee Neighbors*, 4; and "Society Girl's Heart," AHC.

3. G. Coolidge to A. Talbot, January 1, 1897, CHC; and G. Coolidge to A. Talbot, February 28, 1897, CHC.

4. See G. Coolidge to A. Talbot, June 20, 1903; G. Coolidge to A. Talbot, March 13, 1924; and G. Coolidge to A. Talbot, August 4, 1919—all in CHC. In the August 4 letter, Grace, writing from the Claremont Hotel in New York, complains, "The Jews are ubiquitous."

5. G. Coolidge to A. Talbot, November 12, 1899, CHC.

6. G. Coolidge to A. Talbot, February 26, 1903, CHC.

7. Ellis, *Pioneers*, 19–20.

8. G. Coolidge to A. Talbot, March 4, 1902, CHC.

9. Letter fragment, likely dating from the late 1890s, shared by Philip Heinicke, email to author, December 19, 2020.

10. Ellis, *Pioneers*, 18–19, 24. Also see G. Coolidge to A. Talbot, July 4, 1896, CHC.

11. "The Ogontz School 1850–1950," Penn State University Libraries, accessed September 3, 2020, https://libraries.psu.edu/about/collections/ogontz-school-1850-1950.

12. Ellis, *Pioneers*, 18; Gustin, "Arapaho Is Distinguished Churchman," WHSL; and "Society Girl's Heart," AHC.

13. G. Coolidge to A. Talbot, January 1, 1897, CHC. Also see Ellis, *Pioneers*, 18.

14. G. Coolidge to A. Talbot, July 4, 1896, CHC.

15. Ellis, *Pioneers*, 18.

16. "Indian Husband Approved," *New York Times*, CHC.

17. "Society Girl's Heart," AHC.

18. "Shoshone Agency," 162.

19. Gustin, "Arapaho Is Distinguished Churchman," WHSL; "Publisher's Notes," in Coolidge, *Teepee Neighbors*, 4; and "Society Girl's Heart," AHC.

20. Ellis, *Pioneers*, 19.

21. Reid, "Westerners," 47.

22. "Anne Harvey Talbot Donaldson," Find a Grave, accessed September 3, 2020, https://www.findagrave.com/memorial/58268941/anne-harvey-donaldson.

23. G. Coolidge to A. Talbot, January 1, 1897, CHC; and G. Coolidge to A. Talbot, February 28, 1897, CHC.

24. See G. Coolidge to A. Talbot, November 4, 1897, CHC.

25. G. Coolidge to A. Talbot, February 9, 1932, CHC.

26. G. Coolidge to A. Talbot, November 5, 1897, CHC.

27. See, for instance, Laura A. Roberts to G. Coolidge, May 13, 1901, CHC.

28. G. Coolidge to Coolidge, January 19, 1899, CHC.

29. In this fragment of a letter shared by Philip Heinicke, Grace expresses great concern over hearing that Washakie had been injured in an incident involving a horse. The letter is addressed to Anne Talbot. Philip Heinicke, email to author, December 19, 2020.

30. G. Coolidge to A. Talbot, March 8, 1897, CHC.

31. G. Coolidge to A. Talbot, March 21, 1897, CHC. Also see preface to Hansson, *Six Modern Women*.

32. G. Coolidge to A. Talbot, February 28, 1897, CHC; and G. Coolidge to A. Talbot, March 15, 1897, CHC.

33. G. Coolidge to A. Talbot, February 28, 1897, CHC.

34. G. Coolidge to A. Talbot, March 21, 1897, CHC.

35. G. Coolidge to A. Talbot, April 2, 1897, CHC.

36. G. Coolidge to A. Talbot, April 30, 1897, CHC.

37. G. Coolidge to A. Talbot, May 18, 1897, CHC.

38. G. Coolidge to A. Talbot, April 30, 1897, CHC.

39. G. Coolidge to A. Talbot, April 2, CHC; and G. Coolidge to A. Talbot, April 30, 1897, CHC.

40. G. Coolidge to A. Talbot, June 24, 1897, CHC.

41. G. Coolidge to A. Talbot, November 4, 1897, CHC.

42. G. Coolidge to A. Talbot, April 26, 1897, CHC.

43. G. Coolidge to Coolidge, November 5, 1897, CHC.

44. Coolidge to G. Coolidge, November 1897, CHC.

45. G. Coolidge to A. Talbot, October 8, 1898, CHC; and G. Coolidge to A. Talbot, October 28, 1898, CHC.

46. G. Coolidge to A. Talbot, December 15, 1898, CHC.

47. G. Coolidge to A. Talbot, March 7, 1898, CHC.

48. Armentrout and Slocum, "Talbot, Ethelbert," in *Episcopal Dictionary*, accessed September 5, 2020, https://www.episcopalchurch.org/glossary/talbot-ethelbert/.

49. G. Coolidge to A. Talbot, September 18, 1898, CHC.

50. G. Coolidge to A. Talbot, December 15, 1898, CHC. Also see G. Coolidge to Coolidge, January 19, 1899, CHC. Grace writes that she went to see the Talbots around New Year's.
51. G. Coolidge to A. Talbot, January 2, 1899, CHC.
52. G. Coolidge to A. Talbot, January 16, 1899, CHC.
53. G. Coolidge to A. Talbot, January 30, 1899, CHC.
54. G. Coolidge to A. Talbot, February 1, 1899, CHC.
55. G. Coolidge to A. Talbot, February 6, 1899, CHC.
56. G. Coolidge to A. Talbot, March 30, 1899, CHC.
57. G. Coolidge to A. Talbot, April 16, 1899, CHC.
58. G. Coolidge to A. Talbot, May 9, 1899, CHC.
59. G. Coolidge to A. Talbot, May 19, 1899, CHC. Also see Ellis, *Pioneers*, 18.
60. G. Coolidge to Coolidge, July 27, 1899, CHC.
61. G. Coolidge to Coolidge, January 19, 1899, CHC.
62. G. Coolidge to A. Talbot, August 20, 1899, CHC. Also see G. Coolidge to Coolidge, July 27, 1899, CHC.
63. G. Coolidge to A. Talbot, June 4, 1899, CHC.
64. G. Coolidge to Coolidge, January 19, 1899, CHC.
65. Coolidge to G. Coolidge, ca. January 1899, CHC.
66. G. Coolidge to Coolidge, August 26, 1899, CHC.
67. G. Coolidge to A. Talbot, August 20, 1899, CHC.
68. G. Coolidge to Coolidge, August 26, 1899, CHC.
69. G. Coolidge to A. Talbot, September 10, 1899, CHC.

7. PROVING HERSELF

1. G. Coolidge to A. Talbot, October 4, 1899, CHC.
2. Armentrout and Slocum, "New York Training School for Deaconesses (NYTSD)," in *Episcopal Dictionary*, https://www.episcopalchurch.org/glossary /new-york-training-school-deaconesses-nytsd/. St. Faith's closed in 1948.
3. G. Coolidge to A. Talbot, June 1, 1901, CHC.
4. G. Coolidge to A. Talbot, March 1900, CHC; and G. Coolidge to A. Talbot, March 16, 1900, CHC.
5. G. Coolidge to A. Talbot, February 26, 1900, CHC.
6. G. Coolidge to A. Talbot, November 12, 1899, CHC.
7. G. Coolidge to A. Talbot, December 5, 1899, CHC.
8. G. Coolidge to A. Talbot, ca. May 1900, CHC.
9. G. Coolidge to A. Talbot, March 16, 1900, CHC.
10. G. Coolidge to A. Talbot, November 12, 1899, CHC; and G. Coolidge to A. Talbot, November 26, 1899, CHC. The November 26 letter reads: "I can't go to bed without writing you to tell you how I do long for that Wednesday night

when I can come over to you. It does seem as tho' I wanted to come to you so much more than I even have before. I want you and need you so."

11. G. Coolidge to A. Talbot, December 5, 1899, CHC. Grace sometimes discussed her teachers with Anne. In one letter, Grace wrote, "I do want you to meet that Miss Hopkins. She's fiercely attractive. Make a fine wife for somebody. I can't think why she's not married."

12. G. Coolidge to A. Talbot, December 10, 1899, CHC.

13. G. Coolidge to A. Talbot, May 1900, CHC.

14. G. Coolidge to A. Talbot, March 27, 1900, CHC.

15. G. Coolidge to A. Talbot, May 4, 1900, CHC.

16. L. Roberts to G. Coolidge, May 13, 1901, CHC.

17. G. Coolidge to A. Talbot, January 13, 1901, CHC. Also see G. Coolidge to A. Talbot, February 6, 1901, CHC, for evidence that Grace and Anne were meeting regularly.

18. G. Coolidge to A. Talbot, May 6, 1901, CHC.

19. G. Coolidge to A. Talbot, May 1901, CHC.

20. G. Coolidge to A. Talbot, May 1901, CHC.

21. G. Coolidge to A. Talbot, May 1901, CHC.

22. G. Coolidge to A. Talbot, ca. May 1901, CHC.

23. Lewandowski, *Red Bird, Red Power*, 66, 88.

24. Lucy N. Carter to G. Coolidge, May 26, 1901, CHC.

25. G. Coolidge to A. Talbot, June 1, 1901, CHC.

26. G. Coolidge to A. Talbot, June 10, 1901, CHC.

27. G. Coolidge to A. Talbot, June 9, 1901, CHC. Also see G. Coolidge to Coolidge, December 25, 1906, CHC.

28. G. Coolidge to A. Talbot, June 10, 1901, CHC.

29. G. Coolidge to A. Talbot, June 21, 1901, CHC.

30. G. Coolidge to A. Talbot, July 24, 1901, CHC.

31. G. Coolidge to A. Talbot, August 22, 1901, CHC.

32. Simmons, *Ute Indians of Utah*, 208, 223.

33. G. Coolidge to A. Talbot, July 24, 1901, CHC; and G. Coolidge to A. Talbot, August 22, 1901, CHC.

34. G. Coolidge to A. Talbot, August 6, 1901, CHC.

35. G. Coolidge to A. Talbot, July 24, 1901; G. Coolidge to A. Talbot, August 22, 1901; and G. Coolidge to A. Talbot, October 31, 1901—all in CHC.

36. G. Coolidge to A. Talbot, July 24, 1901, CHC.

37. G. Coolidge to A. Talbot, August 6, 1901, CHC.

38. G. Coolidge to A. Talbot, August 22, 1901, CHC.

39. G. Coolidge to A. Talbot, July 24, 1901, CHC.

40. G. Coolidge to A. Talbot, August 30, 1901, CHC.

41. Carter to G. Coolidge, May 26, 1901, CHC.
42. G. Coolidge to A. Talbot, October 31, 1901, CHC.
43. G. Coolidge to A. Talbot, November 3, 1901, CHC. This letter also mentions that Grace had briefly glimpsed a visiting Sherman while at St. Faith's. She was in class, heard people outside the door of her room, and looked out. In back was Sherman boasting a "cheerful grin." He then disappeared, and when she looked for him later, he had gone.
44. G. Coolidge to A. Talbot, November 24, 1901, CHC.
45. G. Coolidge to A. Talbot, January 11, 1902, CHC.
46. G. Coolidge to A. Talbot, January 15, 1902, CHC.
47. G. Coolidge to A. Talbot, March 4, 1902, CHC. Bishop Funsten had replaced Ethelbert Talbot upon Talbot's election as the bishop of central Pennsylvania. He continued Talbot's work at Wind River when not tending to his own flock of five children. See Hawley, *History of Idaho*, 381–82.
48. G. Coolidge to A. Talbot, March 17, 1902, CHC.
49. G. Coolidge to A. Talbot, March 21, 1902, CHC.
50. G. Coolidge to A. Talbot, April 25, 1902, CHC.
51. G. Coolidge to A. Talbot, May 29, 1902, CHC.
52. G. Coolidge to A. Talbot, June 25, 1902, CHC.
53. G. Coolidge to A. Talbot, ca. June 1902, CHC.

8. TWOSING

1. G. Coolidge to A. Talbot, June 13, 1902, CHC.
2. G. Coolidge to A. Talbot, June 25, 1902, CHC.
3. G. Coolidge to A. Talbot, July 7, 1902, CHC; and G. Coolidge to A. Talbot, September 10, 1902, CHC. The quote is from the July 7 letter.
4. G. Coolidge to A. Talbot, June 25, 1902, CHC. Grace elsewhere compared the Shoshones to "sunflowers," being "round and foolish." See G. Coolidge to A. Talbot, August 5, 1902, CHC.
5. G. Coolidge to A. Talbot, June 25, 1902, CHC. Also see "Julia Felter Hereford." Julia was married to John R. Hereford, born June 18, 1874, in Sweetwater, Wyoming. Hereford died on October 3, 1941, at age sixty-seven. He is buried in Washakie Cemetery alongside his wife. See "John H. Hereford," Find a Grave, accessed June 20, 2020, https://www.findagrave.com /memorial/146659736/john-r-hereford.
6. G. Coolidge to A. Talbot, July 2, 1902, CHC.
7. G. Coolidge to A. Talbot, June 25, 1902, CHC.
8. G. Coolidge to A. Talbot, July 2, 1902, CHC.
9. G. Coolidge to A. Talbot, July 7, 1902, CHC.
10. G. Coolidge to A. Talbot, July 31, 1902, CHC.

11. G. Coolidge to A. Talbot, July 7, 1902, CHC.

12. G. Coolidge to A. Talbot, August 5, 1902, CHC.

13. G. Coolidge to A. Talbot, July 21, 1902, CHC.

14. G. Coolidge to A. Talbot, August 5, 1902, CHC.

15. G. Coolidge to A. Talbot, August 20, 1902, CHC.

16. G. Coolidge to A. Talbot, August 20, 1902, CHC.

17. G. Coolidge to A. Talbot, September 1, 1902, CHC.

18. G. Coolidge to A. Talbot, September 10, 1902, CHC.

19. G. Coolidge to A. Talbot, September 24, 1902, CHC.

20. G. Coolidge to A. Talbot, October 22, 1902, CHC.

21. G. Coolidge to A. Talbot, September 24, 1902, CHC.

22. G. Coolidge to A. Talbot, October 22, 1902, CHC.

23. Gardner Wetherbee to G. Coolidge (telegram), October 6, 1902, CHC.

24. G. Coolidge to A. Talbot, October 22, 1902, CHC.

25. G. Coolidge to A. Talbot, November 2, 1902, CHC.

26. Gustin, "Arapaho Is Distinguished Churchman," WHSL.

27. G. Coolidge to A. Talbot, November 2, 1902, CHC.

28. G. Coolidge to A. Talbot, October 22, 1902, CHC.

29. "Society Girl's Heart," AHC.

30. "Indian Husband Approved," CHC.

31. "Rev. Sherman Coolidge Married."

32. "Society Girl's Heart," AHC. The *Denver Post*'s use of the phrase "Poor Lo" was in reference to Alexander Pope's "Essay on Man," line 99. It reads: "Lo, the poor Indian!" S. Alice Callahan (Creek) popularized this phrase with her novel, *Wynema*. See Callahan, *Wynema*, 52, 110.

33. G. Coolidge to A. Talbot, November 20, 1902, CHC.

34. G. Coolidge to A. Talbot, October 22, 1902, CHC.

35. Talbot to Coolidge, October 18, 1902, CHC.

36. "Col. Meade Invalided at Home"; "General Coolidge Dies; Was in Three Wars"; and "News and Notes of the Month," 304.

37. *United States Army and Navy Journal*, November 1902, 253.

38. *United States Army and Navy Journal*, June 1903, 1025.

39. *United States Army and Navy Journal*, July 1903, 1059.

40. *United States Army and Navy Journal*, August 1903, 1284.

41. G. Coolidge to A. Talbot, November 20, 1902, CHC.

42. Uncle Nye to G. Coolidge, November 12, 1902, CHC.

43. G. Coolidge to A. Talbot, November 20, 1902, CHC.

44. G. Coolidge to A. Talbot, October 22, 1902, CHC.

45. G. Coolidge to A. Talbot, November 25, 1902, CHC.

46. G. Coolidge to A. Talbot, December 8, 1902, CHC.

47. G. Coolidge to A. Talbot, February 21, 1903, CHC.
48. G. Coolidge to A. Talbot, November 25, 1902, CHC.
49. G. Coolidge to A. Talbot, December 8, 1902, CHC.
50. G. Coolidge to A. Talbot, February 26, 1903, CHC.
51. G. Coolidge to A. Talbot, December 8, 1902, CHC.
52. G. Coolidge to A. Talbot, November 20, 1902, CHC.
53. G. Coolidge to A. Talbot, December 27, 1902, CHC. Sherman's relative who made the comment to Grace was named Paul Revere. The Coolidges would later adopt his daughter, Virginia.

9. DEATH AND LIFE

1. G. Coolidge to A. Talbot, October 26, 1902, CHC.
2. G. Coolidge to A. Talbot, November 20, 1902, CHC.
3. G. Coolidge to A. Talbot, October 26, 1902, CHC.
4. G. Coolidge to A. Talbot, November 20, 1902, CHC.
5. G. Coolidge to A. Talbot, November 25, 1902, CHC.
6. G. Coolidge to A. Talbot, February 26, 1903, CHC.
7. G. Coolidge to A. Talbot, November 25, 1902, CHC.
8. See Coolidge to G. Coolidge, July 2, 1909, CHC. Sherman notes that his salary has just been raised to $600. Also see G. Coolidge to A. Talbot, November 25, 1902, CHC.
9. Coolidge, "Death of Brave Heart," CHC.
10. G. Coolidge to A. Talbot, January 15, 1903, CHC.
11. G. Coolidge to A. Talbot, November 25, 1902, CHC.
12. G. Coolidge to A. Talbot, July 2, 1902, CHC.
13. G. Coolidge to A. Talbot, February 26, 1903, CHC.
14. G. Coolidge to A. Talbot, November 25, 1902, CHC.
15. G. Coolidge to A. Talbot, January 15, 1903, CHC.
16. G. Coolidge to A. Talbot, January 26, 1903, CHC.
17. G. Coolidge to A. Talbot, January 15, 1903, CHC.
18. G. Coolidge to A. Talbot, October 14, 1903, CHC.
19. G. Coolidge to A. Talbot, January 15, 1903, CHC.
20. Philip Heinicke, email to author, December 16, 2020.
21. G. Coolidge to A. Talbot, April 21, 1903, CHC.
22. G. Coolidge to A. Talbot, April 25, 1903, CHC.
23. G. Coolidge to A. Talbot, May 30, 1903, CHC.
24. G. Coolidge to A. Talbot, March 13, 1903, CHC.
25. Coolidge, *Teepee Neighbors*, 9–10.
26. G. Coolidge to A. Talbot, March 5, 1904, CHC.
27. G. Coolidge to A. Talbot, February 26, 1903, CHC.

28. G. Coolidge to A. Talbot, May 13, 1903, CHC; and Photographic albums 1902–4, Ethelbert Talbot Papers, American Heritage Center, University of Wyoming–Laramie (hereafter ETP).

29. See, for instance, A. A. Abbott to Coolidge, January 7, 1904, CHC.

30. "Indian Priest from Wyoming," 495. Also see "Canon Coolidge Dies," *Hobart Herald*, February 18, 1932, 4.

31. *Churchman* 88, no. 11 (November 1903): 576; and "American Church News," 417. Also see James Bowen Funsten to Coolidge, May 28, 1903, CHC. The letter invites him to Washington.

32. "Missionary Council," 883.

33. *Churchman* 88, no. 12 (December 1903): 699.

34. *City and State*, December 10, 1903, 381.

35. Matthew K. Sniffen to Coolidge, ca. 1903, CHC. The letter discusses how Coolidge had asked that the Arapahos be allotted lands before Wind River was opened to further white settlement.

36. Talbot, "Bishop's Diary," 91.

37. Coolidge, "Arapahoe Christmas Tree," 113–15.

38. Coolidge, "Christmas Tree that Bore Souls," 280–83.

39. "Society Belle Turns Squaw," GHP. The article was reprinted as "Very Silly Woman or Exaggerated Story" in the *Albuquerque Indian* 1, no. 8 (January 1906): 21. The *Albuquerque Indian* was published by the Albuquerque Indian School. The story is attributed to the *Detroit Free Press*. The date is not provided but was likely 1904 because the article references the Coolidges' having met six years prior.

40. Coolidge, *Teepee Neighbors*, 11–12, 16.

41. G. Coolidge to A. Talbot, February 26, 1903, CHC.

42. G. Coolidge to A. Talbot, March 28, 1903, CHC.

43. G. Coolidge to A. Talbot, February 26, 1903, CHC.

44. G. Coolidge to A. Talbot, April 25, 1903; G. Coolidge to A. Talbot, May 30, 1903; and G. Coolidge to A. Talbot, June 20, 1903—all from CHC.

45. G. Coolidge to A. Talbot, August 20, 1903, CHC; and "Coolidge Family," Finding Aid, CHC. According to the Finding Aid, Louis was born April 14, 1904, and died on October 21, 1904.

46. G. Coolidge to A. Talbot, November 22, 1904, CHC; and "Coolidge Family," Finding Aid, CHC. According to the Finding Aid, Grace Ann was born prematurely on August 10, 1904, and died April 5, 1905, at nearly eight months. Though Grace's transcribed correspondence suggests these dates are correct, it seems impossible that she could have given birth again just four months after having Louis. It is possible that the transcription is faulty due to Grace's borderline-illegible handwriting.

47. G. Coolidge to A. Talbot, November 22, 1904, CHC.

48. G. Coolidge to A. Talbot, November 22, 1904, CHC; and "Coolidge Family," Finding Aid, CHC.

49. G. Coolidge to A. Talbot, January 9, 1905, CHC.

50. G. Coolidge to A. Talbot, April 9, 1905, CHC; and "Coolidge Family," Finding Aid, CHC.

51. G. Coolidge to A. Talbot, November 22, 1904; Coolidge to Funsten, November 6, 1905; and "Coolidge Family," Finding Aid—all from CHC.

52. G. Coolidge to A. Talbot, November 2, 1905, CHC. Sherman wrote to Bishop Funsten of Philip's death: "On the 17th of October my little son was born who was destined to stay only 12 days with us. While I was away at the Sunday School and at the Agency Church service he passed away, quietly in his mother's arms. Just before he died Mrs. Coolidge baptized him. He was apparently such a strong baby we both thought he would be Christened in the Church in due time as the others were." See Coolidge to Funsten, November 6, 1905, CHC. Funsten replied to Coolidge, writing that he was "exceedingly sorry to hear of the affliction that has come into the home of Mrs. Coolidge and yourself." He enclosed twenty-five dollars for expenses incurred by the sad situation and closed the letter, writing, "Praying to God will overrule all things in his glory." See Funsten to Coolidge, November 8, 1905, CHC. Around this time, it appears that Gardner Wetherbee had taken steps to secure his daughter's future in the event of his death. See Wetherbee to G. Coolidge, October 12, 1905, CHC. Wetherbee's letter explains that Grace will have no trouble receiving her property should something happen to him.

53. G. Coolidge to A. Talbot, October 25, 1905, CHC.

54. G. Coolidge to A. Talbot, December 8, 1905, CHC.

55. Thomas, "Some Children of Wyoming," 120.

56. G. Coolidge to A. Talbot, December 26, 1906, CHC. The letter contains the first mention of Effie.

57. Application for Enrollment in a Non-reservation School, Effie Coolidge, Student Files, Carlisle Indian School Digital Resource Center, Archives & Special Collections, Waidner-Spahr Library, Dickinson College PA (hereafter ECSF).

58. It proved difficult to determine when the Coolidges adopted Virginia. The first mention of her in a letter to Anne Talbot is Spring 1907. See G. Coolidge to A. Talbot, May 2, 1907, CHC.

59. Application for Enrollment in a Non-reservation School, Virginia Coolidge, Student File, Carlisle Indian School Digital Resource Center, Archives & Special Collections, Waidner-Spahr Library, Dickinson College PA (VCSF).

60. G. Coolidge to A. Talbot, October 1, 1908, CHC.
61. G. Coolidge to A. Talbot, May 11, 1906, CHC.
62. "General Coolidge Dies; Was in Three Wars."
63. Goodnough, "Sherman Coolidge," AHC.
64. "Coolidge Family," Finding Aid, CHC; and "Sarah Lucy Coolidge Row-lodge," Find a Grave, accessed May 20, 2020, https://www.findagrave
   .com/memorial/79480274/sarah-lucy-rowlodge. Also see G. Coolidge to
   Coolidge, December 25, 1906, CHC.
65. G. Coolidge to A. Talbot, May 6, 1907, CHC.
66. G. Coolidge to A. Talbot, May 2, 1907, CHC.
67. Uncle Nye to G. Coolidge, November 12, 1902, CHC.
68. Aunt Sarah to G. Coolidge, January 29, 1907, CHC. Less than a year later,
   Uncle Nye died. In his will, he left Grace over $3,000, the equivalent of
   roughly $85,000 in today's terms. See G. Coolidge to A. Talbot, November 15,
   1908, CHC. The letter also mentions that Grace's father had just sent her $500.

10. MALCONTENTS

1. Nicholson, "To Advance a Race," 1, 14–15.
2. Though McKenzie was meticulous in preserving his letters, correspondence
   between him and the Coolidges does not appear to exist from 1904 to 1911.
   See "Scope and Contents," Fayette Avery McKenzie Papers, Tennessee
   State Library and Archives, Nashville, accessed March 24, 2020, https://tsla
   .tnsosfiles.com/history/manuscripts/findingaids/McKENZIE_FAYETTE
   _AVERY_PAPERS_1894-1957.pdf.
3. McKenzie apparently disliked the agent at Wind River, and the feeling was
   mutual. He wrote Coolidge in 1905, "Sometimes I have feared that efforts
   have not been lacking to lessen my reputation on the Reservation—as
   they were not lacking to block my work and ruin my comfort while I was
   there. I understand the late superintendent is now willing to recognize my
   good qualities 'outside the Indian Service'—which means, I suppose, that
   he regards me as a failure in the Service." See Fayette Avery McKenzie to
   Coolidge, August 2, 1905, CHC.
4. Larner, "Society of American Indians," in Davis, *Native America in the Twentieth Century*, 603.
5. Nicholson, "To Advance a Race," 56–57.
6. Fowler, *Arapahoe Politics*, 93–94; and Funsten, "Indian as a Worker," 877.
7. "Indian Troubles in Boise," 248.
8. Fowler, *Arapahoe Politics*, 94–96.
9. J. M. Cooper to Alfred Heinicke, December 19, 1947. Philip Heinicke shared
   this letter in a private email to the author, December 20, 2020. Cooper's

letter also reveals that Sherman Coolidge's two biological daughters, Sallie and Rose, received allotments of 151.87 and 109.96 acres, respectively.

10. Fowler, *Arapahoe Politics*, 94–96.

11. Fowler, *The Arapaho*, 79.

12. Fowler, *Arapahoe Politics*, 96. Not long afterward, Wadsworth was caught cheating the Arapahos and Shoshones of their own monies and was terminated. See G. Coolidge to A. Talbot, September 18, 1906, CHC. Also see Fowler, *The Arapaho*, 79; and D. E. Coon, "Map of Wind River Indian Reservation, Wyoming: Showing Indian Allotments that Will Be Sold and Leased on the Ceded and Diminished Reservation," 1908, Historic Map Collection, University of Wyoming Libraries, https://uwdigital.uwyo.edu /islandora/object/wyu%3a121102.

13. Funsten often wrote Coolidge, sent him funds, and was pleased to hear of the Indian marriages he had performed at Wind River. See Coolidge to Funsten, November 6, 1905, CHC. For instances where Funsten sent Coolidge extra funds, see Funsten to Coolidge, March 4, 1905; Funsten to Coolidge, June 15, 1907; Funsten to Coolidge, August 30, 1907; and Funsten to Coolidge, March 3, 1909—all in CHC. Most of the extra funds came in sums of $100.

14. Funsten, "Indian as a Worker," 876–78.

15. G. Coolidge to A. Talbot, February 26, 1903, CHC.

16. "Indian Troubles in Boise," 248.

17. Fowler, *Arapahoe Politics*, 96.

18. Funsten, "Report of the Bishop," in *Annual Report*, 91–92.

19. "Year's Work," 506.

20. Funsten, "Five Thousand Miles," 873.

21. Kirshbaum, "Far West," 229.

22. Thomas, "Red Men of Wyoming," 759–62.

23. Fowler, *Arapahoe Politics*, 107, 324n59.

24. Duncombe, "Church and the Native American Arapahoes," 366–69.

25. Coolidge to G. Coolidge, July 2, 1909, CHC.

26. Duncombe, "Church and the Native American Arapahoes," 366.

27. Nathaniel S. Thomas to Coolidge, June 13, 1910, CHC. One could question whether the Episcopal hierarchy had really given up on Coolidge. In 1912 there was talk in church literature about the possibility he could become the first Indian bishop. See "First Indian Bishop May Be Named by Episco- pals," 1912, Sherman Coolidge File, Cathedral of St. John in the Wilderness Archives, Denver (hereafter SJWA).

28. Thomas to Coolidge, June 13, 1910, CHC; and *Indian's Friend* 13, no. 4 (December 1910): 1. A book written in 1911 by Rev. David A. Sanford, the

Episcopal missionary to the Southern Cheyennes and Arapahos from 1904 to 1907, states that Coolidge was "transferred" to Oklahoma. See Sanford, *Indian Topics*, 18. The real reasons for Coolidge's departure never seem to have appeared in print.

29. See G. Coolidge to Coolidge, September 10, 1910, CHC. Also see G. Coolidge to A. Talbot, April 16, 1913, CHC.
30. Thomas to Coolidge, January 6, 1910, CHC.
31. Philip Heinicke, email to author, December 16, 2020.
32. Goodnough, "Sherman Coolidge," AHC.
33. Fowler, *The Arapaho*, 61–77, 80–85.
34. Markley and Crofts, *Walk Softly*, 158–59; and Murphy, "Reverend John Roberts."

11. A NEW MISSION, A NEW SOCIETY

1. Wetherbee to G. Coolidge, January 12, 1910, CHC. Also see "Anna G. Wetherbee," Find a Grave, accessed August 17, 2020, https://www.findagrave.com/memorial/184290404/anna-g_-wetherbee. Hanna Nye Wetherbee died on December 30, 1909, aged sixty-nine.
2. S. Coolidge to G. Coolidge, May 19, 1910, CHC. In a later letter to Grace, Sophie discussed her thoughts on "how unjustly our Indians have been and are treated," and how Indians are "cheated" by the reservation system. Sophie writes, "I [illegible] hope to live to see the day when the Reservation is no longer in existence and when the Indian can become one of the best and most trustworthy citizens of these United States." See S. Coolidge to G. Coolidge, January 5, 1918, CHC.
3. Francis Key Brooke to Coolidge, July 4, 1910, CHC.
4. Brooke to Coolidge, December 26, 1911, CHC; and G. Coolidge to Coolidge, September 10, 1910, CHC. The latter letter was posted from Denver.
5. Coolidge to G. Coolidge, September 2, 1910, CHC.
6. Coolidge to G. Coolidge, November 28, 1910, CHC.
7. Coolidge and Dwyer, "Report of the Committee," in *Journal*, 20.
8. See "Announcements," 165. Also see Coolidge, "Indian Leaders in Council," 1004. Though the *Spirit of Missions* described him as being "in charge of field work" on the Cheyenne and Arapaho Indian Reservation, Owanah Anderson's research shows that Coolidge had no duties as a missionary at Whirlwind. Church records only list his signatures for marriages, baptisms, and services. See Anderson, *400 Years*, 162. A report from this period in New York's *Rushville Chronicle* tells of a visit Coolidge made to St. Mark's Church in Penn Yann, New York, during the summer of 1911. See *Rushville Chronicle*,

June 16, 1911, 5. The article calls Coolidge an "Arapaho Indian Chief" and mentions that he is a missionary in Oklahoma.

9. Coolidge to G. Coolidge, August 22, 1911, CHC.

10. Coolidge to G. Coolidge, September 21, 1910, CHC; and Coolidge to G. Coolidge, November 17, 1910, CHC. It seems that Gardner Wetherbee had begun to support financially his son-in-law and daughter following his wife's death. See G. Coolidge to Coolidge, September 7, 1911, CHC. The letter indicates that Grace's father had sent a check to Sherman in Oklahoma. Also see Anderson, *400 Years*, 150–65.

11. Coolidge to G. Coolidge, October 27, 1910, CHC; "Indian Work," in *Journal*, 16; "Our Indian Children," 160; and "Our Letter Box," 242.

12. Coolidge to G. Coolidge, September 5, 1910, CHC; and Coolidge to G. Coolidge, November 30, 1910, CHC.

13. Coolidge to G. Coolidge, October 5, 1910, CHC.

14. G. Coolidge to Coolidge, October 8, 1910, CHC.

15. G. Coolidge to Coolidge, September 17, 1911, CHC.

16. G. Coolidge to Coolidge, October 2, 1910, CHC.

17. G. Coolidge to Coolidge, October 28, 1910, CHC.

18. G. Coolidge to Coolidge, October 8, 1910, CHC.

19. G. Coolidge to A. Talbot, May 7, 1911, CHC.

20. G. Coolidge to Coolidge, September 25, 1911, CHC.

21. Coolidge to G. Coolidge, October 5, 1910, CHC. Italics in original.

22. Coolidge to G. Coolidge, October 27, 1910, CHC.

23. Coolidge to G. Coolidge, November 17, 1910; Coolidge to G. Coolidge, November 24, 1910; and Coolidge to G. Coolidge, April 13, 1911—all in CHC.

24. Coolidge to G. Coolidge, October 15, 1910; Coolidge to G. Coolidge, November 30, 1910; and G. Coolidge to A. Talbot, ca. Spring 1911—all in CHC.

25. Coolidge to G. Coolidge, November 17, 1910; Coolidge to G. Coolidge, February 27, 1910; Coolidge to G. Coolidge, February 28, 1911—all in CHC. The quote about the Oklahoma climate is from the November 17 letter.

26. Coolidge to G. Coolidge, February 28, 1911, CHC.

27. Draft letter from Coolidge to Brooke, April 1911, CHC. The draft is a response to a letter from Brooke dated April 20, 1911.

28. G. Coolidge to A. Talbot, April 8, 1912, CHC.

29. Coolidge to G. Coolidge, April 10, 1911, CHC. Italics in original.

30. Lanternari, *Religions of the Oppressed*, 65–67, 97–100. Peyote is a small cactus indigenous to the lands of present-day Mexico. Its top, or button, is edible and contains alkaloids such as mescaline, lophophorine, and anhaline. When ingested, these elements bring on effects such as hallucination and levitation.

Peyote is not considered addictive or a narcotic. Also see La Barre, *Peyote Cult*, 43–56.

31. Coolidge to G. Coolidge, April 10, 1911, CHC. Italics in original.
32. G. Coolidge to A. Talbot, January 25, 1912, CHC.
33. G. Coolidge to A. Talbot, June 16, 1912, CHC.
34. G. Coolidge to A. Talbot, November 15, 1911, CHC; and G. Coolidge to A. Talbot, ca. November 1911, CHC.
35. G. Coolidge to A. Talbot, ca. May 1911, CHC.
36. See Coolidge to G. Coolidge, May 9, 1911, CHC; and Coolidge to G. Coolidge, February 6, 1912, CHC.
37. Coolidge to G. Coolidge, June 14, 1911, CHC; and G. Coolidge to A. Talbot, July 14, 1911, CHC.
38. Harriet M. Bedell to Coolidge, July 7, 1911, CHC. Also see Bedell to Coolidge, August 25, 1911, CHC.
39. G. Coolidge to A. Talbot, October 17, 1911, CHC.
40. Larner, "Society of American Indians," in Davis, *Native America in the Twentieth Century*, 603; and Nicholson, "To Advance a Race," 1–2, 14, 56, 61–62, 323–24.
41. Coolidge to G. Coolidge, November 18, 1908, CHC. Public interest had not been great. Coolidge told Grace of how few people attended the lectures. No surviving record of Coolidge's speeches during that week at Ohio State exists, but Eastman discussed the Battle of Little Big Horn. McKenzie was disappointed with the press coverage that followed the lectures. He felt "small space" was devoted to the lectures' actual contents.
42. Perhaps Eastman's most famous book, the autobiography *From the Deep Woods to Civilization*, was published in 1916. For a brief discussion of Eastman's output, see Miller, "Charles Alexander Eastman," in Liberty, *American Indian Intellectuals*, 61–70.
43. Hertzberg, *American Indian Identity*, 43–45; and Speroff, *Carlos Montezuma, MD*, 1–2, 24–30, 47–63, 117, 201–3.
44. See, for instance, Super, "Indian Education at Carlisle," 220.
45. Speroff, *Carlos Montezuma, MD*, 333.
46. Nicholson, "To Advance a Race," 62–63.
47. Hertzberg, *American Indian Identity*, 71; and Speroff, *Carlos Montezuma, MD*, 333–34.
48. *Report of the Executive Council*, 19, 174.
49. "Full-Blood Indian Now a Missionary," PSAI.
50. Larner, "Society of American Indians," 604.
51. Hertzberg, *American Indian Identity*, 37, 45.

52. See Maddox, *Citizen Indians*, 11–16, for a discussion of the SAI activists' primary concerns. For those SAI leaders critical of white society, one might cite Arthur C. Parker or Gertrude Bonnin, both of whom regularly condemned white society as individualistic and driven by greed. See, for instance, Parker's March 1917 letter to Philip Gordon, in which he criticizes "modern business ethics" and states: "I rather honor [Indians] for not becoming commercial hearted." Arthur C. Parker to Philip Gordon, March 23, 1917, PSAI. The attorney Thomas Sloan (Omaha) went to great lengths to protect the peyote religion. See Hertzberg, *American Indian Identity*, 174, 249, 255, 268. Bonnin often celebrated Native values and argued for their preservation in her writings. See her articles "Indian Praying," 92; and "Heart to Heart Talk," *San Francisco Bulletin*, 1922. For some of Bonnin's harshest criticisms of whites' treatment of Native peoples, see her "Our Sioux People," 1923, Gertrude and Raymond Bonnin Collection, L. Tom Perry Special Collections, Harold B. Library, Brigham Young University, Provo (hereafter GRBC). Charles Eastman often indicated, with subtlety, that Native values were superior to white hypocrisies. See the discussion in Hoxie, *This Indian Country*, 171–75, 178.
53. Hertzberg, *American Indian Identity*, 31.
54. Maddox, *Citizen Indians*, 10–11.
55. Hoxie, *Talking Back to Civilization*, 11.
56. Leonard, *Illiberal Reformers*, 142, 152, 156.
57. In the brief entry Folkmar devotes to American Indians, he states that they are likely related to Mongolians. See Folkmar, *Dictionary of Races or Peoples*, 77–78.
58. Born in 1863, Marie Louise Bottineau Baldwin was of French and Ojibwe extraction. Her father, Jean Baptiste Bottineau, was a wealthy lawyer who fought diligently for the land claims of his Turtle Mountain Band of Ojibwe. Baldwin moved with her father to Washington DC to aid his legal practice, and she later earned a degree from Washington College of Law. See Cahill, "Marie Louise Bottineau Baldwin," 65, 69–70, 73. Charles E. Dagenett was born in present-day Oklahoma around 1872. At Carlisle, he worked as the school's printer, and upon graduation in 1887 he enrolled in neighboring Dickinson College, completing his degree at Eastman College in Poughkeepsie, New York. He joined the Indian Service in 1904 and in 1907 became its highest-ranking Native employee as the supervisor of employment. See Speroff, *Carlos Montezuma, MD*, 337. Laura Cornelius (later Kellogg), born in 1888, later published *Our Democracy and the American Indian* (1920). The monograph criticized Euro-American society for its treatment of Indians and laid out "a practical plan based on real values, with the singleness of

purpose of bringing new life to a whole people." See Kellogg, *Our Democracy*, 10. Henry Roe Cloud, born in 1884, graduated from Yale in 1910 and joined the SAI at just twenty-five years old. He would go on to found a preparatory school for Indian boys in Wichita, Kansas, the Roe Institute, later named the American Indian Institute. In 1933 he was appointed superintendent at Haskell. Roe Cloud died in 1950. See Speroff, *Carlos Montezuma*, MD, 336. Born in 1868 or '69 in present-day Nebraska, Angel De Cora, later De Cora Dietz, attended Hampton as a child and later became one of the best-known Native artists of her generation. See Waggoner, *Fire Light*, 3, 23–29. She provided illustrations for Gertrude Bonnin's 1901 book, *Old Indian Legends*. Upon her death in 1919, De Cora Deitz donated $3,000 to the Society of American Indians. See Lewandowski, *Red Bird, Red Power*, 57, 217n60.

59. Hertzberg, *American Indian Identity*, 46; Hoxie, *This Indian Country*, 238–40; and Porter, *To Be Indian*, 111, 118, 122.

60. Speroff, *Carlos Montezuma*, MD, 334–36.

61. Valentine, "Address," in *Report of the Executive Council*, 27–28.

62. Kellogg, "Industrial Organization for the Indian," in *Report of the Executive Council*, 43–55.

63. Baldwin, "Modern Home Making," in *Report of the Executive Council*, 58–67.

64. Parker, "Philosophy of Indian Education," in *Report of the Executive Council*, 68–76.

65. "Discussion on Indian Education," in *Report of the Executive Council*, 79–80.

66. De Cora Dietz, "Native Indian Art," in *Report of the Executive Council*, 84, 87.

67. *Report of the Executive Council*, 88, 91.

68. Coolidge contributed his knowledge to a volume on sign language published in 1918. See Seton, *Sign Talk*, xiii, 106. Also see Coolidge to G. Coolidge, ca. January 1899, CHC.

69. *Report of the Executive Council*, 91–92.

70. See discussion in Maddox, *Indian Citizens*, 1–17, regarding how participation in the SAI strengthened the Native perspectives of the membership.

71. "The Public Entertainment," in *Report of the Executive Council*, 110–11.

72. Sloan, "Reservation System—Administration," in *Report of the Executive Council*, 115–16.

73. *Report of the Executive Council*, 127–29.

74. *Report of the Executive Council*, 174.

75. "Indians Will Speak from Church Pulpits," 1911, PSAI. Coolidge's role in the Society of American Indians was later reported on at his alma mater, Hobart College. See "Alumni Notes," *Hobart Herald*, November 15, 1911, 5.

76. See, for instance, "Indian Has His Cause"; "A New Type of Red Man"; and "Rally of Red Men"—all quoted in *Report of the Executive Council*, 165–70.

77. Parker to Joseph Keppler, November 5, 1911, quoted in Hertzberg, *American Indian Identity*, 59.

78. *Report of the Executive Council*, 157–58.

79. Coolidge to G. Coolidge, October 12, 1911, CHC; and "Full-Blood Indian Now a Missionary," PSAI.

80. Speroff, *Carlos Montezuma*, MD, 339.

81. Bedell to Coolidge, November 15, 1911, CHC; and Coolidge to G. Coolidge, December 27, 1911, CHC.

82. Coolidge to G. Coolidge, December 4, 1911, CHC.

83. Sophie Hope Austin (later known as Rosie) Coolidge would be born September 5, 1912, in Faribault, Minnesota. See "Coolidge Family," Finding Aid, CHC.

84. Coolidge to G. Coolidge, February 6, 1912, CHC.

85. See, for instance, Parker to Coolidge, April 6, 1911, PSAI.

86. Parker to Coolidge, November 20, 1911, PSAI.

87. Parker to Coolidge, December 5, 1911, PSAI.

88. Coolidge to Parker, December 14, 1911, PSAI.

89. Hertzberg, *American Indian Identity*, 79–82.

90. Coolidge to G. Coolidge, February 6, 1912, CHC.

91. Coolidge to G. Coolidge, February 10, 1912, CHC.

92. Coolidge to G. Coolidge, February 6, 1912, CHC.

93. Coolidge to G. Coolidge, February 10, 1912, CHC.

94. Coolidge to G. Coolidge, February 13, 1912, CHC.

95. See Parker to Coolidge, February 5, 1912, PSAI.

96. G. Coolidge to Coolidge, March 3, 1912, CHC; and Coolidge to G. Coolidge, March 6, 1912, CHC.

97. Coolidge to G. Coolidge, March 9, 1912, CHC.

98. G. Coolidge to Coolidge, ca. March 1912, CHC.

99. Coolidge to G. Coolidge, February 13, 1912, CHC.

100. "Objects of the Society," in *Report of the Executive Council*, 14.

101. *Platform of the Third Annual Conference of the Society of American Indians*, 1913, PSAI.

102. Effie Agnes Coolidge, Application for Membership, 1912; Sallie Coolidge, Application for Membership, 1912; Virginia Coolidge, Application for Membership, 1912—all in PSAI. Sallie Coolidge signed her own application in a childlike script.

12. THE SOCIETY ASCENDANT

1. G. Coolidge to A. Talbot, April 22, 1912, CHC.

2. G. Coolidge to A. Talbot, April 16, 1913, CHC.

3. G. Coolidge to A. Talbot, April 22, 1912, CHC. As noted previously, following his wife's death, Gardner Wetherbee evidently began offering Sherman and Grace financial support. Coolidge's move to Faribault, incidentally, was recorded in "Alumni Notes," *Hobart Herald*, October 1, 1912, 5.

4. "Henry Benjamin Whipple."

5. See Ehrenhalt and Laskey, *Precious and Adored*.

6. "Conference Evening," 300. Just a single periodical refers to Coolidge's serving as a rector in Faribault. See Kinney, "Indian YMCA Conference," 654–55.

7. "Reports of the Clergy," *Journal of the Fifty-Ninth Annual Convention, Diocese of Minnesota*, 1916, 141.

8. S. Coolidge to Hebard, December 29, 1930, GHP. Goodnough records the use of the nickname "Rosie." "Coolidge Family," Finding Aid, CHC; Goodnough, "Sherman Coolidge," AHC; and "Rose Austin Coolidge Heinicke," Find a Grave, accessed May 29, 2020, https://www.findagrave.com/memorial /34858869/rose-austin-heinicke.

9. G. Coolidge to A. Talbot, September 5, 1912, CHC.

10. *Quarterly Journal of the Society of American Indians* 1, no. 1 (January–April 1913): 115.

11. See Parker to Coolidge, December 5, 1911, PSAI.

12. Coolidge to Parker, December 14, 1911, PSAI.

13. Parker to Coolidge, December 30, 1911, PSAI.

14. Parker to Coolidge, February 5, 1912, PSAI; and Parker to Coolidge, February 23, 1912, PSAI.

15. Parker corresponded frequently with Coolidge on financial matters and other society business throughout 1912. See Parker to Coolidge, March 5, 1912, PSAI; and Parker to Coolidge, May 14, 1912, PSAI.

16. Parker to Coolidge, April 6, 1911, PSAI.

17. Hertzberg, *American Indian Identity*, 83; Larner, "Society of American Indians," 604; and *Report of the Executive Council*, 15.

18. Hertzberg, *American Indian Identity*, 84, 92, 96–97; and *Quarterly Journal of the Society of American Indians* 1, no. 1 (January–April 1913): 115.

19. Society of American Indians, *Proceedings of the Second Annual Conference*, 118–19. Printed as a supplement to *Quarterly Journal of the Society of American Indians* 1, no. 1 (January–April 1913).

20. Hill, "Some Social and Moral Conditions," in Society of American Indians, *Proceedings of the Second Annual Conference*, 119–25; and Parker, "Modern Indian Council," 54.

21. Society of American Indians, *Proceedings of the Second Annual Conference*, 125, 136.

22. Hertzberg, *American Indian Identity*, 85.

23. Society of American Indians, *Proceedings of the Second Annual Conference*, 183. The speech was later reprinted in the *Journal of History*, in slightly modified form, as well as in the SAI *Quarterly*. See Coolidge, "Use Your Citizenship Worthily," 298–301.

24. Coolidge, "Indian American," 20–24. Coolidge's speech was printed in the *Quarterly*, not the *Proceedings of the Second Annual Conference*.

25. Parker to Coolidge, May 1, 1913, PSAI.

26. Pratt, "Solution to the Indian Problem," in Society of American Indians, *Proceedings of the Second Annual Conference*, 199–202.

27. Adams, *Education for Extinction*, 320–23; and Hertzberg, *American Indian Identity*, 17–18.

28. Society of American Indians, *Proceedings of the Second Annual Conference*, 135–36.

29. Hertzberg, *American Indian Identity*, 97. Laura Cornelius Kellogg and her fellow Oneida, the conductor and cornet virtuoso Dennison Wheelock, filled the other two posts of vice president.

30. "Platform of the Second Annual Conference," 71–74. The society also listed a number of urgent matters that the members demanded be addressed, including the unprosecuted murder of a Seminole Indian in Palm Beach, Florida; the securing of the title of the Mescalaro Apache Indians to their reservation; and the restitution of lands to the Turtle Mountain Band of North Dakota.

31. Coolidge to G. Coolidge, October 5, 1912, CHC.

32. Parker to Coolidge, November 8, 1912, PSAI; and Coolidge to Parker, February 9, 1913, PSAI.

33. Parker to Coolidge, December 1, 1912, PSAI. Parker writes: "I have not been writing you very much because of the feeling which I have in my bones that you should glue yourself to a chair, take a quart of ink and supply of pens and finish that biography of yours. If you do not do it when I come to Minnesota, I shall put the quart of ink in a squirt gun, point it at you and see how fast you can run."

34. G. Coolidge to A. Talbot, March 1, 1913, CHC. Also see Coolidge to Parker, March 7, 1913, PSAI. Also see *Indian's Friend* 15, no. 6 (March 1913): 2. Grace's aunt Sarah had died a few months before in November 1912 following a week spent ill in the hospital. See G. Coolidge to A. Talbot, December 14, 1912, CHC.

35. G. Coolidge to A. Talbot, April 16, 1913, CHC.

36. Coolidge to Parker, March 7, 1913, PSAI. See Parker to Coolidge, March 10, 1913, PSAI, for the quote regarding the "clan."

37. Coolidge to Carlos Montezuma, April 30, 1913, Carlos Montezuma Papers, Wisconsin State Historical Society, Madison (hereafter CMP); and Coolidge

to Richard Henry Pratt, May 1, 1913, Richard Henry Pratt Papers, Beinecke Rare Book and Manuscript Library, Yale University, New Haven CT (hereafter RHPP).

38. Coolidge to Montezuma, May 5, 1913, CMP.

39. Coolidge to Pratt, May 17, 1913, RHPP. Coolidge assured Pratt: "I am not, and never was, in favor of the Wild West Show type of Indian." Also see "Leaders of Indians to Hold Convention in Denver Oct. 7–12," 1914, CMP.

40. Coolidge to Montezuma, May 20, 1913, CMP. Italics in original.

41. Parker to Coolidge, August 19, 1913, PSAI; and Parker to Coolidge, September 6, 1913, PSAI.

42. Parker to Coolidge, July 1, 1913, PSAI.

43. Parker to Coolidge, July 7, 1913, PSAI.

44. Parker to Coolidge, April 24, 1913, PSAI.

45. John Hewitt to Parker, August 25, 1913, PSAI.

46. J. H. Norris to Coolidge, July 31, 1913, CHC. Also see Coolidge to G. Coolidge, November 9, 1916, CHC. The letter gives the allotment's size.

47. Coolidge to G. Coolidge, May 31, 1913, CHC. In Washington DC, Coolidge also took care to ensure that Virginia Coolidge's allotment at Wind River had been guaranteed water rights. Sherman spent ten days in the capital seeing to these tasks. See G. Coolidge to A. Talbot, June 1, 1913, CHC.

48. Hertzberg, *American Indian Identity*, 97, 112–15; and Larner, "Society of American Indians," 603. Also see the untitled article in *Trail* 6, no. 5 (October 1913): 6–9, for the location of the headquarters. Parker and Coolidge had chosen the conference theme, which was originally formulated as "What the Indian Can Do for Himself." See Parker to Coolidge, July 7, 1913, PSAI.

49. McKenzie, "Cooperation of the Two Races," 23–32.

50. Coolidge, "American Indian of Today," 33–35.

51. See untitled article, *Trail*, 6–9. The *Trail* was a monthly published for the Society of Sons of Colorado.

52. "Indians Plead for Justice in Local Pulpits," 1913, PSAI. One newspaper later made the claimed that in Denver, Coolidge had met the man who killed his father. Though it is possible, no other source indicates that this meeting occurred. See "Real Americans at Meeting of Indian Society," 1914, PSAI.

53. At the conference's end, Sloan lost his vice presidency to another attorney, a Menominee named William J. Kershaw. Dagenett was elected one of the vice presidents, along with Representative Carter and Potawatomi school teacher Emma Johnson Goulette. See Hertzberg, *American Indian Identity*, 117–18. Goulette was a welcome choice in the wake of Laura Cornelius Kellogg's controversial departure. In the summer of 1913, she and her husband had been arrested for allegedly conning several businessmen out of money for

use on Indian reservations. Parker then accused her of "dancing almost in the nude for the benefit of Indian people." See Maddox, *Citizen Indians*, 193. (The quote is found in a letter from Parker to J. N. B. Hewitt, August 30, 1913, PSAI.) The escalating situation was Parker's biggest concern prior to Denver. He told Coolidge that Kellogg was lobbying him for "one hour in which to berate 'our policy,'" while noting that "twenty minutes is sufficient if the good lady wishes to give us a scolding." Parker ended up banning her entirely just before the conference's start but feared the possible consequences. "She writes to me that if we ask her to resign," he warned Coolidge, "we better look out." See Parker to Coolidge, September 24, 1913, PSAI. No such retribution occurred. Representative Stephens, incidentally, was a Democrat and chairman of the Committee on Indian Affairs. See Speroff, *Carlos Montezuma, MD*, 289.

13. HARMONY IN JEOPARDY

1. Parker to Coolidge, December 31, 1913, PSAI.
2. G. Coolidge to A. Talbot, March 28, 1914, CHC.
3. G. Coolidge to A. Talbot, April 16, 1913, CHC.
4. G. Coolidge to A. Talbot, March 28, 1914, CHC.
5. Parker, "Quaker City Meeting," 56–59.
6. Coolidge to G. Coolidge, February 15, 1914, CHC.
7. Coolidge to G. Coolidge, February 18, 1914, CHC. Days later, Coolidge learned in a meeting with Commissioner Sells that the mission in Whirlwind, Oklahoma, would likely be shuttered. The reservation superintendent felt it was keeping Indians away from their farms and families because of its remote location. Coolidge noted that the news would be "a hard blow" to Miss Bedell. Her students were to be enrolled in a government school. See Coolidge to G. Coolidge, February 18, 1914, CHC. After the stay in Washington DC, Coolidge traveled to Carlisle to visit Virginia. There, he learned of "a great shake-up." Grace told Anne Talbot of the incident, noting, "The govt. employees are a credit to any country, really, aren't they? The children say that the immediate result is that the food is a little better and that they have two mattresses on the beds instead of one!" See G. Coolidge to A. Talbot, March 28, 1914, CHC.
8. Parker, "Quaker City Meeting," 56.
9. Montezuma, "Reservation Is Fatal," 69–74.
10. Coolidge, "American Indians," 251–55. Also see the advertisement in the *American Issue*, September 1913, 1. The conference's title, the "Monster Twentieth-Century Jubilee Convention of the Anti-Saloon League of America," is recorded there. Part of Coolidge's speech was later quoted in "Lo, the Poor, Rich Indian," 609.

11. Coolidge, "Function of the Society," 186–90.

12. Coolidge, "Indian of To-Day," 93.

13. See Coolidge, "Function of the Society," 185. Coolidge quotes Eastman directly: "To use Dr. Eastman's words: 'The North American Indian was the highest type of pagan and uncivilized man. He possessed not only a superb physique but a remarkable mind.'" For a taste of Parker's contempt for capitalism, which he surely shared with Coolidge, see Parker to Philip Gordon, March 23, 1917, PSAI. Parker writes regarding reservation Indians: "I do not want them to have their land and resources stolen because of their failure to understand 'modern business ethics.' I rather honor them for not becoming commercial hearted. But without some form of protection and property restriction their lands are going to go. The pauper Indian has no friends. The drifting tramp Indian is no better than any other tramp, except in ancestry. I, therefore, shrink from the thought of having the weak and poor, the ignorant and old thrust weaponless into a commercial sea filled with long fanged sharks. 'They will learn to fight?' No they won't, not that way. They must enter the fight with a blade in hand, which if not as sharp will acquire an edge soon enough. The favored and capable such as you and perhaps me, need no protection and no special mercy. We can get along with this 'Civilization,' defective as it is."

14. Parker, "Study in the Complexities," 220–24.

15. Kenny L. Brown, "Owen, Robert Latham (1856–1947)," *The Encyclopedia of Oklahoma History and Culture*, accessed June 3, 2020, https://www.okhistory .org/publications/enc/entry.php?entry=ow003; and Coolidge to Parker, February 1914, PSAI. Also see Parker to Coolidge, September 26, 1914, PSAI. The letter discusses Owen.

16. Parker to Coolidge, September 26, 1914, PSAI.

17. Coolidge to Montezuma, April 24, 1913, CMP.

18. Parker to Coolidge, May 14, 1914, PSAI.

19. Coolidge to Montezuma, July 14, 1914, CMP.

20. Edmund Menger to Moses Friedman, November 19, 1913, ECSF. The letter states that Effie entered Carlisle on September 10, 1913. In the school paper, the *Carlisle Arrow*, there is a report of Virginia giving a presentation on "Incidents in the Life of Rev. Sherman Coolidge." See *Carlisle Arrow* 12, no. 36 (May 19, 1916): 5. Another report records how Grace visited the school in 1916 to take Virginia and Effie on a trip to Atlantic City. See *Carlisle Arrow* 12, no. 31 (April 14, 1916): 3.

21. G. Coolidge to A. Talbot, March 28, 1914, CHC.

22. G. Coolidge to A. Talbot, December 1, 1915, CHC.

23. G. Coolidge to A. Talbot, April 16, 1913, CHC.

24. G. Coolidge to A. Talbot, April 16, 1913, CHC.

25. G. Coolidge to A. Talbot, August 11, 1915, CHC.

26. See Grace Coolidge, "Two Indian Stories," *Outlook*, March 23, 1912, 651–55. *Collier's* ran such writings as a handsomely illustrated series titled "Teepee Neighbor Sketches." See Coolidge, "The Victory," 16–17.

27. Coolidge, *Teepee Neighbors*, 9, 17–18. For the stories referenced, see, respectively, "The Other Mad Man," 218–25; "A Venture into Hard Hearts," 102–8; and "Ghosts," 28–35.

28. G. Coolidge to A. Talbot, December 14, 1912, CHC.

29. Quoted in Cornell, introduction to *Teepee Neighbors*, by Coolidge, xxiv–xxv. The book's publisher, Four Seas Company in Boston, was a small press known for printing the early works of modernists such as William Faulkner and William Carlos Williams—not bad company.

30. Coolidge, *Teepee Neighbors*, 9, 17–18. Grace also served on the SAI's advisory board in 1917 and on the board of the *American Indian Magazine* from 1913 to 1915 and 1917–18. Larner, introduction, PSAI.

31. Coolidge to Montezuma, April 20, 1914, CMP.

32. "Members Constituting the Fourth Conference," 319.

33. Parker, "Editorial Comment," July–September 1914, 165–66. The Coolidges' connections to wealthy Episcopal reformers may have helped raise donations. Correspondence suggests that the couple often—and successfully—solicited financial support for the society. See Parker to G. Coolidge, November 16, 1914, PSAI.

34. See McKenzie, "Results of the Madison Conference," 230; and Parker to Coolidge, October 27, 1914, PSAI.

35. Parker, "Awakened American Indian," 270–71.

36. Parker to Coolidge, November 14, 1914, PSAI.

37. Parker, "Awakened American Indian," 269–74.

38. Woodrow Wilson to Society of American Indians, December 10, 1914, PSAI.

39. See Hertzberg, *American Indian Identity*, 128. Hertzberg notes that the 1914 meeting with Wilson "seems to have had no effect whatsoever."

40. See Parker to Coolidge, December 15, 1914, PSAI; and Parker to Coolidge, January 20, 1915, PSAI.

41. Coolidge to Parker, January 29, 1915, PSAI.

42. Parker to Coolidge, January 7, 1915, PSAI.

43. Coolidge to Parker, January 15, 1915, PSAI. Also see Parker to G. Coolidge, April 10, 1915, PSAI.

44. Coolidge to Montezuma, April 16, 1914, CMP.

45. Speroff, *Carlos Montezuma, MD*, 258, 286, 299.

46. Coolidge to Montezuma, April 16, 1915, CMP.

47. Montezuma to Coolidge, April 17, 1915, CMP. No response from Coolidge is found in Montezuma's papers.

48. See "Conference Evening," 300–302; "Indian YMCA Conference," 240; and "Indian Progress Conference," 240.

49. Coolidge to G. Coolidge, August 12, 1915, CHC; and Coolidge to G. Coolidge, August 17, 1915, CHC.

50. See "Conference Evening," 300–302. In that piece, Coolidge also mentions attending the Indian Government Service Employees Conference and a conference of the Episcopal Church of the Pacific Coast states and Alaska, the Hawaiian Islands, and the Philippines.

51. Child, *Boarding School Seasons*, 27, 30, 33, 93; and Milk, *Haskell Institute*, 76–77, 127–67.

52. Parker to John R. Wise, August 24, 1913, PSAI.

53. Coolidge to Parker, January 23, 1913, PSAI.

54. "Members and Associate Members," 313–15; and Hertzberg, *American Indian Identity*, 135.

55. Wilson to Parker, September 24, 1915, PSAI.

56. Lewandowski, *Red Bird, Red Power*, 11–13. Coolidge admired Bonnin's community center initiative but felt it was redundant because missionaries had been doing that type of work for years. See Coolidge to G. Coolidge, November 9, 1916, CHC.

57. Lewandowski, *Ojibwe, Activist, Priest*, 4, 45–46.

58. Parker to Philip Gordon, May 18, 1915, PSAI; and Lewandowski, *Red Bird, Red Power*, 103.

59. "Indian Progress Conference," 240.

60. "Conference Evening," 302. The anecdote about the Digger boys appears to have been widely circulated in Indian reform circles. Matthew Sniffen, the long-term secretary of the Indian Rights Association, mentioned the quote in *Meaning of the Ute "War,"* 7.

61. Parker, "Fifth Conference," 282.

62. Hertzberg, *American Indian Identity*, 136–37.

63. Montezuma, "Let My People Go," 33–34.

64. Parker to Coolidge, June 7, 1916, PSAI.

65. See "Annual Conference of Society of American Indians," *Indian Leader*, November 1914, 6. Coolidge is quoted as saying that reservations "are not the best place" for Indians and that "there are other lives better than these passed on the reservation."

66. Hertzberg, *American Indian Identity*, 140, 144; and Parker to Coolidge, April 16, 1915, PSAI.

67. See Gordon to Charles S. Lusk, October 4, 1915, BCIM. Gordon's nomination of Sloan for SAI president is discussed in Parker to Gordon, November 19, 1915, PSAI. Also see Gordon, "Opposition to the Indian Bureau," 259–60, in which Gordon references the "nasty" comments he made about the Indian Bureau at Lawrence. Also see Parker to Coolidge, April 16, 1915, PSAI. Parker refers to Sloan's statements at Lawrence: "Some of their brutal and corrupt Superintendents need outing and Sloan is both familiar with these men and fearless in his attack."

68. Hertzberg, *American Indian Identity*, 137. Also see G. Coolidge to A. Talbot, December 1, 1915, CHC.

69. G. Coolidge to A. Talbot, December 1, 1915, CHC.

70. "Platform of the Fifth Conference," 285–89.

71. "The Sunday Evening Meeting," *Carlisle Arrow*, March 6, 1914, 2.

72. Parker, "Editor's Viewpoint," 8–14.

73. Society of American Indians, *Proceedings of the Second Annual Conference*, 119.

14. STATE OF CHAOS, STATE OF WAR

1. Parker to Coolidge, October 11, 1915, PSAI.

2. Parker to Coolidge, November 4, 1915, PSAI.

3. Parker to Coolidge, May 11, 1916, PSAI. Sloan had also advocated a "Rights to Nomination" bill that would allow Indians to elect their own superintendents. The Ojibwes were in favor. Coolidge opposed the idea because he feared "mixed-bloods" might try and exploit the situation to take power and enrich themselves. See Coolidge to G. Coolidge, April 11, 1916, CHC.

4. Parker to Coolidge, December 3, 1915, PSAI.

5. U.S. Senate Committee on Indian Affairs, *Hearings*, 93–95.

6. "Gardner Wetherbee," Find a Grave, accessed August 22, 2020, https://www.findagrave.com/memorial/130563888/gardner-wetherbee.

7. G. Coolidge to Coolidge, March 30, 1916, CHC.

8. G. Coolidge to Coolidge, April 26, 1916, CHC.

9. G. Coolidge to Coolidge, March 30, 1916, CHC.

10. G. Coolidge to Coolidge, March 27, 1916, CHC.

11. G. Coolidge to Coolidge, March 30, 1916, CHC.

12. G. Coolidge to Coolidge, April 26, 1916, CHC.

13. "Conference Helped," 221.

14. See Parker to Coolidge, April 4, 1916, PSAI; and Parker to Coolidge, April 12, 1916, PSAI.

15. See Parker to Coolidge, April 24, 1916, PSAI.

16. Hertzberg, *American Indian Identity*, 146.

17. Parker to Coolidge, June 7, 1916, PSAI.

18. Coolidge, "Opening Address," 227–28.

19. Larson, "Indian and His Liquor Problem," 237. Also see Hertzberg, *American Indian Identity*, 149.

20. Pratt, "Pratt Regarding Peyote," 237–38.

21. Lewandowski, *Red Bird, Red Power*, 12–13, 92, 133, 136.

22. Lone Wolf, "How to Solve the Problem," 257–59.

23. "Cedar Rapids Platform," 224.

24. "Open Debate on the Loyalty," 252–56. As suggested by his statements in the Cedar Rapids debate, Coolidge's views on the reservation system remained paternalistic. In 1916 the Indian Rights Association had come out against the Johnson bill, which would have allowed the democratic election of reservation agents by a majority vote of Indian men over eighteen years of age who were residents. The Indian Rights Association feared that under this scheme older Indians would "become the easy prey of conniving mixed bloods and unscrupulous whites." Coolidge agreed, stating: "By such law the very worst elements will seek to control Indian tribes." See "Legislation Proposed," in *Fourth Annual Report*, 26–27.

25. "Newspaper Comment," 266–67.

26. "Tribal War Averted at Indian Meeting," 1916, PSAI. Parker later tried to paper over the incident in the *American Indian Magazine* by denying rumors of "bad blood." See "Newspaper Comment," 266.

27. Gordon, "Opposition to the Indian Bureau," 259–60.

28. Montezuma, "Address before the Sixth Conference," 160–62.

29. "Indians Talk to Student Body of Coe on Their Aim," 1916, PSAI.

30. "Escaped Massacre," PSAI.

31. See "The Cedar Rapids Platform," 223–24. For use of the term "radical" and SAI election results, see "Important Topics Considered," 218–19.

32. Coolidge to G. Coolidge, October 2, 1916, CHC. This letter mentions that Coolidge had visited the Tama Indian reservation while in Iowa. He had heard bad reports but found the situation less dire than expected. "These Indians are perhaps more backward than they ought to be surrounded as they are by civilization," he told Grace.

33. Coolidge to G. Coolidge, October 8, 1916, CHC; and Coolidge to G. Coolidge, November 9, 1916, CHC. The second letter states, "I have given out notice that we are willing to take any child without home or parents."

34. Coolidge to G. Coolidge, November 4, 1916, CHC; and Coolidge to G. Coolidge, November 9, 1916, CHC.

35. Coolidge to G. Coolidge, October 23, 1916, CHC.

36. Coolidge to G. Coolidge, November 4, 1916, CHC.

37. Coolidge to G. Coolidge, October 23, 1916, CHC.

38. Coolidge to G. Coolidge, November 9, 1916, CHC.

39. Coolidge to G. Coolidge, October 8, 1916, CHC. Documents shared by Philip Heinicke with the author via email, December 16, 2020, indicate the ranch property became Coolidge's on August 25, 1916.

40. See Speroff, *Carlos Montezuma, MD*, 361.

41. Gertrude Bonnin to Montezuma, December 10, 1916, CMP.

42. Speroff, *Carlos Montezuma, MD*, 361–62.

43. Kennedy, *Over Here*, 3–11.

44. Zinn, *People's History of the United States*, 134.

45. Kennedy, *Over Here*, 145–49.

46. Boyer et al., *Enduring Vision*, 663–67.

47. Schaffer, *America in the Great War*, 25–26.

48. Fite and Peterson, *Opponents of War*, 204.

49. Kennedy, *Over Here*, 80.

50. Rawlings, *Second Coming*, 77–78; and Speroff, *Carlos Montezuma, MD*, 461.

51. Kennedy, *Over Here*, 85–86.

52. Boyer et al., *Enduring Vision*, 663–67.

53. Kennedy, *Over Here*, 39–40, 88–89, 91, 145–49. The quote is by George Creel, head of the Committee on Public Information.

54. Lewandowski, *Red Bird, Red Power*, 126.

55. Britten, *American Indians*, 43–44, 62–63, 177–78; and Speroff, *Carlos Montezuma, MD*, 413–14.

56. Hertzberg, *American Indian Identity*, 170.

57. Parker, "Editorial Comment," July–September 1917, 147.

58. Bonnin to Parker, August 6, 1917, PSAI.

59. See, for instance, "Five Civilized Tribes," 143; and "What Indians Are Thinking," 143–44.

60. Parker, "Editorial Comment," 147. Coolidge expressed the desire to go to France as a chaplain but never made any attempt to do so. See Reid, "Westerners," 47.

61. Parker to Coolidge, October 2, 1917, PSAI.

62. Larner, "Society of American Indians," 604.

63. Reid, "Westerners," 47.

64. G. Coolidge to A. Talbot, January 11, 1916, CHC.

65. G. Coolidge to A. Talbot, February 8, 1918, CHC.

66. Barrett, *Subversive Peacemakers*, 98.

67. G. Coolidge to A. Talbot, February 8, 1918, CHC.

68. Hertzberg, *American Indian Identity*, 171–72; and Parker to Bonnin, July 5, 1917, PSAI.

69. See, for instance, Parker to Coolidge, October 2, 1917; and Parker to Coolidge, February 6, 1918, PSAI.
70. Parker to Coolidge, February 20, 1918, PSAI.
71. Parker to Grace Coolidge, October 12, 1917, PSAI.
72. Parker, "Editorial Comment," Spring 1918, 18; and Parker to Grace Coolidge, October 12, 1917, PSAI.
73. G. Coolidge to Coolidge, September 24, 1917, CHC.
74. Coolidge to G. Coolidge, September 29, 1917, CHC.
75. Coolidge to G. Coolidge, October 5, 1917, CHC. Coolidge also inquired at other hospitals in the area. He felt the one in Sheridan might be better for Virginia. See Coolidge to G. Coolidge, October 7, 1917, CHC.
76. G. Coolidge to Coolidge, November 18, 1917, CHC.
77. Coolidge to G. Coolidge, December 8, 1917, CHC. Unfortunately, it was impossible for Virginia to transfer to the hospital in Sheridan because she did not hold the right qualifications. Also see G. Coolidge to A. Talbot, April 6, 1919, CHC.
78. G. Coolidge to Coolidge, October 2, 1917, CHC. Grace also writes of her plans to chastise McDonough by missive before she learned of Sherman's visit: "I was going to answer it and tell her gently but firmly in what light, socially and intellectually, she and her nurses showed themselves by their prejudice, but since your letter came I think there has been enough said and I will simply not answer at all." She also mentions how she told Bishop Funsten of the troubles Virginia had encountered.
79. G. Coolidge to A. Talbot, April 20, 1921; and G. Coolidge to A. Talbot, March 10, 1922, CHC.
80. G. Coolidge to Coolidge, November 13, 1917, CHC.
81. Coolidge to G. Coolidge, October 29, 1917, CHC.
82. Coolidge to G. Coolidge, October 19, 1917, CHC.
83. G. Coolidge to A. Talbot, February 8, 1918, CHC.
84. G. Coolidge to A. Talbot, April 29, 1918, CHC.
85. G. Coolidge to A. Talbot, February 8, 1918, CHC. Coolidge's transfer took place on March 16, 1918. See Diocese of Minnesota, *Journal of the Sixty-First Annual Convention*, 77.
86. G. Coolidge to A. Talbot, April 29, 1918, CHC.
87. Parker to G. Coolidge, October 12, 1917, PSAI.
88. See Parker to Coolidge, February 6, 1918, PSAI.
89. Parker to Coolidge, February 20, 1918, PSAI.
90. Parker to G. Coolidge, October 12, 1917, PSAI; and Speroff, *Carlos Montezuma, MD*, 363, 420–25.
91. Coolidge to G. Coolidge, June 15, 1918, CHC.

92. Coolidge to G. Coolidge, August 14, 1918, CHC.

93. Lewandowski, *Red Bird, Red Power*, 119, 130–31; Parker to Coolidge, February 6, 1918, PSAI; and Speroff, *Carlos Montezuma*, MD, 242.

94. Crosby, *America's Forgotten Pandemic*, 56–65; and Hertzberg, *American Indian Identity*, 175–76.

95. Coolidge to G. Coolidge, November 10, 1918, CHC.

96. "At the Indian Convention," 120–22.

97. Speroff, *Carlos Montezuma*, MD, 413–15.

98. "At the Indian Convention," 121–22.

99. Speroff, *Carlos Montezuma*, MD, 264.

100. "Election of Officers," 125; and Hertzberg, *American Indian Identity*, 175–76. Coolidge noted in a letter to Grace that giving up the *American Indian Magazine* had been a "relief" to Parker. Coolidge also warned Bonnin that the editorship would be "no light burden." He had secretly wanted Parker to continue, but Bonnin "did things quickly and evidently we were too slow." See Coolidge to G. Coolidge, November 8, 1918, CHC.

101. Coolidge to G. Coolidge, November 8, 1918, CHC. Coolidge writes that he had written Montezuma a "stiff letter," likely about the dangers of bureau abolition, but was surprised to have gotten a "pleasant answer." Regarding citizenship, see "Platform and Resolutions," *American Indian Magazine* 6, no. 3 (July–September 1918): 138–40.

102. Speroff, *Carlos Montezuma*, MD, 242.

103. Coolidge to G. Coolidge, August 14, 1918, CHC.

104. Coolidge to G. Coolidge, October 14, 1918, CHC.

105. Coolidge to G. Coolidge, November 8, 1918, CHC.

106. Coolidge to G. Coolidge, October 14, 1918; and Coolidge to G. Coolidge, October 28, 1918, CHC. The October 28 letter mentions, "Schools are glad of the vacation."

107. Coolidge to G. Coolidge, November 8, 1918, CHC.

108. Bonnin to Montezuma, October 22, 1918, CMP.

109. Gertrude Bonnin apparently caught the virus in March 1919. See Bonnin to Montezuma, March 12, 1919, CMP.

110. G. Coolidge to Coolidge, December 16, 1918, CHC.

111. G. Coolidge to Coolidge, August 4, 1919, CHC. Also see "Coolidge Family," Finding Aid, CHC; and G. Coolidge to A. Talbot, August 4, 1919, CHC.

112. G. Coolidge to A. Talbot, March 3, 1920, CHC.

113. Hertzberg, *American Indian Identity*, 184–85; and Speroff, *Carlos Montezuma*, MD, 266. Sloan played a role in the 1918 founding of the Native American Church, which sought to legally protect peyote's ingestion as a sacrament in religious ceremonies and establish the peyote religion's connections to

Christianity. Sloan died in 1940. See Hertzberg, *American Indian Identity*, 149; and Maroukis, *Peyote and the Yankton Sioux*, 131.

114. Hertzberg, *American Indian Identity*, 177.

115. Gordon, "Address by Father Philip Gordon," 152–53; and Ahern, "Experiment Aborted," 264.

116. Lewandowski, *Red Bird, Red Power*, 157.

117. See Wilson, *Ohiyesa*, 162. Upon resigning, Eastman deemed the society "a political pressure group with patronage interests." Two years later, Eastman separated from his wife, Elaine. In his old age, he built a cabin on Lake Huron so he could be close to nature. He died in 1939. Elaine died in 1953. See Miller, "Charles Alexander Eastman," in Liberty, *American Indian Intellectuals*, 61–70.

118. See "Officers of the Society," 56.

119. "At the Indian Convention," 121–22.

120. Speroff, *Carlos Montezuma, MD*, 415.

121. Britten, *American Indians*, 149.

122. S. Coolidge, "Ye Cannot Serve God and Mammon," CHC.

123. Hertzberg, *American Indian Identity*, 190.

EPILOGUE

1. G. Coolidge to A. Talbot, November 11, 1918, CHC.

2. "Hobart Centennial Fund Campaign," WHSL.

3. G. Coolidge to A. Talbot, December 16, 1918, CHC.

4. Robert I. Woodward, "Notes about the Reverend Sherman Coolidge," August 4, 1996, SJWA. Also see "In Memoriam," 1932, SJWA. This clipping is from the *Episcopal Convention Journal* for the year ending 1931.

5. G. Coolidge to A. Talbot, March 5, 1920, CHC.

6. G. Coolidge to A. Talbot, December 30, 1919, CHC.

7. Hertzberg, *American Indian Identity*, 193–94.

8. Speroff, *Carlos Montezuma, MD*, 415.

9. Hertzberg, *Indian Identity*, 193, 197–98, 220–21.

10. Speroff, *Carlos Montezuma, MD*, 367.

11. Charles H. Burke to Everett Sanders, July 18, 1928, PSAI.

12. Hertzberg, *American Indian Identity*, 200–201.

13. Coolidge to G. Coolidge, October 27, 1910, CHC.

14. See Bonnin, Fabens, and Sniffen, *Oklahoma's Poor Rich Indians*, 1–41.

15. Hertzberg, *American Indian Identity*, 201–2; Hoxie, *This Indian Country*, 269; and Speroff, *Carlos Montezuma, MD*, 369–70. Also see Huebner, "Unexpected Alliance," 337–66. Collier led a life of activism. In 1917 he founded the National Community Center Association in New York, establishing contacts

among many progressive intellectuals and reformers of his era, including the wealthy patron Mabel Dodge. Following World War I, Collier relocated to California, where he worked as a community organizer and teacher at San Francisco State College. His life changed when Dodge invited him to her literary retreat in Taos, New Mexico, where he encountered the Pueblos. Their communal lifestyle so impressed Collier that he shifted the core of his activism to protecting Native rights. See Taylor, *New Deal*, 12–13, 120–21. After her resignation from the Society of American Indians, Bonnin remained in Washington DC and joined the Indian Welfare Committee of the General Federation of Women's Clubs in 1921. Four years later, she founded her own Native rights organization, the National Council of American Indians. She spent the following decade traveling the United States, inspecting reservations, and reporting the findings to Congress. She died in 1938. See Davidson and Norris, introduction to *American Indian Stories*, xi–xxxv.

16. Olson and Wilson, *Native Americans*, 98–99.

17. Hertzberg, *American Indian Identity*, 202–3. Parker later became the director of the Rochester Museum of Arts and Sciences in 1925. He spent the remainder of his life in upstate New York. During the Great Depression, he became involved in the Work Progress Administration, where he promoted an Indian arts project. In later life, Parker was elected the first president of the Society for American Archaeology. He passed away in 1955. See Porter, *To Be Indian*, 167–71, 200–201, 239.

18. Parker, "Ruth Margaret Muskrat," 320.

19. Harry B. Hunt, "This Little World: Washington," *Daily News* (San Francisco), September 18, 1923, 16.

20. Messer, *Henry Roe Cloud*, 99.

21. Hertzberg, *American Indian Identity*, 203.

22. Hoxie, *This Indian Country*, 274.

23. See Elaine Eastman, *Pratt*, 271–72. According to Eastman, Pratt died skeptical that any progress would ever be made in the area of Indian policy reform.

24. See Davidson and Norris, introduction, xxvii; Hertzberg, *American Indian Identity*, 204; and Speroff, *Carlos Montezuma, MD*, 370.

25. G. Coolidge to A. Talbot, March 13, 1924, CHC.

26. G. Coolidge to A. Talbot, July 28, 1920, CHC.

27. G. Coolidge to A. Talbot, December 20, 1920, CHC.

28. See "Coolidge Family," Finding Aid, CHC. Effie had two children with Tibbetts, Grace Katharine (born 1923) and Harold Ralph (born 1927). Her mental troubles began in the 1930s. Her last place of residence is recorded as Ypsilanti State Hospital, Michigan, in the year 1940. It is possible she was later buried in Ethete, Wyoming. See Goodnough, "Sherman Coolidge,"

AHC. Goodnough mentions that both Effie and Virginia "sleep at Ethete," where Rev. John Roberts established St. Michael's Episcopal Mission in 1919. Grace sometimes visited Effie after she was institutionalized. In one letter, she writes: "My visit to Effie, wh. I dreaded really went off all right. She is in a charming place, 80 acre grounds, a fascinating big house, tile floors and lovely old furniture, no locks or bars or anything like that visible. I liked the whole tone of the place and Effie looked as young and pretty and cheerful as cd be. Of course, she was perfectly irrational. Told me the wildest yarns, but didn't seem to be much impressed by them. I stayed over an extra day to see her Doctor in Phila. A Dr. Ludlum, teaches at the University and seems to be quite a big person. A quite fascinating personality and one that inspired confidence. And when I tell you that on his sofa he had a little dusty white dog, just like my own Cluffie, you can imagine how at home I felt! He said she had drifted in a year ago and just stayed. Well, what he said about Effie was very interesting. Her trouble seems to come from a tremendously over gland secretion. He has been giving her ovarian [illegible] and other gland stuff, but with not much result however. Now he is going to try bringing in the menopause with X ray treatments. I know some of the T.B. girls here who have had that done, of course for other reasons. . . . Effie didn't seem to be concerning herself at all about husband or children and didn't beg at all to come away with me wh I had feared she might do." See G. Coolidge to A. Talbot, November 23, 1931, CHC. Also see G. Coolidge to A. Talbot, December 12, 1922, CHC; and G. Coolidge to A. Talbot, October 23, 1932, CHC.

29. G. Coolidge to A. Talbot, December 12, 1922, CHC.
30. "Indian Buys Broadmoor Home; Moves Family Here: Full-Blooded Navajo Is Canon of the Episcopal Church in Colorado; Is Well Known Here," *Colorado Springs Gazette*, CHC.
31. Philip Heinicke, email to author, December 16, 2020. The ground-floor den, which had barred windows before the Coolidges moved in, served as a Cub Scout meeting room for Philip Heinicke. Rosie acted as den mother.
32. Woodward, "Notes about the Reverend," SJWA.
33. Philip Heinicke, email to author, December 16, 2020.
34. G. Coolidge to A. Talbot, December 20, 1922, CHC.
35. G. Coolidge to A. Talbot, March 13, 1924, CHC. It is possible that Virginia was buried in Ethete, Wyoming. See Goodnough, "Sherman Coolidge," AHC.
36. "Coolidge Family," Finding Aid, CHC.
37. G. Coolidge to A. Talbot, March 25, 1925, CHC; and "Coolidge Family," Finding Aid, CHC. Also see G. Coolidge to A. Talbot, March 9, 1928, CHC, for more comments on Sallie's health.
38. "Coolidge Family," Finding Aid, CHC.

39. "A. B. Club Bears Inspection," 32.

40. See, for instance, Espey, *Citizen, Jr.*, 78.

41. Olden, *Shoshone Folk Lore*, 58.

42. Markley and Crofts, *Walk Softly*, 147.

43. G. Coolidge to A. Talbot, December 29, 1926, CHC.

44. Gustin, "Arapaho Is Distinguished Churchman," WHSL; and "Hobart Centennial Fund Campaign," WHSL.

45. Hertzberg, *American Indian Identity*, 217.

46. Gustin, "Arapaho Is Distinguished Churchman," WHSL. Grace's grandmother and Gardner's mother, Sarah Coolidge, was born June 4, 1810, in Charleston, Massachusetts, and died at age ninety on July 4, 1900, in Harvard, Massachusetts. See "Sarah Coolidge Wetherbee," Find a Grave, accessed August 28, 2020, https://www.findagrave.com/memorial/161370089 /sarah-wetherbee.

47. "Scenario Wanted," 44.

48. See "Coolidge Family," Finding Aid, CHC. Gathered from the little information available in the CHC, the American Indian Film Company appears to have existed until the mid-1930s, though it did not produce films. Instead, the Coolidges represented Native actors in Hollywood.

49. "Coolidge Decries Injustice in Barring Native Indians from American Citizenship," *Colorado Springs Gazette*, June 13, 1927, 10.

50. Coolidge, "Ye Cannot Serve God and Mammon," CHC. Italics in original.

51. Goodnough, "Sherman Coolidge," AHC. Also see G. Coolidge to A. Talbot, October 1, 1931, CHC.

52. "Canon Coolidge Is Claimed by Death," AHC.

53. Reid, "Westerners," 47.

54. "Coolidge Decries Injustice," 10.

55. "General Coolidge Dies; Was in Three Wars"; and "Brig. Gen. Charles Coolidge Dies in Detroit, Mich.," GHP.

56. "Canon Coolidge Pays His Debt of Love," CHC.

57. "Sophia Wagner Lowry Coolidge."

58. G. Coolidge to A. Talbot, October 23, 1928, CHC; and "Coolidge Family," Finding Aid, CHC.

59. G. Coolidge to A. Talbot, January 15, 1929, CHC.

60. G. Coolidge to A. Talbot, October 23, 1928, CHC.

61. "Many Alumni Back for Commencement," *Hobart Herald*, June 16, 1931, 6. The *Herald* noted that Coolidge had traveled the greatest distance to join the celebrations.

62. G. Coolidge to A. Talbot, July 15, 1931, CHC; and G. Coolidge to A. Talbot, July 24, 1931, CHC.

63. G. Coolidge to A. Talbot, October 1, 1931, CHC.

64. G. Coolidge to A. Talbot, February 9, 1932, CHC.

65. "Coolidge Family," Finding Aid, CHC. Also see Woodward, "Notes about the Reverend," SJWA; and Goodnough, "Sherman Coolidge," AHC.

66. G. Coolidge to A. Talbot, January 1, 1933, CHC.

67. G. Coolidge to A. Talbot, February 9, 1932, CHC.

68. Irving P. Johnson, eulogy for Sherman Coolidge, CHC.

69. "Canon Coolidge Dies"; and "Canon Coolidge Is Claimed by Death," AHC.

70. See Gustin, "Arapaho Is Distinguished Churchman," WHSL; and "In Memoriam," SJWA.

71. G. Coolidge to A. Talbot, February 9, 1932, CHC.

72. Child, *Boarding School Seasons*, 40; Porter, *To Be Indian*, 140–41; Speroff, *Carlos Montezuma, MD*, 373; and Taylor, *New Deal*, 12–13.

73. G. Coolidge to A. Talbot, April 25, 1937, CHC; and Goodnough, "Sherman Coolidge," AHC.

74. "Coolidge Family," Finding Aid, CHC. One of Grace's last acts was making a $7,000 donation to St. Michael's Mission in Wind River. See Goodnough, "Sherman Coolidge," AHC; and "Grace Darling Wetherbee Coolidge," Find a Grave, accessed June 20, 2020, https://www.findagrave.com/memorial /34466606/grace-darling-coolidge. In 1953 a woman named Helen Butler published a fictionalized account of Grace and Sherman's marriage, *A Stone upon His Shoulder.* Also see "St. Michael's Mission," Wyoming State Historic Preservation Office, accessed March 26, 2021, https://wyoshpo.wyo.gov/index .php/programs/national-register/wyoming-listings/view-full-list/572-st -michael-s-mission.

75. Ellis, *Pioneers*, 29.

76. G. Coolidge to A. Talbot, May 19, 1934, CHC.

77. "Coolidge Family," Finding Aid, CHC.

78. Philip Heinicke, email to author, December 16, 2020.

79. "Coolidge Family," Finding Aid, CHC. As an artist, Sallie called herself "Comes Back Woman." She married Vance on May 7, 1934, in Reno, Nevada. The couple's store was located at 1710 North Wilcox Avenue in Hollywood, California. Sallie gave birth to a son in May 1934, but he died at two months. Afterward Sallie was ill for some time. She divorced Vance in 1940. Sallie experienced poor health and later moved to Oklahoma (despite her well-documented hatred of the state). There, she met and married Chief Jesse Rowlodge in 1953. They remained married until her death. Sallie gave birth to a boy in 1934, but he unfortunately died. Grace wrote in one of her letters, "Sallie's baby has come and gone. It came at 6 mos. and lived 3 hours. She had an awful time having it, instruments at the last. It was a little boy. They

feel awfully badly. But I wrote to her the only thing to do is to begin as soon as she can having another one. And find out what made her miscarry. I am thankful it was alive for a little while anyhow. Now it will always be a real person to her." See G. Coolidge to A. Talbot, July 17, 1934, CHC. Rosie and Alfred Heinicke produced four children: Philip (born 1938), Nye (born 1940), Cynthia (born 1941), and Diana (born 1944). Rosie's husband served in the army, and she lived mostly in Colorado Springs, where she was well known for her volunteer work.

80. See "Rose Austin Coolidge Heinicke"; and "Sarah Lucy Coolidge Rowlodge."

81. S. Coolidge to Hebard, December 29, 1930, GHP.

BIBLIOGRAPHY

UNPUBLISHED SOURCES

AHC. Coolidge, Sherman, Biographical File. American Heritage Center, University of Wyoming, Laramie.

BCIM. Bureau of the Catholic Indian Missions Records. Raynor Memorial Libraries, Marquette University Archives, Milwaukee.

CHC. Coolidge-Heinicke Collection. Colorado Springs Pioneers Museum, Colorado Springs.

CMP. Montezuma, Carlos. Papers. Wisconsin State Historical Society, Madison.

ECSF. Coolidge, Effie. Student File. Carlisle Indian School Digital Resource Center, Archives & Special Collections, Waidner-Spahr Library, Dickinson College PA.

ETP. Talbot, Ethelbert. Papers. American Heritage Center, University of Wyoming, Laramie.

GHP. Hebard, Grace Raymond. Papers. American Heritage Center, University of Wyoming, Laramie.

GRBC. Bonnin, Gertrude and Raymond. Collection. L. Tom Perry Special Collections, Harold B. Library, Brigham Young University, Provo.

HWP. Whipple, Henry Benjamin. Papers. Gale Family Library, Minnesota Historical Society, St. Paul.

PSAI. Society of American Indians. Papers. Cornell University Library, Ithaca NY.

RBIA. Records of the Bureau of Indian Affairs. National Archives and Records Administration, Washington DC.

RHPP. Pratt, Richard Henry. Papers. Beinecke Rare Book and Manuscript Library, Yale University, New Haven CT.

SJWA. Coolidge, Sherman. File. Cathedral of St. John in the Wilderness Archives, Denver.

VCSF. Coolidge, Virginia. Student File. Carlisle Indian School Digital Resource Center, Archives & Special Collections, Waidner-Spahr Library, Dickinson College PA.

WHSL. Coolidge, Sherman. File. Warren Hunting Smith Library, Hobart and William Smith Colleges, Geneva NY.

PUBLISHED SOURCES

"A. B. Club Bears Inspection." *Monitor* 17, no. 7 (July 1922): 32.

Adams, David Wallace. *Education for Extinction: American Indians and the Boarding School Experience, 1875–1928.* Wichita: University Press of Kansas, 1995.

Agonito, Joseph. *Brave Hearts: Indian Women of the Plains.* New York: Rowman & Littlefield, 2017.

Ahern, Wilbert H. "An Experiment Aborted: Returned Students in the Indian Service, 1881–1909." *Ethnohistory* 44, no. 2 (Spring 1997): 263–304.

Allen, Anne. *And the Wilderness Shall Blossom: Henry Benjamin Whipple, Churchman, Educator, Advocate for the Indians.* Afton MN: Afton Historical Society Press, 2008.

"American Church News." *Churchman* 88, no. 10 (October 1903): 417–19.

Anderson, Jeffrey D. *The Four Hills of Life: Northern Arapaho Knowledge and Life Movement.* Lincoln: University of Nebraska Press, 2001.

Anderson, Owanah. *400 Years, Anglican/Episcopal Mission among American Indians.* Cincinnati: Forward Movement Publications, 1997.

"Announcements." *Spirit of Missions* 77, no. 1 (January 1912): 164–65.

"The Annual Diocesan Council." *Church Times* 8, no. 3 (November 1897): 1–2.

"The Annual Meeting." *Indian's Friend* 16, no. 5 (January 1904): 10.

Archuleta, Margaret L., Brenda J. Child, and Tsianina K. Lomawaima, eds. *Away from Home: American Indian Boarding School Experiences, 1879–2000.* Phoenix: Heard Museum, 2000.

Armentrout, Don S., and Robert Boak Slocum, eds. *An Episcopal Dictionary of the Church: A User-Friendly Reference for Episcopalians.* New York: Church Publishing, 2021.

"At the Indian Convention." *American Indian Magazine* 5, no. 3 (July–September 1917): 120–22.

Baldwin, Marie L. "Modern Home Making and the Indian Woman." In *Report of the Executive Council,* 58–67.

Barnes, Erinn. "Between Two Worlds." Thesis, University of Colorado–Colorado Springs, 2009.

Barrett, Clive. *Subversive Peacemakers: War-Resistance 1914–1918, an Anglican Perspective.* Cambridge: Lutterworth Press, 2014.

Barrows, Isabel C. *A Sunny Life: The Biography of Samuel June Barrows.* Boston: Little, Brown, 1913.

Barrows, Samuel J., ed. *Proceedings of the Seventh Annual Meeting of the Lake Mohonk Conference of the Friends of the Indian.* New York: Lake Mohonk, 1889.

Bonnin, Gertrude. "An Indian Praying on the Hilltop." *American Indian Magazine* 7, no. 2 (Summer 1919): 92.

Bonnin, Gertrude, Charles H. Fabens, and Matthew K. Sniffen. *Oklahoma's Poor Rich Indians: An Orgy of Graft and Exploitation of the Five Civilized Tribes— Legalized Robbery*. Philadelphia: Indian Rights Association, 1924.

Boyer, Paul S., Clifford E. Clark Jr., Joseph F. Kett, Neal Salisbury, Harvard Sitkoff, and Nancy Woloch. *The Enduring Vision: A History of the American People*. Vol. 2, *From 1865*. Boston: Houghton Mifflin, 2000.

Britten, Thomas A. *American Indians in World War I: At Home and at War*. Albuquerque: University of New Mexico Press, 1997.

Brown, Dee Alexander. *The Fetterman Massacre*. Lincoln: University of Nebraska Press, 1984.

Butler, Helen. *A Stone upon His Shoulder*. Philadelphia: Westminster Press, 1953.

Cahill, Cathleen D. "Marie Louise Bottineau Baldwin: Indigenizing the Federal Indian Service." *Studies in American Indian Literatures* 25, no. 2 (Summer 2013): 63–86.

Callahan, S. Alice. *Wynema: A Child of the Forest*. 1891. Reprinted, edited and with an introduction by A. LaVonne Brown Ruoff. Lincoln: University of Nebraska Press, 1997.

Carlson, Paul H. *The Plains Indians*. College Station: Texas A&M University Press, 1998.

"The Cedar Rapids Platform." *American Indian Magazine* 4, no. 3 (July– September 1916): 223–24.

Chalcraft, Edwin L. "Report of Superintendent of Wind River School." In *Annual Reports of the Department of the Interior for the Fiscal Year Ended June 30, 1900*, edited by U.S. Department of the Interior, 415–16. Washington DC: Government Printing Office, 1900.

"Chicago." *Churchman* 71, no. 5 (May 1895): 727.

"Chicago Letter." *Church Standard* 4, no. 11 (November 1897): 91.

Child, Brenda J. *Boarding School Seasons: American Indian Families, 1900–1940*. Lincoln: University of Nebraska Press, 1998.

Churchman 88, no. 11 (November 1903): 576.

Churchman 88, no. 12 (December 1903): 699.

"Church Periodical Club." *Church Standard* 74, no. 1 (January 1898): 441.

Clark, D. Anthony Tyeeme. "At the Headwaters of a Twentieth-Century 'Indian Political Agenda': Rethinking the Origins of the Society of American Indians." In *Beyond Red Power: American Indian Politics and Activism since 1900*, edited by Daniel M. Cobb and Loretta Fowler, 70–91. Santa Fe NM: School for Advanced Research Press, 2007.

"Conference Evening at Haskell Indian School: An Extract from the Haskell *Indian Leader.*" *Quarterly Journal of the Society of American Indians* 3, no. 4 (October–December 1915): 292–302.

"Conference Helped by Cedar Rapids Friends." *American Indian Magazine* 4, no. 3 (July–September 1916): 221.

"Connecticut Letter." *Church Standard* 74, no. 11 (November 1897): 91.

Coolidge, Grace. "An Arapahoe Christmas Tree." *Spirit of Missions* 68, no. 1 (January 1903): 113–15.

———. "A Christmas Tree that Bore Souls." *Spirit of Missions* 70, no. 4 (April 1905): 280–83.

———. *Paddy-Paws: Four Adventures of the Prairie Dog with a Red Coat.* Chicago: Rand McNally, 1914.

———. *Teepee Neighbors.* Boston: Four Seas Press, 1917.

———. "The Victory." *Collier's* 50, no. 25 (September 1913): 16–17.

———. "Wanted: To Save the Babies." *American Indian Magazine* 5, no. 1 (January–March 1917): 17–22.

Coolidge, Sherman. "The American Indian of Today." *Quarterly Journal of the Society of American Indians* 2, no. 4 (January–March 1914): 33–35.

———. "American Indians for the Honor of Their Race." *Red Man* 6, no. 7 (March 1914): 251–55.

———. "Education of Indians." *Churchman* 55, no. 5 (May 1887): 594–95.

———. "The Function of the Society of American Indians." *Quarterly Journal of the Society of American Indians* 2, no. 3 (July–September 1914): 186–90.

———. "The Indian American: His Duty to His Race and to His Country, the United States of America." *Quarterly Journal of the Society of American Indians* 1, no. 1 (January–April 1913): 20–24.

———. "Indian Leaders in Council." *Spirit of Missions* 76, no. 12 (December 1911): 1003–5.

———. "The Indian of To-Day." *Colorado Magazine* 1, no. 2 (May 1893): 87–94.

———. "Indian Speeches." In Barrows, *Proceedings*, 98, 100.

———. "Indians in Wyoming." In *Eleventh Census: 1890*, 628–29, edited by U.S. Census Office, 627–34. Vol. 10 of *Report on Indians Taxed and Indians Not Taxed in the United States (Except Alaska).* Washington DC: Government Printing Office, 1894.

———. "Opening Address of the President." *American Indian Magazine* 4, no. 3 (July–September 1916): 227–28.

———. "Report from Sherman Coolidge." *Spirit of Missions* 50, no. 8 (August 1885): 424–25.

———. "Report from Sherman Coolidge." *Spirit of Missions* 51, no. 8 (August 1886): 57.

———. "Report from Sherman Coolidge." *Spirit of Missions* 61, no. 3 (March 1896): 118.

———. "Report from Sherman Coolidge." *Spirit of Missions* 62, no. 7 (July 1897): 550.

———. "Report from Sherman Coolidge." *Spirit of Missions* 63, no. 12 (December 1898): 598.

———. "Report from Sherman Coolidge." *Spirit of Missions* 64, no. 1 (January 1899): 14.

———. "Report from Sherman Coolidge." *Spirit of Missions* 64, no. 5 (May 1899): 229.

———. "Use Your Citizenship Worthily of the Gospel of Christ." *Journal of History* 7, no. 1 (January 1914): 298–301.

Coolidge, Sherman, and Thomas S. Dwyer. "Report of the Committee on the State of the Church." In *Journal of the Seventeenth Annual Convocation of the Missionary District of Oklahoma Held at Shawnee, Oklahoma, May 16, 17, 18, 1911*, 20. Chickasha OK: Queen City Print, 1911.

Cornell, George L. "Coolidge, Sherman." In *Encyclopedia of North American Indians*, edited by D. L. Birchfield, 133–34. Boston: Houghton Mifflin, 1996.

———, ed. Introduction to *Teepee Neighbors*, by Grace Coolidge, xv–xxvi. Norman: University of Oklahoma Press, 1984.

Cozzens, Peter. *Eyewitnesses to the Indian Wars, 1865–1890.* Vol. 4, *The Long War for the Northern Plains.* Mechanicsburg PA: Stackpole Books, 2004.

Crosby, Alfred W. *America's Forgotten Pandemic: The Influenza of 1918.* Cambridge: Cambridge University Press, 2003.

Crum, Steven. "Almost Invisible: The Brotherhood of North American Indians (1911) and the League of North American Indians (1935)." *Wičazo Ša Review* 21, no. 1 (Spring 2006): 43–59.

Davidson, Cathy N., and Ada Norris, eds. Introduction to *American Indian Stories, Legends, and Other Writings*, by Zitkala-Ša, xi–xxxvi. New York: Penguin Books, 2003.

De Cora Deitz, Angel. "Native Indian Art." In *Report of the Executive Council*, 82–87.

"Diocese News." *Churchman* 71, no. 4 (April 1885): 494–95.

"Diocese News." *Churchman* 71, no. 5 (May 1885): 658.

Diocese of Minnesota. *Journal of the Sixty-First Annual Convention, Diocese of Minnesota.* Minneapolis: Dahlen, 1918.

"Discussion on Indian Education." In *Report of the Executive Council*, 79–80.

Douglas, Ian T. "'A Light to the Nations': Episcopal Foreign Missions in Historical Perspective." *Anglican and Episcopal History* 61, no. 4 (December 1992): 449–81.

Duncombe, Edward S. "The Church and the Native American Arapahoes. Part II: Toward Assimilation." *Anglican and Episcopal History* 66, no. 3 (September 1997): 354–82.

———. "The Northern Arapahoe Experience of Episcopal Mission Work and United States Policy, 1883–1925. Part I: Background." *Anglican and Episcopal History* 66, no. 2 (June 1997): 175–98.

Eastman, Charles. *The Indian of Today: The Past and Future of the First American.* New York: Doubleday, Page, 1915.

Eastman, Elaine. *Pratt: The Red Man's Moses.* Norman: University of Oklahoma Press, 1935.

The Echo. Geneva NY: W. F. Humphrey for Hobart College, 1889.

The Echo. Geneva NY: W. F. Humphrey for Hobart College, 1890.

"Educational Notes." *Religious Telescope* 64, no. 16 (April 1898): 15.

Ehrenhalt, Lizzie, and Tilly Laskey, eds. *Precious and Adored: The Love Letters of Rose Cleveland and Evangeline Simpson Whipple, 1890–1918.* St. Paul: Minnesota Historical Society Press, 2019.

Eick, Gretchen Cassel. *They Met at Wounded Knee: The Eastmans' Story.* Reno: University of Nevada Press, 2020.

"Election of Officers." *American Indian Magazine* 6, no. 3 (July–September 1918): 125.

Ellis, Amanda M. *Pioneers.* Colorado Springs: Dentan Printing, 1955.

Espey, Clara Ewing. *Citizen, Jr.* New York: Abingdon Press, 1922.

"The Far West." *Sunday at Home: A Family Magazine for Sabbath Reading*, 1908–9, 229–30.

Fear-Segal, Jacqueline. "Nineteenth-Century Indian Education: Universalism versus Evolutionism." *Journal of American Studies* 33, no. 2 (August 1999): 323–41.

Fite, Gilbert C., and Harriet C. Peterson. *Opponents of War, 1917–1918.* Santa Barbara: Greenwood Press, 1986.

"Five Civilized Tribes Doing Their Bit." *American Indian Magazine* 5, no. 3 (July–September 1917): 143.

Folkmar, Daniel. *Dictionary of Races or Peoples.* Washington DC: Government Printing Office, 1911.

Fowler, Loretta. "Arapaho." In *Plains*, edited by Raymond J. Demallie, 840–62. Vol. 13 of *Handbook of North American Indians.* Washington DC: Smithsonian Institution Scholarly Press, 2001.

———. *The Arapaho.* New York: Chelsea House, 1989.

———. *Arapahoe Politics, 1851–1978: Symbols in Crises of Authority.* Lincoln: University of Nebraska Press, 1982.

Funsten, James Bowen. "Five Thousand Miles through Idaho and Wyoming." *Spirit of Missions* 73, no. 9 (November 1908): 869–75.

————. "Report of the Bishop of the Missionary District of Boise." In *The Annual Report of the Board of Missions of the Protestant Episcopal Church in the United States of America, 1906/07*, 88–93. New York: Domestic and Missionary Society, 1907.

Gordon, Philip. "Address by Father Philip Gordon, Vice-President." *American Indian Magazine* 7, no. 3 (Fall 1919): 152–53.

————. "Opposition to the Indian Bureau." *American Indian Magazine* 4, no. 3 (July–September 1916): 259–60.

Greene, Jerome A. *American Carnage: Wounded Knee, 1890*. Norman: University of Oklahoma Press, 2014.

Hansson, Laura Marholm. *Six Modern Women: Psychological Sketches*. Translated by Hermione Ramsden. Boston: Roberts' Brothers, 1896.

Hatch, Thom. *Black Kettle: The Cheyenne Chief Who Sought Peace but Found War*. Hoboken NJ: John Wiley & Sons, 2004.

Hawley, James H. *History of Idaho: The Gem of the Mountains*. Vol. 4. Chicago: S. J. Clarke, 1920.

Hebard, Grace Raymond. *Marking the Oregon Trail, the Bozeman Road and Historic Places in Wyoming, 1908–1920*. Washington DC: State Regents of the Daughters of the American Revolution, 1921.

Hedren, Paul L. *Powder River: Disastrous Opening of the Great Sioux War*. Norman: University of Oklahoma Press, 2016.

Hertzberg, Hazel W. *The Search for an American Indian Identity: Modern Pan-Indian Movements*. Syracuse: Syracuse University Press, 1971.

Hill, Asa. "Some Social and Moral Conditions of the Reservation." In Society of American Indians, *Proceedings of the Second Annual Conference*, 119–25.

Hoig, Stan. *The Sand Creek Massacre*. Norman: University of Oklahoma Press, 2005.

Hoxie, Frederick E. *A Final Promise: The Campaign to Assimilate the Indians, 1880–1920*. Lincoln: University of Nebraska Press, 1984.

————, ed. *Talking Back to Civilization: Indian Voices from the Progressive Era*. New York: Bedford/St. Martin's Press, 2001.

————. *This Indian Country: American Indian Activists and the Place They Made*. New York: Penguin, 2012.

Huebner, Karen L. "An Unexpected Alliance: Stella Atwood, the California Clubwomen, John Collier, and the Indians of the Southwest, 1917–1934." *Pacific Historical Review* 78, no. 3 (January 2009): 337–66.

"Important Topics Considered." *American Indian Magazine* 4, no. 3 (July–September 1916): 217–19.

"An Indian Priest from Wyoming." *Churchman* 88, no. 10 (October 1903): 495.

"Indian Progress Conference." *Quarterly Journal of the Society of American Indians* 3, no. 3 (July–September): 239–40.

Indian's Friend 13, no. 4 (December 1910): 1.

"Indian Society Is Welcomed to City, Opening Meeting Held Last Night." *American Indian Magazine* 6, no. 3 (July–September 1918): 117–20.

"Indian Troubles in Boise." *Churchman* 95, no. 2 (February 1907): 248.

"Indian Work." In *Journal of the Seventeenth Annual Convocation of the Missionary District of Oklahoma Held at Shawnee, Oklahoma, May 16, 17, 18, 1911,* 16. Chickasha OK: Queen City Print, 1911.

"Indian YMCA Conference." *Quarterly Journal of the Society of American Indians* 3, no. 3 (July–September 1915): 240.

Iverson, Peter. *Carlos Montezuma and the Changing World of American Indians.* Albuquerque: University of New Mexico Press, 1982.

Jackson, Helen Hunt. *A Century of Dishonor: A Sketch of the United States Government's Dealings with Some of the Indian Tribes.* 1881. Revised edition of 1885. Norman: University of Oklahoma Press, 1995.

Jorgenson, Joseph G. *The Sun Dance Religion: Power for the Powerless.* Chicago: University of Chicago Press, 1972.

Journal of the Forty-First Annual Council of the Protestant Episcopal Church of the Diocese of Minnesota, which Assembled in St. Mark's Church, Minneapolis, June 1–2, 1898. Stillwater MN: Washington County Journal, 1898. https://babel.hathitrust.org/cgi/pt?id=wu.89077217818&view=1up&seq=5.

Kellogg, Laura Cornelius. "Industrial Organization for the Indian." In *Report of the Executive Council,* 43–55.

———. *Our Democracy and the American Indian: A Comprehensive Presentation of the Indian Situation as It Is Today.* Kansas City: Burton, 1920.

Kendall, Henry. "Indian Speeches." In Barrows, *Proceedings,* 99–100.

Kennedy, David M. *Over Here: The First World War and American Society.* Oxford: University Press, 1980.

Kinney, Bruce. "The Indian YMCA Conference." *Missions: American Baptist International Magazine* 6, no. 8 (September 1915): 654–55.

Kirshbaum, S. "The Far West." *Sunday at Home: A Family Magazine for Sabbath Reading,* 1908–9, 229–30.

Klapper, Charles J., ed. *Indian Affairs: Laws and Treaties.* Vol. 2, *Treaties.* Washington DC: Government Printing Office, 1904.

Kroeber, Alfred Louis. *The Arapaho.* 1902. Reprint. Lincoln: University of Nebraska Press, 1983.

La Barre, Weston. *The Peyote Cult.* 1938. Reprint, 5th ed., Norman: University of Oklahoma Press, 1989.

Lanternari, Vittorio. *The Religions of the Oppressed: A Study of Modern Messianic Cults.* Translated by Lisa Sergio. New York: Mentor Books, 1963.

Larner, John W. "Society of American Indians." In *Native America in the Twentieth Century: An Encyclopedia*, edited by Mary B. Davis, 603–4. New York: Garland, 1994.

Larson, Henry A. "The Indian and His Liquor Problem." *American Indian Magazine* 4, no. 3 (July–September 1916): 234–37.

Larson, T. A. *History of Wyoming*. Lincoln: University of Nebraska Press, 1990.

Lazarus, Edward. *Black Hills/White Justice: The Sioux Nation versus the United States, 1775 to the Present*. Lincoln: University of Nebraska Press, 1999.

"Legislation Proposed." In *Fourth Annual Report of the Executive Committee of the Indian Rights Association for the Year Ending December 14, 1916*, 25–28. Philadelphia: Indian Rights Association, 1916.

Leonard, Thomas. *Illiberal Reformers: Race, Eugenics & American Economics in the Progressive Era*. Princeton: Princeton University Press, 2017.

"Letter, Minneapolis." *Indian's Friend* 16, no. 1 (October 1913): 1.

Lewandowski, Tadeusz. *Ojibwe, Activist, Priest: The Life of Father Philip Gordon, Tibishkogijik*. Madison: University of Wisconsin Press, 2019.

———. *Red Bird, Red Power: The Life and Legacy of Zitkala-Ša*. Norman: University of Oklahoma Press.

Linn, Mary S., Tessie Narango, Sheilah Nicholas, Inée Slaughter, Akira Yamamoto, and Ofelia Zepeda. "Awaking the Languages: Challenges of Enduring Language Programs: Field Reports from Fifteen Program from Arizona, New Mexico and Oklahoma." In *Indigenous Languages across the Community*, edited by Barbara Burnaby and Jon Reyhner, 105–26. Flagstaff: Northern Arizona University, 2002. https://jan.ucc.nau.edu/jar/ILAC/ILAC_13.pdf.

Lone Wolf, Delos. "How to Solve the Problem." *American Indian Magazine* 3, no. 4 (Fall 1916): 257–59.

"Lo, the Poor, Rich Indian." *Relief Society Magazine* 5, no. 11 (November 1918): 609–16.

Maddox, Lucy. *Citizen Indians: Native American Intellectuals, Race, and Reform*. Ithaca: Cornell University Press, 2005.

Markley, Elinor R., and Beatrice Crofts. *Walk Softly, This Is God's Country: Sixty-Six Years on the Wind River Indian Reservation, Compiled from the Letters and Journals of the Rev. John Roberts, 1883–1949*. Lander WY: Mortimore, 1997.

Maroukis, Thomas Constantine. *Peyote and the Yankton Sioux: The Life and Times of Sam Necklace*. Norman: University of Oklahoma Press, 2004.

———. *We Are Not a Vanishing People: The Society of American Indians, 1911–1923*. Tucson: University of Arizona Press, 2021.

McDermott, John D. *Forlorn Hope: The Battle of White Bird Canyon and the Beginning of the Nez Perce War*. Boise: Idaho State Historical Society, 1978.

McKenzie, Fayette A. "The Cooperation of the Two Races." *Quarterly Journal of the Society of American Indians* 2, no. 1 (January–March 1914): 23–32.

———. "Results of the Madison Conference." *Quarterly Journal of the Society of American Indians* 2, no. 3 (July–September 1914): 229–30.

Meisenheimer, D. K., Jr. "Regionalist Bodies/Embodied Regions: Sarah Orne Jewett and Zitkala-Ša." In *Breaking Boundaries: New Perspectives on Women's Regional Writing*, edited by Sherrie A. Inness and Diana Royer, 109–23. Iowa City: University of Iowa Press, 1997.

"Members and Associate Members of the Society of American Indians Who Registered at the Lawrence Conference, September 28 to October 3, 1915." *Quarterly Journal of the Society of American Indians* 3, no. 4 (October–December 1915): 313–15.

"Members Constituting the Fourth Conference." *Quarterly Journal of the Society of American Indians* 2, no. 4 (October–December 1914): 319.

Messer, David W. *Chauncey Yellow Robe: A Biography of the American Indian Educator, Ca. 1870–1930.* Jefferson NC: McFarland, 2019.

———. *Henry Roe Cloud: A Biography.* New York: Hamilton Books, 2009.

Meyers, Jeffery. *Converging Stories: Race, Ecology, and Environmental Justice in American Literature.* Athens: University of Georgia Press, 2005.

Milk, Theresa. *Haskell Institute: 19th Century Stories of Sacrifice and Survival.* Lawrence KS: Mammoth, 2007.

Miller, David Reed. "Charles Alexander Eastman, The 'Winner': From Deep Woods to Civilization." In *American Indian Intellectuals*, edited by Margot Liberty, 61–70. St. Paul MN: West, 1978.

"The Missionary Council: The Third Day, Thursday, October 29th." *Spirit of Missions* 68, no. 12 (December 1903): 880–85.

Montezuma, Carlos. "Address before the Sixth Conference." *American Indian Magazine* 4, no. 3 (July–September 1916): 160–62.

———. "Let My People Go." *American Indian Magazine* 4, no. 1 (January–March 1916): 32–33.

———. "The Reservation Is Fatal to the Development of Good Citizenship." *Quarterly Journal of the Society of American Indians* 2, no. 1 (January–March 1914): 69–74.

"Newark." *Church Standard* 74, no. 12 (December 1897): 169.

"News and Notes." *Indian's Friend* 10, no. 7 (March 1898): 4–5.

"News and Notes of the Month." *Spirit of Missions* 65, no. 5 (May 1900): 304.

"Newspaper Comment." *American Indian Magazine* 4, no. 3 (July–September 1916): 266–67.

Nicholson, Christopher L. "To Advance a Race: A Historical Analysis of the Personal Belief, Industrial Philanthropy and Black Liberal Arts Higher

Education in Fayette McKenzie's Presidency at Fisk University, 1915–1925."
PhD diss., Loyola University, Chicago, 2011.

Nickerson, Herman G. "Report Concerning Indians in Wyoming." In *Annual Reports of the Department of the Interior for the Fiscal Year Ended June 30, 1900*, 414–17. Washington DC: Government Printing Office, 1900.

"Objects of the Society." In *Report of the Executive Council*, 14–15.

Office of Archeology and Historic Preservation. "Shoshone Episcopal Mission: Photographs, Written Historical and Descriptive Data." American Historic Buildings Survey. Washington DC: National Park Service, ca. 1970.

"Officers of the Society." *American Indian Magazine* 7, no. 1 (Spring 1919): 56.

Olden, Sarah Emilia. *Shoshone Folk Lore, as Discovered from the Rev. John Roberts, a Hidden Hero, on the Wind River Indian Reservation in Wyoming*. Milwaukee: Morehouse, 1923.

Olson, James C. *Red Cloud and the Sioux Problem*. Lincoln: University of Nebraska Press, 1965.

Olson, James S., and Raymond Wilson. *Native Americans in the Twentieth Century*. Urbana: University of Illinois Press, 1984.

"Open Debate on the Loyalty of Indian Employees in the Indian Service." *American Indian Magazine* 4, no. 3 (July–September 1916): 252–56.

Ostler, Jeffrey. *The Plains Sioux and U.S. Colonialism from Lewis and Clark to Wounded Knee*. Cambridge: Cambridge University Press, 2004.

"Our Indian Children." *Spirit of Missions* 77, no. 2 (February 1912): 159–62.

"Our Letter Box." *Spirit of Missions* 76, no. 3 (March 1911): 240–43.

Parker, Arthur C. "The Awakened American Indian: An Account of the Washington Meeting." *Quarterly Journal of the Society of American Indians* 2, no. 4 (October–December 1914): 269–74.

———. "Editorial Comment." *American Indian Magazine* 5, no. 3 (July–September 1917): 146–53.

———. "Editorial Comment." *Quarterly Journal of the Society of American Indians* 2, no. 3 (July–September 1914): 165–66.

———. "Editorial Comment." *Quarterly Journal of the Society of American Indians* 3, no. 4 (October–December 1915): 251–64.

———. "Editorial Comment: The American Indian in the World Crisis." *American Indian Magazine* 6, no. 1 (Spring 1918): 15–24.

———. "The Editor's Viewpoint: The Functions of the Society of American Indians." *Quarterly Journal of the Society of American Indians* 4, no. 1 (January–March 1916): 8–14.

———. "The Fifth Conference." *Quarterly Journal of the Society of American Indians* 3, no. 4 (October–December 1915): 281–83.

———. "A Modern Indian Council." *Red Man* 5, no. 2 (October 1912): 54.

———. "The Philosophy of Indian Education." In *Report of the Executive Council*, 76–80.

———. "The Quaker City Meeting of the Society of American Indians." *Quarterly Journal of the Society of American Indians* 2, no. 1 (January–March 1914): 56–59.

———. "A Study in the Complexities of an Indian's Legal Status." *Quarterly Journal of the Society of American Indians* 3, no. 3 (July–September 1915): 220–24.

Parker, Robert Dale, ed. "Ruth Margaret Muskrat, Cherokee, 1897–1982." *Changing Is Not Vanishing: A Collection of American Indian Poetry to 1930*, 320–30. Philadelphia: University of Pennsylvania Press, 2011.

"Pennsylvania." *Churchman* 77, no. 3 (March 1898): 444.

Peyer, Bernd C., ed. *American Indian Nonfiction: An Anthology of Writings, 1760s–1930s.* Norman: University of Oklahoma Press, 2007.

———, ed. *What the Elders Wrote: An Anthology of Early Prose by North American Indians.* Berlin: Dietrich Reimer, 1982.

Pfister, Joel. *The Yale Indian: The Education of Henry Roe Cloud.* Durham NC: Duke University Press, 2009.

Philbrick, Nathaniel. *The Last Stand: Custer, Sitting Bull, and the Battle of the Little Bighorn.* New York: Penguin, 2011.

"Platform and Resolutions." *American Indian Magazine* 5, no. 3 (July–September 1918): 138–40.

"Platform of the Fifth Conference." *Quarterly Journal of the Society of American Indians* 3, no. 4 (October–December 1915): 285–89.

"Platform of the Second Annual Conference of the Society of American Indians." *Quarterly Journal of the Society of American Indians* 1, no. 1 (January–April 1913): 71–74.

Porter, Joy. *To Be Indian: The Life of Iroquois-Seneca Arthur Caswell Parker.* Norman: University of Oklahoma Press, 2001.

Powers, Thomas. *The Killing of Crazy Horse.* New York: Knopf, 2010.

Pratt, Richard Henry. "Origin and History of Work at Carlisle." *American Missionary* 37, no. 4 (May 1883): 108–11.

———. "Remarks and Motion of Gen. Pratt Regarding Peyote." *American Indian Magazine* 4, no. 3 (July–September 1916): 237–38.

———. "The Solution to the Indian Problem." In Society of American Indians, *Proceedings of the Second Annual Conference*, 197–204.

Pritzker, Barry M. *A Native American Encyclopedia: History, Culture, People.* Oxford: Oxford University Press, 2000.

Progressive Men of the State of Wyoming. Chicago: A. W. Bowen, 1901.

"The Public Entertainment." In *Report of the Executive Council*, 110–11.

Rahill, Peter J. "The Catholic Indian Missions and Grant's Peace Policy, 1870–1884." PhD diss., Catholic University of America, Washington DC, 1953.

Ramirez, Renya. *Standing Up to Colonial Power*. Lincoln: University of Nebraska Press, 2018.

Rawlings, William. *The Second Coming of the Invisible Empire: The Ku Klux Klan of the 1920s*. Macon GA: Mercer University Press, 2016.

Reid, Mabel. "Westerners." *Sunset: The Pacific Monthly* 41, no. 5 (November 1918): 47.

Report of the Executive Council on the Proceedings of the First Annual Conference of the Society of American Indians. Washington DC, 1912.

Roberts, John. "Letter (August 13, 1885)." *Spirit of Missions* 50, no. 10 (October 1885): 531.

———. "Report from John Roberts." *Spirit of Missions* 49, no. 3 (March 1884): 125–26.

———. "Report from John Roberts." *Spirit of Missions* 49, no. 6 (June 1884): 281.

———. "Report from John Roberts." *Spirit of Missions* 50, no. 7 (July 1885): 363–64.

———. "Report from John Roberts." *Spirit of Missions* 50, no. 9 (September 1885): 467.

———. "Report from John Roberts." *Spirit of Missions* 61, no. 3 (March 1896): 118.

———. "Report from John Roberts." *Spirit of Missions* 64, no. 8 (August 1899): 408.

Sanford, David A. *Indian Topics: Or, Experiences in Indian Missions with Selections from Various Sources*. New York: Broadway, 1911.

"Scenario Wanted for Great Indian Film." *American Indian Magazine* 7, no. 4 (August 1920): 44.

Schaffer, Ronald. *America in the Great War: The Rise of the War Welfare State*. Oxford: Oxford University Press, 1991.

Schultz, Jeffrey D., Andrew L. Aoki, Kerry L. Haynie, and Anne M. McCulloch, eds. *Encyclopedia of Minorities in American Politics: Hispanic Americans and Native Americans*. Westport CT: Greenwood, 2000.

Seton, Ernest Thompson. *Sign Talk: A Universal Signal Code, without Apparatus, for Use in the Army, the Navy, Camping, Hunting, and Daily Life*. Garden City NY: Doubleday, Page, 1918.

"Shoshone Agency." *Churchman* 82, no. 8 (August 1902): 162.

"The Shoshone Indians." *Spirit of Missions* 83 (1918): 599.

Simmons, Virginia McConnell. *The Ute Indians of Utah, Colorado, and New Mexico*. Boulder: University of Colorado Press, 2000.

Sloan, Thomas. "Reservation System—Administration." In *Report of the Executive Council*, 112–21.

Smith, Andrea. *Indigenous People and Boarding Schools: A Comparative Study*. New York: Secretariat of the United Nations Permanent Forum on Indigenous Issues, January 26, 2009. https://www.un.org/esa/socdev/unpfii/documents/E _C_19_2009_crp1.pdf.

Smith, Gene. "Lost Bird." *American Heritage* 47, no. 2 (April 1996). https://www .americanheritage.com/lost-bird#1.

Sniffen, Matthew K. *The Meaning of the Ute "War."* Philadelphia: Indian Rights Association, 1915.

Society of American Indians. *Proceedings of the Second Annual Conference, Held at Columbus, Ohio, October 2–7, 1912, at Ohio State University.* In *Quarterly Journal of the Society of American Indians* 1, no. 1 (January–April 1913): 115–222.

Spalding, John. "First Annual Report of the Missionary Jurisdiction of Wyoming, Territory." *Spirit of Missions* 49, no. 11 (November–December 1884): 586–88.

———. "A Remarkable Opportunity." *Churchman* 52, no. 8 (August 1885): 208.

———. "Second Annual Report of the Jurisdiction of Wyoming." *Spirit of Missions* 50, no. 11 (November–December 1885): 617–19.

———. "Second Annual Report of the Missionary Bishop of Wyoming and Idaho." In *Annual Report of the Board of Missions for the Fiscal Year, 1885/86,* 90–92. New York: Domestic and Foreign Missionary Society of the Protestant Episcopal Church in the USA, 1886.

Speroff, Leon. *Carlos Montezuma, MD, a Yavapai American Hero: The Life and Times of an American Indian, 1866–1923.* Portland OR: Arnica, 2005.

Stamm, Henry E. *People of the Wind River: The Eastern Shoshones, 1825–1900.* Norman: University of Oklahoma Press, 1999.

Stone, Wilbur Fiske, ed. *History of Colorado.* Chicago: S. J. Clarke, 1918.

Super, O. B. "Indian Education at Carlisle." *New England Magazine* 18, no. 2 (April 1895): 224–40.

Talbot, Ethelbert. "The Bishop's Diary." *Diocese of Central Pennsylvania Journal of Convention* 33 (1904): 91.

———. "Fourth Annual Report of the Missionary Bishop of Wyoming and Idaho." In *Annual Report of the Board of Missions for the Fiscal Year, 1889/90,* 79–83. New York: Domestic and Foreign Missionary Society of the Protestant Episcopal Church in the USA, 1890.

———. *My People of the Plains.* New York: Harper & Brothers, 1906.

———. "Second Annual Report of the Missionary Bishop of Wyoming and Idaho." In *Annual Report of the Board of Missions for the Fiscal Year, 1887/88,* 86–88. New York: Domestic and Foreign Missionary Society of the Protestant Episcopal Church in the USA, 1888.

———. "The Shoshone Indian School in Wyoming." *Spirit of Missions* 58 (1893): 125.

Taylor, Graham D. *The New Deal and American Indian Tribalism: The Administration of the Indian Reorganization Act, 1934–45.* Lincoln: University of Nebraska Press, 1980.

The Thirty-Fourth Annual Report of the Executive Committee of the Indian Rights Association, for the Year Ending December 14, 1916. Philadelphia: Indian Rights Association, 1916.

Thomas, Nathaniel S. "The Red Men of Wyoming." *Spirit of Missions* 75, no. 9 (September 1910): 759–62.

———. "Some Children of Wyoming." *Spirit of Missions* 75, no. 2 (February 1910): 119–23.

Thompson, Jerry D. *A Civil War History of the New Mexico Volunteers and Militia.* Albuquerque: University of New Mexico Press, 2015.

Tomkins, William. *Universal Indian Sign Language of the Plains Indians.* California: William Tomkins, 1931.

Trafzer, Clifford E., Jean A. Keller, and Lorene Sisquoc, eds. *Boarding School Blues: Revisiting American Indian Educational Experiences.* Lincoln: Bison Books, 2006.

Treuer, Anton. *Atlas of Indian Nations.* Washington DC: National Geographic, 2014.

United States Army and Navy Journal and Gazette of the Regular and Armed Forces 40 (November 1902): 253.

United States Army and Navy Journal and Gazette of the Regular and Armed Forces 40 (June 1903): 1025.

United States Army and Navy Journal and Gazette of the Regular and Armed Forces 40 (July 1903): 1059.

United States Army and Navy Journal and Gazette of the Regular and Armed Forces 40 (August 1903): 1284.

United States Army and Navy Journal and Gazette of the Regular and Volunteer Forces 32 (September 1894): 55.

United States Army and Navy Journal and Gazette of the Regular and Volunteer Forces 32 (October 1894): 85.

United States Army and Navy Journal and Gazette of the Regular and Volunteer Forces 32 (March 1895): 452.

United States Army and Navy Journal and Gazette of the Regular and Volunteer Forces 40 (January 1903): 454.

Urbanek, Mae. *Chief Washakie.* Boulder: Johnson, 1971.

U.S. Senate. *Report of the Philippine Commission to the President.* Vol. 4. Washington DC: Government Printing Office, 1901.

U.S. Senate Committee on Indian Affairs. *Hearings before the Committee in Indian Affairs, United States Senate, Sixty-Fourth Congress, First Session, H. R. 10385, an Act Making Appropriations for the Current and Contingent Expenses of the Bureau of Indian Affairs, for Fulfilling Treaty Stipulations with Various Indian Tribes, and for Other Purposes, for the Fiscal Year Ending June 30, 1917.* Washington DC: Government Printing Office, 1917.

Utley, Robert M. *The Last Days of the Sioux Nation.* New Haven: Yale University Press, 2004.

Valentine, Robert G. "Address of Hon. Robert G. Valentine, Commissioner of Indian Affairs." In *Report of the Executive Council*, 23–28.

Van Orsdale, J. T. "Rev. Sherman Coolidge, D.D." *Colorado Magazine* 1, no. 2 (May 1893): 85–86.

"Very Silly Woman or Exaggerated Story." *The Albuquerque Indian* 1, no. 8 (January 1906): 21.

Waggoner, Linda. *Fire Light: The Life of Angel De Cora, Winnebago Artist*. Norman: University of Oklahoma Press, 2008.

Wagner, David E., ed. *Powder River Odyssey: Nelson Cole's Western Campaign of 1865: The Journals of Lyman G. Bennett and Other Eyewitness Accounts*. Norman: Arthur H. Clark, 2009.

Wells, Merle. "The Nez Perce and Their Way." *Pacific Northwest Quarterly* 55, no. 1 (1964): 35–37.

"What Indians Are Thinking about the War." *American Indian Magazine* 5, no. 3 (July–September): 143–44.

Whipple, Henry. "Bishop Whipple's Address to the Twenty-Eighth Annual Council of the Diocese of Minnesota." In *Journal of the Proceedings of the Twenty-Eighth Annual Convention of the Diocese of Minnesota*, 32–46. Minneapolis: Johnson, Smith & Harrison Printers, 1885.

———. *Lights and Shadows of a Long Episcopate: Being Reminiscences and Recollections of the Right Reverend Henry Benjamin Whipple, D.D., LL. D., Bishop of Minnesota*. New York: Macmillan, 1899.

———. Preface to *Century of Dishonor*, by Jackson, ix–xxiv.

———. "A Worthy Object." *Churchman* 52, no. 7 (July 1885): 96.

Wilkinson, Charles F. *Blood Struggle: The Rise of Modern Indian Nations*. New York: W. W. Norton, 2005.

Wilson, Raymond. *Ohiyesa: Charles Eastman, Santee Sioux*. Urbana: University of Illinois Press, 1981.

Wolfe, Patrick. "Settler Colonialism and the Elimination of the Native." *Journal of Genocide Research* 8, no. 4 (2006): 387–409.

"Worth Knowing About." *The Indian's Friend* 16, no. 7 (March 1904): 8.

"A Year's Work in the District of Wyoming." *Churchman* 98, no. 10 (October 1908): 506.

Yenne, Bill. *Sitting Bull*. Yardley PA: Westholme, 2008.

Zinn, Howard. *A People's History of the United States*. New York: Harper Collins, 1993.

INDEX

Larrabee-Allen, Philip Sheridan
(Nee-netch-a), 59, 126, 132–33, 237n26,
237n27, 238n39; name changes of, 21, 26;
as Nee-netch-a, 11–13, 16, 20; as Philip
Sheridan Larrabee-Allen, 26–28
Leonard, Abiel, 101
"Let My People Go" (Montezuma), 192
Lincoln, Abraham, 29, 74
Lippman, Walter, 205
Lone Bear, 69, 78, 138–39
Lone Wolf, Delos, 199
Lowry, Lena, 23

McDonough (nurse), 208, 278n78
McKenzie, Fayette Avery, 137–38, 153–55,
167, 175, 260nn2–3, 264n41
McKinley, William, 75, 249n63
McLaughlin, James, 69, 138, 141
Medicine Man, 13, 24
Meriam, Lewis, 220
Meriam Report, 220
Merritt, E. B., 197
Mexico, 152, 204, 263n30
Modoc War, 23
Montezuma, Carlos, 180–81, 188, 230n19,
274n47; background of, 154; death
of, 218; and SAI, 155, 161, 167–68, 170,
175, 190–92, 195, 198–202, 207, 209–11,
217–18; and Sherman Coolidge,
172–73, 184, 186–88, 199–201, 203, 210,
279n101; and World War I, 209
Mooney, James, 246n7
Mule, 126, 129, 144
My People of the Plains (Ethelbert
Talbot), 47

National Association for the
Advancement of Colored People,
154–55
National Council of American Indians,
281n15

National Indian Welfare Committee,
219, 281n15
Native American Church, 279n113
Nee-netch-a. See Larrabee-Allen, Philip
Sheridan (Nee-netch-a)
New Republic, 205
New York Times, 81, 119,
Nez Perce, 31, 37, 159–60, 237n36
Nickerson, Herman G., 19, 78–82, 103
Nunlist, Ursis, 43, 102, 108
Nye (Grace Coolidge's uncle), 108, 120,
260n68

Oakerhater, David Pendleton, 148
Office of Indian Affairs. See Bureau of
Indian Affairs (BIA)
Ogontz School for Young Ladies, 84
Ohio State University, 153–55, 181, 264n41
Oregon Trail, 13, 17, 86
Outlook, 139, 185
Owen, Robert Latham, 184, 187, 196,
272n15

Paddy-Paws (Grace Coolidge), 185
Paiutes, 63, 191
Parker, Arthur C., 161, 219, 230n19,
265n52, 272n13; background of, 157;
later life of, 281n17; and SAI, 157–59,
162–64, 167, 170, 173–75, 177, 179–80,
183–84, 186–87, 190–92, 194, 198–99,
202, 205–7, 209–10, 268n15, 270n48,
271n53, 276n26; and Sherman
Coolidge, 162, 167, 171–74, 182–83,
187, 195–96, 198–99, 207, 209, 268n15,
269n33, 270n48, 279n100
Parker, Ely S., 157
peyote religion, 202, 218, 231n19, 279n113;
background of, 152, 263n30; and SAI,
157, 191, 194, 199, 207, 213, 265n52; and
Sherman Coolidge, 152, 164
Philippines, 73–74, 119, 249n59, 274n50